THE GIGANTIC ACTIVITY BOOK FOR MINECRAFTERS

Over 200 Activities—Puzzles, Mazes, Dot-to-Dot, Word Search, Spot the Difference, Crosswords, Sudoku, Drawing Pages, and More!

JEN FUNK WEBER

Sky Pony Press
New York

This book is not authorized or sponsored by Microsoft Corp., Mojang AB, Notch Development AB or Scholastic Inc., or any other person or entity owning or controlling rights in the Minecraft name, trademark, or copyrights.

Sky Pony Press books may be purchased in bulk at special discounts for sales promotion, corporate gifts, fund-raising, or educational purposes. Special editions can also be created to specifications. For details, contact the Special Sales Department, Sky Pony Press, 307 West 36th Street, 11th Floor,New York, NY 10018 or info@skyhorsepublishing.com.

Visit our website at www.skyponypress.com.

10 9 8 7 6 5 4 3 2 1

Library of Congress Cataloging-in-Publication Data is available on file.

Puzzles created by Jen Funk Weber
Cover design by Brian Peterson
Cover illustration by Amanda Brack and Bill Greenhead
Interior illustrations by Amanda Brack

Print ISBN: 978-1-5107-6295-4

Printed in China

Portions of this book were previously publishing as *Amazing Activities for Minecrafters* (ISBN: 978-1-5107-2174-6), *Amazing Mazes for Minecrafters* (ISBN: 978-1-5107-4723-4), and *Astounding Activities for Minecrafters* (ISBN: 978-1-5107-4102-7).

INTRODUCTION

This Gigantic Activity Book for Minecrafters workbook teaches kids valuable problem-solving skills while offering them an irresistible puzzling adventure complete with diamond swords, zombies, skeletons, and creepers.

Whether it's the joy of seeing their favorite game characters on every page or the thrill of breaking codes, battling mobs, and using what they know to solve problems, there is something in this workbook for every young gamer! Turn the page to discover hundreds of exciting brain games and challenges.

Inside you'll find:
Amazing Activities for Minecrafters
Amazing Mazes for Minecrafters
Astounding Activities for Minecrafters

Happy adventuring!

AMAZING ACTIVITIES FOR MINECRAFTERS

Puzzles and Games for Hours of Entertainment!

Sky Pony Press
New York

TABLE OF CONTENTS

Going Batty
Steve Says
The Mirror's Image
City Slicker
Take a Guess
Enchanted Chest
See and Solve
Home Sweet Biome
Creeper Twins
Circle of Truth: Crafting Clue
Mob Scene
Squared Up: Mobs in Every Quarter
Watchtower Quest
A Cure for What Ails You
You Can Draw It: Wolf
Piece It Together
Pick, the Right Tool!
Tool Chest
Find the Portal
Crossword Clue Finder
See the Sea
Power Play: Mystery Word
Survival Maze
Blocked!
Connect the Dots: Hostile Mob
Mixed Up
A Small Problem
Crack the Code
Alpha Code
Grab and Go Challenge
Word Mine
Circle of Truth: Fun Fact
Zombie Twins
Can You Dig It?
Squared Up: Farm Mobs
Grow with the Flow
Basic Training
You Can Draw It: Villagers
The Shape of Things to Come
When Pigs Hide
Miner's Block
True or False?
Steve Says: Joke Time
On the Playground
Enchanted Map
Common Code
Every Nook and Cranny
Circle of Truth: Survival Tip
Skeleton Twins
Connect the Dots: Pit of Peril!
Squared Up: Block Party
Hold It!
Collecting Treasure
Circle of Truth: Food for Thought
You Can Draw It: Iron Golem
Tip for Ending Endermen
Word Farm
Connect the Dots: Farm Life
Hunt for Enchantments
Rotten Luck
Multiplayer Mismatch
Twin Mobs
Path of Doom
Truth or Tale?
Connect the Dots: Our Hero
Terms of the Game
Squared Up: Inventory
Fact-Finding Mission
Blackout
Multiplayer CTM Challenge
Here, There, and Everywhere
Deflect This
Down on the (Mob) Farm
Places, People!
Minecraft Puzzle Boss Certificate
Answers

GOING BATTY

There are fourteen bats hidden in this Minecrafter's haunted house. Can you find them all without going batty?

STEVE SAYS...

If you have ever played the game Simon Says, then you know how this game works: follow only the directions that begin with "Steve says" to reveal a fun fact for Minecrafters.

	1	2	3	4	5
A	SPIDERS	ONE	CREEPERS	CREATE	MAGENTA
B	WERE	SILVERFISH	MAKE	VILLAGERS	THE
C	OCELOT	RESULT	CONSTRUCT	GREEN	OF
D	PINK	IS	A	FOREST	SAVANNA
E	CODING	PURPLE	THE	MISTAKE	BE

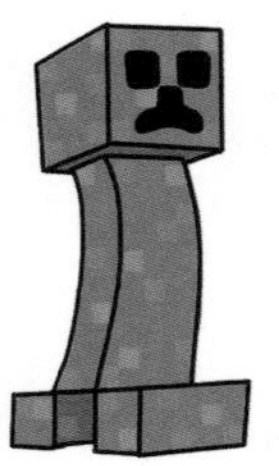

1. **Steve says**, "Cross off all the Mobs in Row B and Column 1."

2. **Steve says**, "Cross off all colors."

3. **Steve says**, "Cross off all biomes."

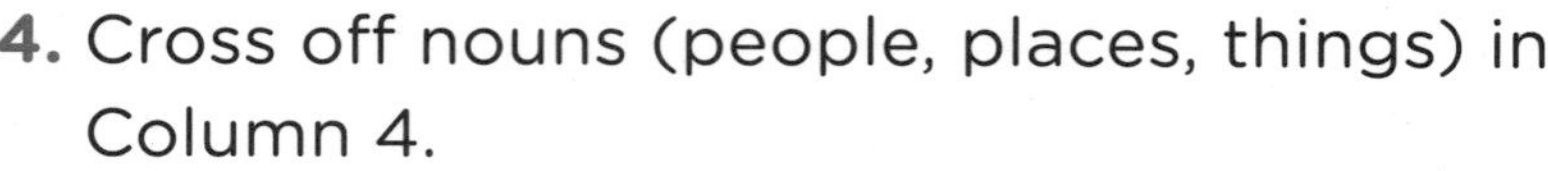

4. Cross off nouns (people, places, things) in Column 4.

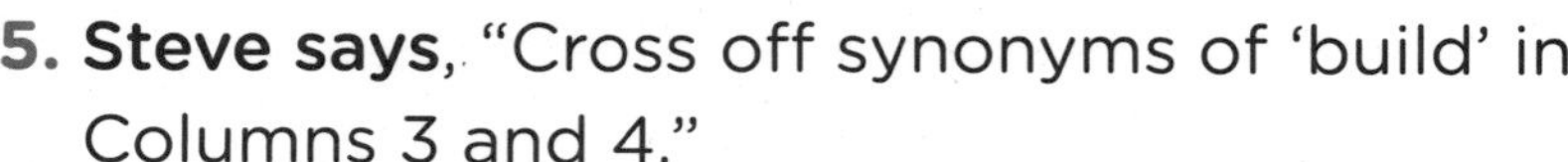

5. **Steve says**, "Cross off synonyms of 'build' in Columns 3 and 4."

6. **Steve says**, "Cross off words with four or fewer letters in Column 2 and Row E."

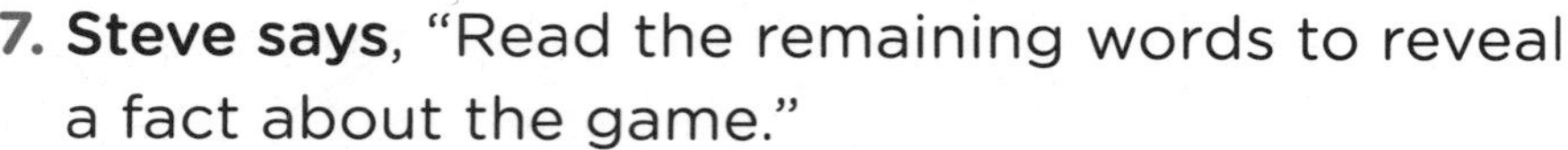

7. **Steve says**, "Read the remaining words to reveal a fact about the game."

THE MIRROR'S IMAGE

Circle letters on the top half of the grid that have correct mirror images on the bottom half. Write the circled letters in order on the spaces provided to reveal a cool fact about Endermen.

E I M N D N E O R T M E K N W I E R E D
C A L D L I E D F N A G R Y L A N O D E
U R P S B E U Z F O R Z L E T E H E P E
N E D W R A S S C R O E A T N E Y D O U

И ∩ D M ꙅ ∀ Ь ꙅ C ꓤ E E ∀ ⊥ O E Ь D Γ E
ꓤ ꓤ E ꙅ B E Ⅎ ∀ Ⅎ O ꓤ B ∩ E ⊥ Γ H E O E
C ∀ Γ Γ Γ V E D Ⅎ E ∀ ꓤ ꓤ ꙅ Γ ∀ И ∀ D E
E Ь ∩ И D Z E Z ꓤ Γ M E E И M ꙅ E ꓤ E O

_ _ _ _ _ _ _ _ _   _ _ _ _   _ _ _ _ _ _ _

“_ _ _ _ _ _ _ _ _ _ _”   _ _ _ _ _ _ _   _ _ _

_ _ _   _ _ _   _ _ _ _ _ _ _ _

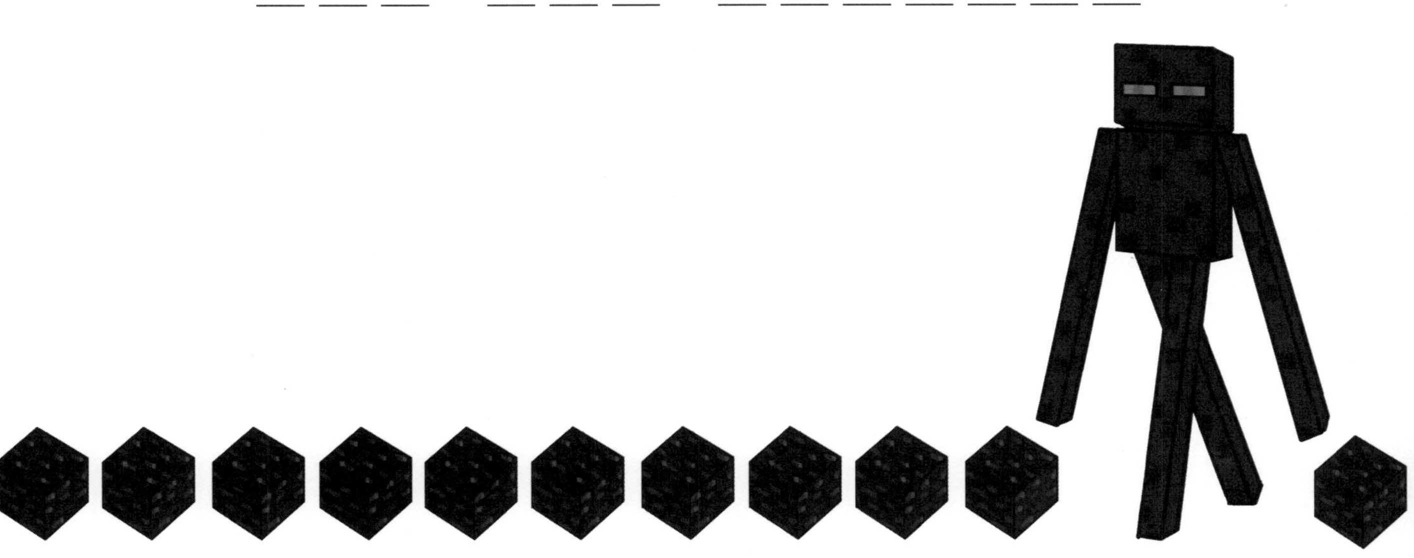

CITY SLICKER

A highly-skilled Minecrafter built the first city below. She logged back in later and made ten changes to her city. Look at the second city on the opposite page. Can you identify all ten changes?

TAKE A GUESS

Write the answers to the clues on the numbered spaces, one letter on each blank. Then transfer the letters to the boxes with the same numbers. A few have already been done for you! If you fill in the boxes correctly, you'll reveal something very useful for Minecrafters.

Clue				
The way out	__ (10)	x (2)	__ (6)	__ (15)
This grows on ears and is sometimes popped	__ (9)	__ (12)	r (5)	__ (8)
A kind of tree	p (11)	__ (13)	__ (14)	__ (1)
To leak through	s (16)	__ (4)	__ (7)	__ (3)

1	2	3	4	5	6	7	8	9	10
	x			r					

11	12	13	14	15	16
p					s

ENCHANTED CHEST

This End City chest is enchanted. To open it, you must press all nine buttons just once, in the correct order.

Follow the directions on the buttons. For instance, 2D means you must move your finger two buttons down. R=right. L=left. U=up. To open the chest, you must land on the F button last.

Which button do you have to press first to land on the F button last?

SEE AND SOLVE

In this crossword puzzle, you get to figure out where each word fits! Use the picture clues to guess the word answers, then see where each word fits best. If you fill in the puzzle correctly, you'll get a funny answer to the question below!

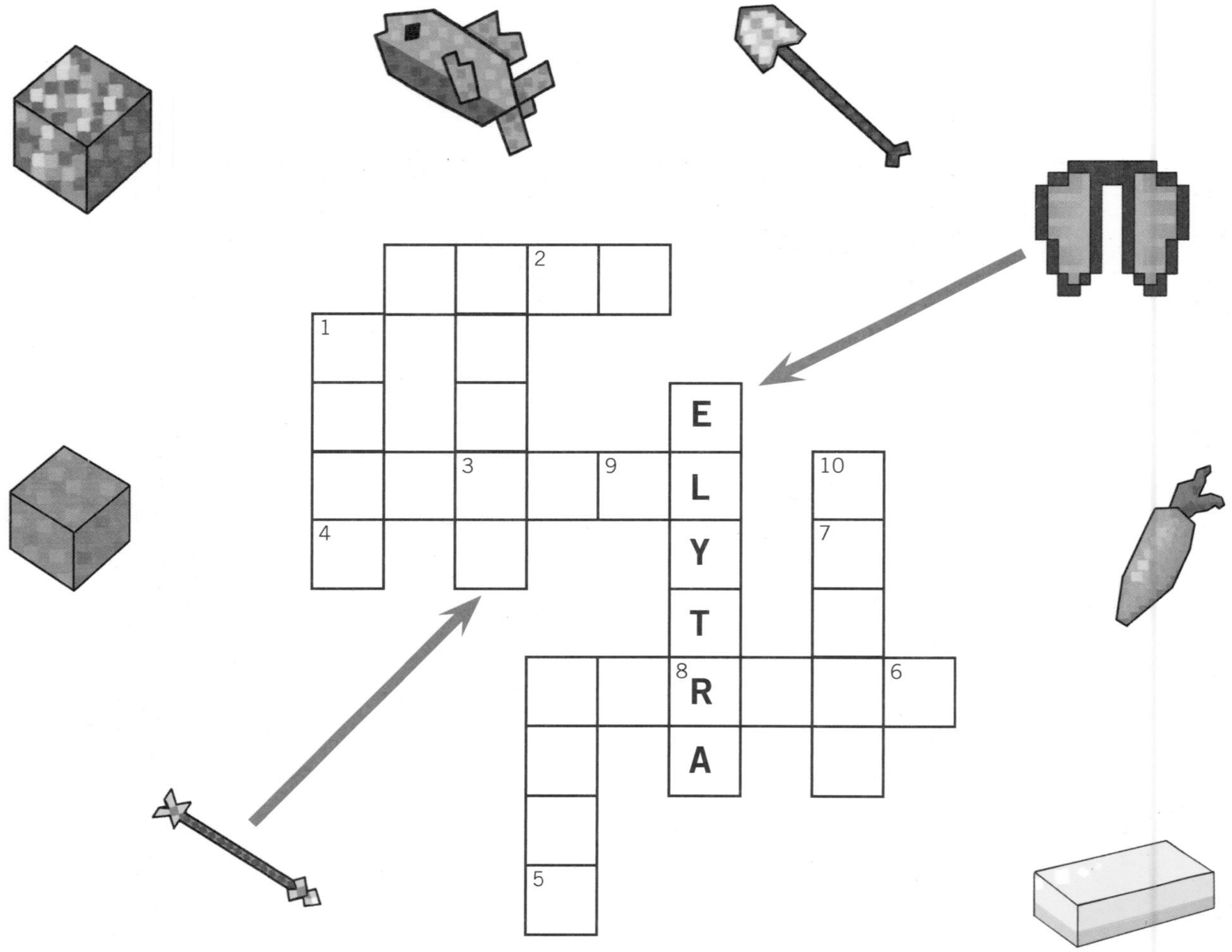

E
L
Y
T
R
A

What happens when blazes are promoted to managers?

__ __ __ __   __ __ __ __   __ __ __ __ __ __ __ __

6 4 9 5   1 10 8 9   9 2 9 8 5 3 7 9

HOME SWEET BIOME

Find and circle the names of fourteen Minecraft biomes in the wordfind below. They might be forward, backward, up, down, or diagonal.

DEEP OCEAN
DESERT
EXTREME HILLS
FROZEN RIVER
JUNGLE
MUSHROOM ISLAND
NETHER
PLAINS
ROOFED FOREST
SAVANNA
STONE BEACH
SWAMPLAND
TAIGA
THE END

J F R O Z E N R I V E R S N
E L G N U J S E N S B L E A
R G E N S N T T E N L S H E
D C A L I L E H D I T A C C
N H E A D M E E H S A V A O
A B L I E O M E E T H A E P
L P E D S I M N S C A N B E
P O M O E E U D N G T N E E
M U S H R O O M I S L A N D
A A I T T N S A I T W A O S
W A X R E H T E N J O K T E
S E R O O F E D F O R E S T

CREEPER TWINS

Only two of these creepers are exactly the same. Which two are identical?

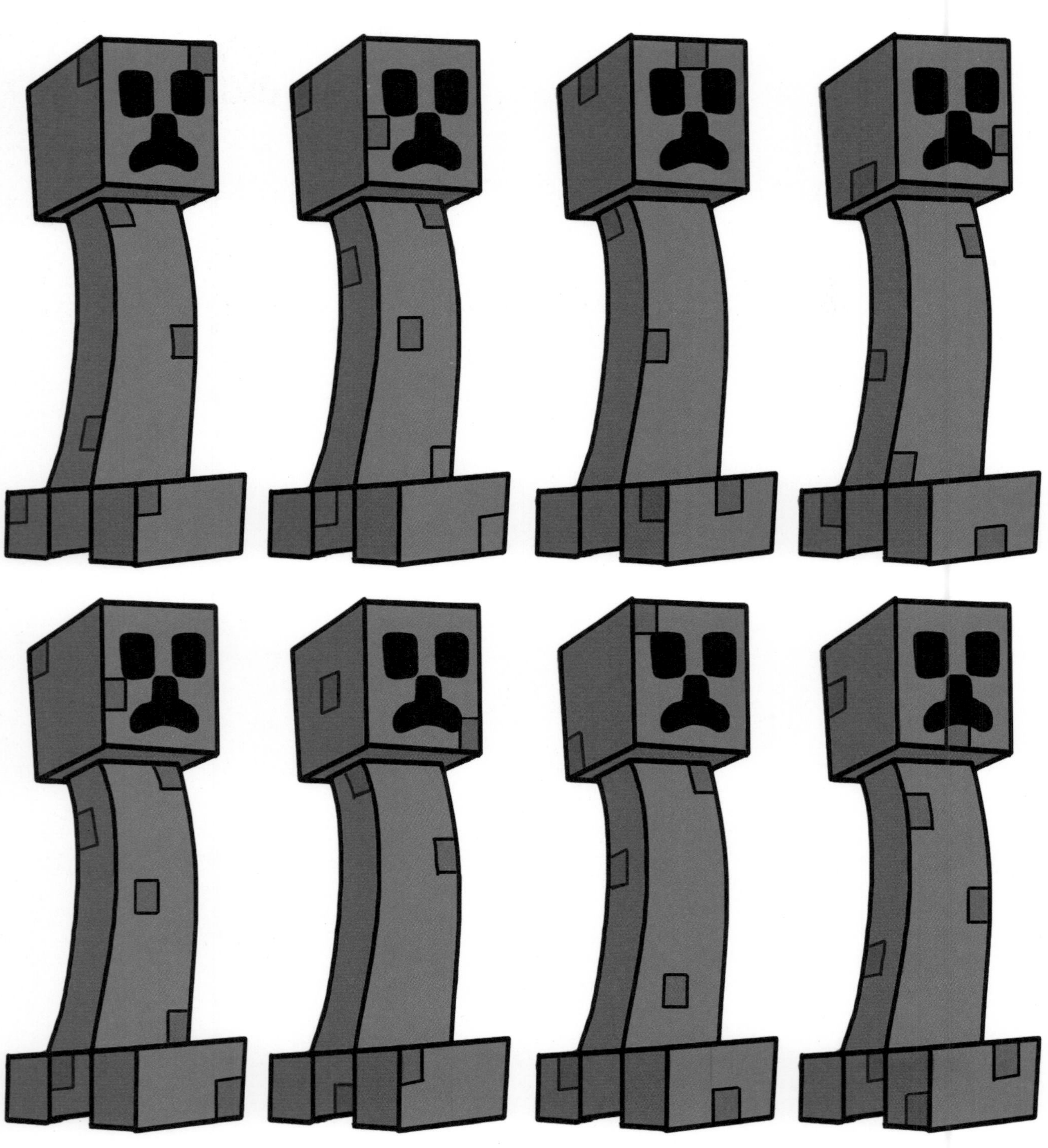

CIRCLE OF TRUTH: CRAFTING CLUE

Start at the ⬇. Write every third letter on the spaces below to reveal a truth that all Minecrafters should know.

D E G I S E A T S M H T O E T N S O D T O M R L A O S K N

D _ _ _ _ _ _ _   _ _ _ _ _ _   _ _ _

_ _ _ _ _ _ _ _ _ _ _   _ _ _ _ _ _

MOB SCENE

Write answers to the clues in the boxes. Read the highlighted boxes downward to reveal a phrase that describes a common Mob scene. Need a hint? The answers are scrambled around the border.

SONIE RACESH TOPUTU REYPAL DRISPE REPEXT GEG DASLED PALSEP

1. To look for something
2. Someone with mad skills
3. Horses and pigs eat these
4. Another word for a Minecrafter
5. The opposite of *input*
6. Use this to ride a pig
7. The eye of this is poisonous and used in brewing
8. Another word for *sound*
9. Use this to spawn a chicken

1.
2.
3.
4.
5.
6.
7.
8.
9.

SQUARED UP: MOBS IN EVERY QUARTER

Each of the four Mobs in this puzzle can appear only once in each row, each column, and the four inside boxes.

B = BABY ZOMBIE VILLAGERS

C = CREEPER

G = GHAST

S = SKELETON

G			B
B	S		
		B	S
	B		G

WATCHTOWER QUEST

Can you find your way back home to where you built the watchtower?

A CURE FOR WHAT AILS YOU

Boxes connected by lines contain the same letter. Some letters are given; others have to be guessed. Fill in all the boxes to reveal a piece of gaming advice.

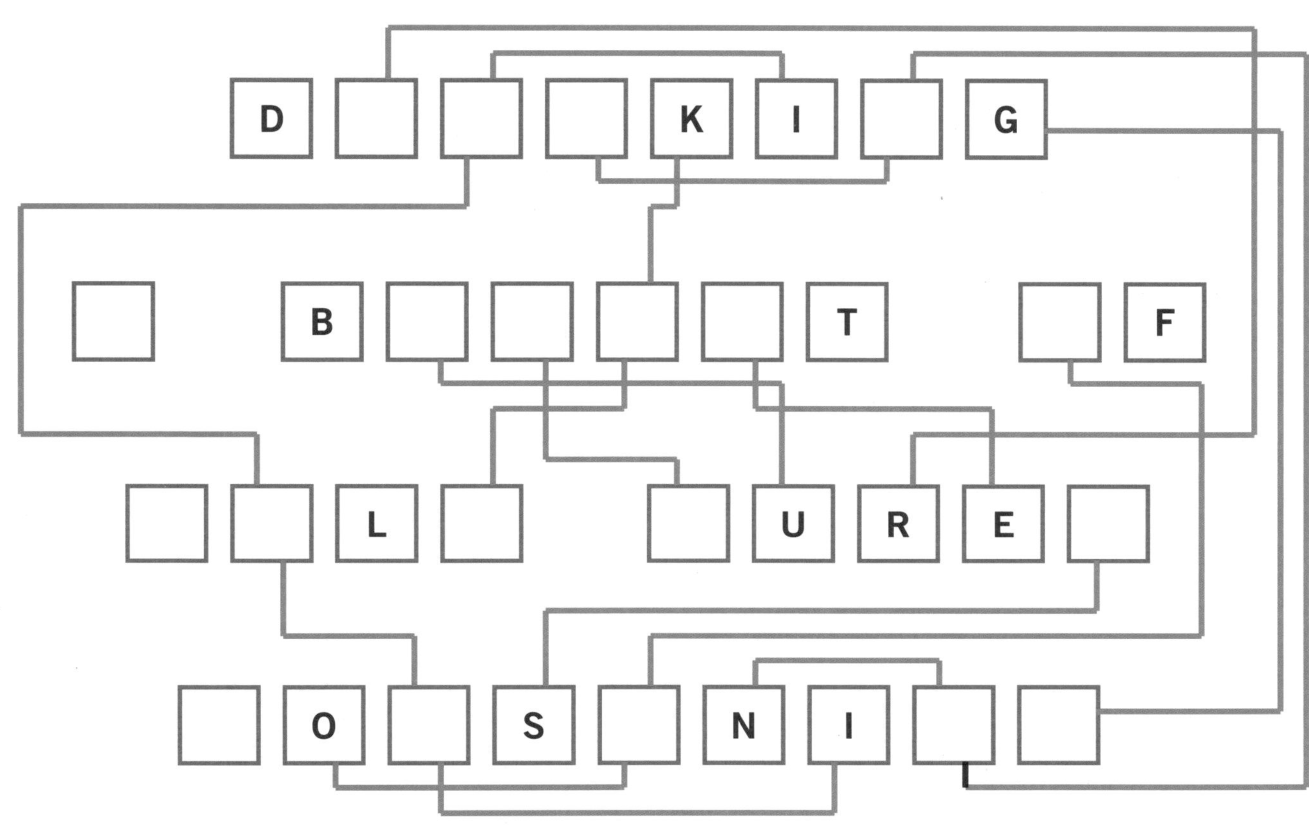

YOU CAN DRAW IT: WOLF

Use the grid to copy the picture one square at a time. Examine the lines in each small square in the top grid then transfer those lines to the corresponding square in the bottom grid. When you finish, you'll have drawn a wolf all your own!

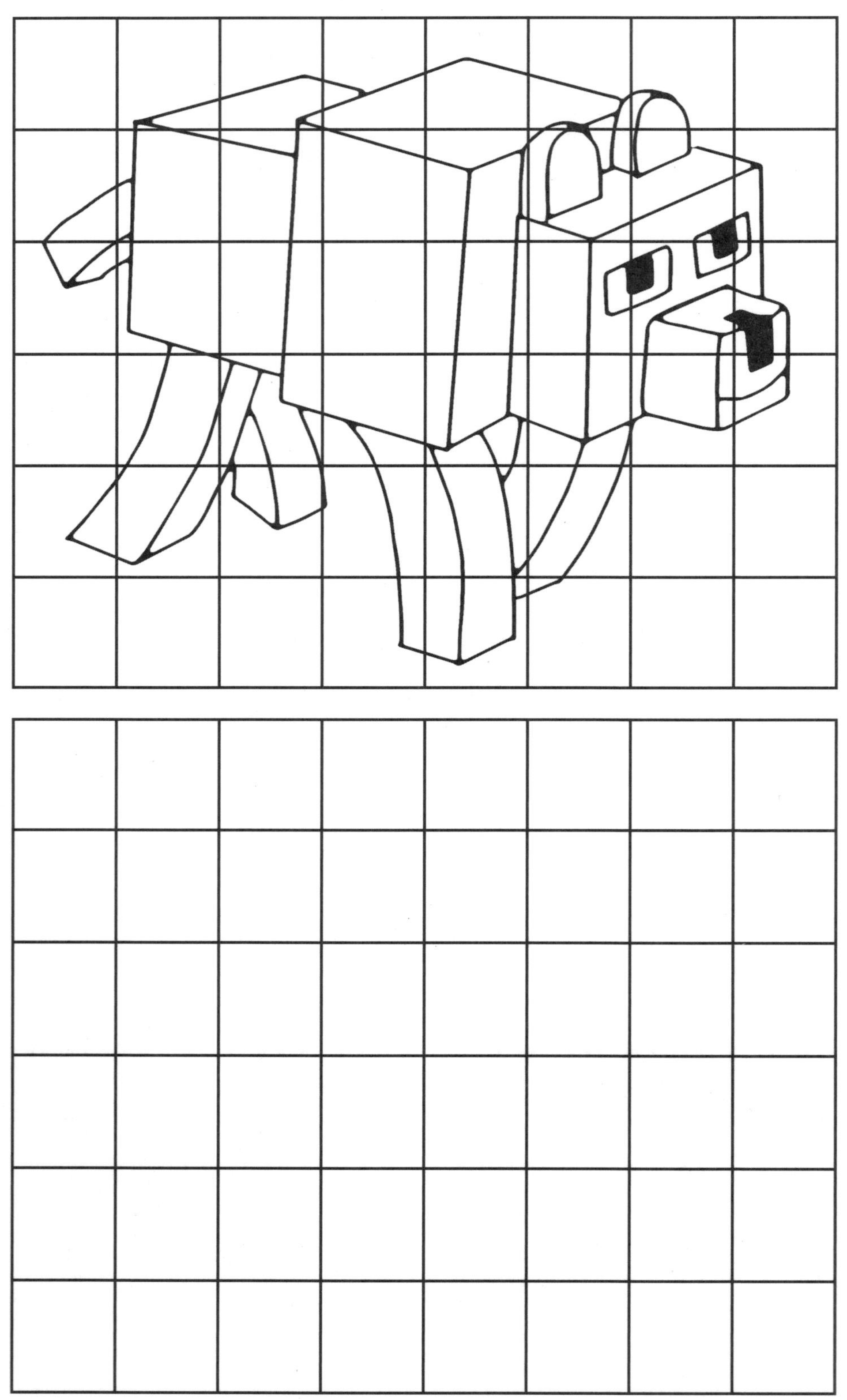

PIECE IT TOGETHER

Identify the seven green puzzle pieces that fit the shapes in the rectangle. Watch out! Pieces might be rotated or flipped. Write the letters of the correct pieces on each space. Not all the pieces will be used.

Read the letters you wrote to reveal the answer to the following question: ***What Mobs make Steve and Alex tremble in fear?***

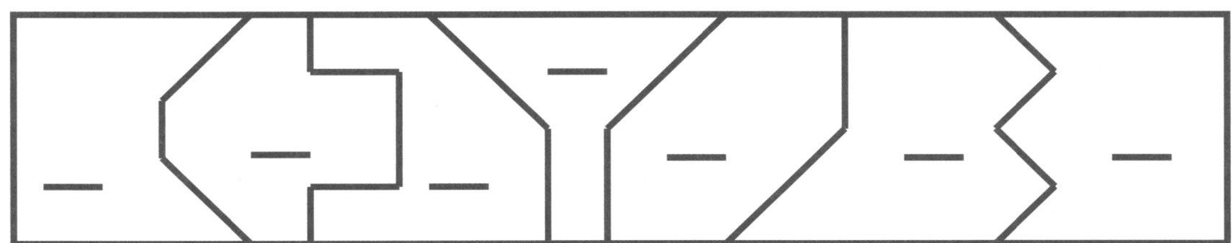

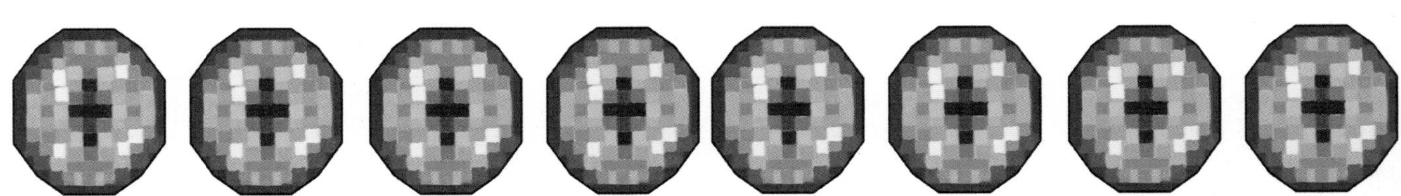

PICK, THE RIGHT TOOL!

There are thirteen pickaxes hidden in this toolshed. Can you pick them all out?

TOOL CHEST

Find and circle the names of nine Minecrafting tools in the letters. They might be forward, backward, up, down, or diagonal. Watch out! Every T, O, and L has been chipped away and replaced by a pickaxe. Can you find all nine tools?

CLOCK	**FLINT AND STEEL**	**PICKAXE**
COMPASS	**IRON AXE**	**SHEARS**
FISHING ROD	**LEAD**	**SHOVEL**

G K C ⛏ ⛏ C W E D ⛏ I S U

I M P E D ⛏ I R ⛏ N A X E

⛏ J B ⛏ S M S P A M ⛏ F H

V U P D N P F ⛏ X S G B ⛏

F ⛏ I N ⛏ A N D S ⛏ E E ⛏

P C C R E S Y U B Q V N W

D W K ⛏ K S H A U ⛏ F C I

A ⛏ A U H V C E H K Y J R

E K X I ⛏ A N S A R ⛏ F ⛏

⛏ X E M U H ⛏ U C R M E I

A ⛏ S D ⛏ R G N I H S I F

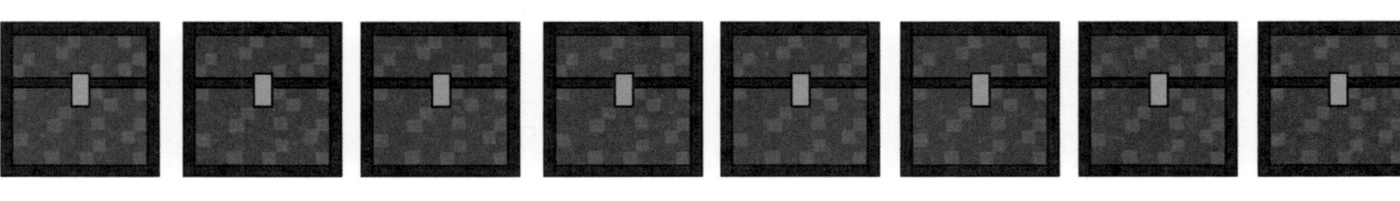

FIND THE PORTAL

Four players are racing to find the End portal. Only one will make it. Follow each player's path, under and over crossing paths, to discover who gets there and who hits a dead end.

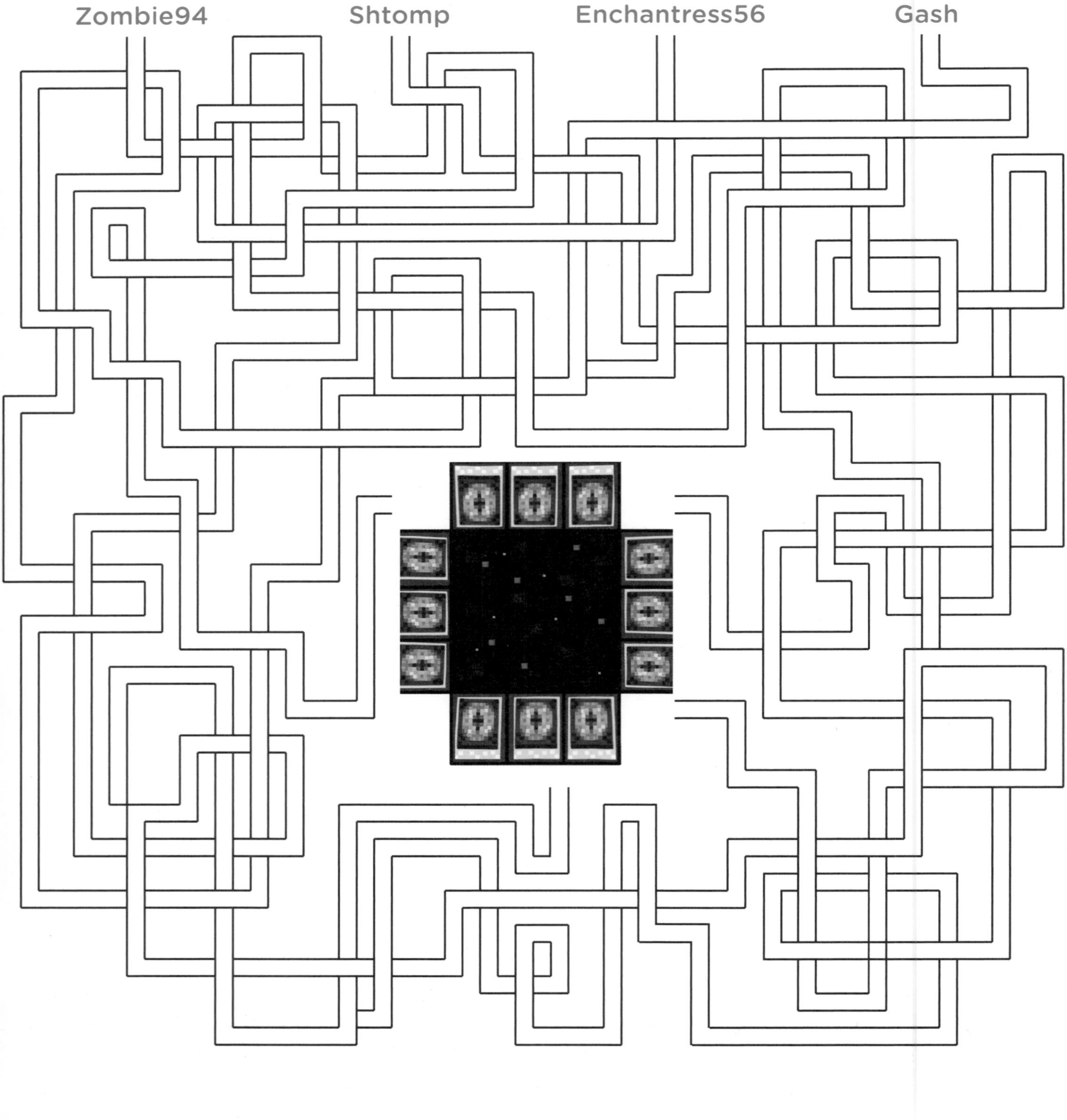

Zombie94 Shtomp Enchantress56 Gash

CROSSWORD CLUE FINDER

Use the pictures and arrows to help you fill in this crossword picture puzzle. Some words can fit in more than one location, so choose carefully!

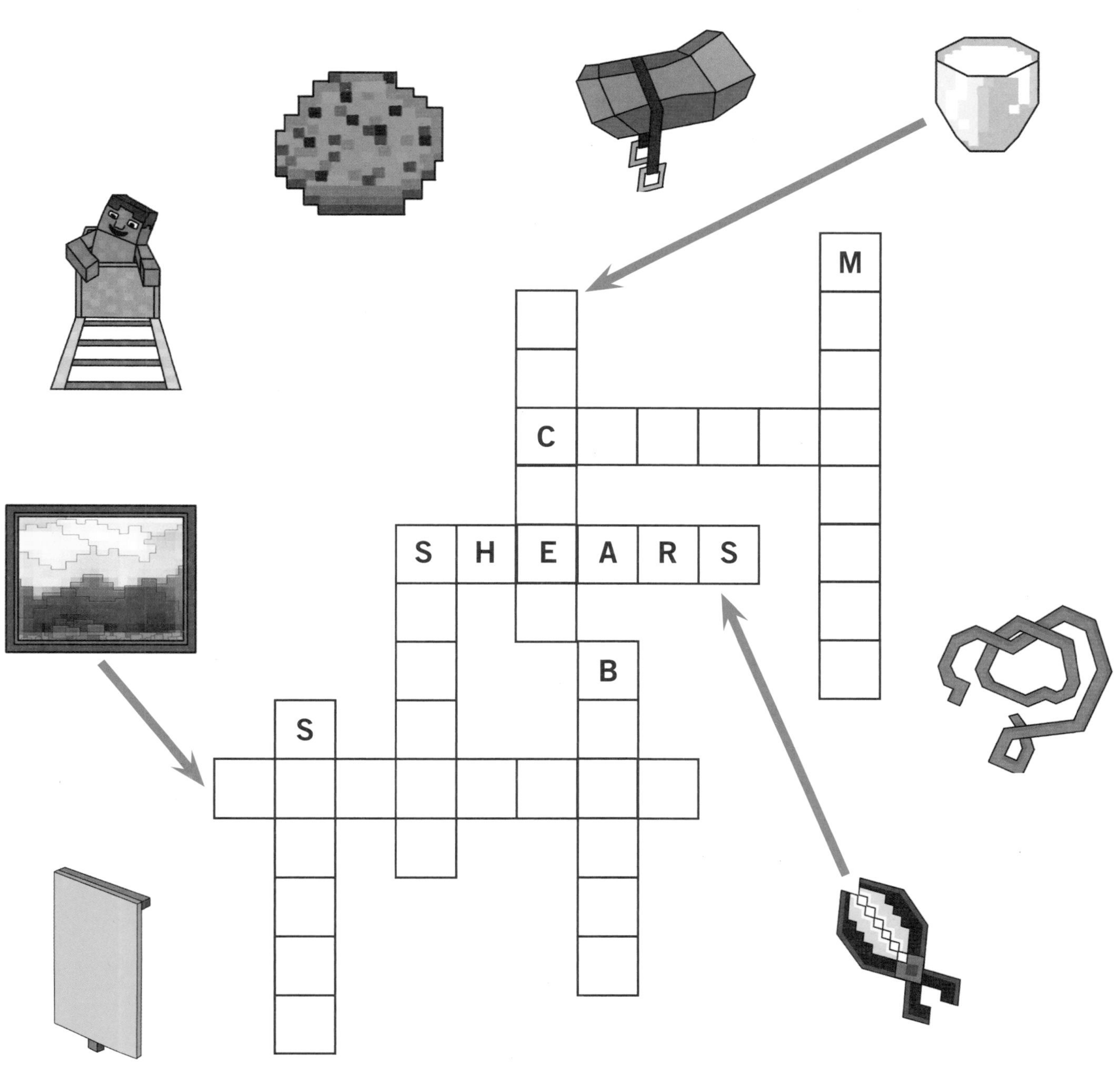

SEE THE SEA

These two pictures seem identical, but there are eleven differences between them. How many can you see?

POWER PLAY: MYSTERY WORD

Every word in Column B contains the same letters as a word in Column A, plus one letter. Draw a line between word "matches," then write the extra letter on the space provided. Unscramble the column of letters to reveal a powerful resource for Minecrafters.

COLUMN A	COLUMN B	EXTRA LETTER
Points	Steve	___
Healer	Diamond	___
Vest	Armor	___
Meander	Hardcore	___
Mentor	Potions	___
Domain	Monster	___
Roam	Enderman	___
Orchard	Leather	___

___ ___ ___ ___ ___ ___ ___ ___

SURVIVAL MAZE

Find your way through this maze from Start to Finish without bumping into a ghast, creeper, zombie, or skeleton.

Start

Finish

BLOCKED!

The names of fourteen Minecraft blocks are hidden below. They might be forward, backward, up, down, or diagonal. For an added challenge, some of the letters are blocked: every D, I, R, and T has been replaced by a ▢. Can you find all fourteen block names?

ANDESITE	**GRANITE**	**OBSIDIAN**
BEACON	**LAPIS LAZULI**	**PRISMARINE**
DIORITE	**MONSTER EGG**	**PUMPKIN**
EMERALD	**MUSHROOM**	**SPONGE**
GLOWSTONE	**NETHER WART**	

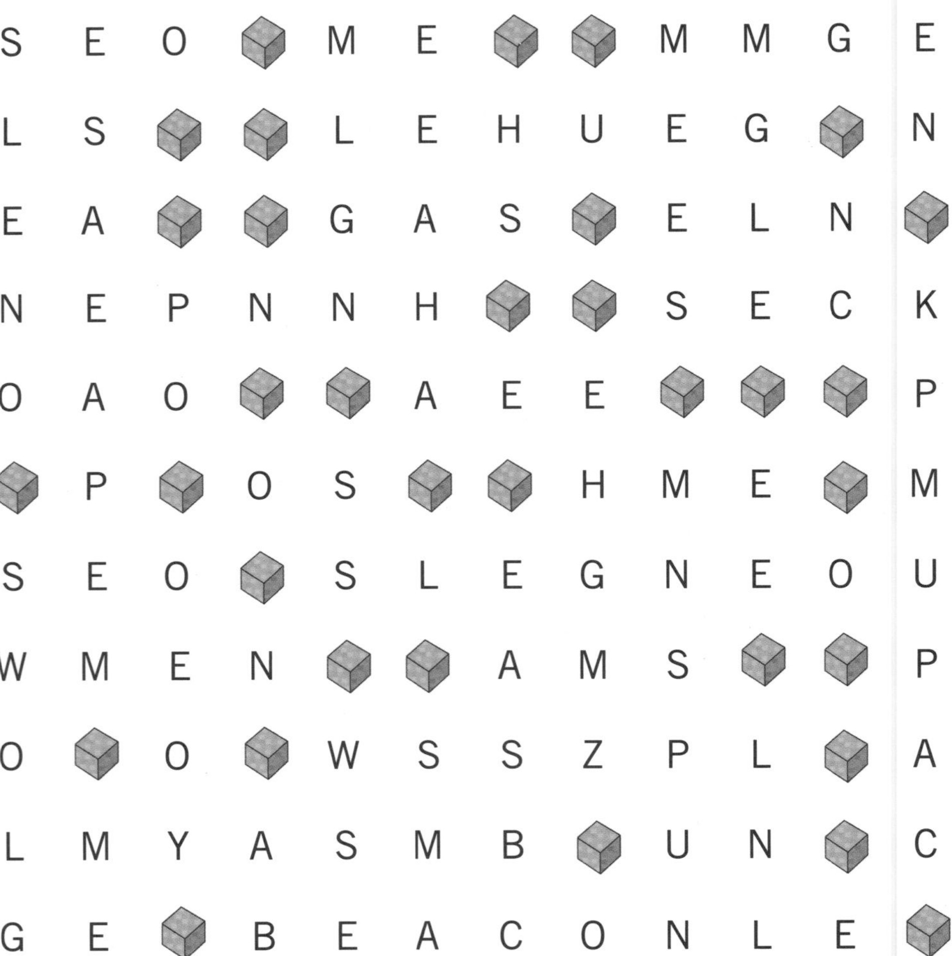

CONNECT THE DOTS: HOSTILE MOB

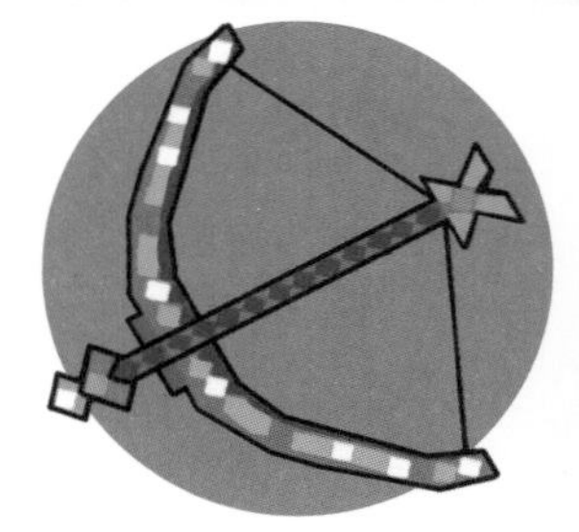

Connect the dots to discover the original boss Mob!

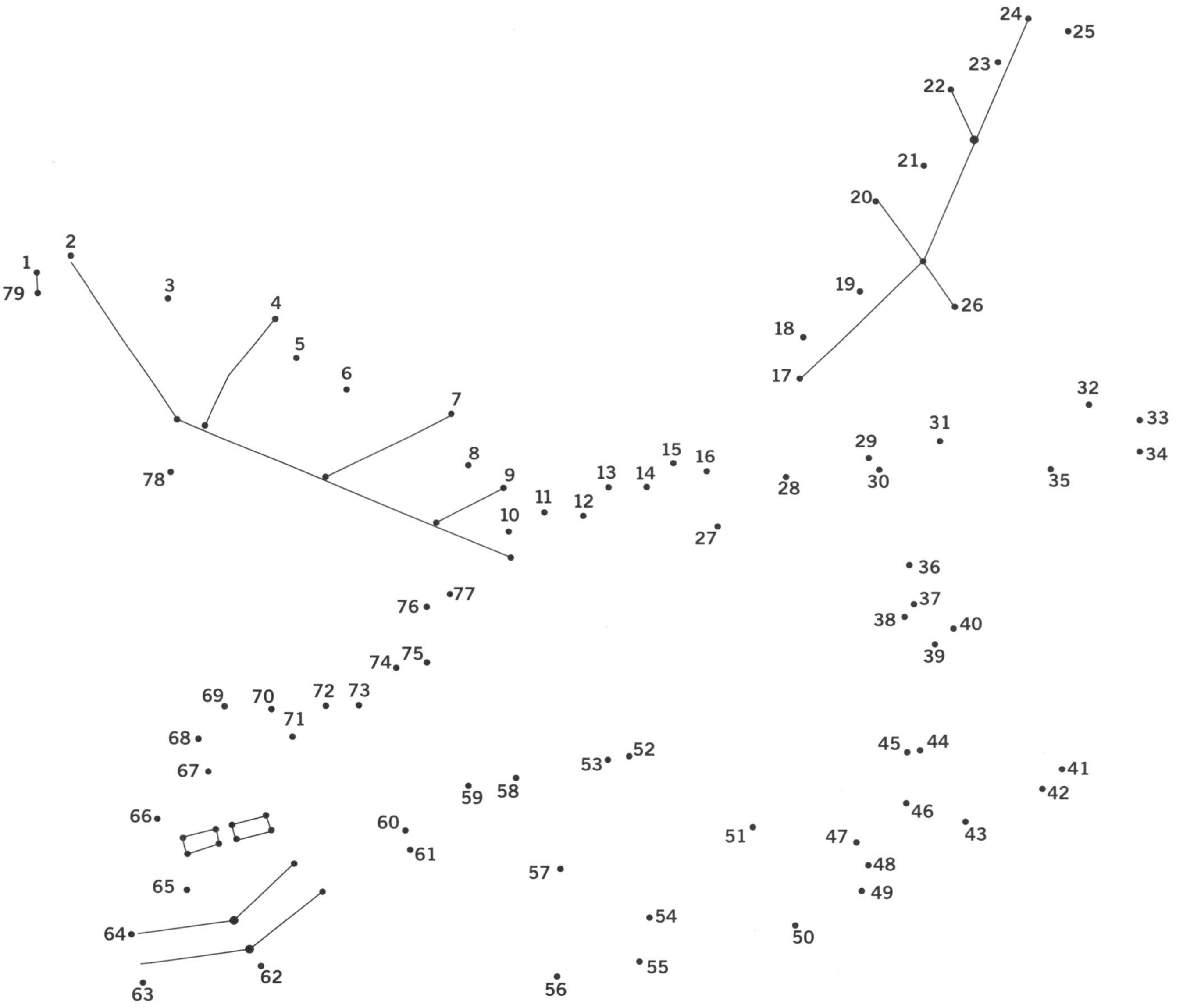

1 2 3 4 5 6 7 8 9 10 11 12 13 14 15 16 17 18 19 20 21 22 23 24 25 26 27 28 29 30 31 32 33 34 35 36 37 38 39 40 41 42 43 44 45 46 47 48 49 50 51 52 53 54 55 56 57 58 59 60 61 62 63 64 65 66 67 68 69 70 71 72 73 74 75 76 77 78 79

MIXED UP

Write the answers to the clues on the spaces, one letter on each blank. Then transfer the letters to the boxes below that have the same numbers. If you fill in the boxes correctly, you'll reveal something Alex loves to brew.

Clue	Blanks
Big smile	_ _ _ _ (9 6 13 3)
12 o'clock p.m.	_ _ _ _ (15 11 14 8)
Pork chop source	_ _ _ (10 2 4)
Ceramic square on a bathroom floor	_ _ _ _ (12 7 1 5)

1	2	3	4	5	6	7	8	9

10	11	12	13	14	15

A SMALL PROBLEM

Every word in Column B contains the same letters as a word in Column A, plus one extra letter. Draw a line between word "matches," then write the extra letter on the space provided.

Unscramble the column of letters to reveal a small problem for Minecrafters.

Column A	Column B	
Drips	Slime	___
Wasp	Tamed	___
Lies	Spider	___
Unreal	Hostile	___
Thaw	Neutral	___
Hotels	Pearl	___
Meat	Wheat	___
Trace	Spawn	___
Leap	Create	___

___ ___ ___ ___ ___ ___ ___ ___ ___

CRACK THE CODE

You don't need a pickaxe to crack this code, just your brain.

Use the code below to find the answer to the joke:

Why did Steve attack the cake with a stick?

W	P	O	C	A	S	T	B	K	U	D	I	N	E	R

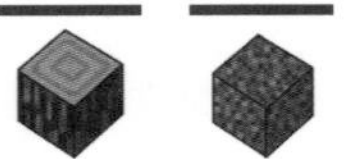 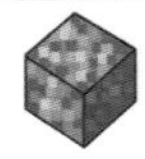   

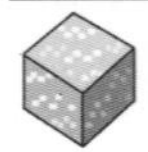  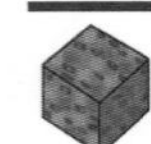   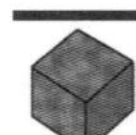  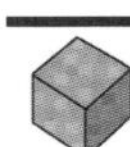 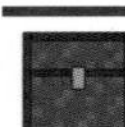

ALPHA CODE

The answer to the joke will be revealed as you add letters to the empty boxes that come before, between, or after the given letters in the alphabet. If you get to Z, start all over again with A. The first letter has already been written for you.

Why was the Ender Dragon book a flop?

B									
C	F	D	B	V	T	F		J	U
D	G	E	C	W	U	G		K	V

R	S	Z	Q	S	D	C
T	U	B	S	U	F	E

Y	R		R	F	C		C	L	B
Z	S		S	G	D		D	M	C

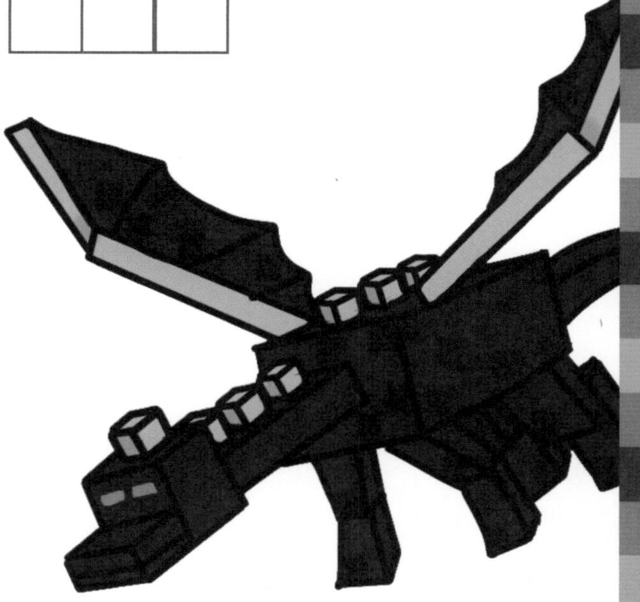

GRAB AND GO CHALLENGE

Pick up every single experience orb in this maze, but do it quickly to escape the zombie chasing you. You'll need to draw a line from Start to Stop that passes through every orb once. Your line can go up, down, left, or right, but not diagonally. On your mark, get set, go!

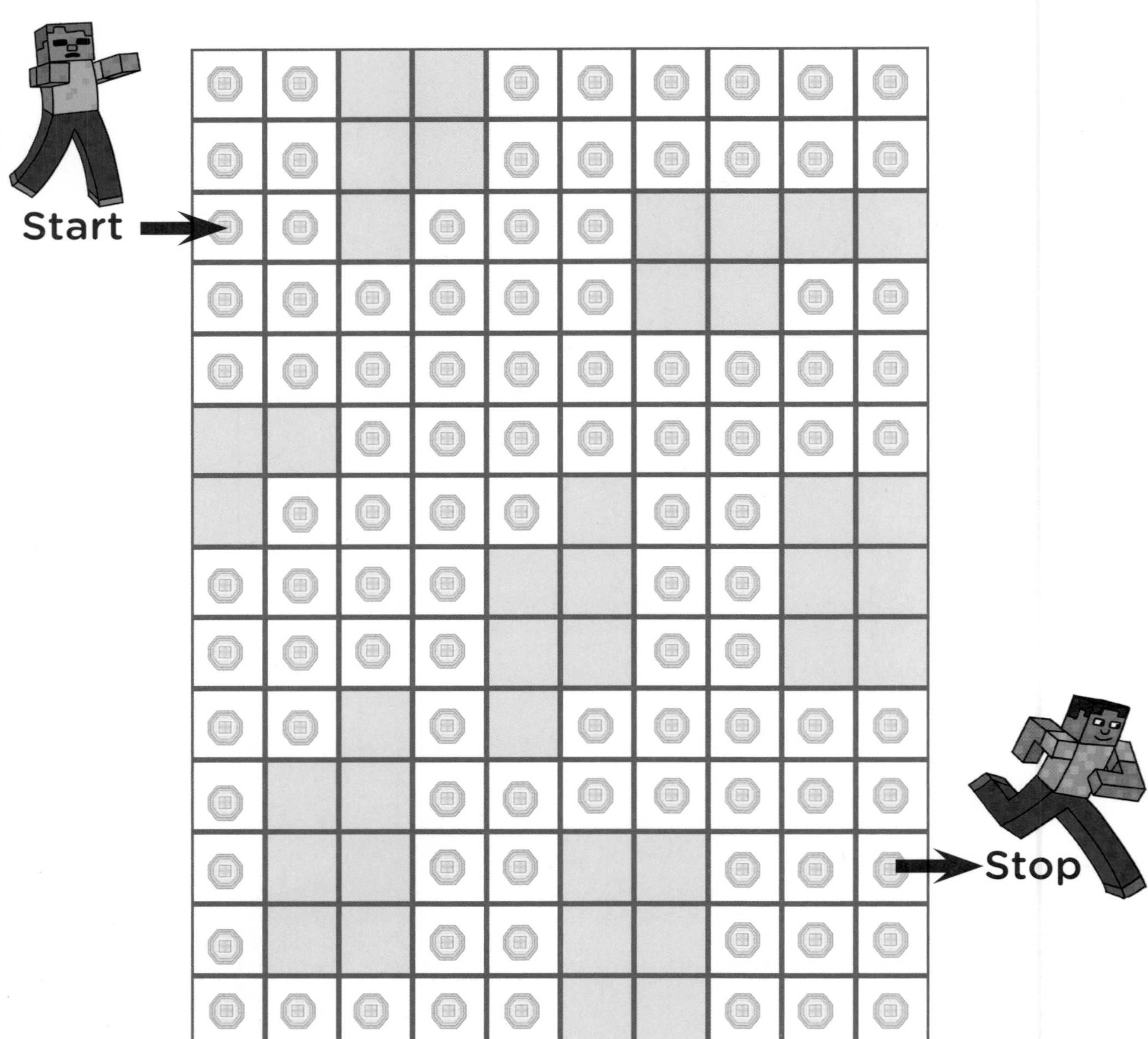

WORD MINE

Find and circle the names of fourteen raw materials in the wordfind. They might be forward, backward, up, down, or diagonal. Watch out! Every R, A, and W has been replaced with a redstone block.

BLAZE ROD
DIAMOND
DRAGON'S BREATH
ENDER PEARL
FEATHER
FLINT
GLOWSTONE DUST
GOLD INGOT
LEATHER
MAGMA CREAM
NETHER WART
PRISMARINE SHARD
REDSTONE
STRING

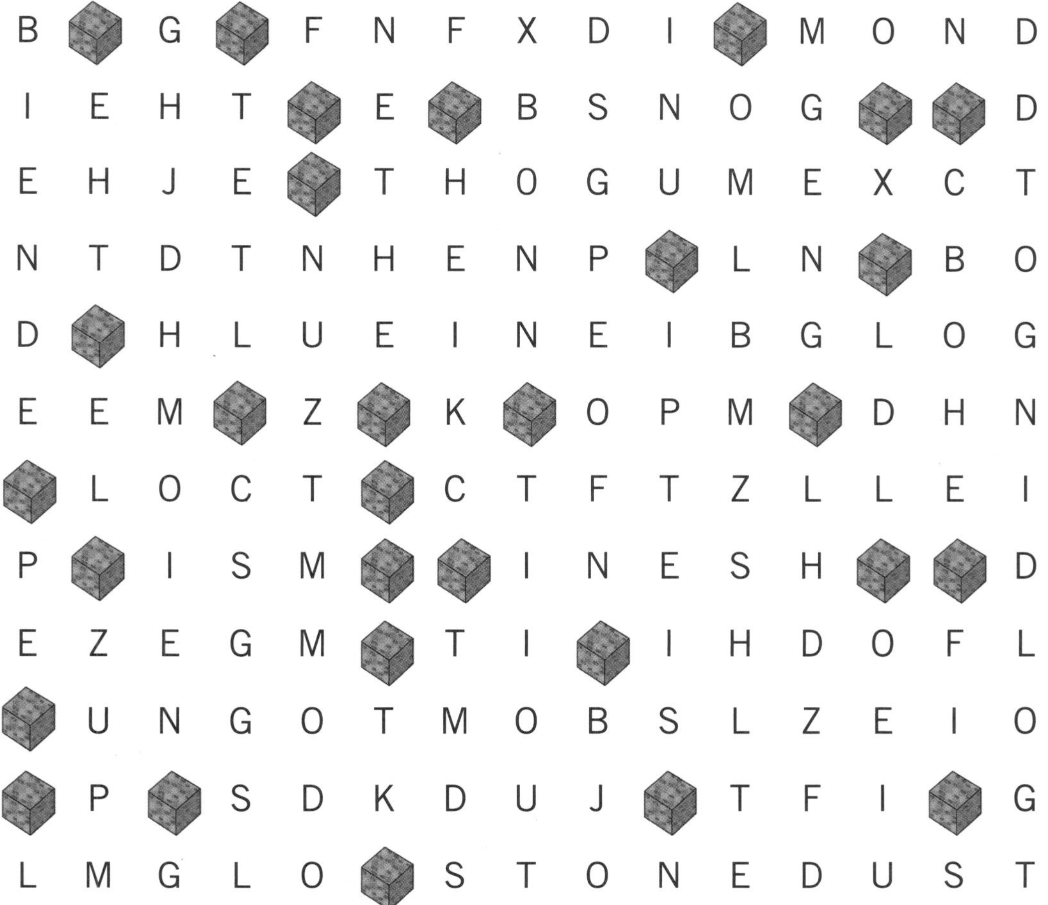

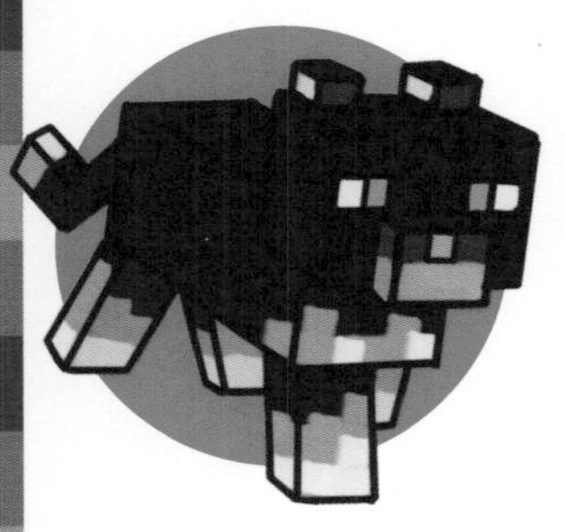

CIRCLE OF TRUTH: FUN FACT

Start at the ▼. Write every third letter on the spaces to reveal a Minecrafting secret.

▼

Y A A O T C U S H C I E A T S N S T T O I O I O N F P I A E T C N

Y _ _   _ _ _ _ ' _   _ _ _ _ _   _   _ _ _ _ _ _

_ _   _   _ _ _   _ _ _ _ _   _ _   _ _

ZOMBIE TWINS

Only two of these zombies are exactly the same. Which two are identical?

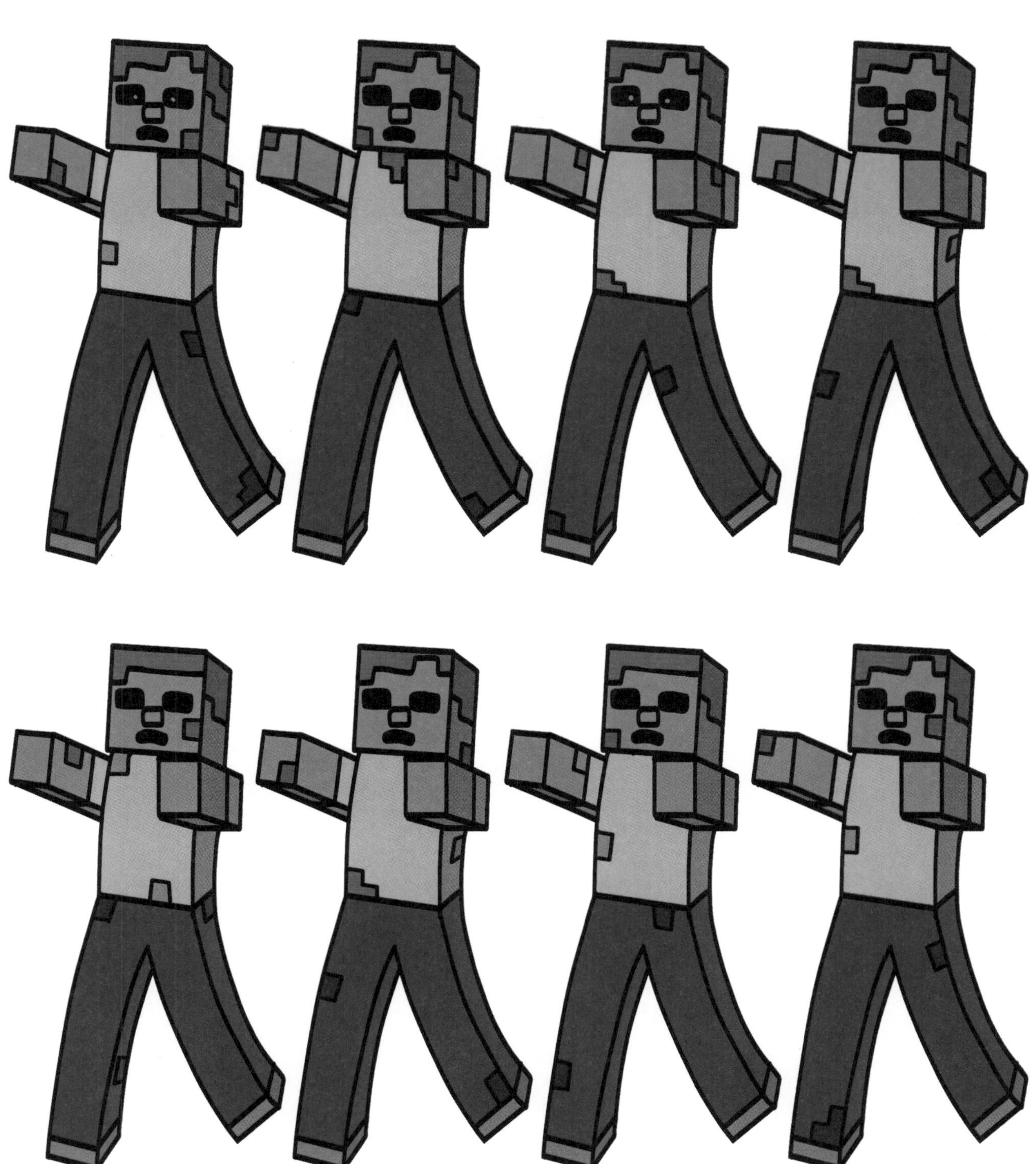

CAN YOU DIG IT?

Turn MINE into ORES one letter at a time. The answer to each clue looks like the word above it, except one letter is different. If you get stuck, try working from the bottom up.

A silent actor

Ten-cent coin

Darkens slowly

Points at a target

Where elbows are found

Greek god of war

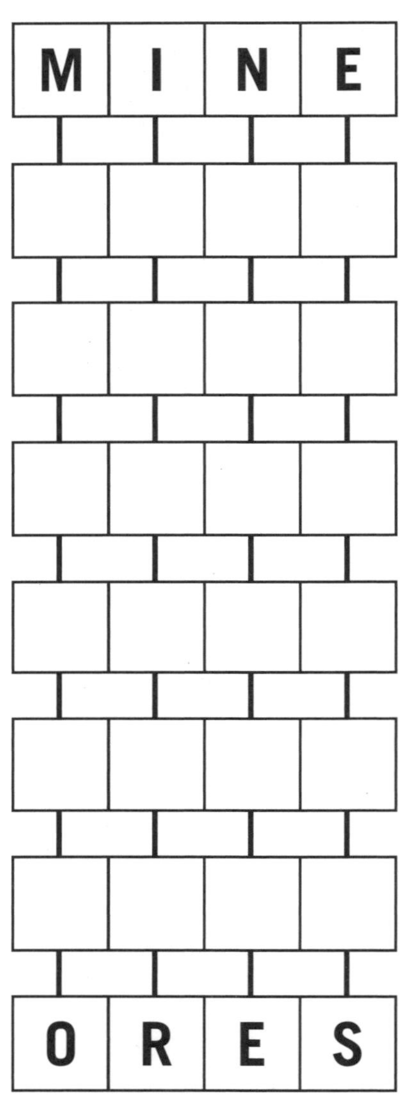

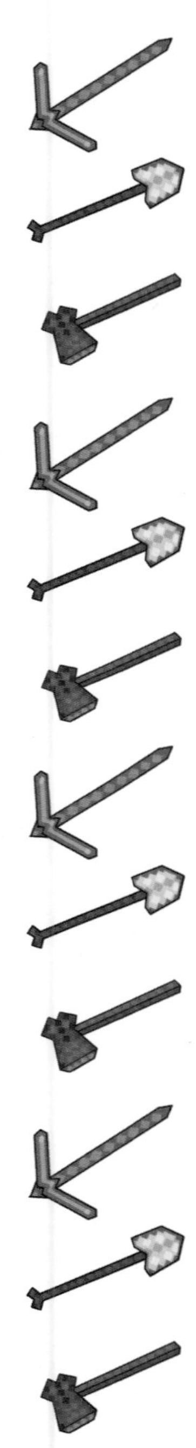

SQUARED UP: FARM MOBS

Each of the four Mobs in this puzzle can appear only once in each row, each column, and the four inside boxes. Fill in the remaining empty boxes with the first letter of a Mob shown below.

C = COW

P = PIG

H = HORSE

S = SHEEP

S	H		P
	C		
C		S	
H			C

GROW WITH THE FLOW

Find the flow of letters that spell out a fun fact for Minecrafters. Start with the corner letter, then read every third letter, moving clockwise around the square, until all the letters are used.

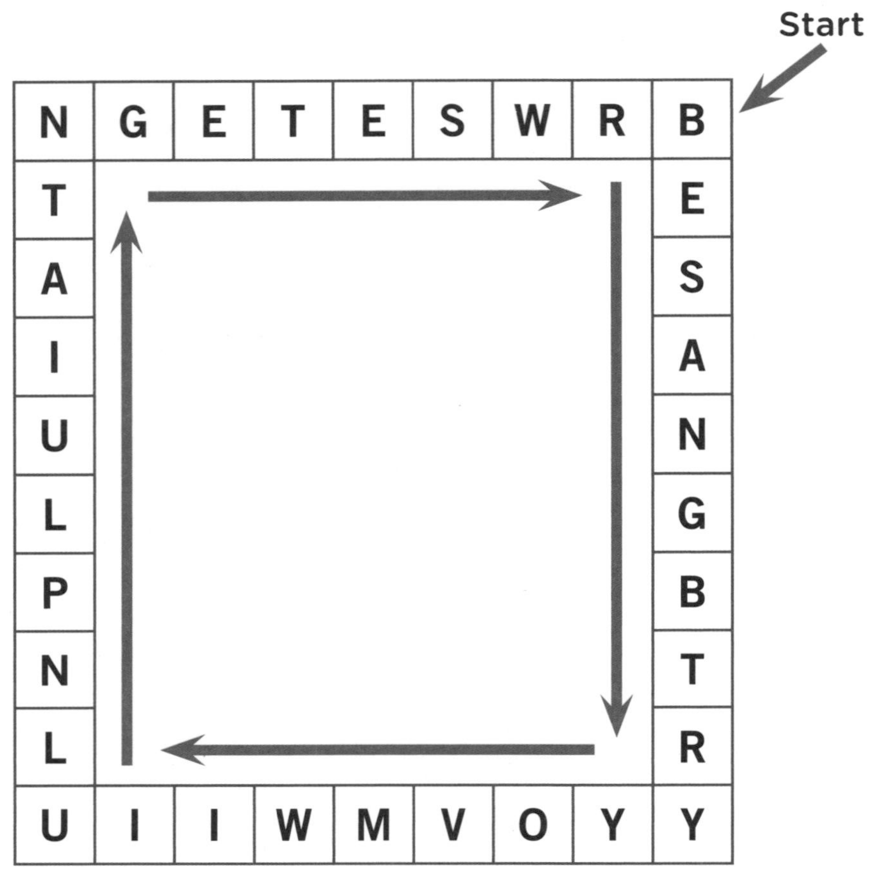

_ _ _ _ _   _ _ _ _ _ _ _ _ _ _   _ _ _ _ _

_ _   _ _   _ _ _ _ _ _ _ _   _ _ _ _ _ _ _ _

BASIC TRAINING

Boxes connected by lines contain the same letter. Some letters are given; others have to be guessed. Fill in all the boxes to reveal a list of items with a connection. Do you know what the connection is?

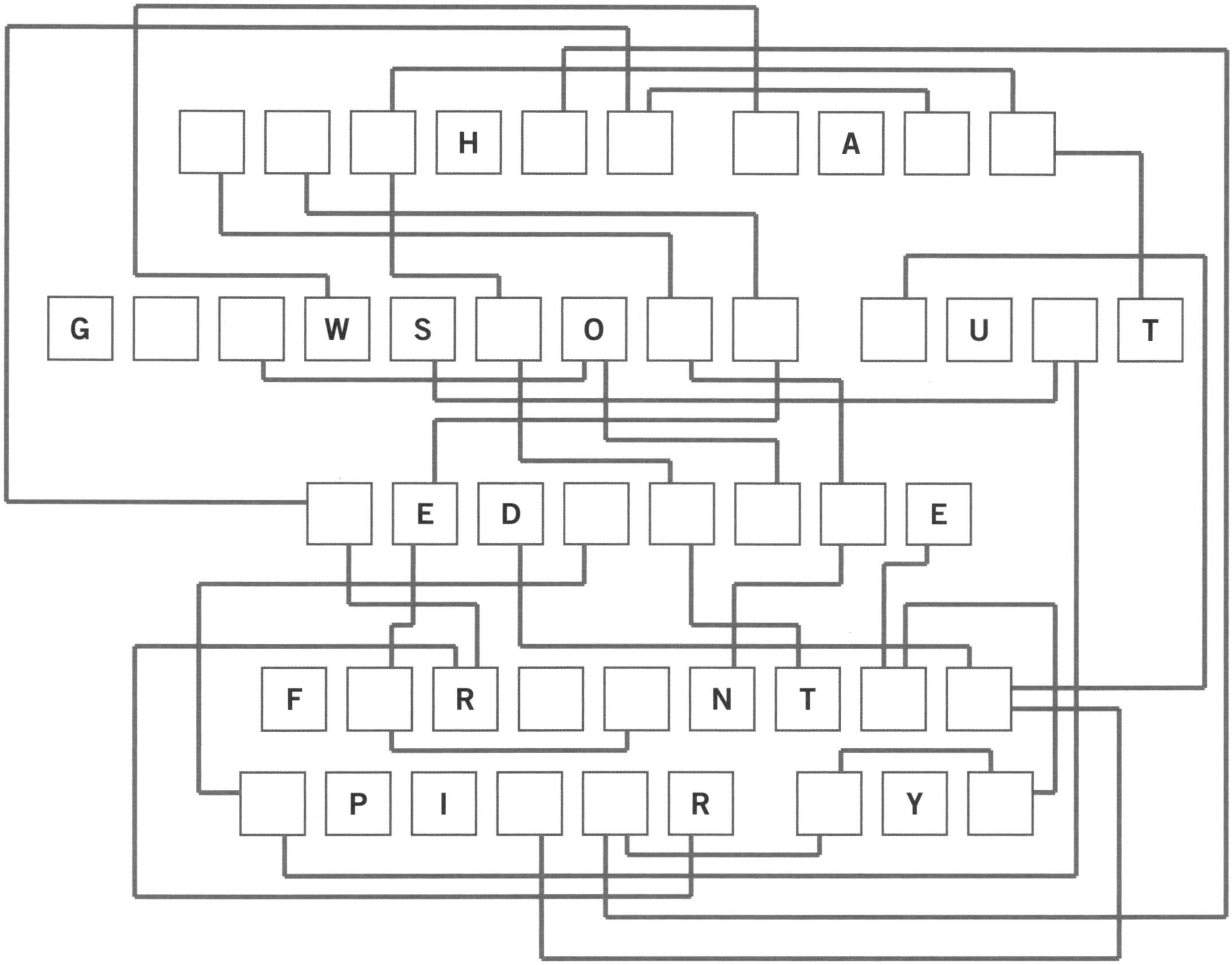

H A

G W S O U T

E D E

F R N T

P I R Y

YOU CAN DRAW IT: VILLAGERS

Use the grid to copy the picture. Examine each small square in the top grid, then transfer those lines to the corresponding square in the bottom grid.

THE SHAPE OF THINGS TO COME

Find the six puzzle pieces that fit the shapes in the rectangle. Watch out! Pieces might be rotated or flipped and not all of them will be used. Write the letters of the correct pieces on the spaces below to answer the question:

What Mob helps keep creepers away?

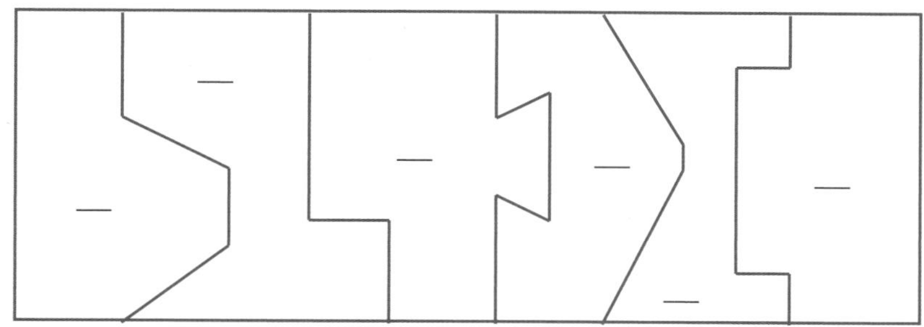

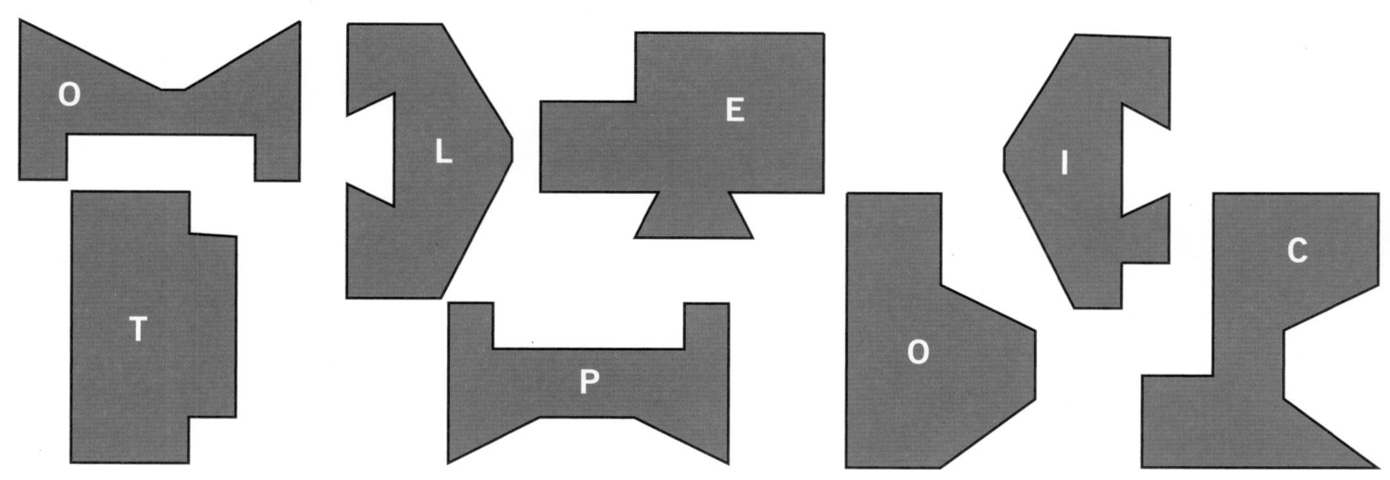

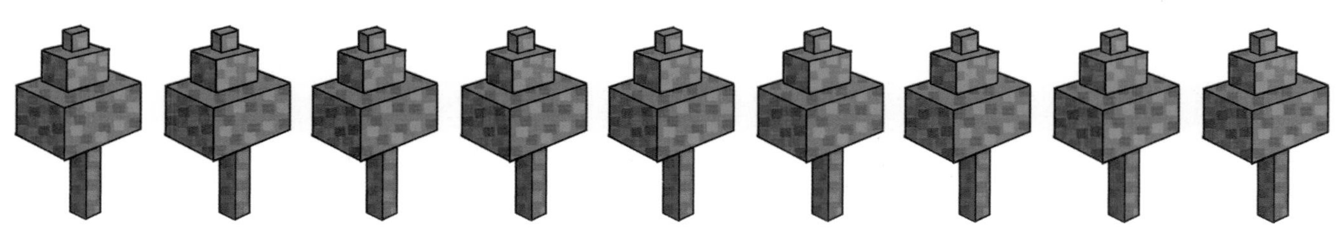

WHEN PIGS HIDE

This pigsty contains thirteen hidden pigs. Can you find them all?

MINER'S BLOCK

Find and circle the names of eight gems in the wordfind below. They might be forward, backward, up, down, or diagonal. Write unused letters on the spaces, in order from top to bottom and left to right, to uncover a tip for mining.

Hint: *Circle individual letters instead of the whole word at once. The first one has been done for you.*

~~COAL~~	EMERALD	IRON	NETHER QUARTZ
DIAMOND	GOLD	LAPIS LAZULI	REDSTONE

R	D	D	I	L	G	A	D	R	O	U	N
E	I	L	U	Z	A	L	S	I	P	A	L
D	D	O	D	I	A	O	A	M	O	N	I
S	D	G	O	R	R	E	C	S	O	R	D
T	I	A	E	M	D	I	A	M	O	N	D
O	O	M	N	D	S	D	O	N	N	T	F
N	E	T	H	E	R	Q	U	A	R	T	Z
E	A	L	L	I	N	T	O	L	A	V	A

_ _ _   _ _ _ _ _ _   _ _ _ _ _ _ _   _ _ _

_ _   _ _ _ _ _ _ _ _   _ _ _, _

_ _ _ _   _ _ _ _   _ _ _ _.

TRUE OR FALSE?

Find your way through this maze from Start to Finish. It will be easier if you answer the questions correctly!

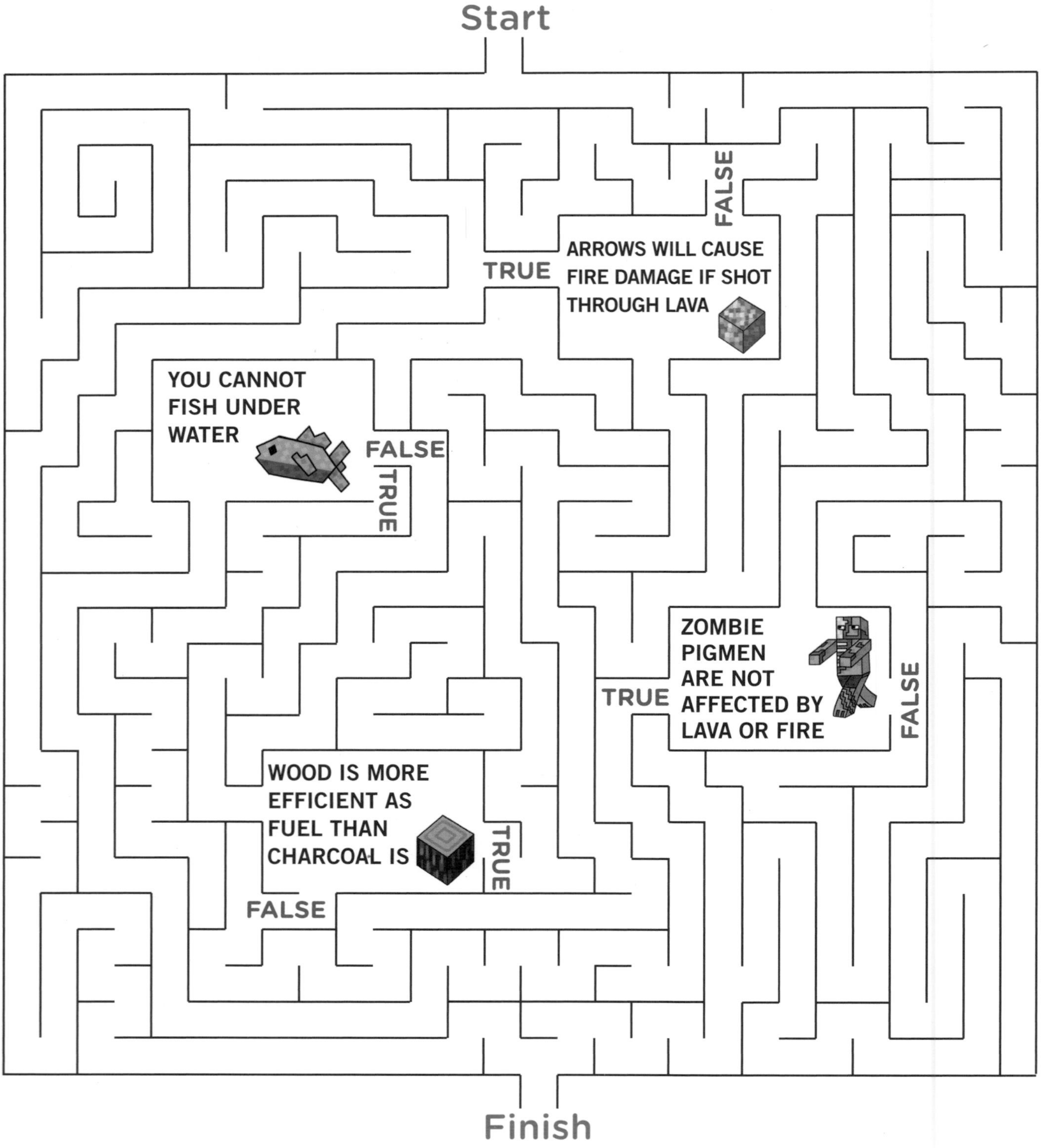

Start

ARROWS WILL CAUSE FIRE DAMAGE IF SHOT THROUGH LAVA

TRUE

FALSE

YOU CANNOT FISH UNDER WATER

FALSE

TRUE

ZOMBIE PIGMEN ARE NOT AFFECTED BY LAVA OR FIRE

TRUE

FALSE

WOOD IS MORE EFFICIENT AS FUEL THAN CHARCOAL IS

TRUE

FALSE

Finish

STEVE SAYS: JOKE TIME

Reveal the answer to the joke by doing what Steve says—and only what Steve says!

	1	2	3	4	5
A	ONE	CRACKS	HEALING	ALL	STRENGTH
B	418	IF	THIRTEEN	WAX	LEAPING
C	ROADS	HISS	ARE	A	BOOM
D	HACKS	THIRTY	INVISIBILITY	ON	7,359,864
E	RATTLE	BLOCKED	MOAN	IT	SWIFTNESS

1. **Steve says**, "Cross off all numbers in Rows B and D and Column 1."
2. **Steve says**, "Cross off all potions in Columns in 3 and 5."
3. **Steve says**, "Cross off words that rhyme with 'axe.'"
4. Cross off words that start or end with vowels.
5. **Steve says**, "Cross off all Mob sounds in Rows C and E."
6. **Steve says**, "Cross off words with fewer than three letters in Columns 2 and 4."
7. **Steve says**, "Write the remaining four words to reveal the answer to the joke."

Why are there no cars in Minecraft?

____________ ____________ ____________ ____________

ON THE PLAYGROUND

Take a good look to find the ten differences between these two pictures.

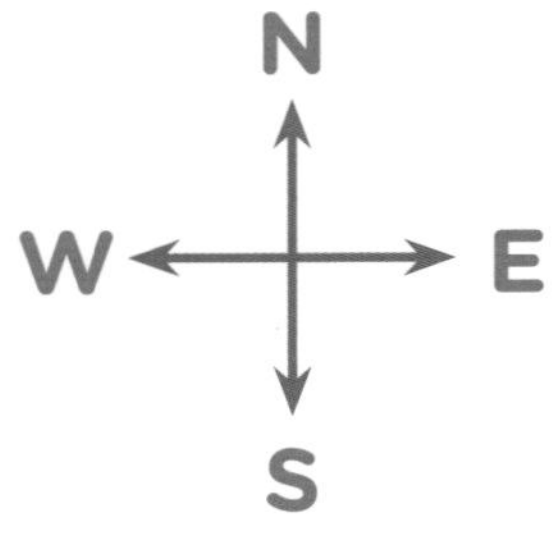

ENCHANTED MAP

This End City map is enchanted. To reveal its contents, you must press all twelve buttons in the right order and land on the F button last. Use the letters and numbers on the buttons to direct you.

Which button must you push first to get to F last?

Hint: *1N means press the button one space north; 2E means move two spaces east. W=west and S=south.*

2S	2S	1W	3W
F	2E	2W	1S
2E	1N	1N	2N

COMMON CODE

Use the key to identify three items that are familiar to Minecrafters. Then use the key to fill in the last set of blank spaces to reveal where all three items are found.

A	C	D	E	G	H	K	L	N	O	R	S	T	U	W

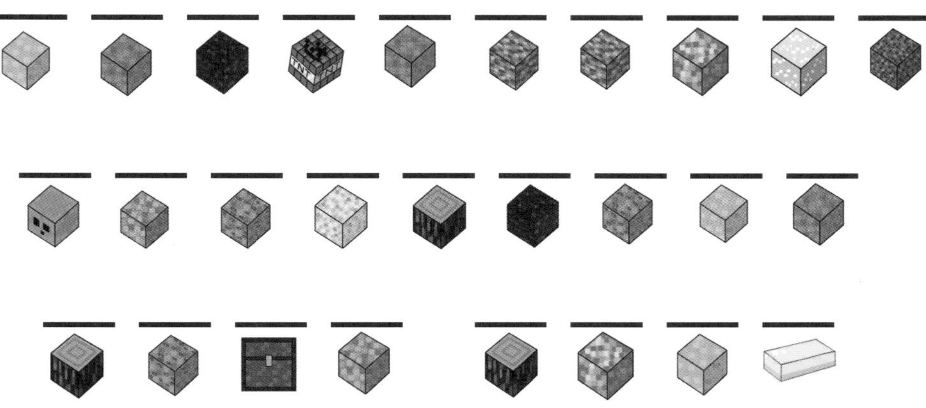

What do the three words above have in common?

They're all found in

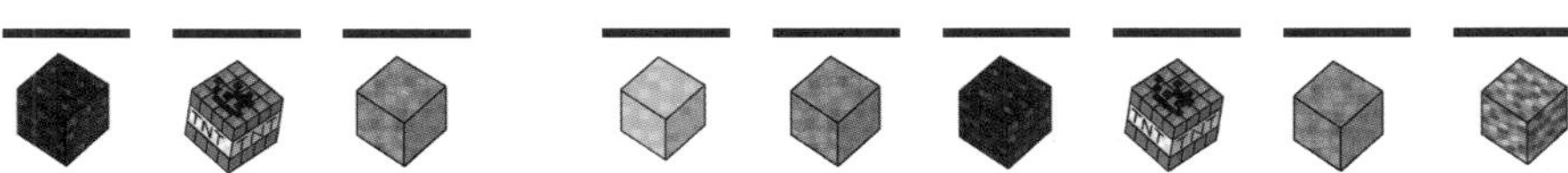

EVERY NOOK AND CRANNY

Draw a line from Start to Stop that passes through every apple once and only once. Your line can go up, down, left, or right, but not diagonally. On your mark, get set, go!

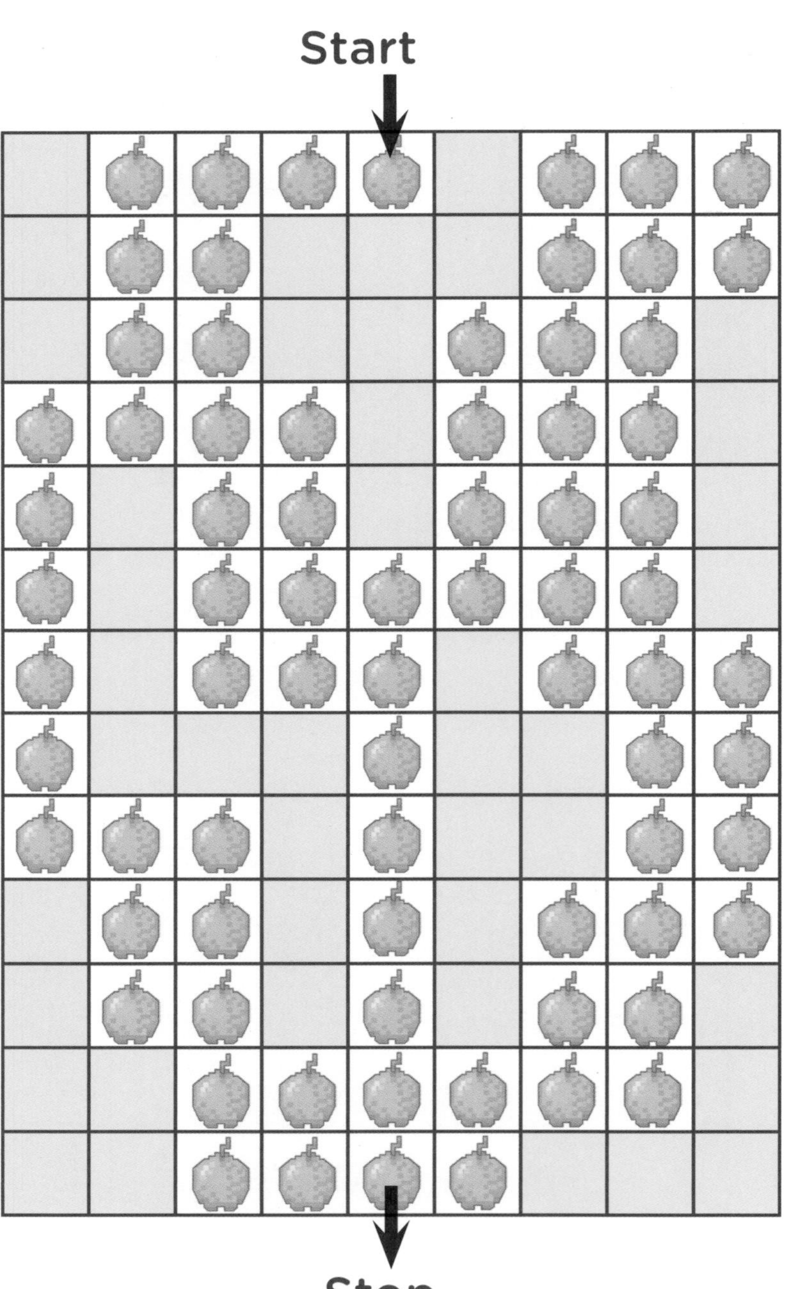

CIRCLE OF TRUTH: SURVIVAL TIP

Start at the ⬇. Write every third letter on the spaces to reveal a truth about Minecraft.

W N H E T E A G A R E D A T A P A N U N D M G E P R N K Y D I W E N I R O T M N H E Y Y N O O W U U O R

W _ _ _   _   _ _ _ _ _ _ _   _ _   _ _ _ _

_ _ _ _   _ _ _   _ _ _ _ _ _ _ _   _ _ _'_

_ _ _   _ _ _ _ _   _ _ _ _   _ _ _

SKELETON TWINS

Only two of these skeletons are exactly the same. Which two are identical? Circle the twins.

CONNECT THE DOTS: PIT OF PERIL!

Connect the dots to complete this perilous scene.

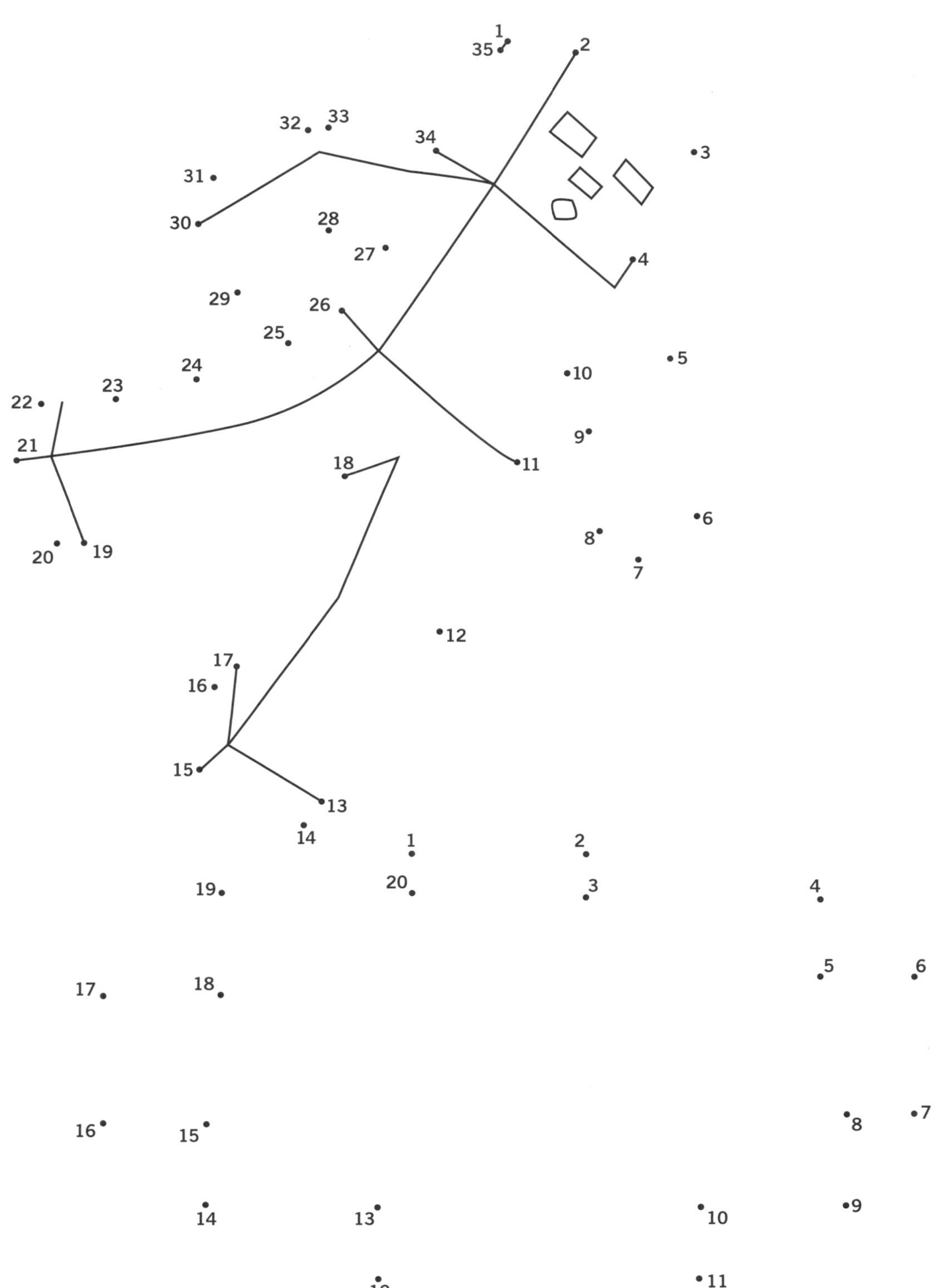

SQUARED UP: BLOCK PARTY

Each of the six blocks in this puzzle can appear only once in each row, each column, and pink rectangle. Use the letter C to represent a clay block, the letter D for a dirt block, and so on. Can you fill every square with the right letter?

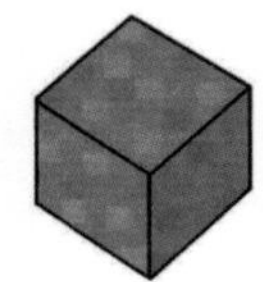

C = Clay

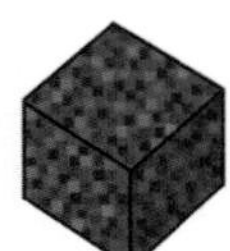

D = Dirt

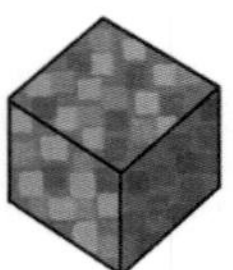

G = Gravel

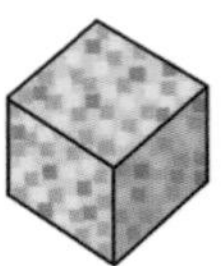

I = Ice

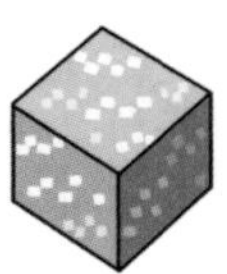

O = Obsidian

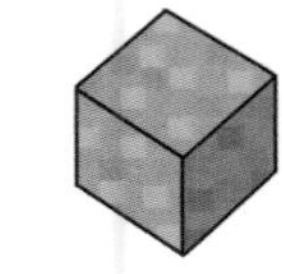

S = Sand

	I	G	C	O	
O	C			G	I
I		S	D		G
D		C	O		S
C	S			D	O
	D	O	I	S	

HOLD IT!

It's time to discuss a weighty matter. Start with the corner letter, then read every third letter, moving clockwise around the square, and write them in the blank spaces below until you solve the mystery message.

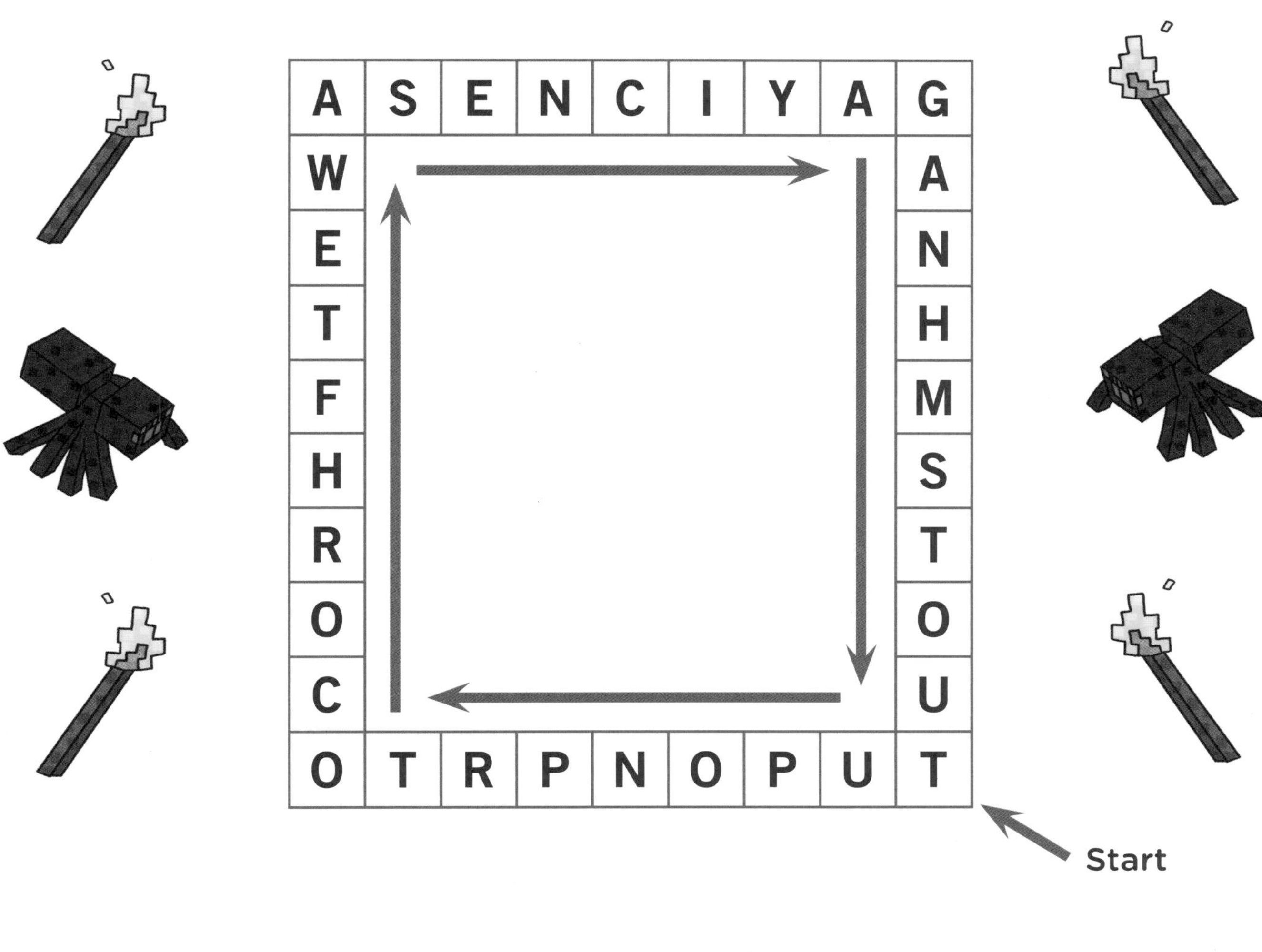

_ _ _ _ _ _ _   _ _ _   _ _ _ _ _ _ _

_ _ _   _ _ _ _ _ _   _ _

_ _ _ _ _ _

COLLECTING TREASURE

Four treasures are yours for the taking—and you want them all! Find the path that allows you to collect the four treasures between Start and Finish. Heads up! Paths go under and over each other.

CIRCLE OF TRUTH: FOOD FOR THOUGHT

Start at the ⬇ *.*

Write every third letter on the spaces to reveal a Minecrafting secret.

E __ __ __ __ __ __   __ __ __ __ __ __ __ __ __ __

__ __ __ __ __ __ __ __   __ __ __ __ __ __ __ __ __,

__ __ __ __ __ __ __,   __ __ __   __ __ __ __ __ __ __

YOU CAN DRAW IT: IRON GOLEM

Use the grid to copy the picture. Examine the lines in each small square in the grid at the left, then transfer those lines to the corresponding square in the grid on the right.

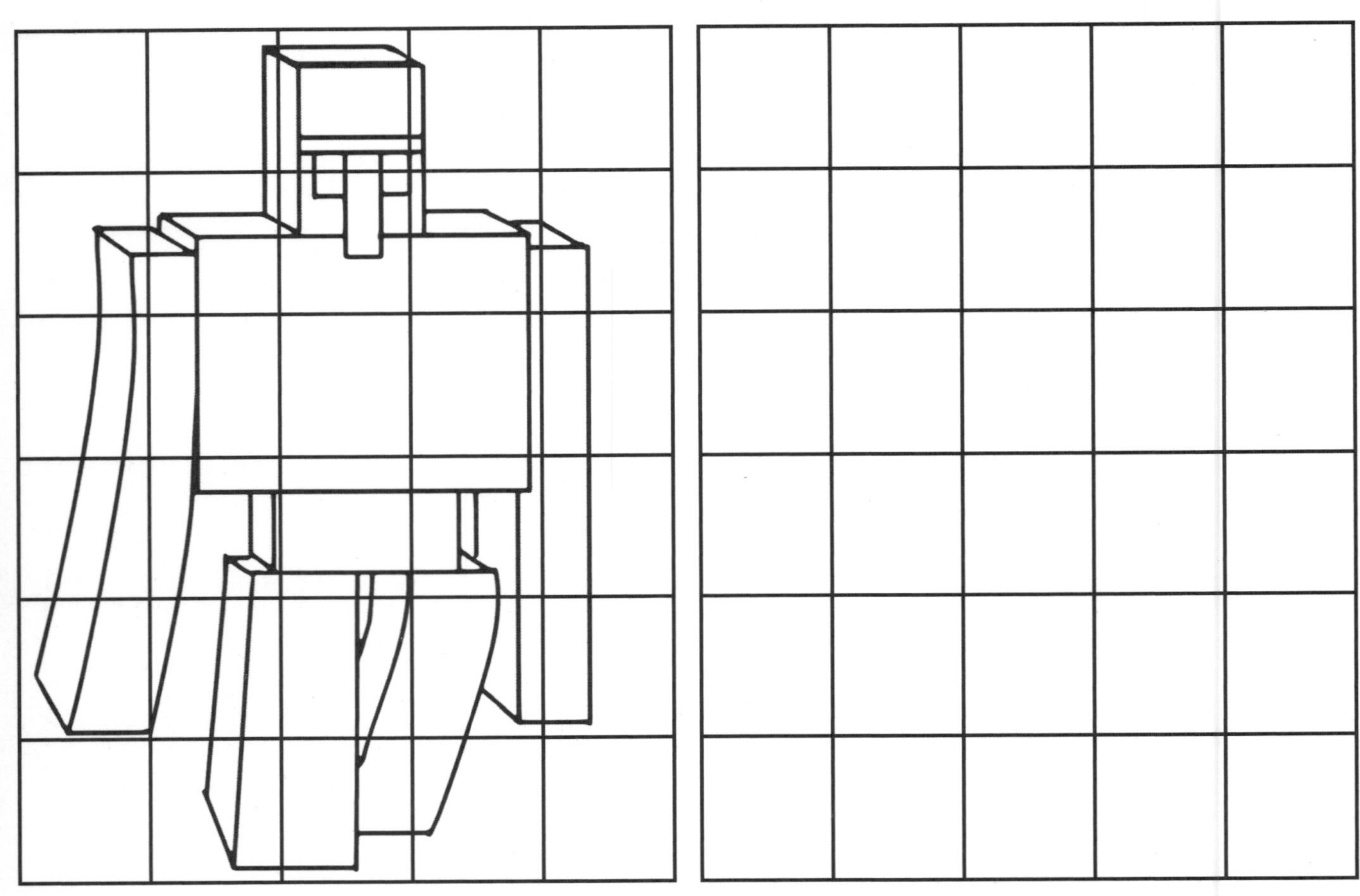

TIP FOR ENDING ENDERMEN

Step 1: Find the ten puzzle pieces that fit the shapes in the rectangle. Watch out! Pieces might be rotated or flipped. Write the letters of the correct pieces on the spaces. Not all pieces are used below.

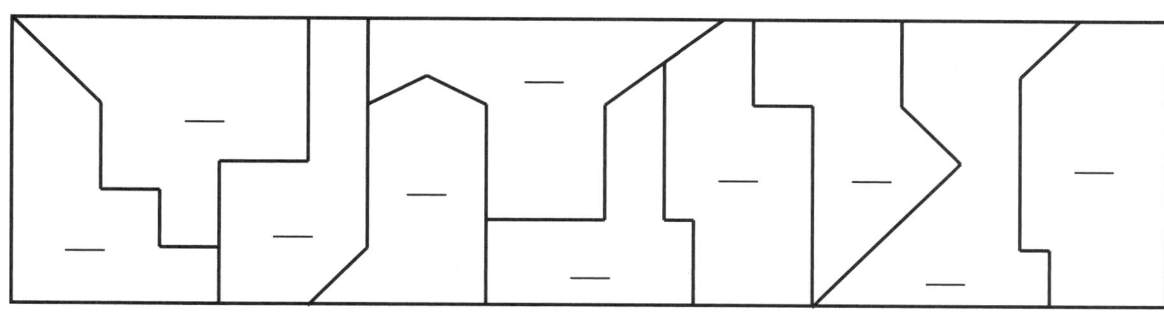

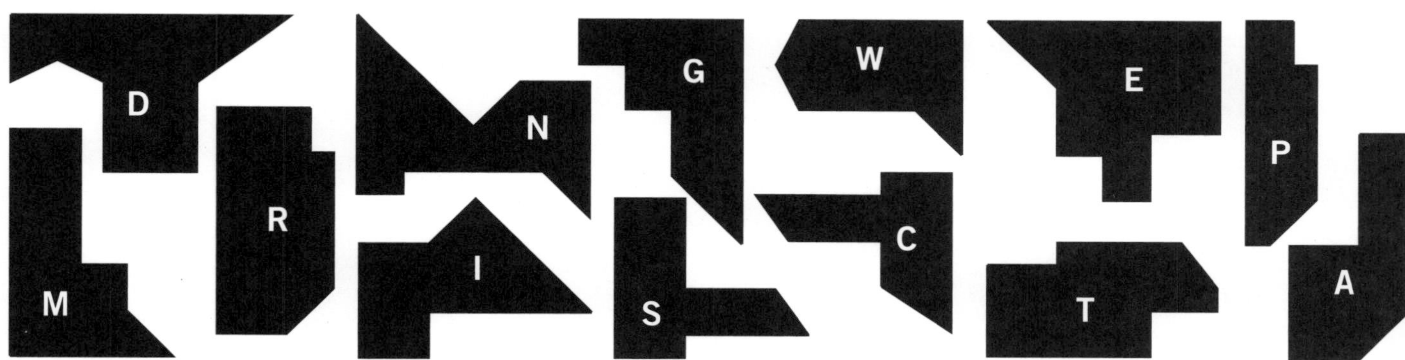

Step 2: Write the letters from the spaces above in the boxes that have the same numbers to reveal something that can help you destroy Endermen.

6	7	3	9	5

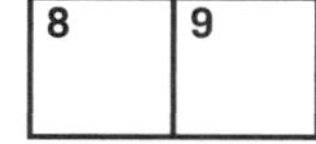

4	3	7	2	10

WORD FARM

The words bat, cow, pig, sheep, spider, squid, chicken, rabbit, donkey, horse, mule, polar bear, ocelot, *and* wolf *are hiding on this farm. How many words can you spot?*

CONNECT THE DOTS: FARM LIFE

Connect the dots to to see what's happening on the Minecrafter's farm.

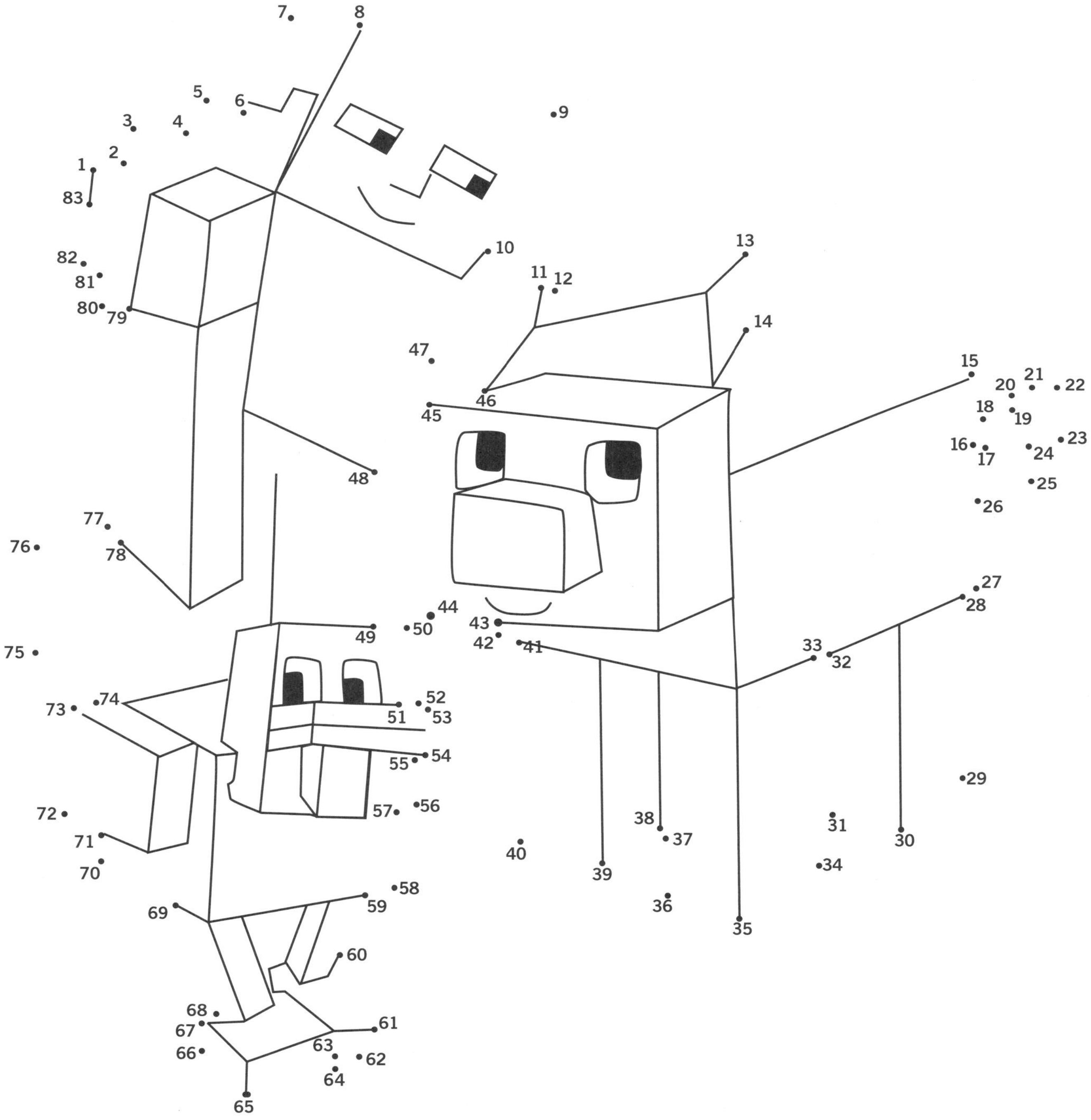

HUNT FOR ENCHANTMENTS

Find and circle the names of fifteen enchantments in the wordfind below. They might be forward, backward, up, down, or diagonal. Write unused letters on the blank spaces, in order from top to bottom and left to right, to discover a fun fact about enchantments.

***Hint:** Circle individual letters instead of whole words. We've found one to get you started.*

H	O	O	K	C	A	B	K	C	O	N	K
E	F	F	I	C	I	E	N	C	Y	K	M
P	O	I	S	M	I	T	E	R	S	I	G
R	E	F	R	I	S	N	H	H	W	N	N
O	E	G	I	E	U	T	A	H	I	F	I
T	M	T	N	T	A	R	H	K	E	I	D
E	A	P	R	I	P	S	A	L	P	N	N
C	L	O	O	N	T	E	P	U	U	I	E
T	F	R	E	W	R	O	E	E	N	T	M
I	E	S	N	B	E	C	O	H	C	Y	A
O	S	N	N	T	M	R	E	L	H	T	N
N	T	U	S	I	L	K	T	O	U	C	H

EFFICIENCY
FIRE ASPECT
FLAME
FORTUNE
INFINITY
KNOCKBACK
~~LOOTING~~
MENDING
POWER
PROTECTION
PUNCH
SHARPNESS
SILK TOUCH
SMITE
UNBREAKING

_ _ _ _   _ _ _ _   _ _ _ _   _ _ _ _

_ _ _   _ _ _ _   _ _ _ _ _ _ _ _ _ _ _

ROTTEN LUCK

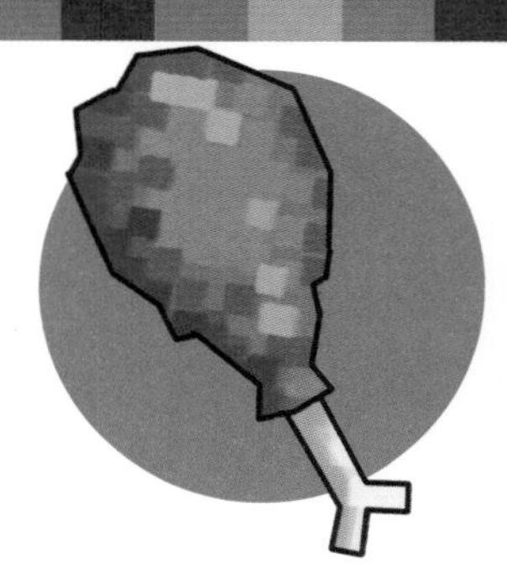

Take your chances with this dangerous maze and avoid food poisoning at all costs. Choose a path from the Start box. There's only one lucky path that leads to a quiet corner and a delicious cookie. The rest lead to the dreaded rotten flesh! Good luck!

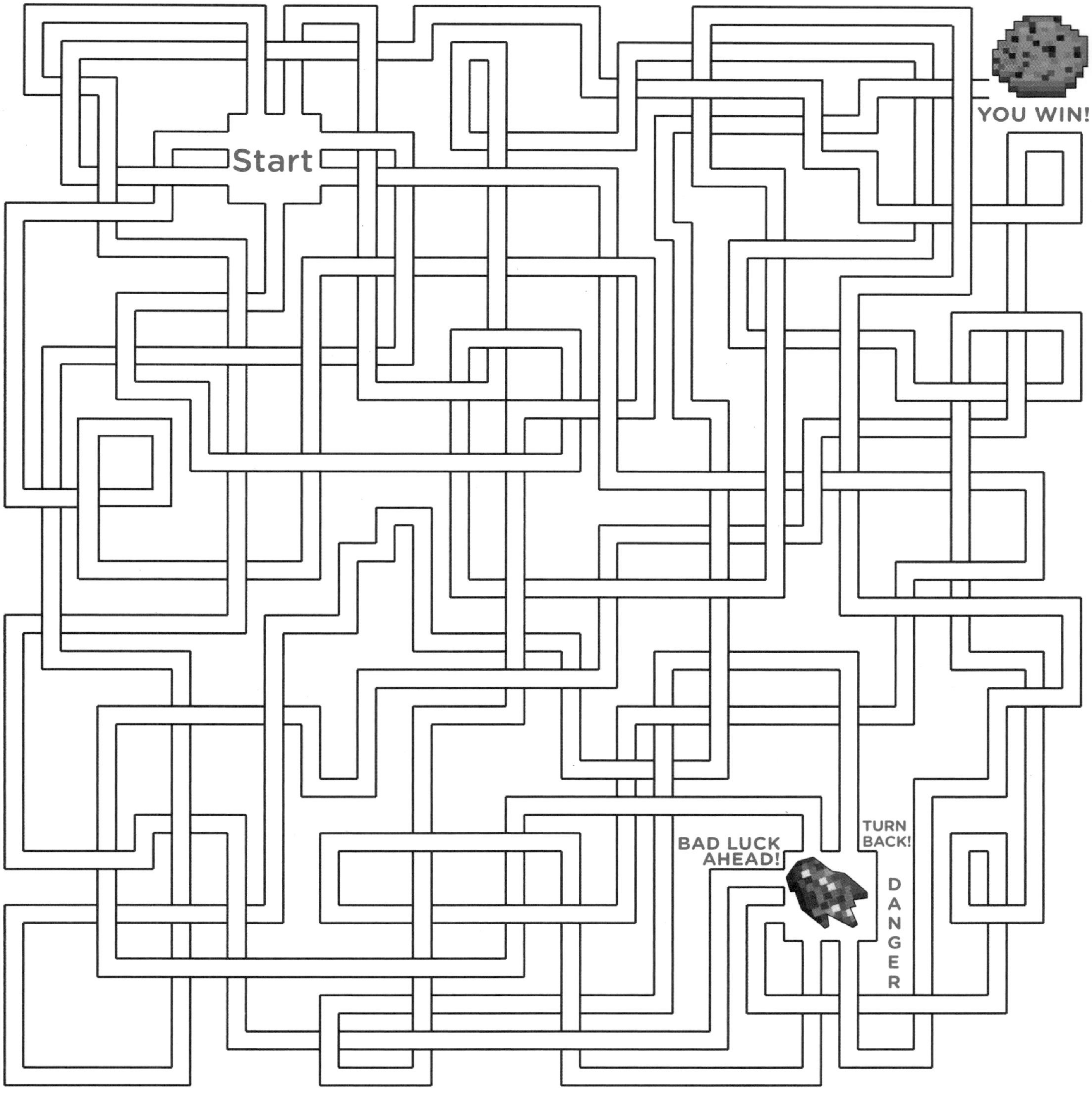

Start

YOU WIN!

BAD LUCK AHEAD!

TURN BACK!

DANGER

MULTIPLAYER MISMATCH

These two pictures are nearly identical, except for ten little differences. How many of these differences can you find?

MINECRAFT
MINECRAFT
TNT

TWIN MOBS

Only two of these villagers are exactly the same. Which two are identical?

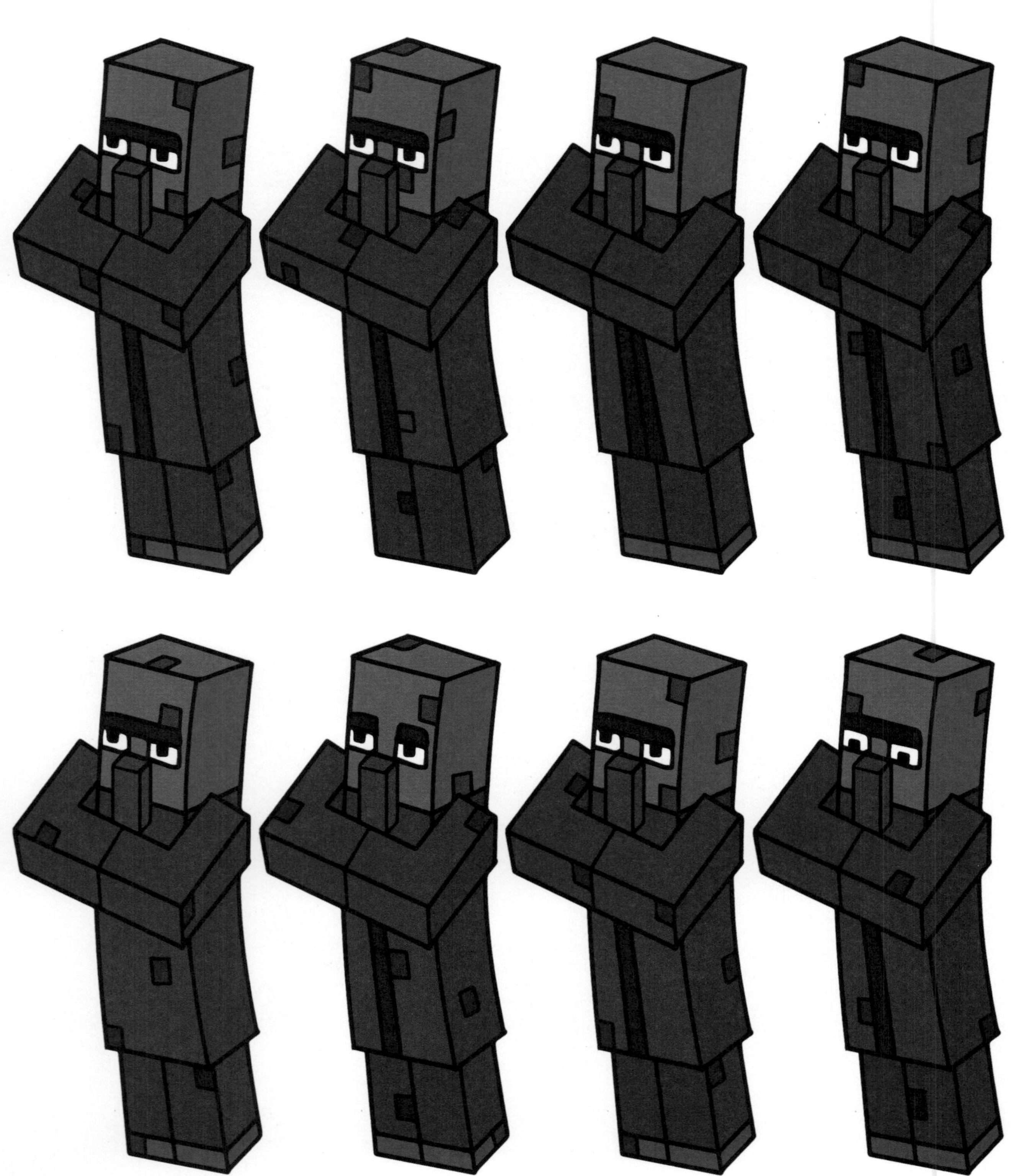

PATH OF DOOM

Begin at the dot below each player's name and work your way down to figure out how each player met their doom. Every time you hit a horizontal line (one that goes across), you must follow it.

Which player was destroyed by an exploding creeper?

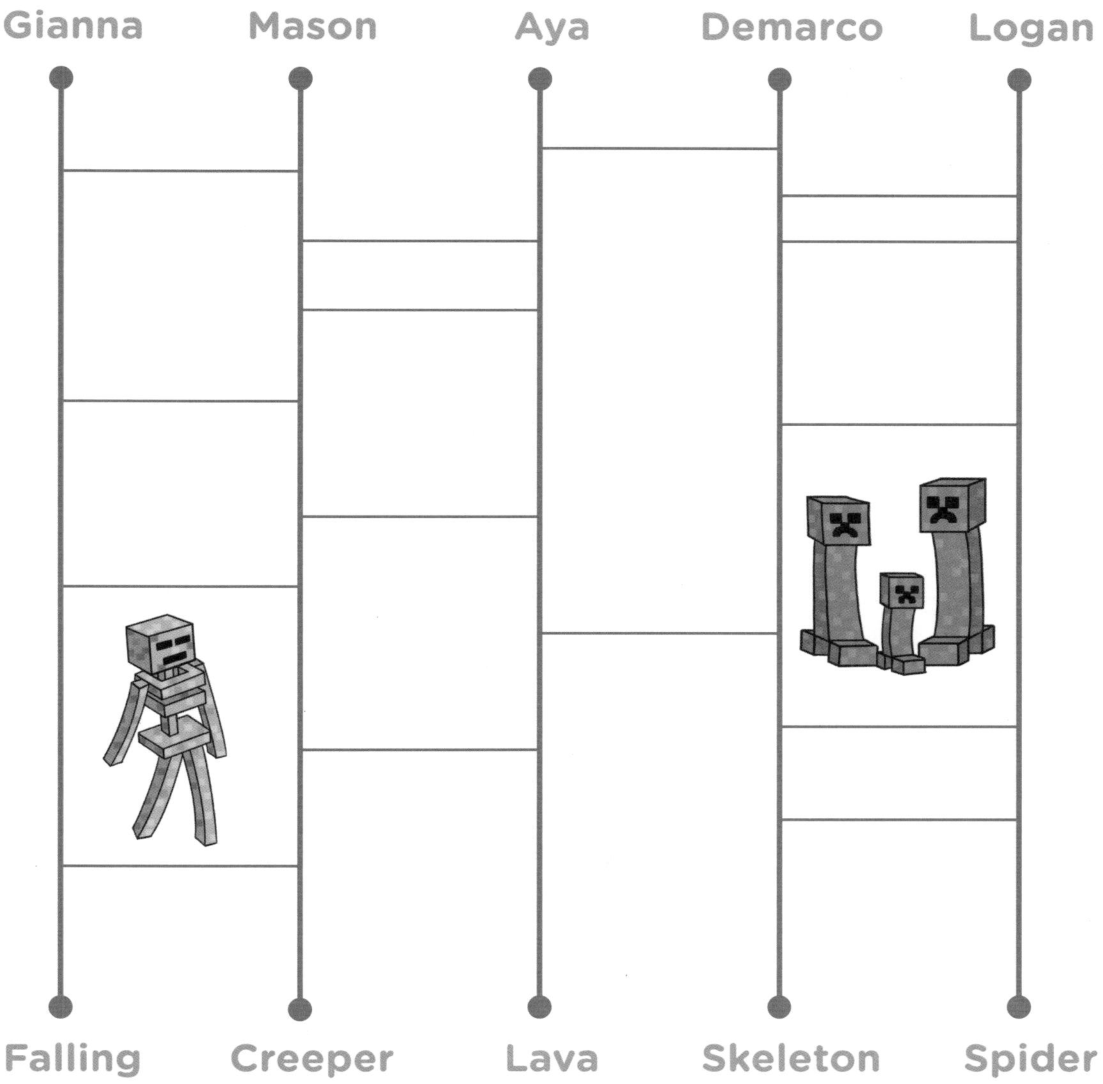

Gianna Mason Aya Demarco Logan

Falling Creeper Lava Skeleton Spider

TRUTH OR TALE?

This is a two-part puzzle. First, name the icons and figure out where each word goes in the crossword. Use the arrows to help you place the first two words. Second, transfer the numbered letters from the crossword to the numbered spaces at the bottom to reveal a claim about Minecraft.

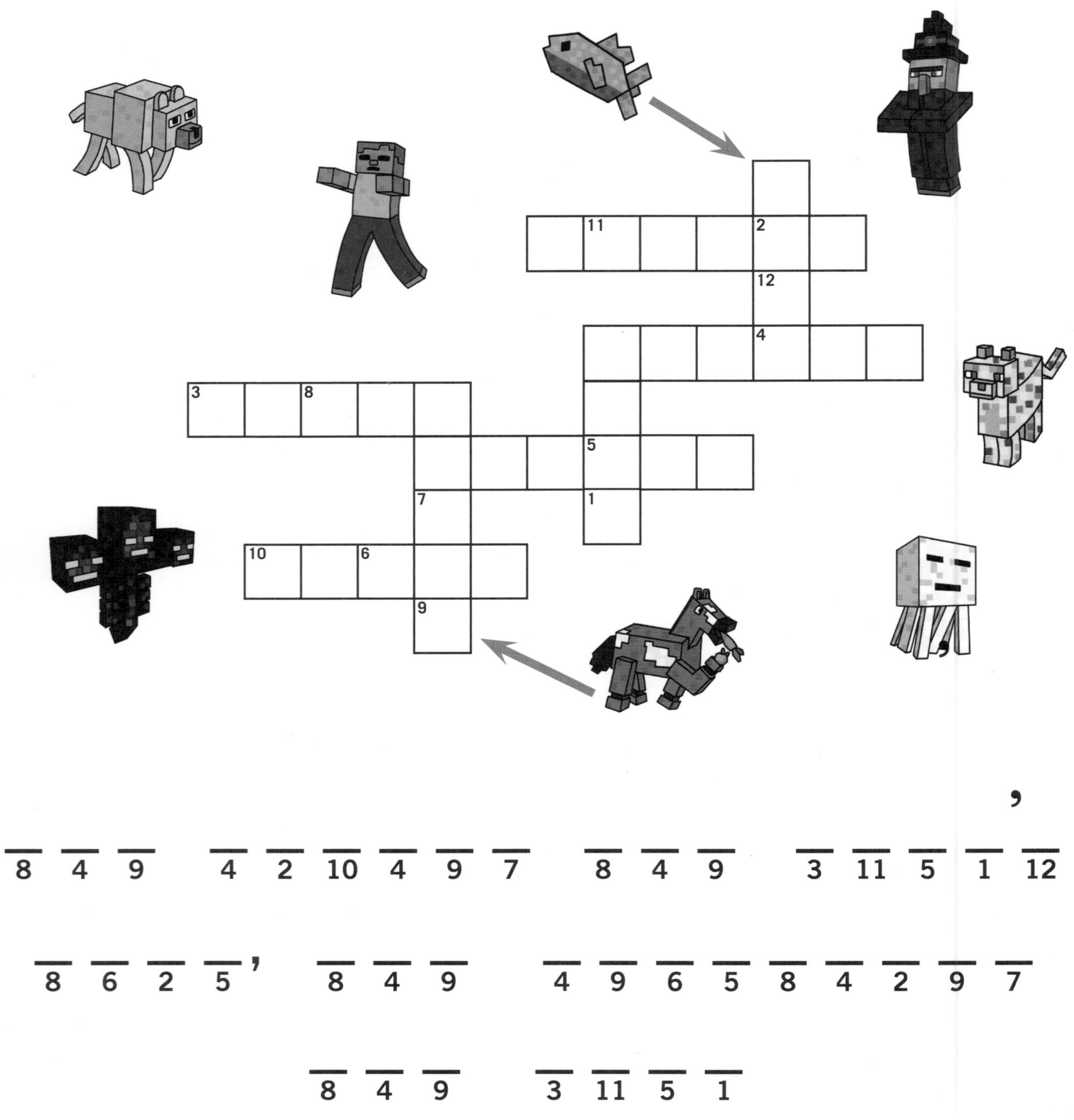

CONNECT THE DOTS: OUR HERO

Connect the dots and find out who always saves the day.

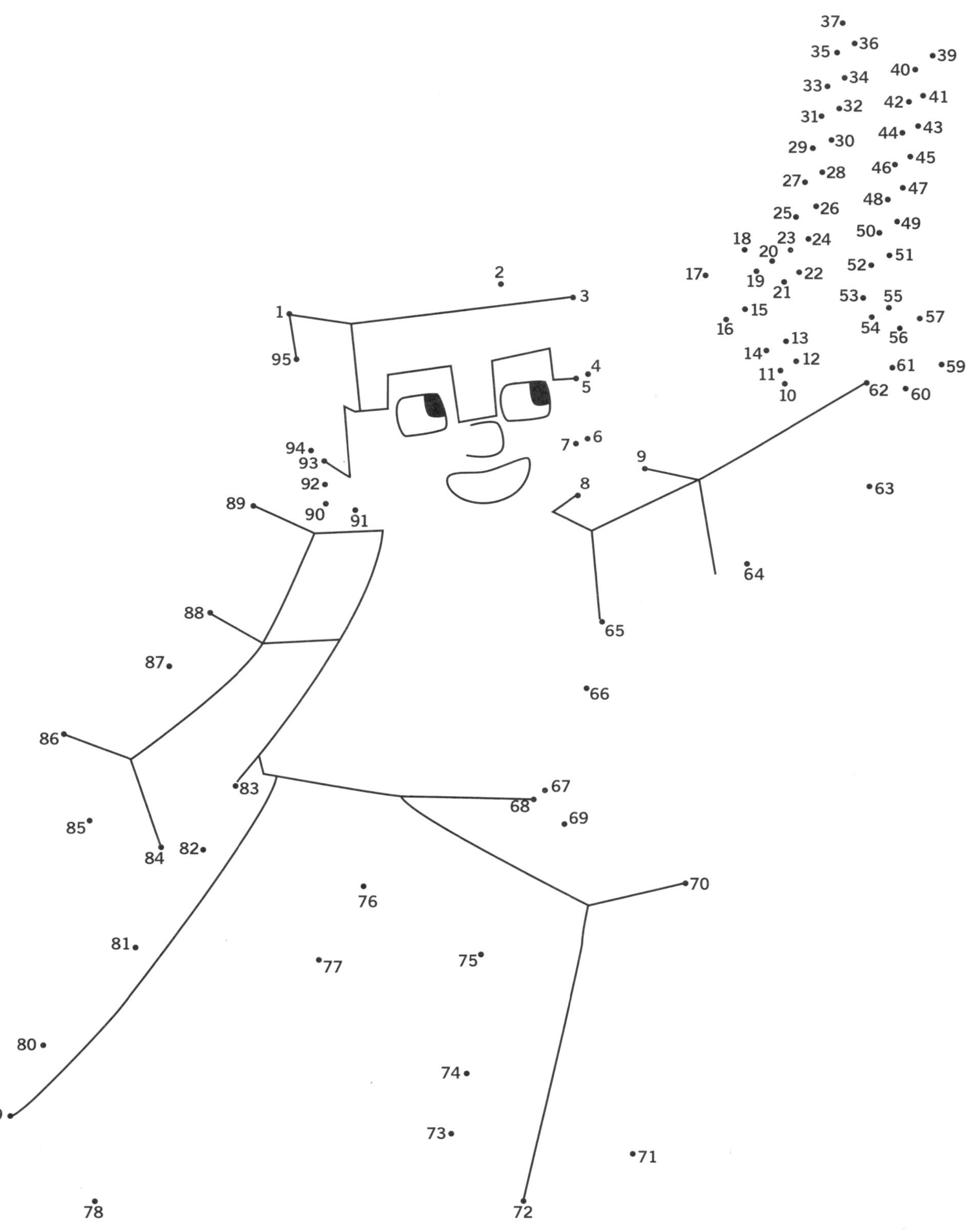

TERMS OF THE GAME

Use the clues (not the pictures this time) to find words that fit in the boxes below.

ACROSS

3 Come to life in the game world

5 An object that is fired at

8 The hunger bar is visible in this mode

9 Begin fighting with

12 Brew potions or power lights with this

15 A C O U R S E E R pack allows players to customize textures, sounds, and more *(Unscramble the word on the space)*

16 This plus cocoa beans makes a cookie

17 Default game character

18 Forest or desert, for example

DOWN

1 Leafless desert plant, often with sharp spikes

2 Entryway to another world

4 Use this to make paper

6 Biome with sand dunes, dead bushes, and cacti

7 Where skin and tools are displayed

10 This type of Mob runs away when hurt

11 Builder's favorite mode

13 Have lava flow on top of water to create this

14 Lava sources and random fires are hazards here

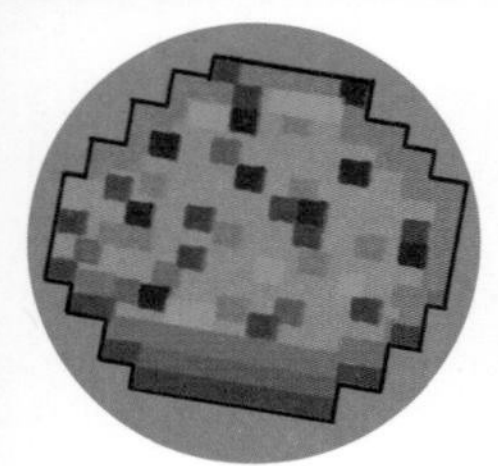

SQUARED UP: INVENTORY

Each of the six inventory items in this puzzle can appear only once in each row, each column, and pink rectangle. Use the letter A to represent apple, the letter C for carrot, and so on. Can you fill every block with the proper item?

A = Apple

C = Carrot

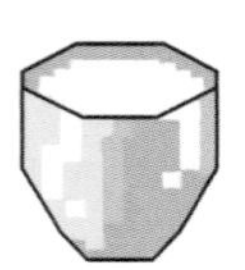

M = Milk

P = Potion

S = Sword

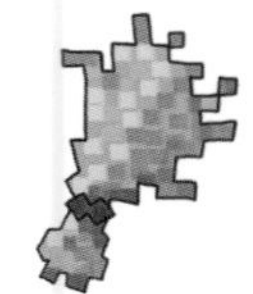

W = Wheat

W	S	P	C	M	
M		A			P
P				C	
C	M		A	P	S
S			P		M
	P	M		W	

FACT-FINDING MISSION

Your mission is find the fact in the letters below. Start with a letter in one of the corners (you have to figure out which one), then read every third letter, going clockwise around the square, until all of the letters are used.

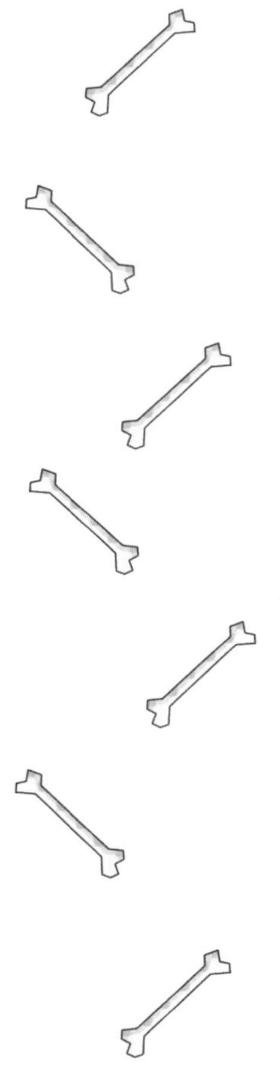

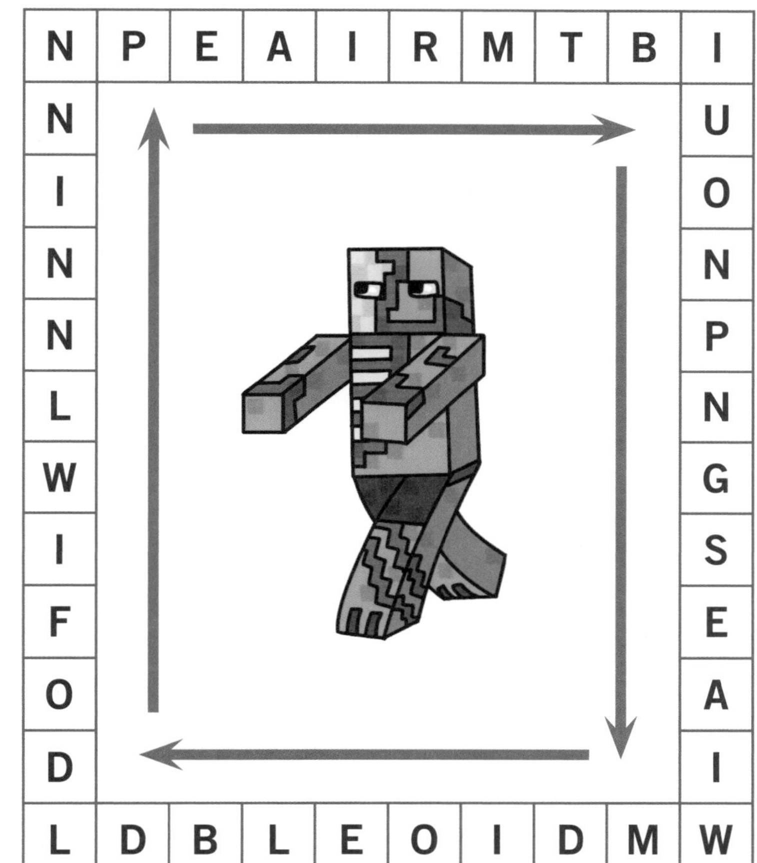

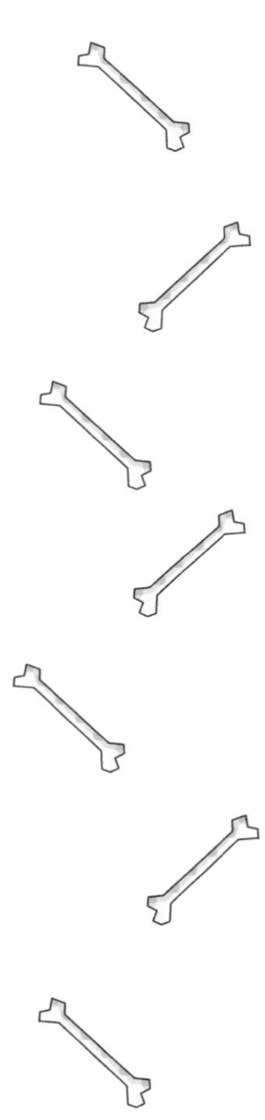

“ ”

BLACKOUT

Read the clues and write the answers across the blank boxes. If you need help, the answers are scrambled around the border.

When all the boxes are full, read the vertical shaded boxes to answer this question:

Which potion is helpful when exploring the Nether and the ocean?

6. D E N

2. C C I I N P

3. S G A R S

4. G A R N I S H

1. R E V E N

5. W O R T H

1. She's got ______, meaning she's got guts

2. Eat outdoors

3. Block you break to get seeds

4. Giving some of what you have to someone else

5. What you do with a splash potion

6. The final dimension

MULTIPLAYER CTM CHALLENGE

Four friends are collecting hardened clay blocks to Complete the Monument.

Which player collected yellow blocks?

To find out, begin at the dot below each player's name and follow it downward. Every time you hit a horizontal line (one that goes across), you must take it. See where each player's path leads.

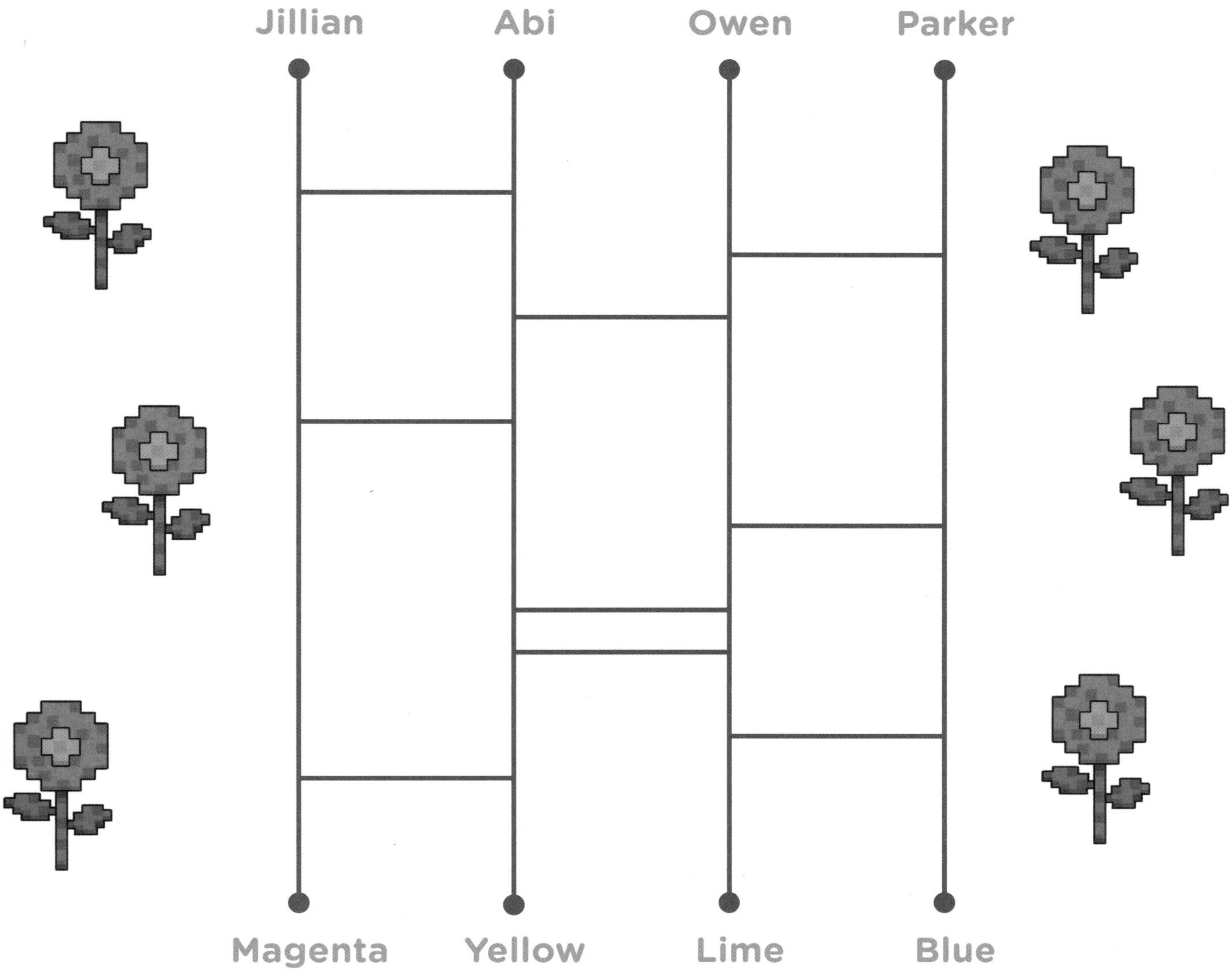

Jillian **Abi** **Owen** **Parker**

Magenta **Yellow** **Lime** **Blue**

HERE, THERE, AND EVERYWHERE

In your search for dropped treasure, you must visit every nook and cranny in this maze before nightfall. Draw a line from Start to Stop that passes through every gold ingot once—and only once. Your line can go up, down, left, or right, but not diagonally. On your mark, get set, go!

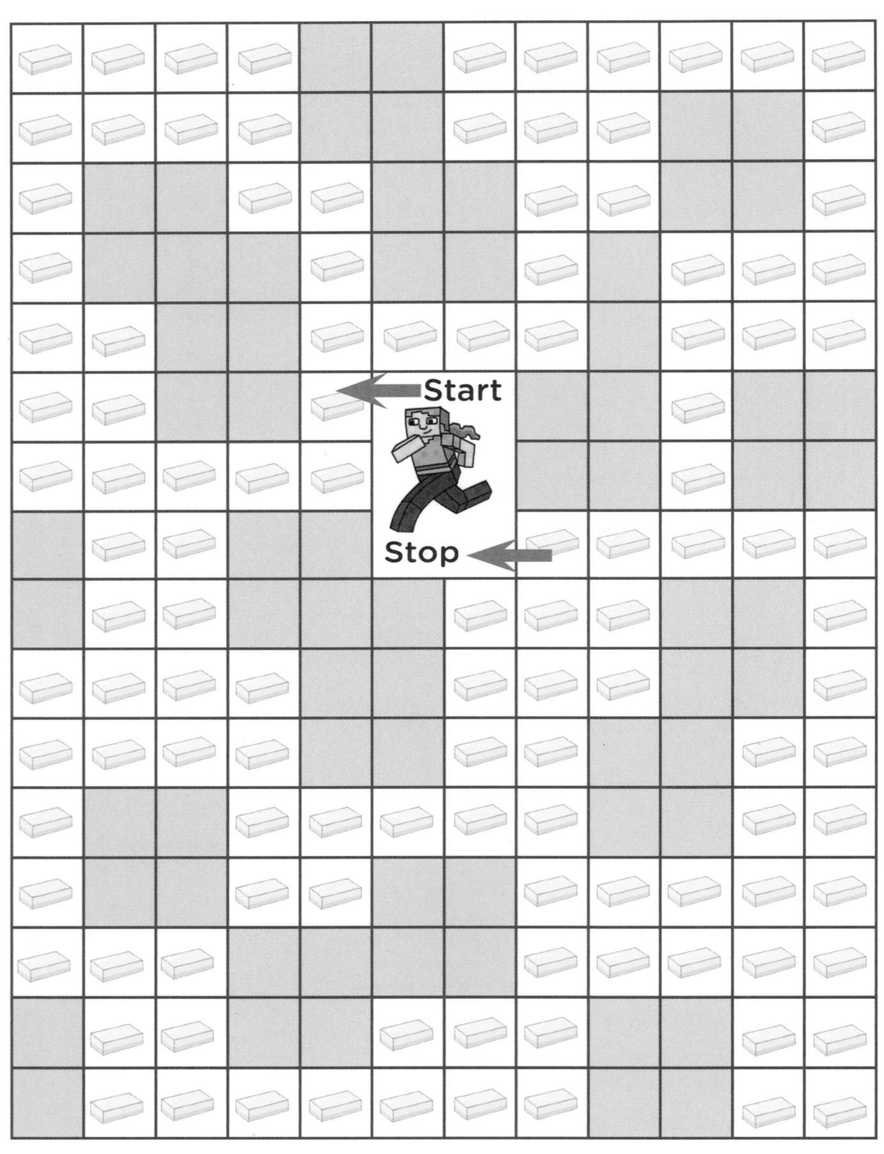

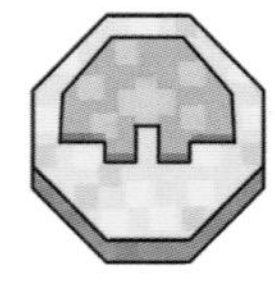
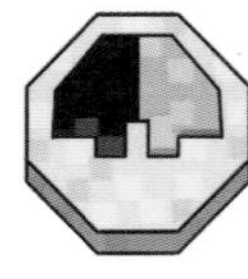

DEFLECT THIS

Every word in Column B contains the same letters as a word in Column A, plus one letter. Draw a line between each pair of "matching" words, then write the extra letter on the space provided. Unscramble the column of letters to reveal something you might want to deflect . . . or not.

COLUMN A	COLUMN B	EXTRA LETTER
Tinge	Bedrock	___
Dread	Wander	___
Meal	Damage	___
Verse	Smelt	___
Drawn	Ladder	___
Corked	Ignite	___
Stem	Flame	___
Gamed	Server	___

___ ___ ___ ___ ___ ___ ___ ___

DOWN ON THE (MOB) FARM

The answer to each clue looks like the word above it, except one letter is different. If you get stuck, try working from the bottom up.

PLACES, PEOPLE!

Use the clues to determine where each of the nine Mobs goes in the three-by-three grid. Write the name of each Mob in pencil inside the box where you think it belongs.

Snow Golem

Zombie Pigman

Wolf

Slime

Pig

Villager

Skeleton

Spider

Sheep

1. *All Mob names that begin with S are in the bottom two rows.*
2. *The pumpkin-headed Mob is in the center box.*

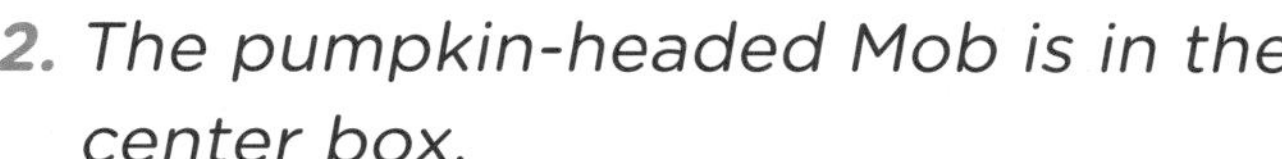

3. *The Mob that can be tamed is in a top corner.*
4. *The zombie and the eight-legged Mob are side-by-side in the bottom row.*
5. *The two farm animals are stacked one on top of the other in the top right.*
6. *The Mob in the bottom center box was a pig who got struck by lightning.*
7. *The arrow-shooting Mob is in a corner.*
8. *The Mob in the top center box might be a blacksmith or a librarian.*

ANSWERS

GOING BATTY

STEVE SAYS...

CREEPERS WERE THE RESULT OF A CODING MISTAKE

(What was supposed to be a pig wound up with extra-long legs, and the result turned into a creeper.)

THE MIRROR'S IMAGE

ENDERMEN WERE CALLED "FARLANDERS" BEFORE THE END WAS CREATED

CITY SLICKER

TAKE A GUESS

EXIT, CORN, PINE, SEEP

EXPERIENCE POINTS

ENCHANTED CHEST

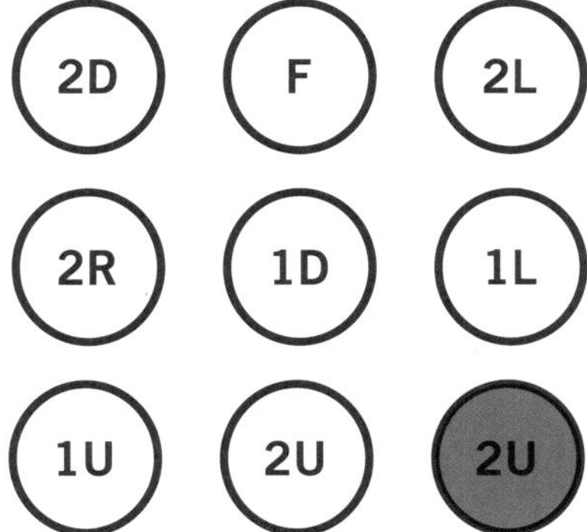

The red button is the first one pressed.

SEE AND SOLVE

LAVA
FISH
ARROW
SHOVEL
ELYTRA
INGOT
CARROT
CLAY

THEY FIRE EVERYONE

HOME SWEET BIOME

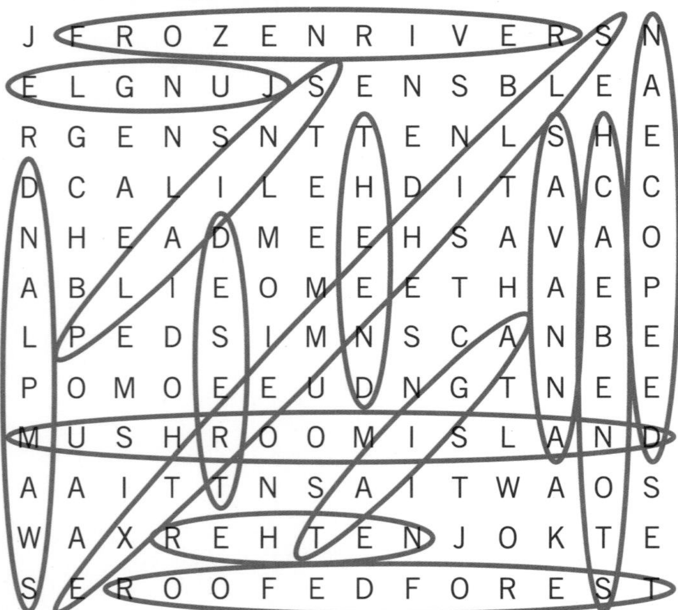

CREEPER TWINS

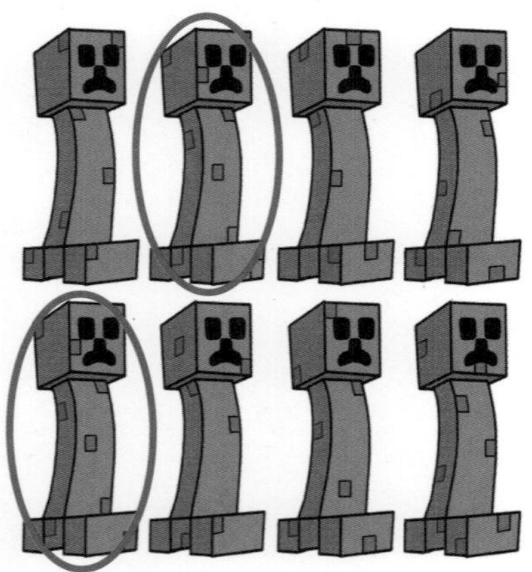

CIRCLE OF TRUTH: CRAFTING CLUE

DIAMOND MAKES THE STRONGEST TOOLS

MOB SCENE

1.		S	E	A	R	C	H	
2.		E	X	P	E	R	T	
3.		A	P	P	L	E	S	
4.		P	L	A	Y	E	R	
5.			O	U	T	P	U	T
6.	S	A	D	D	L	E		
7.	S	P	I	D	E	R		
8.			N	O	I	S	E	
9.	E	G	G					

EXPLODING CREEPERS

SQUARED UP: MOBS IN EVERY QUARTER

G	C	S	B
B	S	G	C
C	G	B	S
S	B	C	G

WATCHTOWER QUEST

A CURE FOR WHAT AILS YOU

DRINKING A BUCKET OF MILK CURES POISONING

PIECE IT TOGETHER

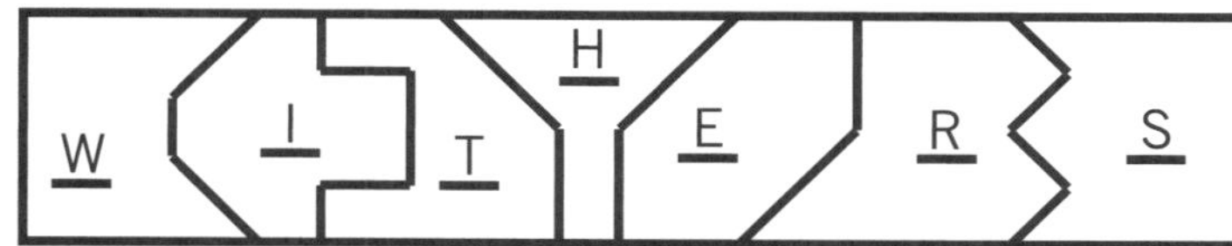

PICK, THE RIGHT TOOL!

TOOL CHEST

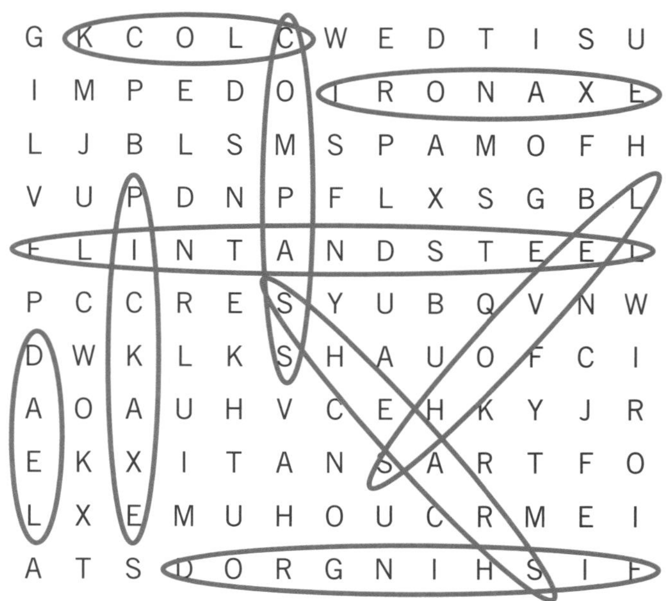

FIND THE PORTAL

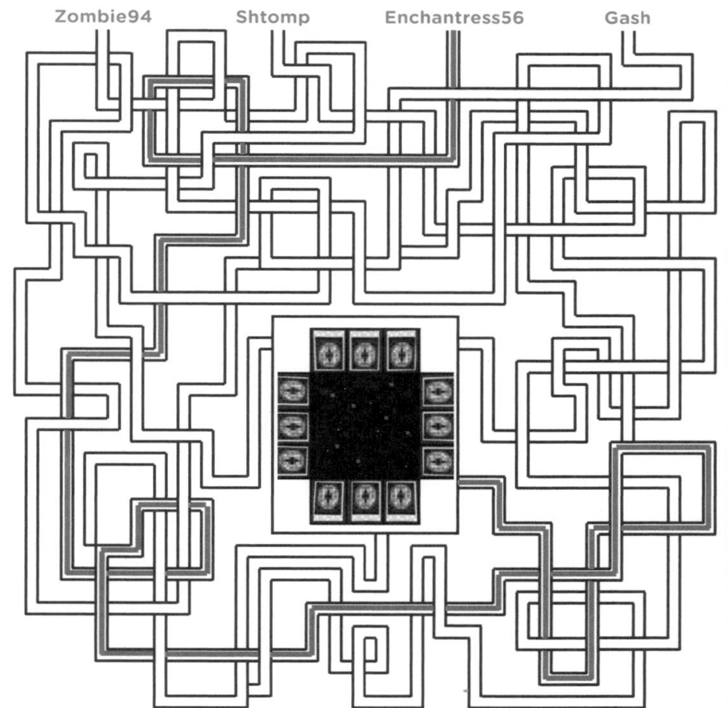

Enchantress56 finds the portal.

CROSSWORD CLUE FINDER

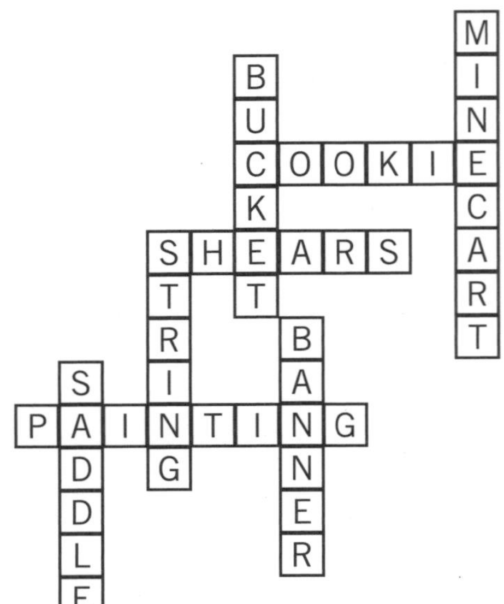

SURVIVAL MAZE

SEE THE SEA

BLOCKED!

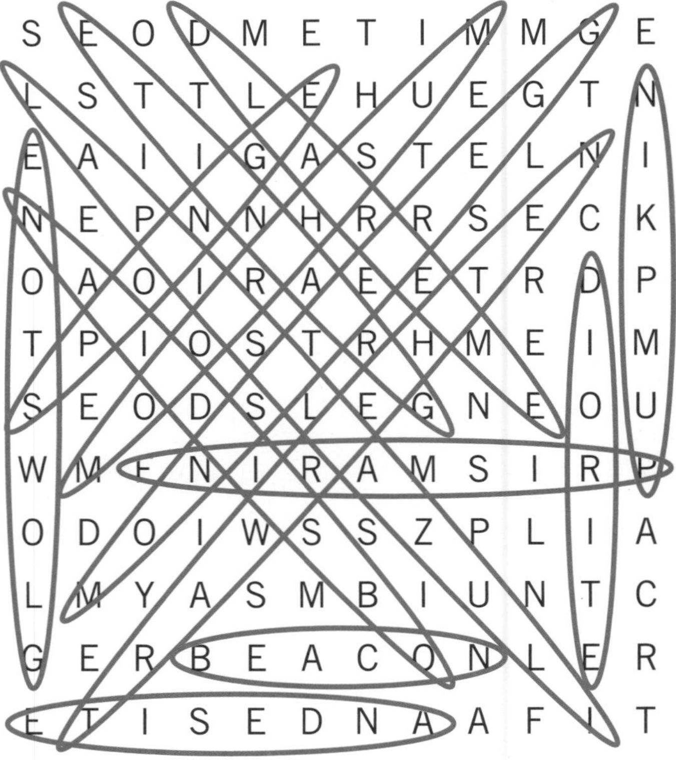

POWER PLAY: MYSTERY WORD

REDSTONE

CONNECT THE DOTS: HOSTILE MOB

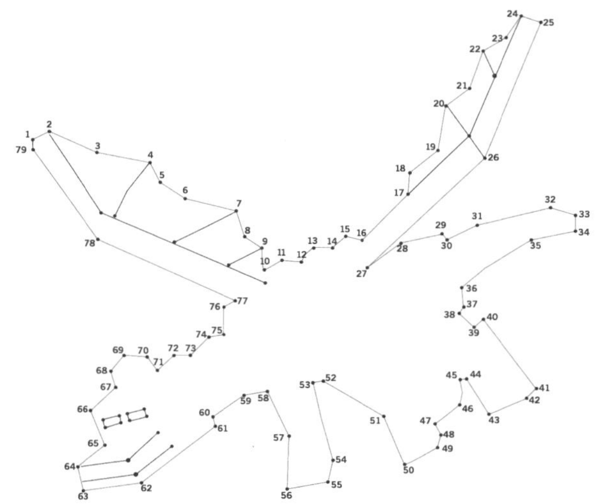

MIXED UP

GRIN, NOON, PIG, TILE

LINGERING POTION

A SMALL PROBLEM

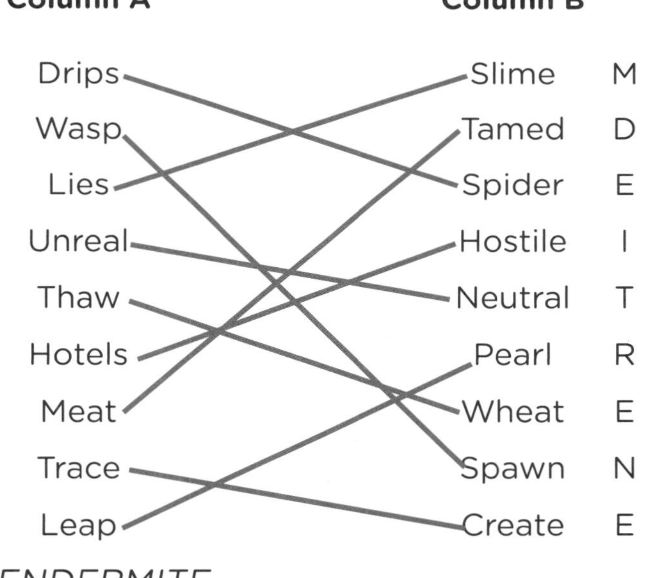

ENDERMITE

CRACK THE CODE

IT WAS A POUND CAKE

ALPHA CODE

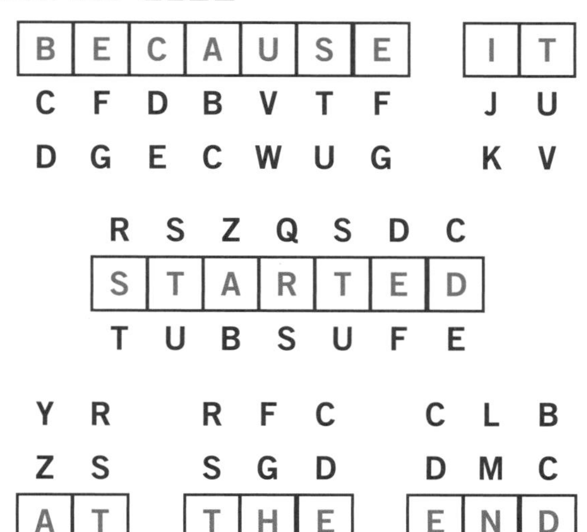

GRAB AND GO CHALLENGE

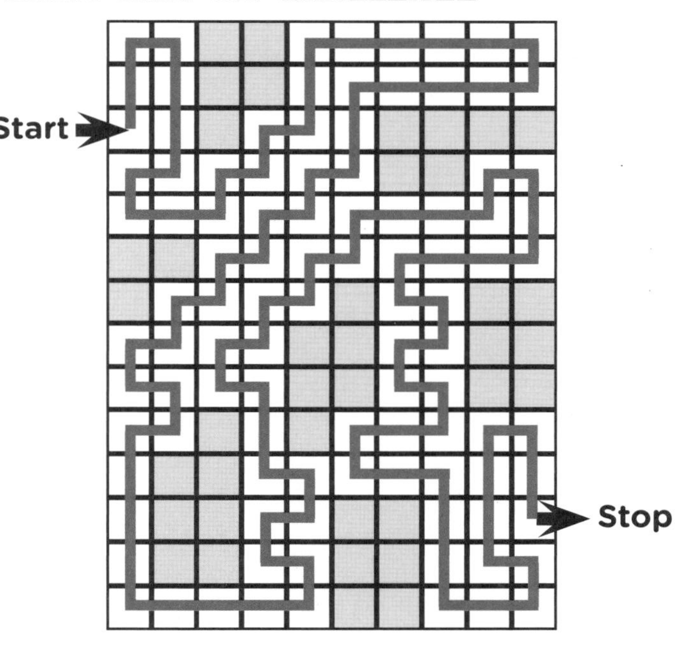

WORD MINE

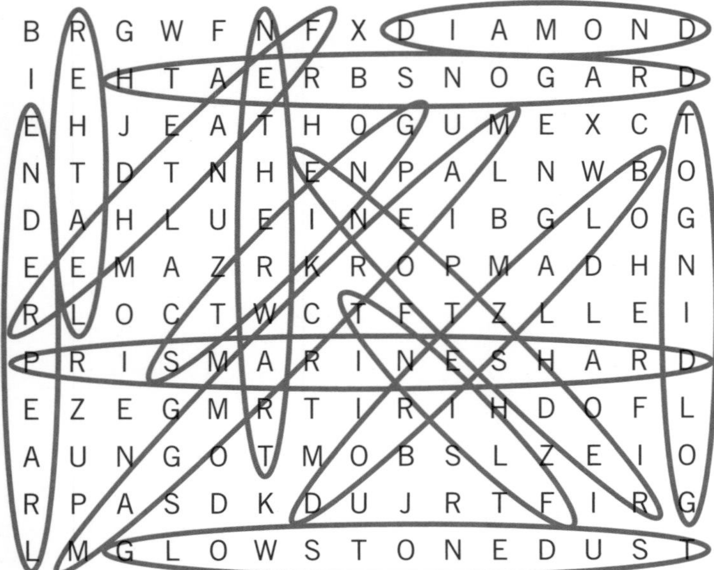

CIRCLE OF TRUTH: FUN FACT

YOU CAN'T OPEN A CHEST IF A CAT SITS ON IT

ZOMBIE TWINS

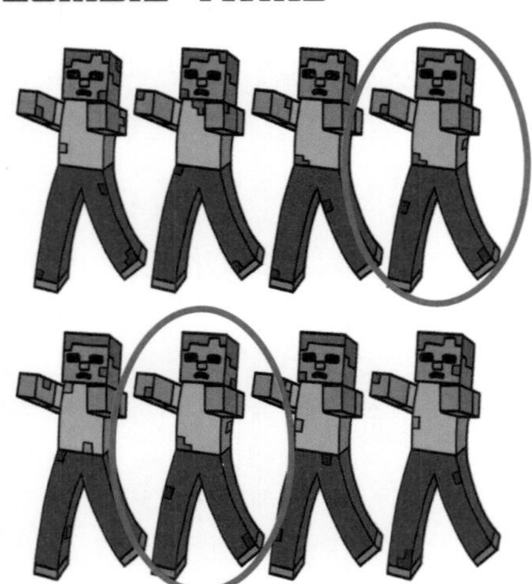

CAN YOU DIG IT?

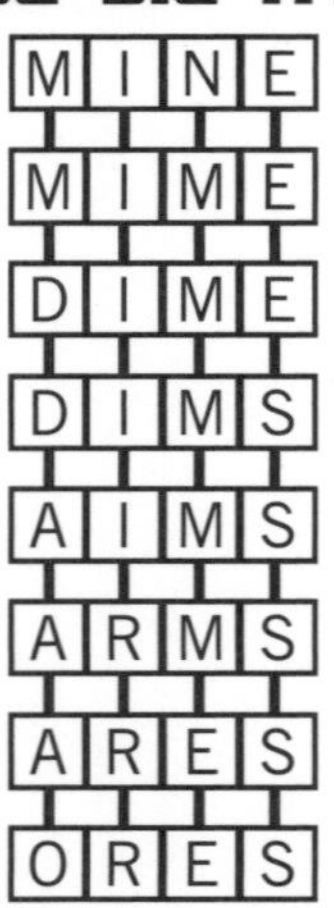

SQUARED UP: FARM MOBS

S	H	C	P
P	C	H	S
C	P	S	H
H	S	P	C

GROW WITH THE FLOW

BABY VILLAGERS GROW UP IN TWENTY MINUTES

You start in the top right corner.

BASIC TRAINING

NETHER WART
GLOWSTONE DUST
REDSTONE
FERMENTED SPIDER EYE
These are the base brewing ingredients.

THE SHAPE OF THINGS TO COME

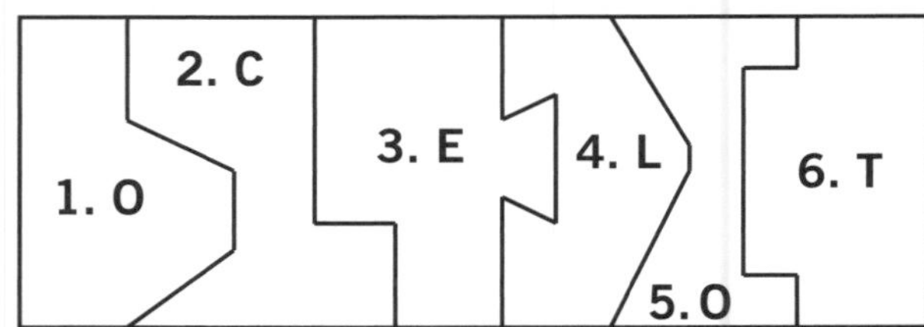

WHEN PIGS HIDE

MINER'S BLOCK

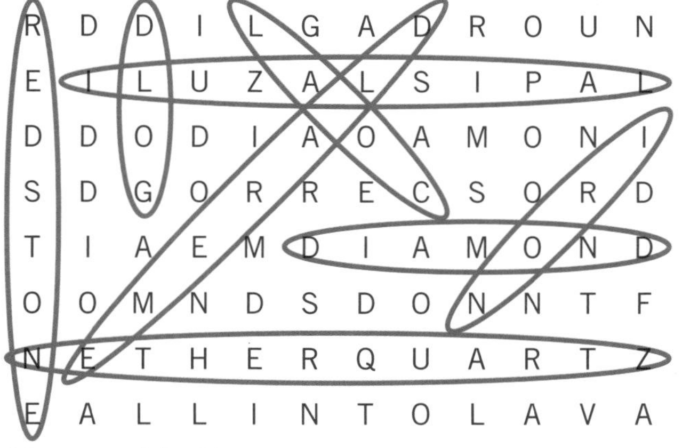

Unused letters:

DIG AROUND DIAMOND ORE SO DIAMONDS DON'T FALL INTO LAVA

TRUE OR FALSE?

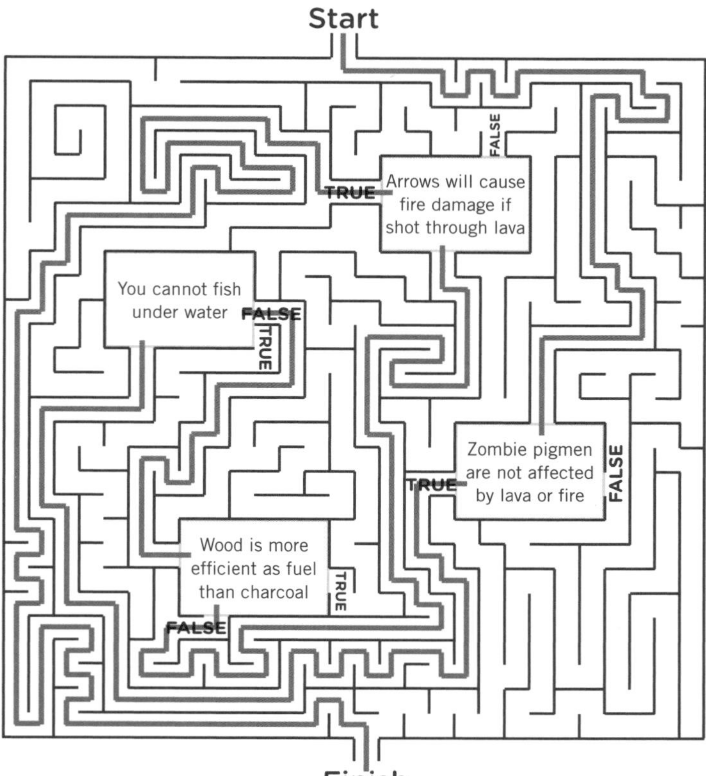

STEVE SAYS: JOKE TIME

ALL ROADS ARE BLOCKED

ON THE PLAYGROUND

ENCHANTED MAP

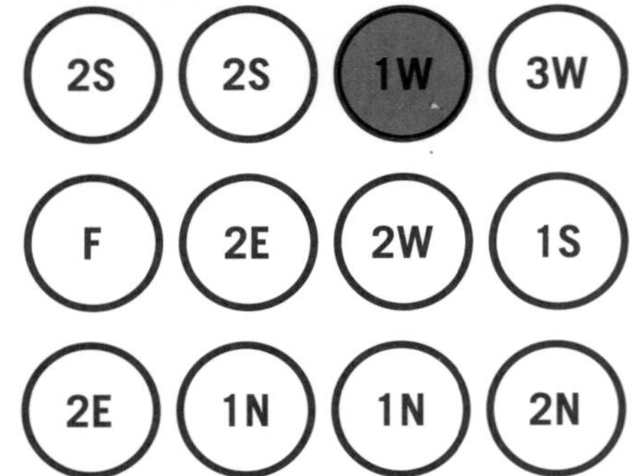

The red button is the first one pressed.

COMMON CODE

NETHERRACK, GLOWSTONE, SOUL SAND
These things are found only in the Nether

EVERY NOOK AND CRANNY

CIRCLE OF TRUTH: SURVIVAL TIP

WEAR A PUMPKIN ON YOUR HEAD AND ENDERMEN WON'T GET ANGRY WITH YOU

SKELETON TWINS

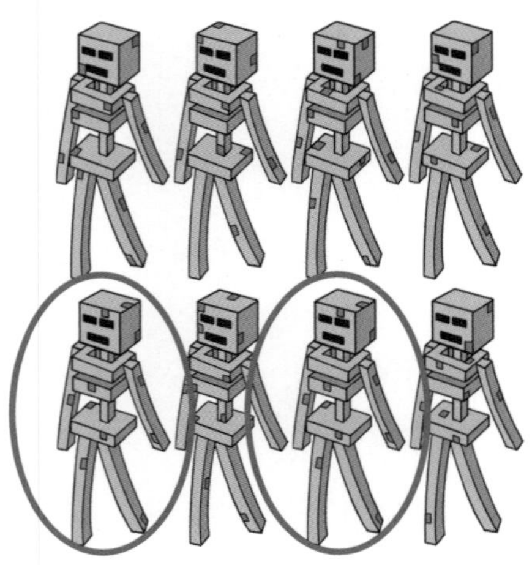

CONNECT THE DOTS: PIT OF PERIL!

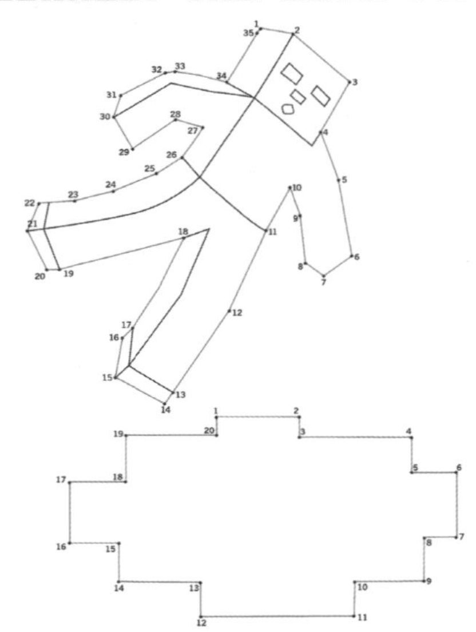

SQUARED UP: BLOCK PARTY

S	I	G	C	O	D
O	C	D	S	G	I
I	O	S	D	C	G
D	G	C	O	I	S
C	S	I	G	D	O
G	D	O	I	S	C

HOLD IT!

TORCHES CAN SUPPORT ANY AMOUNT OF WEIGHT

COLLECTING TREASURE

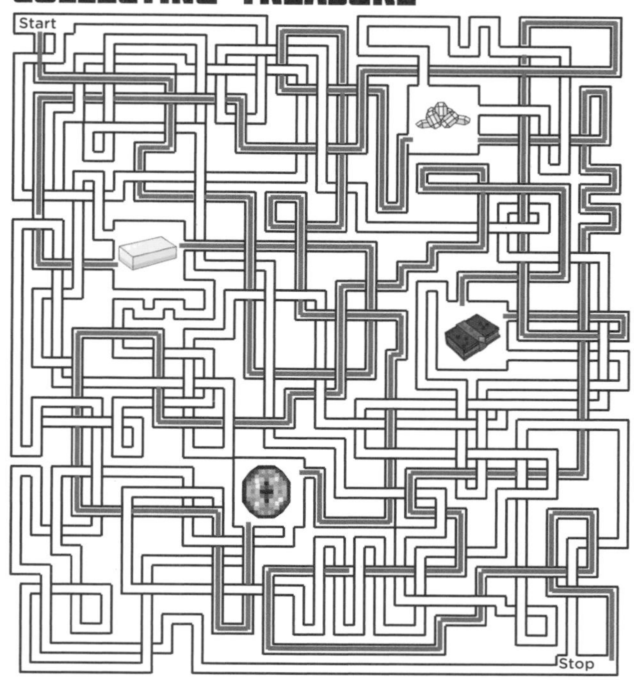

CIRCLE OF TRUTH: FOOD FOR THOUGHT

EATING PUFFERFISH CAUSES POISONING, HUNGER, AND NAUSEA

TIP FOR ENDING ENDERMEN

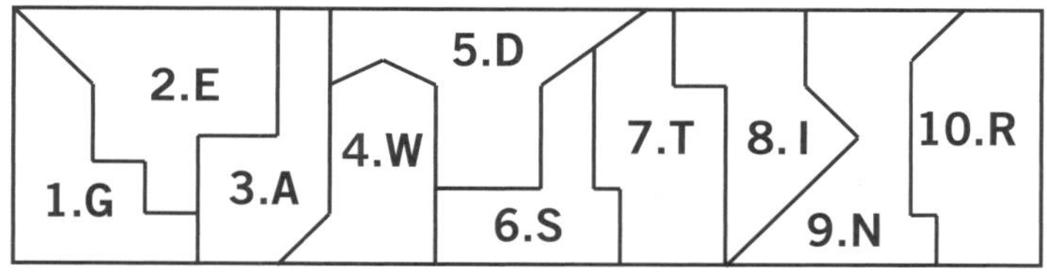

STAND IN WATER

WORD FARM

CONNECT THE DOTS: FARM LIFE

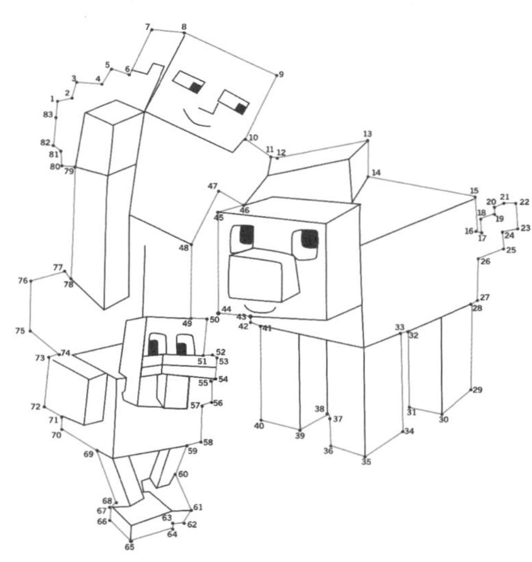

HUNT FOR ENCHANTMENTS

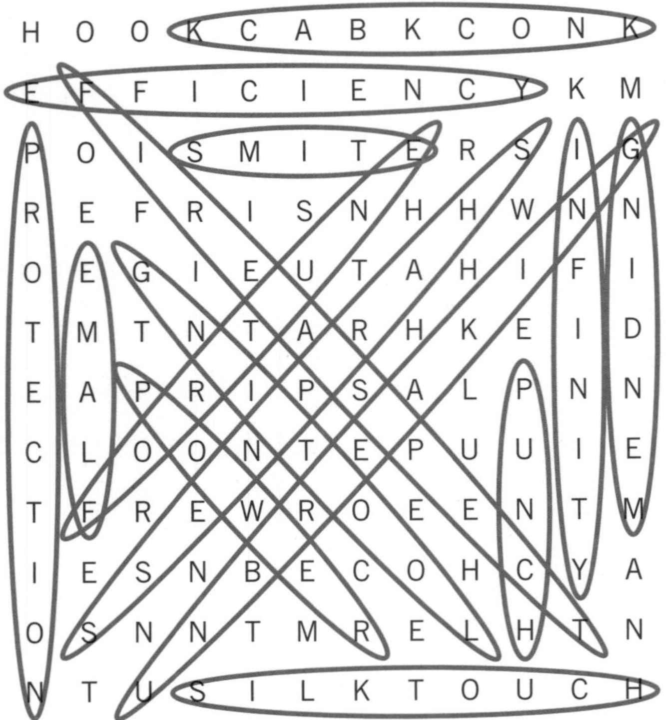

Unused letters:
HOOK MORE FISH WITH THE LURE ENCHANTMENT

ROTTEN LUCK

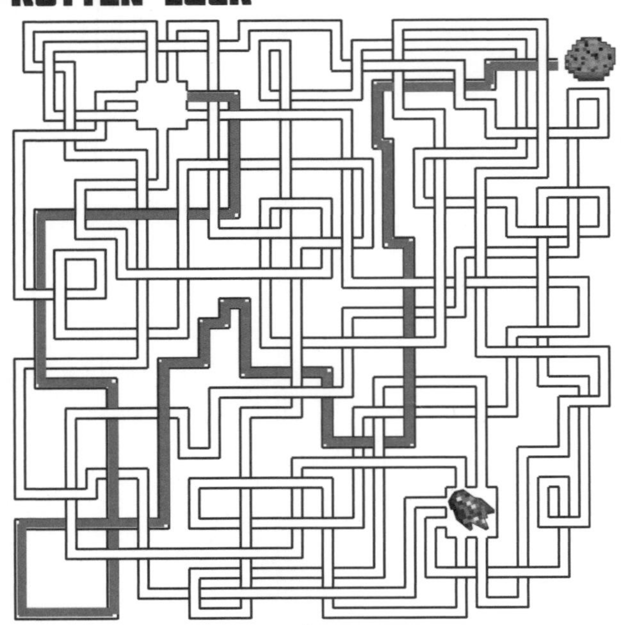

MULTIPLAYER MISMATCH

TWIN MOBS

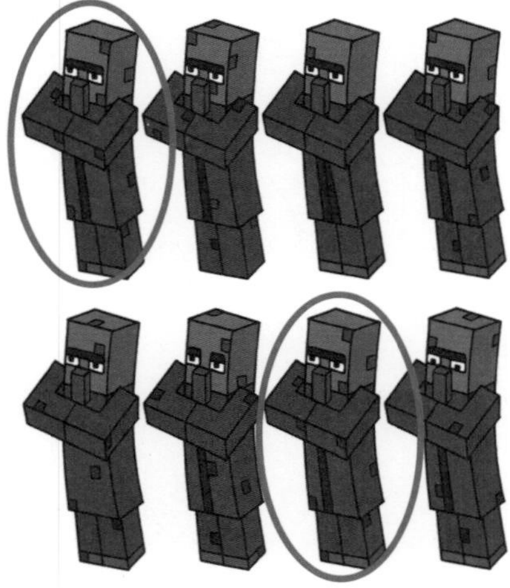

PATH OF DOOM

Gianna - Lava; Mason - Skeleton; Aya - Spider; ***Demarco - Creeper****; Logan - Falling*

TRUTH OR TALE?

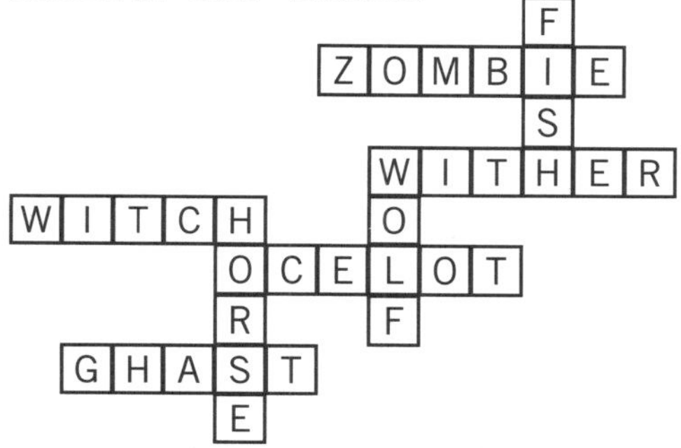

THE HIGHER THE WOLF'S TAIL, THE HEALTHIER IT IS

This tall tale (about a tall tail!) is true.

CONNECT THE DOTS: OUR HERO

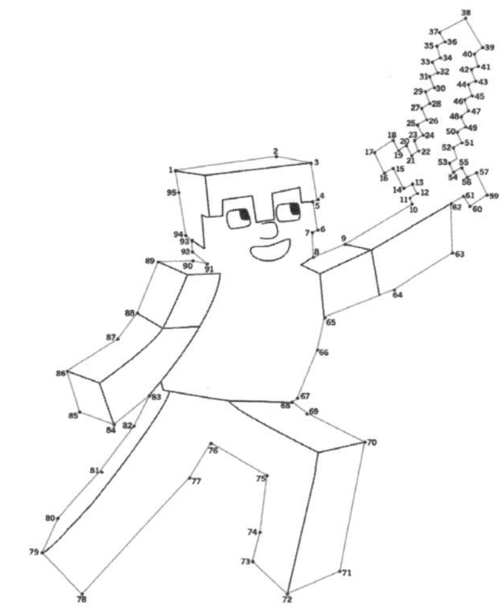

TERMS OF THE GAME

CACTUS
SPAWN
PORTAL
DESERT
SUGARCANE
TARGET
INVENTORY
SURVIVAL
ATTACK
PASSIVE
CREATIVE
REDSTONE
RESOURCE
STONE
NETHER
WHEAT
STEVE
BIOME

SQUARED UP: INVENTORY

W	S	P	C	M	A
M	C	A	W	S	P
P	A	S	M	C	W
C	M	W	A	P	S
S	W	C	P	A	M
A	P	M	S	W	C

FACT-FINDING MISSION

NAMING A MOB "DINNERBONE" WILL FLIP IT UPSIDE DOWN

You start in the top left corner.

BLACKOUT

1.		N	E	R	V	E	
2.	P	I	C	N	I	C	
3.		G	R	A	S	S	
4.	S	H	A	R	I	N	G
5.		T	H	R	O	W	
6.			E	N	D		

NIGHT VISION

MULTIPLAYER CTM CHALLENGE

Jillian - Lime; Abi - Magenta; Owen - Blue; ***Parker - Yellow***

HERE, THERE, AND EVERYWHERE

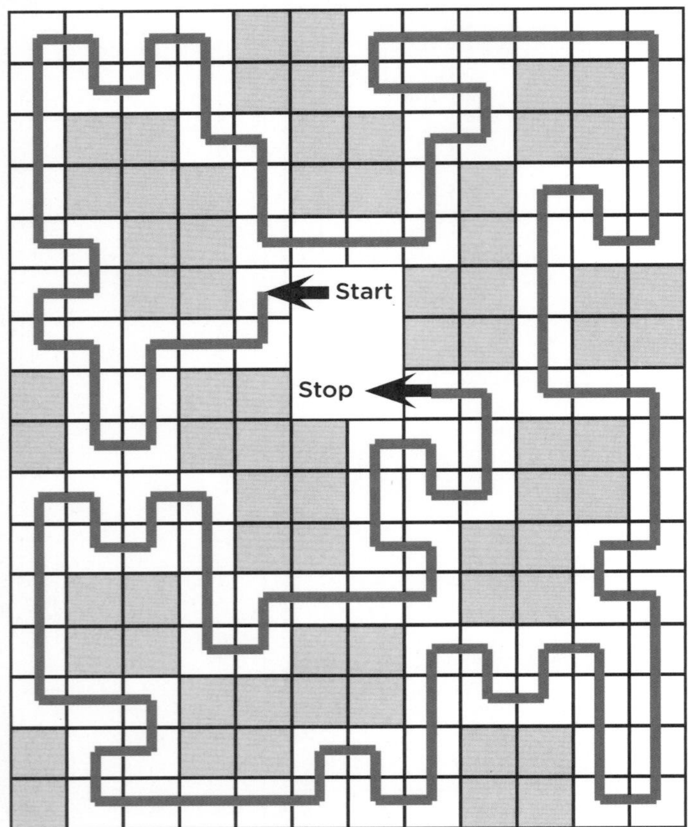

DEFLECT THIS

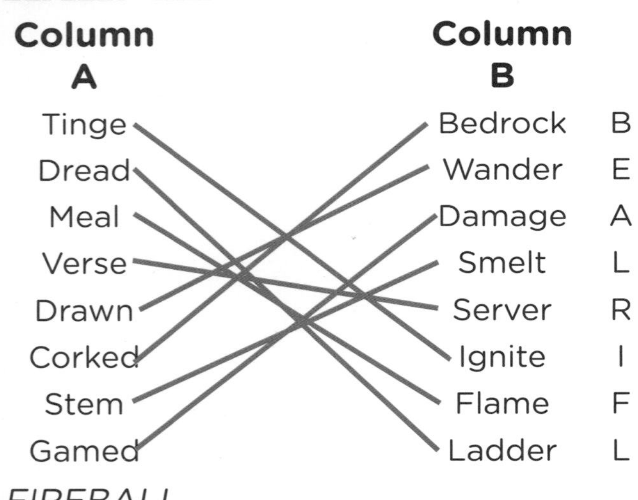

DOWN ON THE (MOB) FARM

PLACES, PEOPLE!

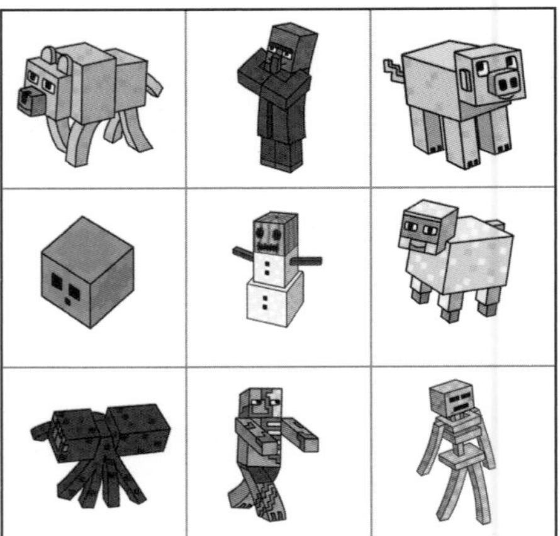

AMAZING MAZES FOR MINECRAFTERS

Challenging Mazes for Hours of Entertainment!

JEN FUNK WEBER

Sky Pony Press
New York

TABLE OF CONTENTS

Cave Explorers
Redstone Roundup
A Dog's Life
Hop to It #1
Capture the Sword
Into the Forest
Tools for the Taking
Safe Slimes
Spelling Bee #1
Favorite Things
Eggceptional Spawning
Around the Blocks
Hop to It #2
Emerald Find
Temple Escape
RUN!
Specimen Collection
Spelling Bee #2
Chest Quest
Frog Fitness
Enchanté
Hop to It #3
Nap Time
Diamond Dash
Good Trades Bad Trade
Smoothies for Six
Spelling Bee #3
Into Battle
Cactus Crop Collection
Lava Knowledge
Hop to It #4
Lost Beacon
An Enchanted Hoe
A Very Smart Pig (and a Funny Girl)
Main Course Mix-up
Spelling Bee #4
A Secret Message
Beds Wanted!
Cobweb Dreams
Saddle Up!
Hop to It #5
The Pearly Path
Mob House
Scavenger Hunt Finds
Mooshroom Shearing
Spelling Bee #5
Where Am I?
'Nother Nether Star, Please
Chest Jests
Hop to It #6
Quick! You Can Save Us All!
Go for Glow
Laugh Lines
Mob School Carpool
Spelling Bee #6
Chicken Herding
Shedding Light on Redstone Torches
Hop to It #7
Go for the Gold
Pursuing Prismarine
Undead Humor
Egg Hunt
Spelling Bee #7
ANSWERS

CAVE EXPLORERS

Four Minecraft players are trying to find their way to a cave where a treasure is hidden. Follow each player's path, under and over crossing paths, to discover which players make it and which one gets lost.

Carlos Cara Cami Camilo

REDSTONE ROUND UP

Alex has plans to build an epic redstone machine. Help her collect all the redstone in the maze. To do this, draw a line from Start to Finish that passes once through every redstone block and dust mound. Your line can go up, down, left, or right, but not diagonally. On your mark, get set, collect!

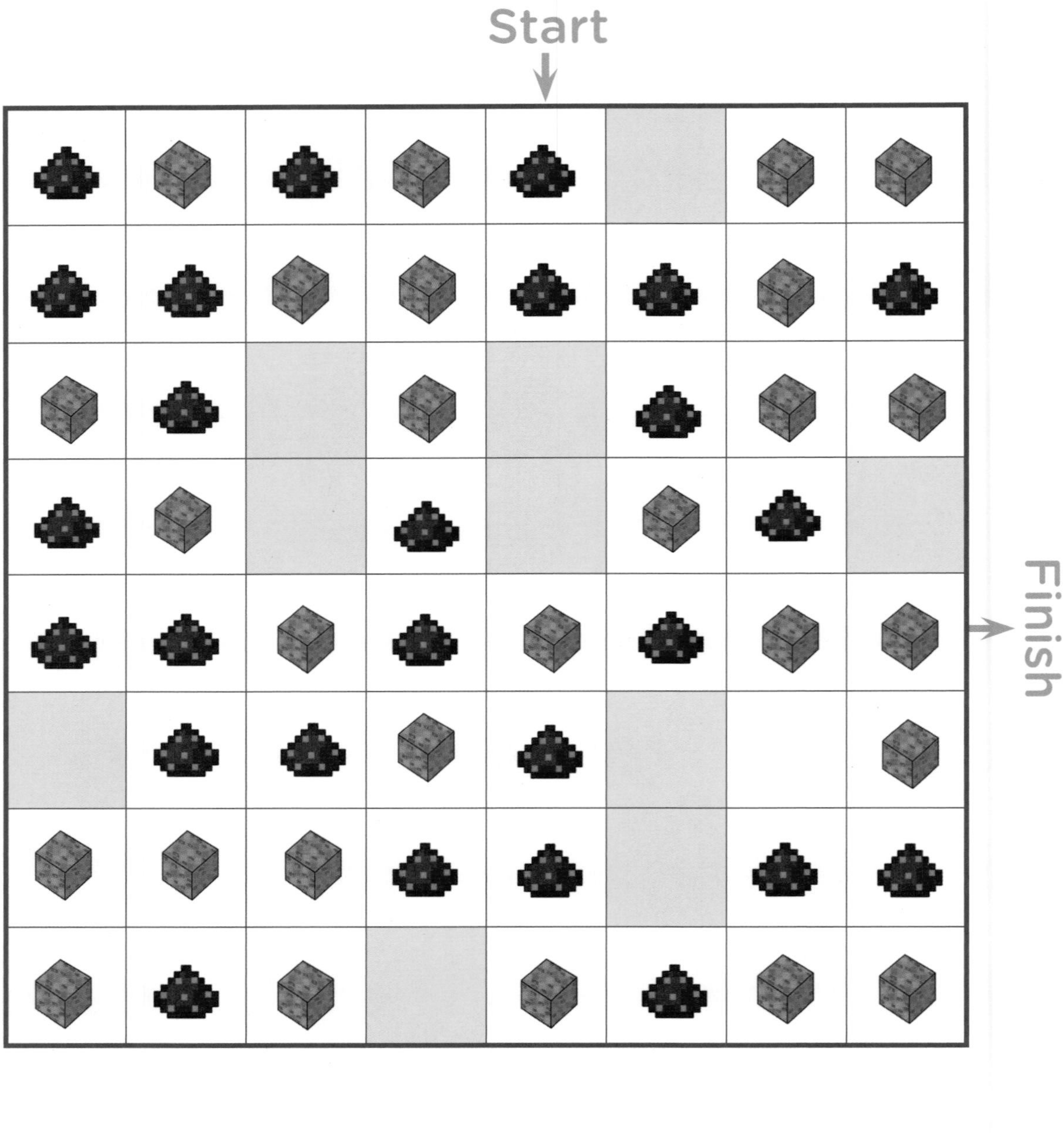

Start

Finish

A DOG'S LIFE

Find your way through this maze from START to FINISH. It will be easier if you correctly identify each statement as true or false.

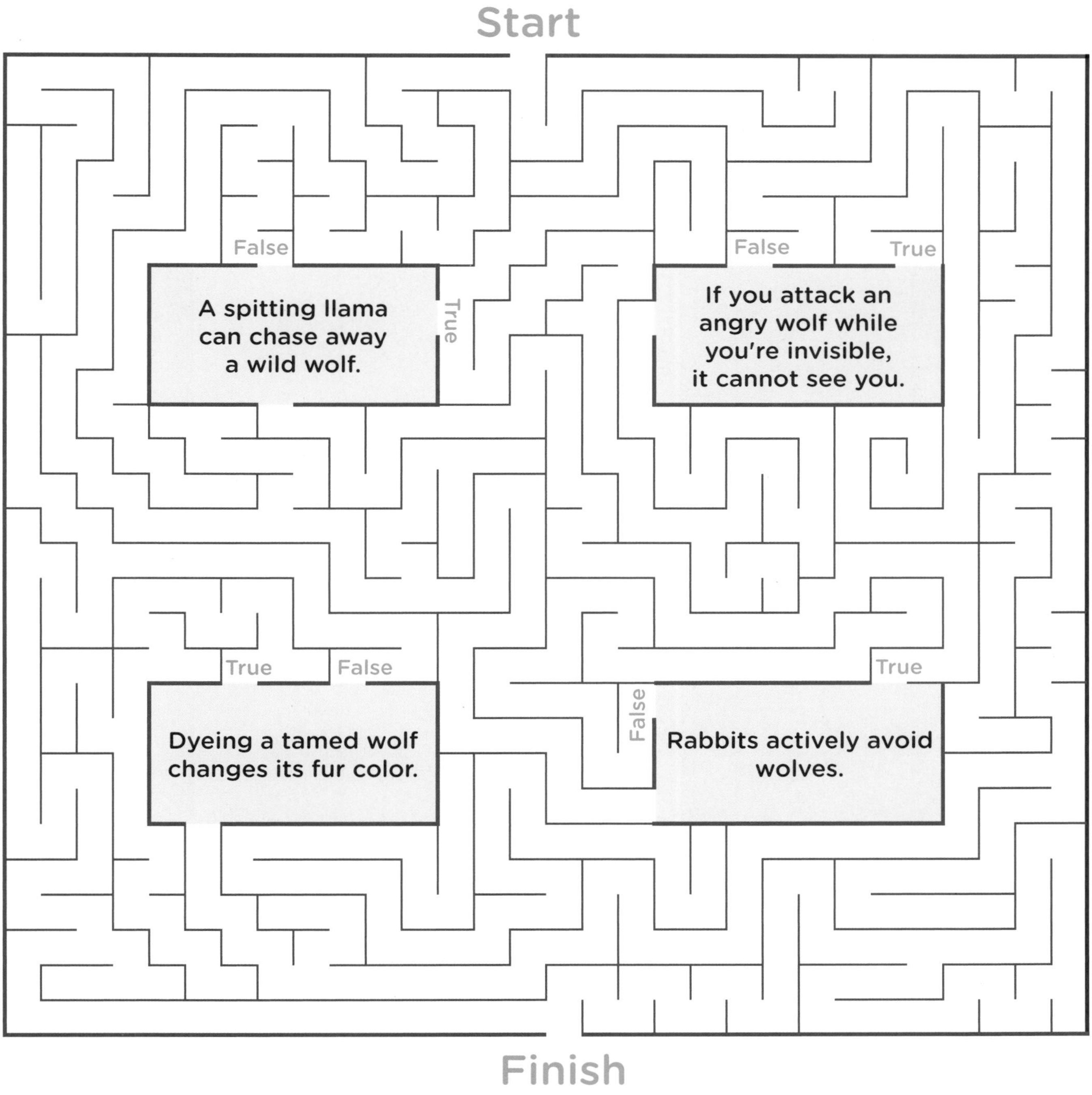

Start

False

True

A spitting llama can chase away a wild wolf.

False

True

If you attack an angry wolf while you're invisible, it cannot see you.

True

False

Dyeing a tamed wolf changes its fur color.

True

False

Rabbits actively avoid wolves.

Finish

HOP TO IT #1

Find your way from the top-left yellow box to the bottom-right yellow box by keeping one icon the same each time you hop boxes. There are two paths to take. See if you pick the right one!

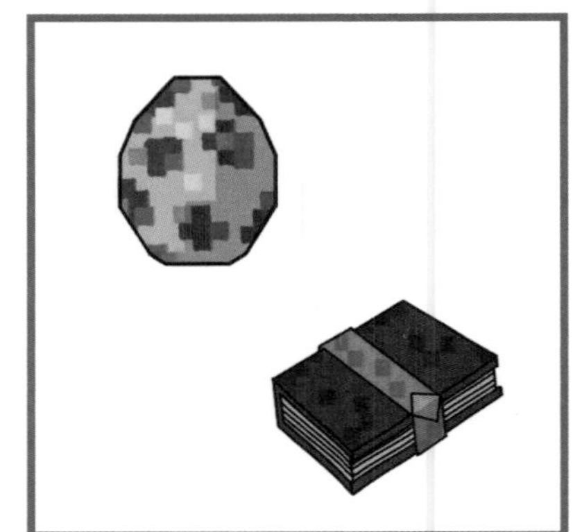
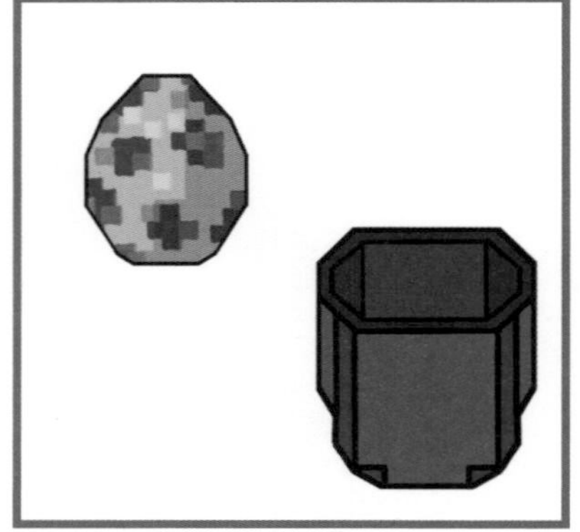

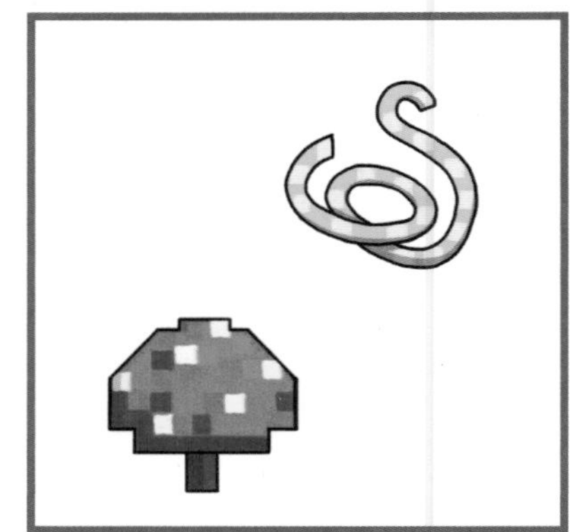

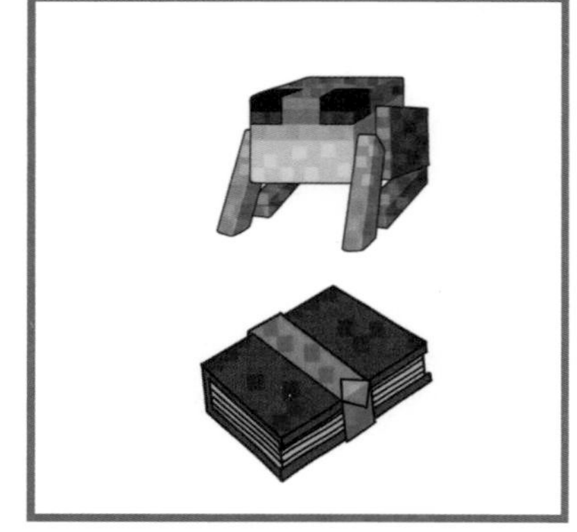
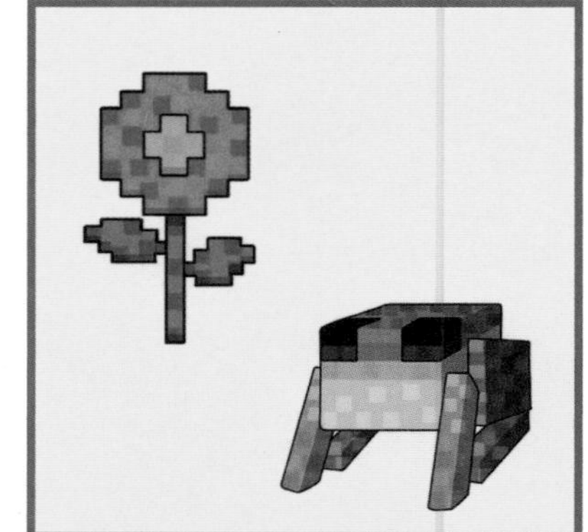

CAPTURE THE SWORD

Navigate this maze to capture the diamond sword in the center. Begin at one corner (you'll have to guess which one), and follow the numbers and arrows.

Each square tells you how many spaces to move and in what direction. Arrows leading off the grid are dead ends. Can you find the path and claim the sword?

3 →	1 →	3 ↓	2 ↓	3 ↓
2 →	4 ↓	3 ↓	1 →	3 ←
2 ↑	2 ↑		3 ←	1 ↑
2 ↑	2 ↓	3 →	1 ←	4 ←
1 →	2 ↑	2 ↑	3 ↑	1 ←

INTO THE FOREST

Your friends are meeting in the forest. Can you get there without running into the skeleton, creeper, enderman, or witch?

START

TOOLS FOR THE TAKING

Four Minecraft players picked up tools. Who collected what? To find out, begin at the dot below each player's name and follow it downward. Every time you hit a horizontal line (one that goes across), you must take it. See where each player's path leads, and write each player's name on the space below the correct tool.

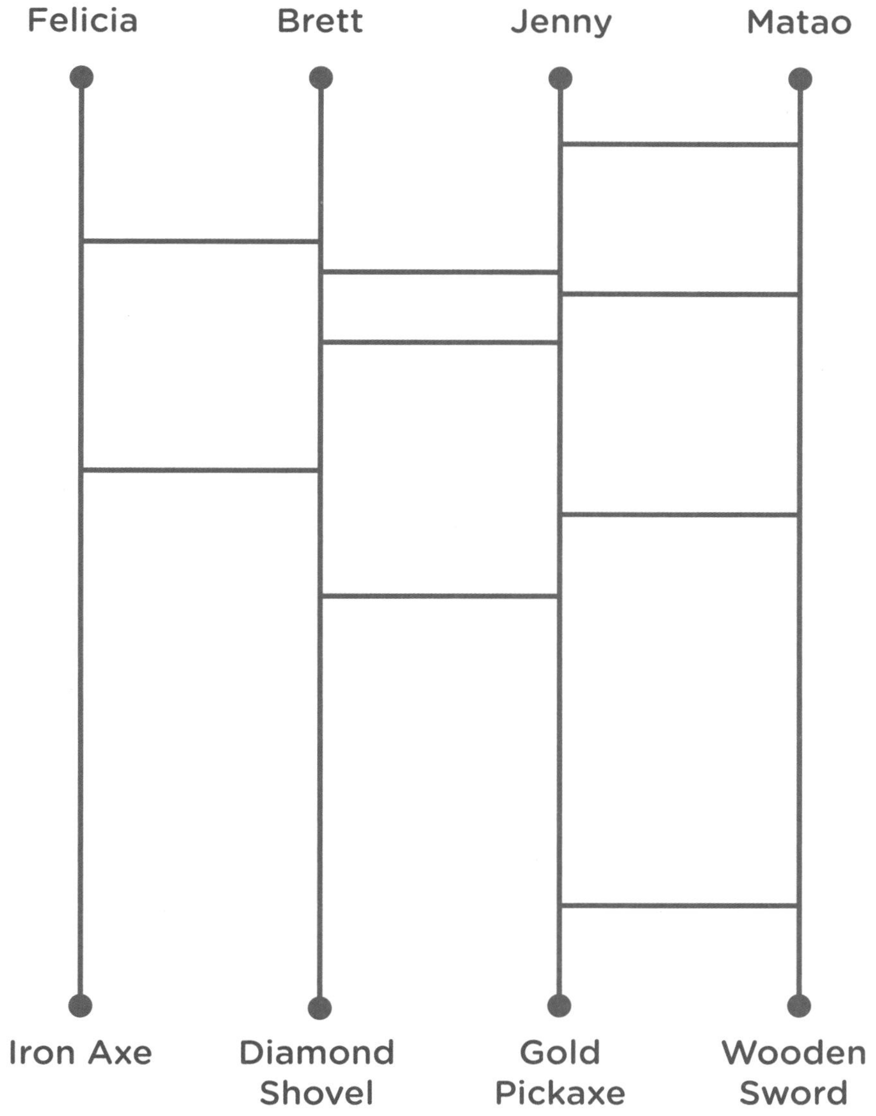

Felicia Brett Jenny Matao

Iron Axe ______

Diamond Shovel ______

Gold Pickaxe ______

Wooden Sword ______

SAFE SLIMES

In this enchanted maze, you can collect slimes safely if you pick up the blocks in a specific order.

Pick up your first block in the top row (you'll have to guess which one!) and your last block in the bottom row. Collect the blocks in this order:

 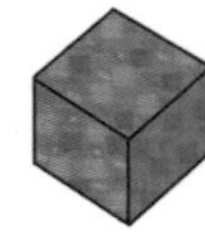 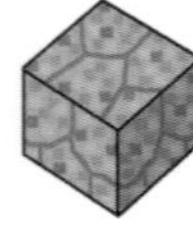

If you bump into a slime out of order, you're destroyed. Start over. Moving only up, down, left, and right, what path must you take?

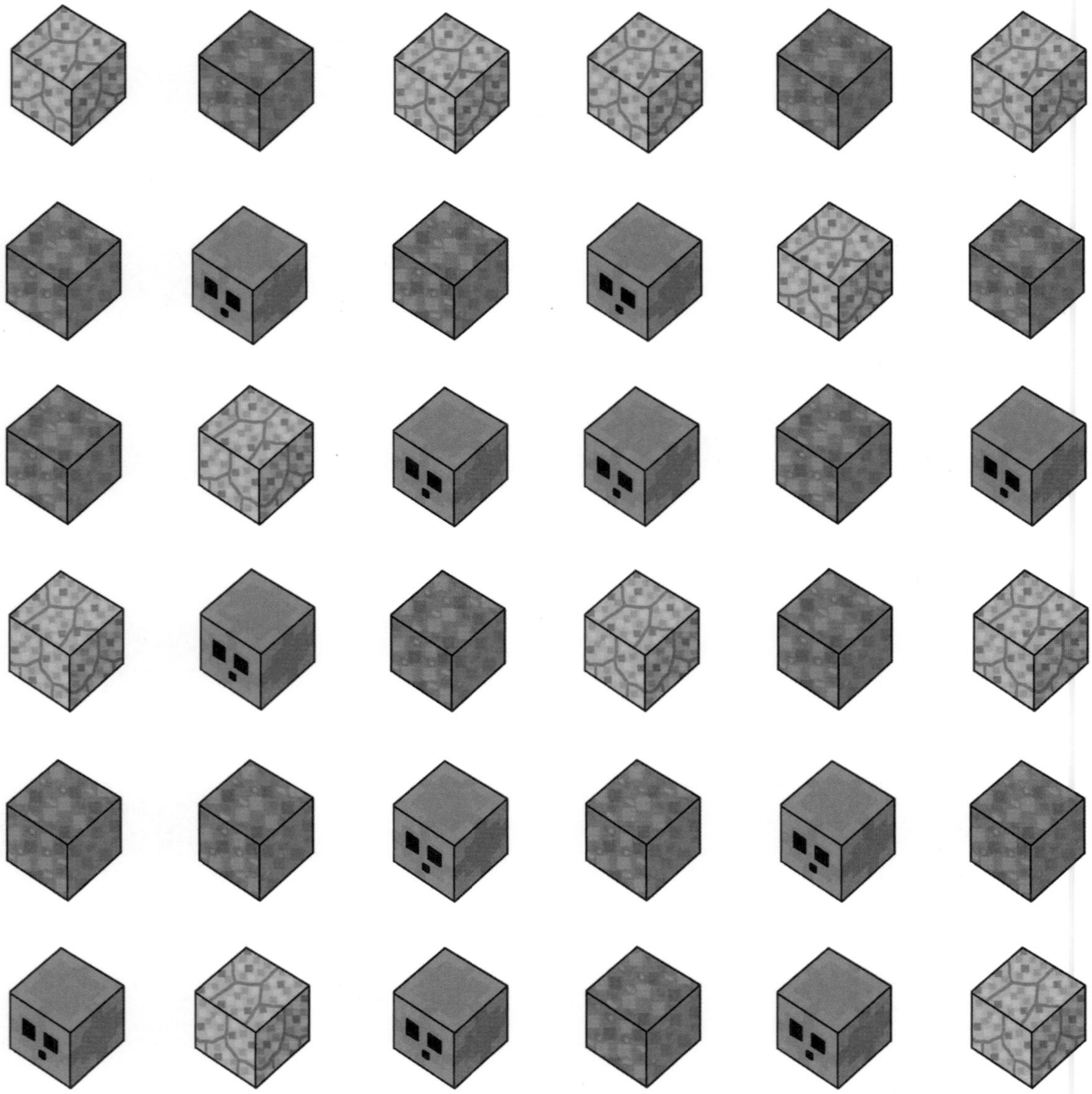

SPELLING BEE #1

Help the bee find its way through this maze to the flowers by spelling 4-letter words.

Make the words by adding MI on the spaces before the given letters. Begin with the word MINE in the top row, and connect the real words until you reach the bottom row. (MIFA is not a real word!)

You can move up, down, left, right, or diagonally.

__FA	MINE	__GO	__BE	__ME	__SO
__OL	__PT	__LK	__LD	__VE	__WN
__AU	__AN	__YO	__CT	__ST	__RD
__SP	__LE	__ND	__LG	__CE	__RT
__LL	__CH	__IZ	__NT	__HY	__OT
__NK	__QO	__PE	__TH	__JU	__UN

FAVORITE THINGS

Follow each player's path, under and over crossing paths, to discover what each likes to do in Minecraft.

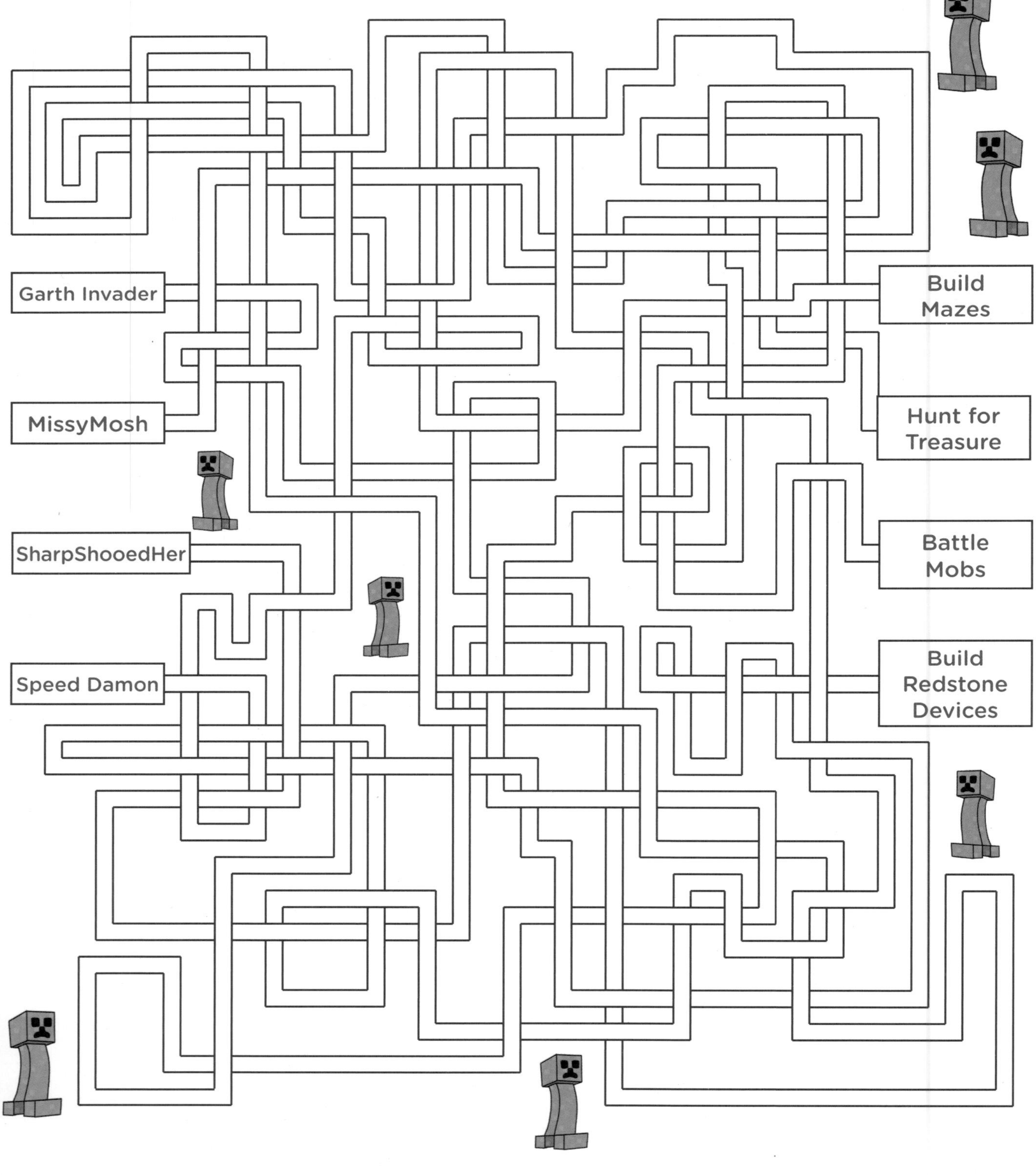

Garth Invader

MissyMosh

SharpShooedHer

Speed Damon

Build Mazes

Hunt for Treasure

Battle Mobs

Build Redstone Devices

EGGCEPTIONAL SPAWNING

Fill the Overworld with mobs of every kind. To do this, draw a line from Start to Finish that passes through every egg once. Your line can go up, down, left, or right, but not diagonally. Get cracking!

Start ←

Finish ←

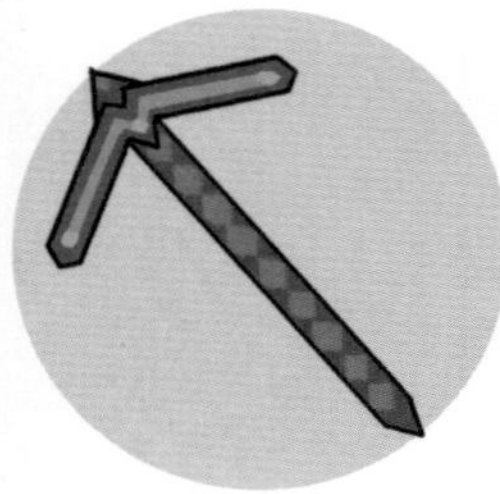

AROUND THE BLOCKS

Do you know your way around the Minecraft blocks?

Find your way through this maze from START to FINISH. It will be easier if you correctly identify each statement as true or false.

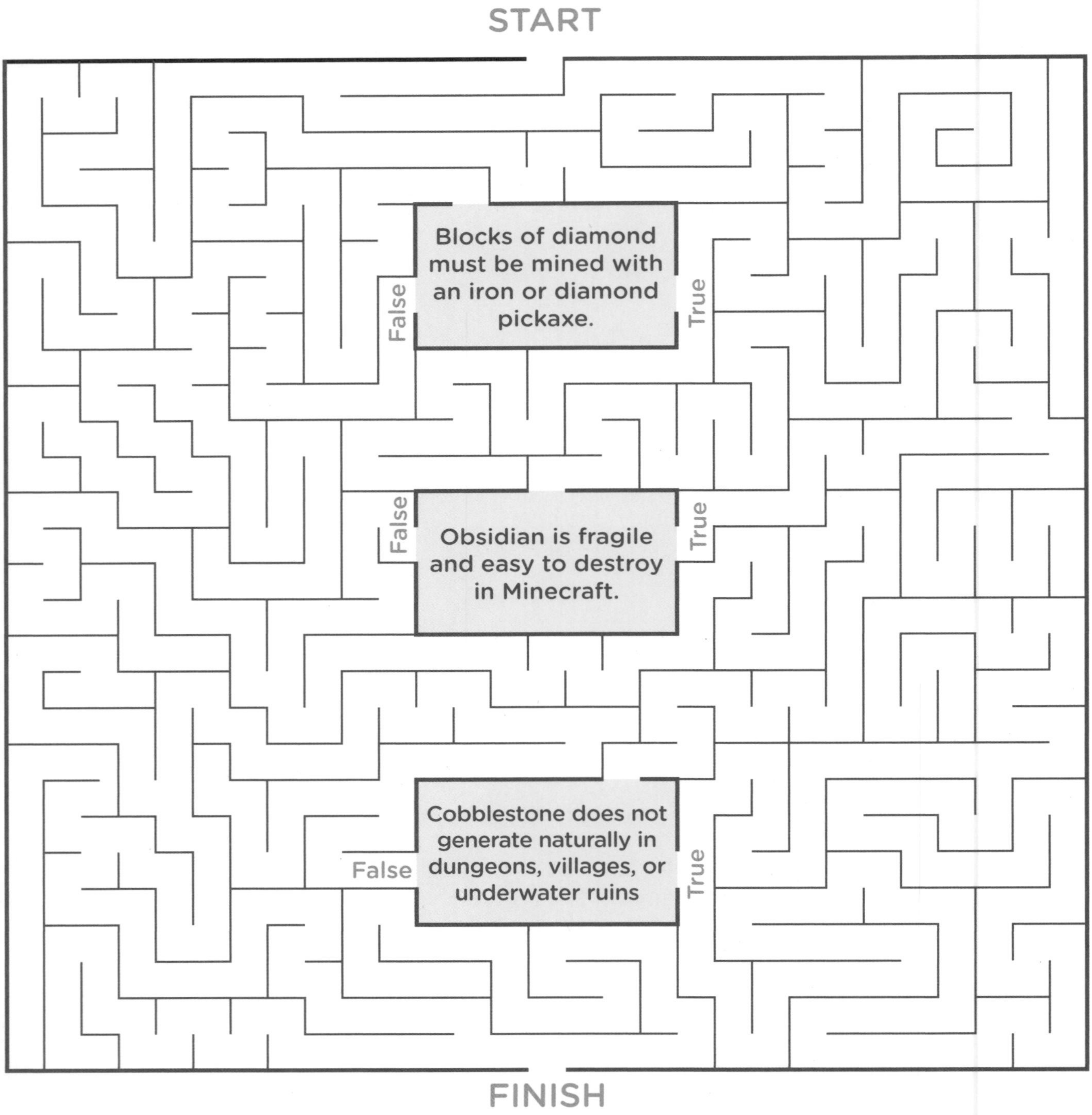

START

Blocks of diamond must be mined with an iron or diamond pickaxe.

False

True

Obsidian is fragile and easy to destroy in Minecraft.

False

True

Cobblestone does not generate naturally in dungeons, villages, or underwater ruins

False

True

FINISH

HOP TO IT #2

Find your way from the top-left yellow box to the bottom-right yellow box by keeping one icon the same each time you hop boxes. There are two paths to take. See if you pick the right one!

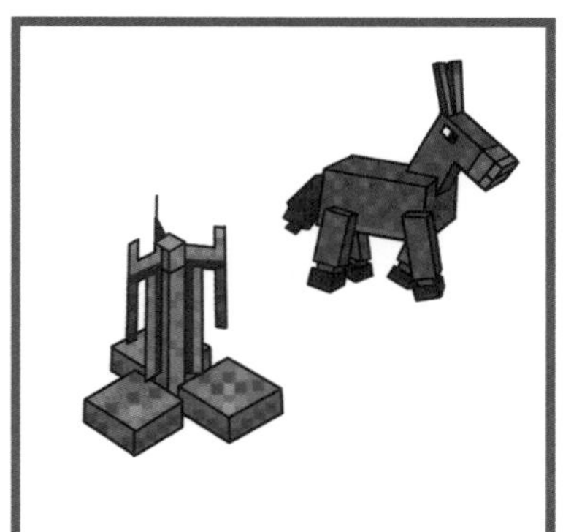

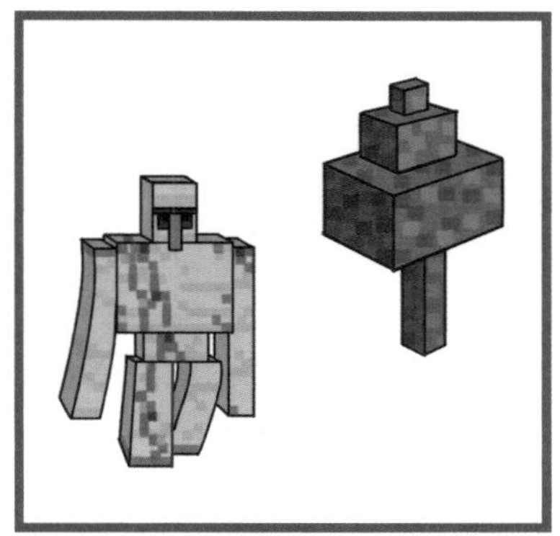

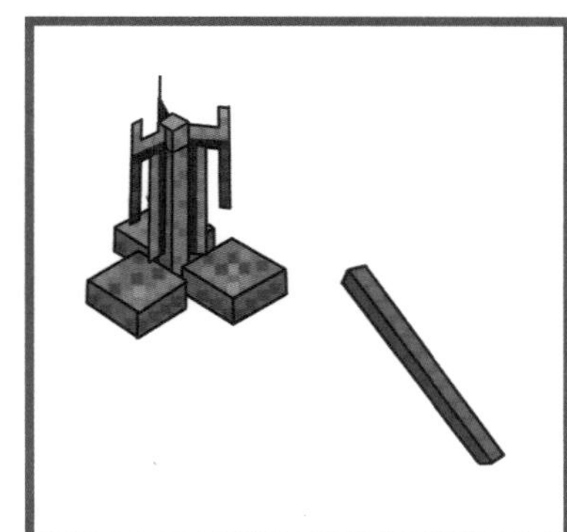

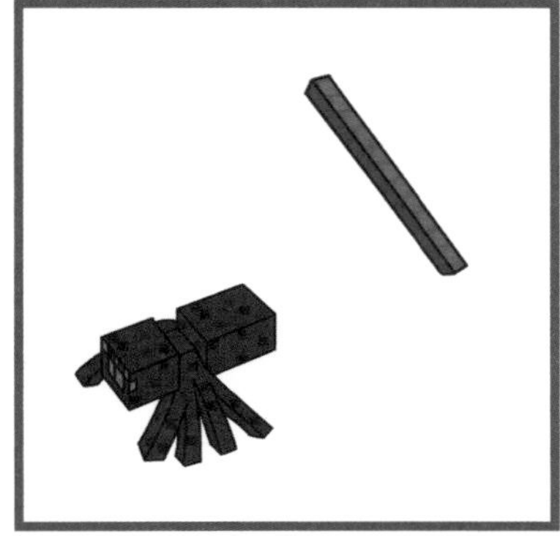

EMERALD FIND

Navigate this maze to find and claim the emeralds.

Begin in a box on the top row (you'll have to guess which one), and follow the numbers and arrows. Each square tells you how many spaces to move and in what direction. Arrows leading off the grid are dead ends.

Can you find the path to the gems?

2↓	4→	3↓	3↓	4↓
2→	3↓	1↓	3←	1↑
2↓	3→	2←	2←	1↓
1→	2↑	2↓	1↑	4←
4↑	1→		3↑	1←

TEMPLE ESCAPE

You are trapped in a desert temple. Can you find your way out?

FINISH

START

RUN!

Four Minecraft players are being chased by mobs. Who is being chased by what? To find out, begin at the dot below each mob and follow it downward. Every time you hit a horizontal line (one that goes across), you must take it. See where each mob's path leads, and write the name of the mob below the person it's chasing.

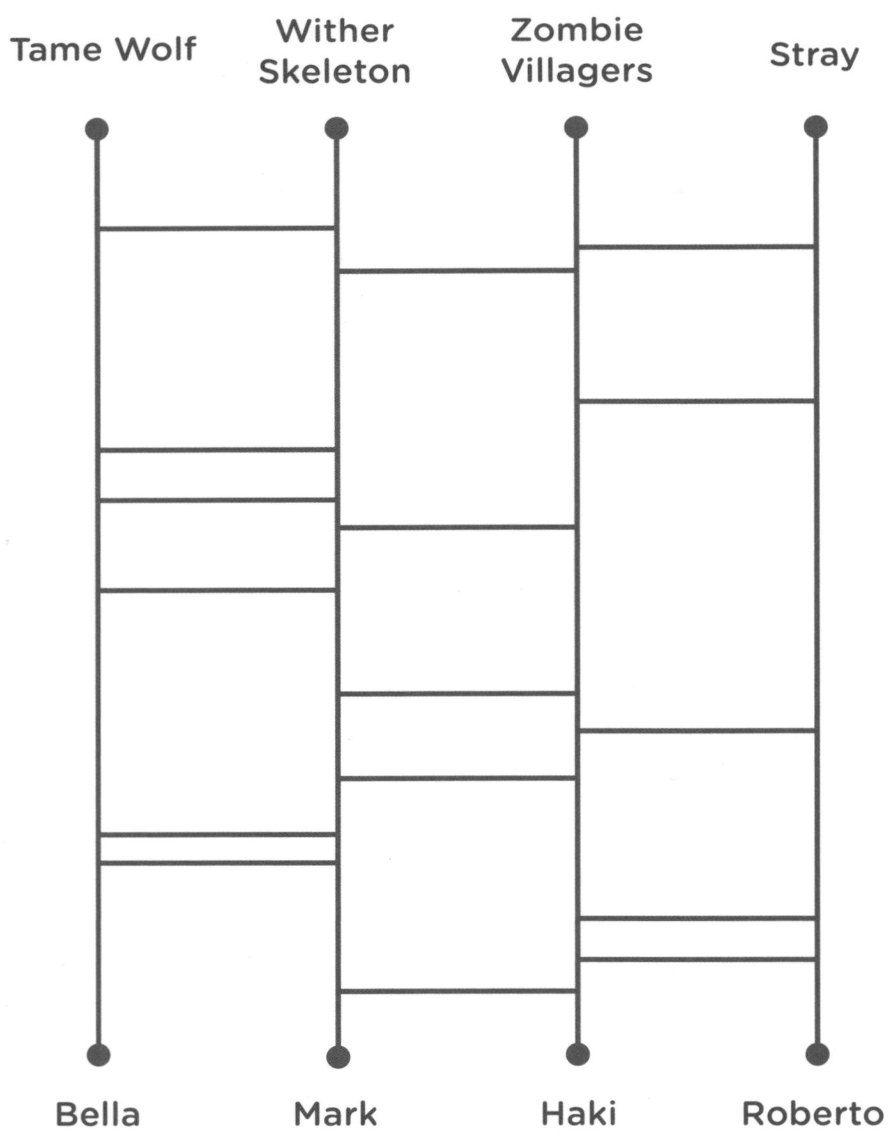

_______________ _______________ _______________ _______________

SPECIMEN COLLECTION

You are collecting specimens for a new aquatic biome. You need: dolphins, squid, and turtles, but they must be collected in this order.

  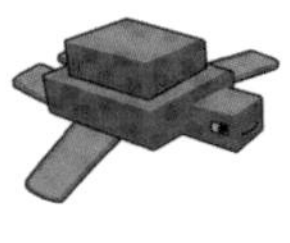

Pick up your first dolphin in the top row and your last turtle in the bottom row. Moving only up, down, left, and right, what path must you take?

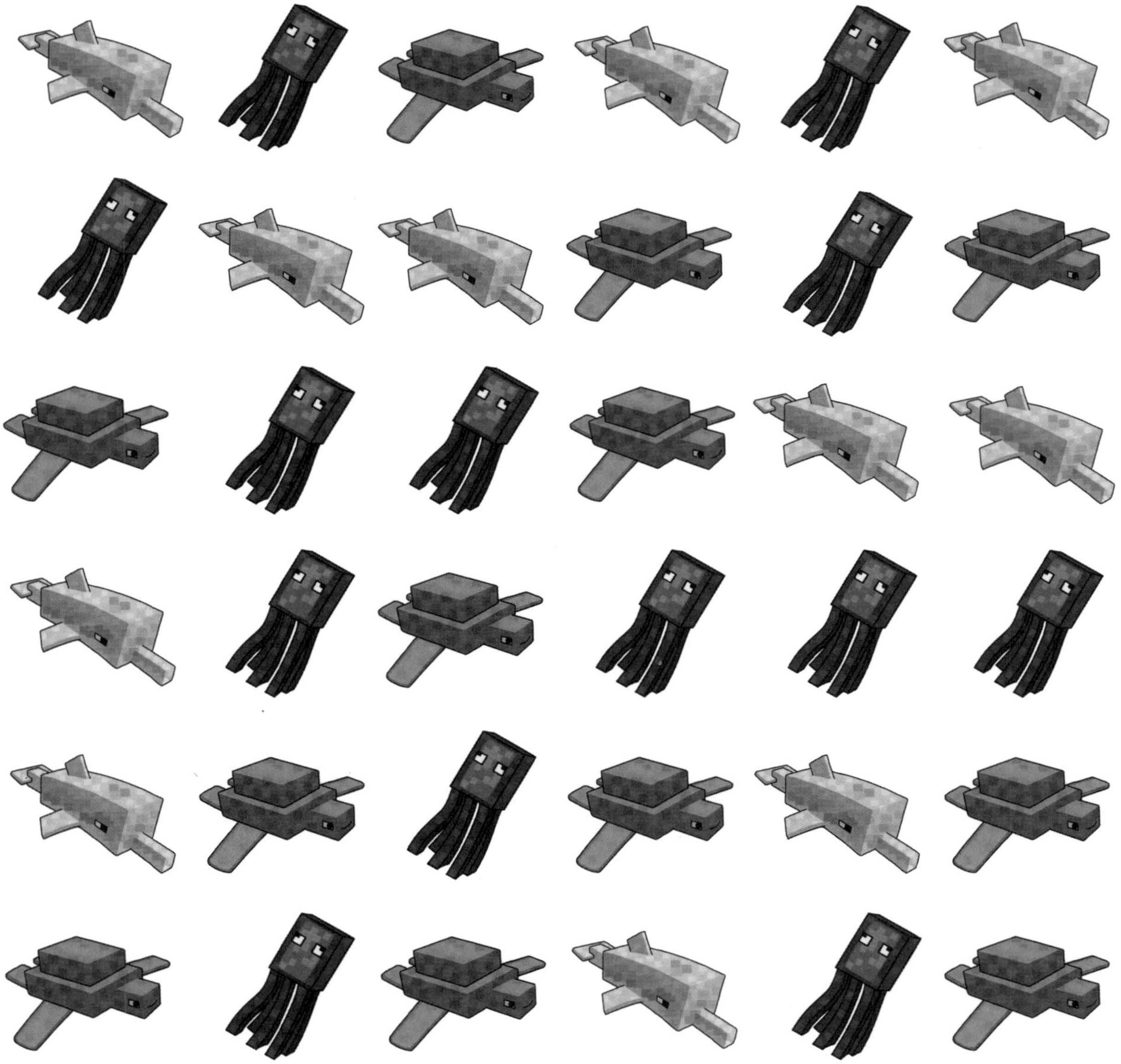

SPELLING BEE #2

Help the bee find its way through this maze to the flowers by spelling 4-letter words.

Make the words by adding M to the first space and N to the second space in the given letters. Begin with the word MINE in the top row, and connect the real words until you reach the bottom row. (MINZ is not a real word!)

You can move up, down, left, right, or diagonally.

_ O _ T	_ E _ G	_ S _ A	_ I _ Z	MINE	_ U _ L
_ I _ O	_ A _ W	_ Z _ K	_ E _ D	_ O _ D	_ A _ F
_ R _ O	_ Y _ A	_ U _ R	_ O _ K	_ I _ H	_ E _ B
_ I _ X	_ P _ E	_ A _ Y	_ J _ I	_ E _ K	_ O _ O
_ A _ Q	_ O _ Z	_ E _ U	_ Y _ V	_ U _ N	_ A _ T
_ U _ F	_ I _ T	_ W _ O	_ A _ V	_ E _ K	_ U _ P

CHEST QUEST

Six Minecraft players are trying to find an enchanted chest. Follow each player's path, under and over crossing paths, to discover which players, if any, find it.

Miney Mo

Nofraido

MC Jammer

CrazyQ

Finder Keeper

Captain E

FROG FITNESS

Help the frog hop to safety. Draw a line from Start to Finish that includes each and every lily pad in the pond. Your line can go up, down, left, or right, but not diagonally. Get hopping!

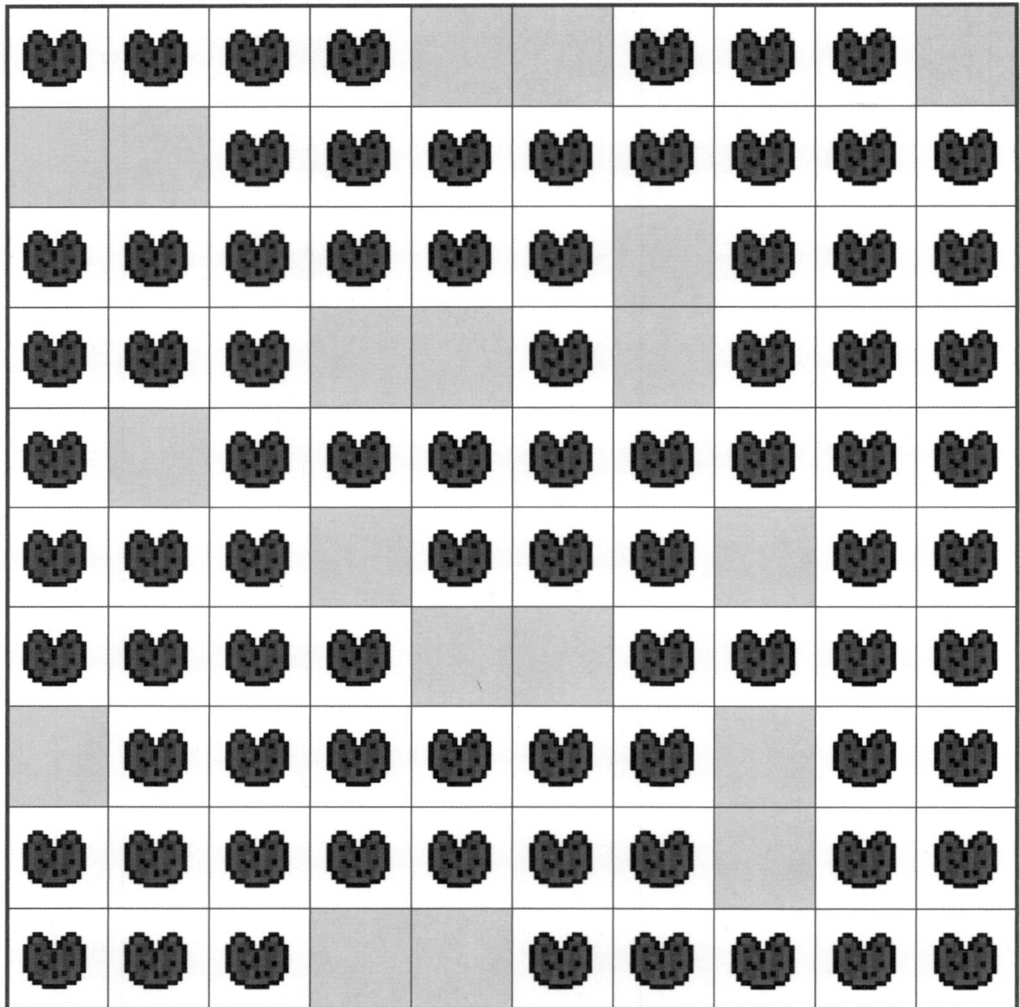

ENCHANTÉ

Find your way through this enchanting maze from START to FINISH. It will be easier if you correctly identify each statement as true or false.

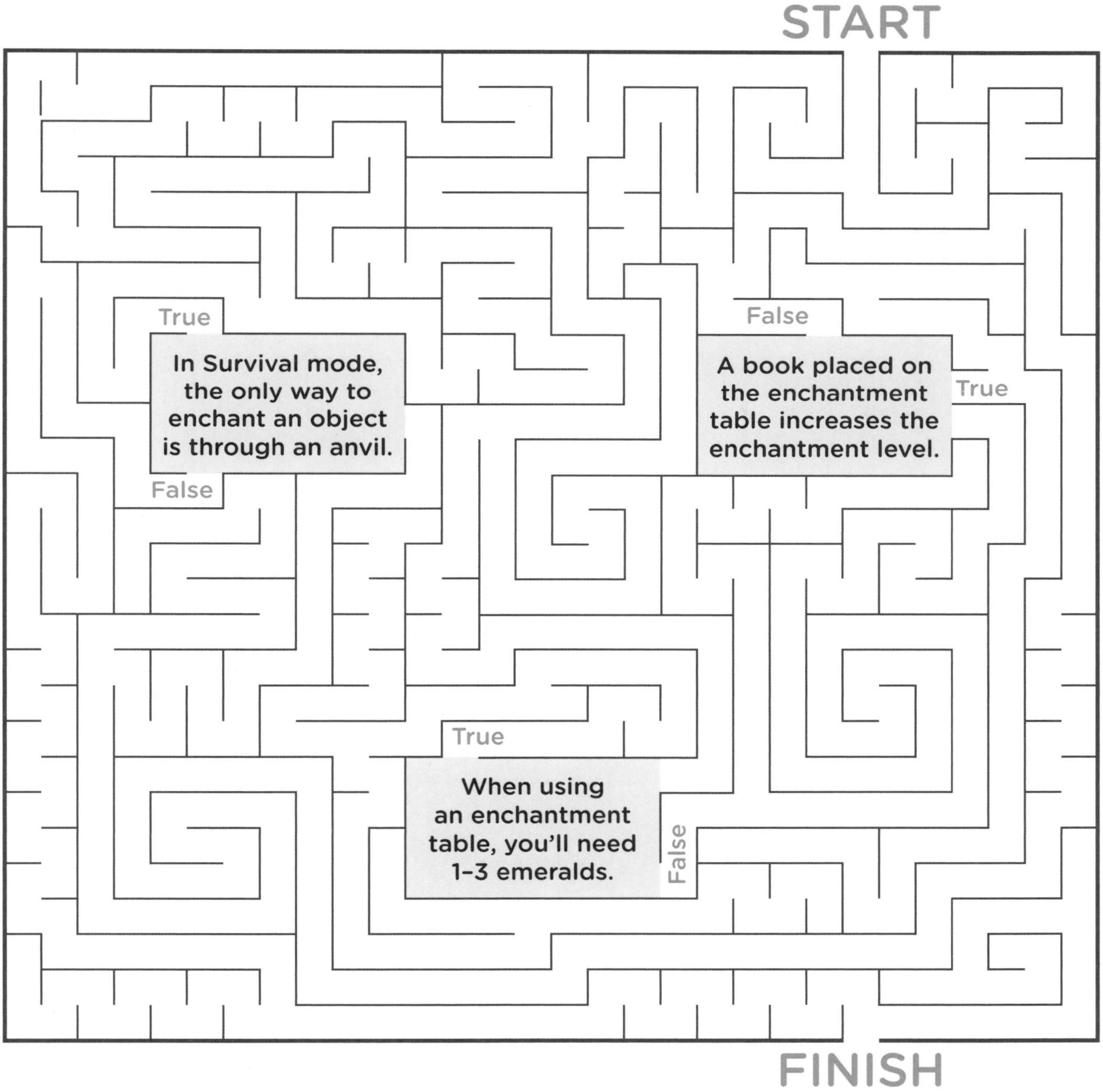

START

True

In Survival mode, the only way to enchant an object is through an anvil.

False

False

A book placed on the enchantment table increases the enchantment level.

True

True

When using an enchantment table, you'll need 1–3 emeralds.

False

FINISH

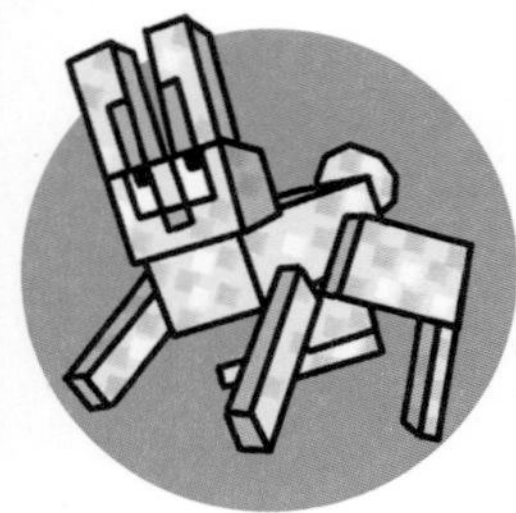

HOP TO IT #3

Find your way from the top-left yellow box to the bottom-right yellow box by keeping one icon the same each time you hop boxes. There are several paths to take. See if you can find the right one!

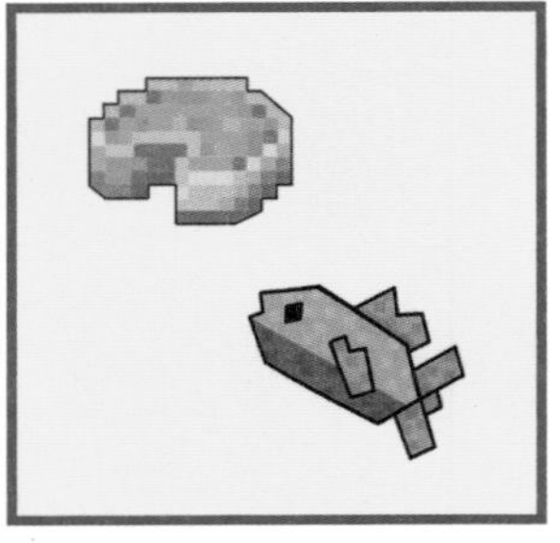

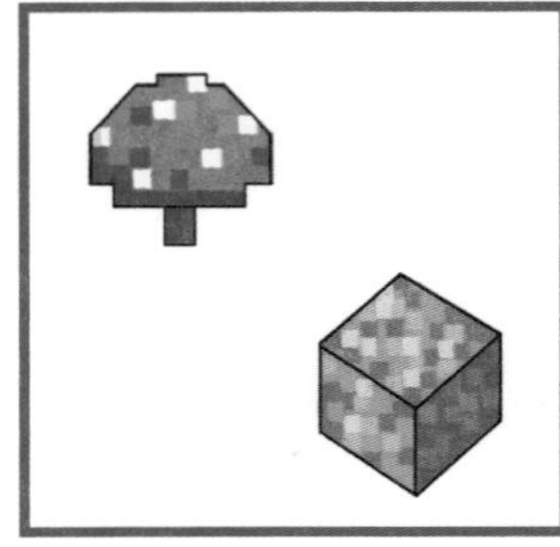
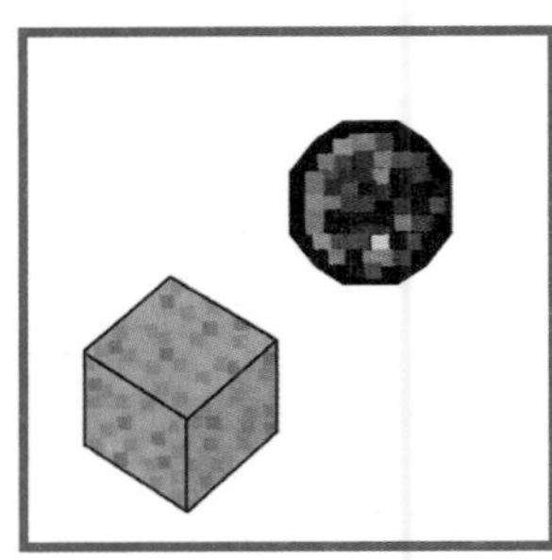
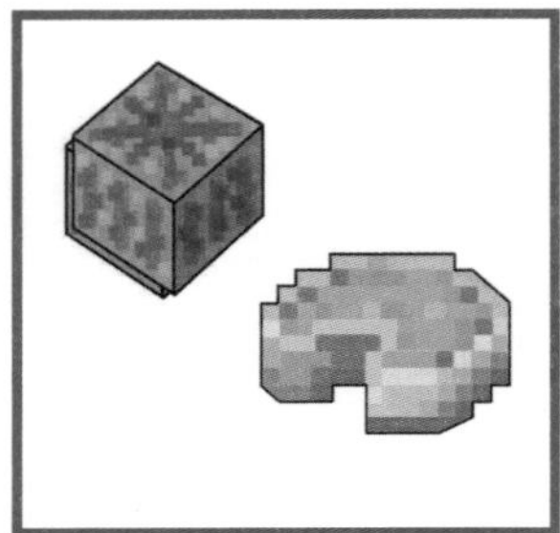

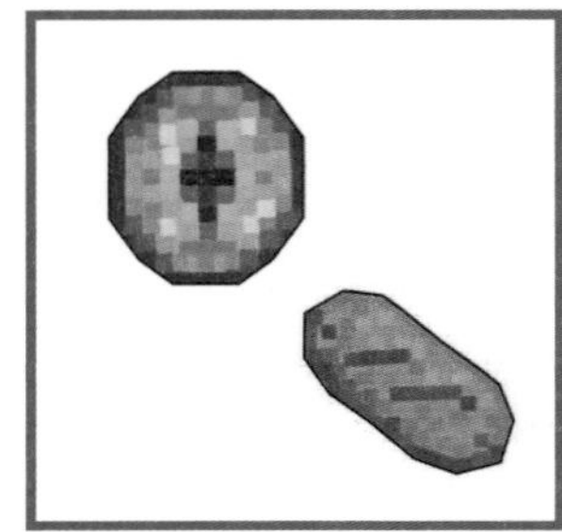
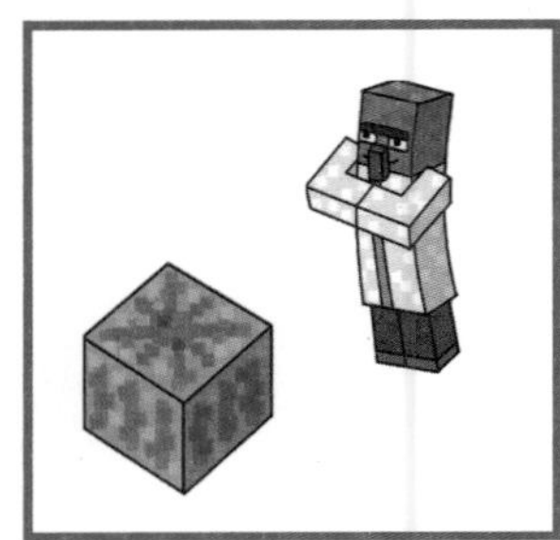
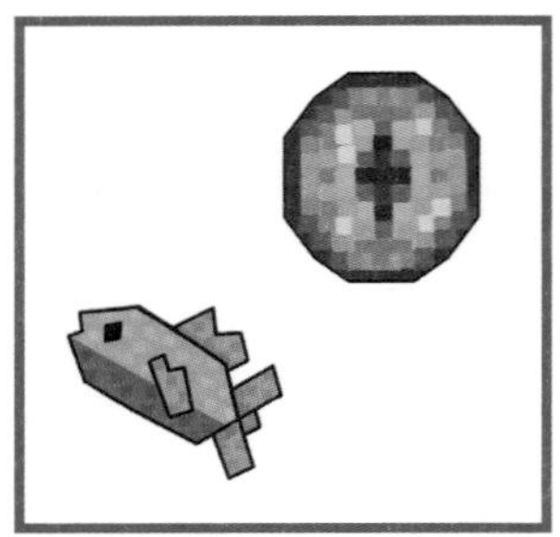
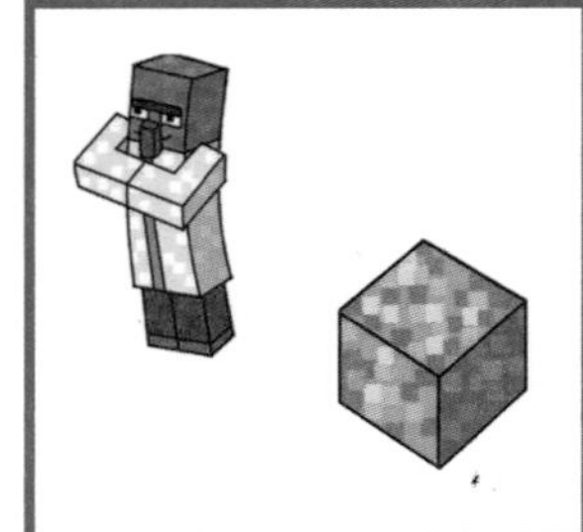
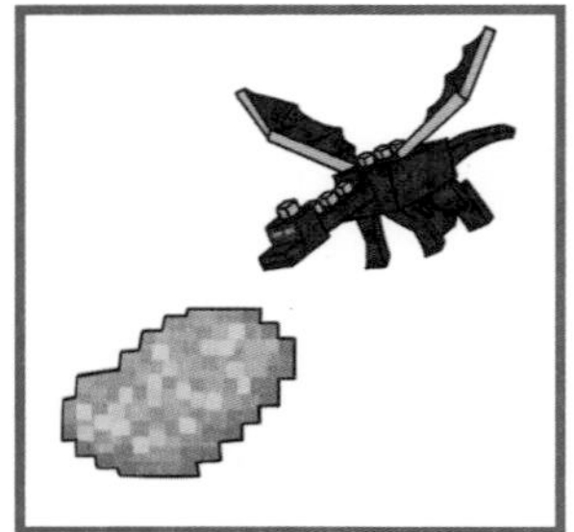

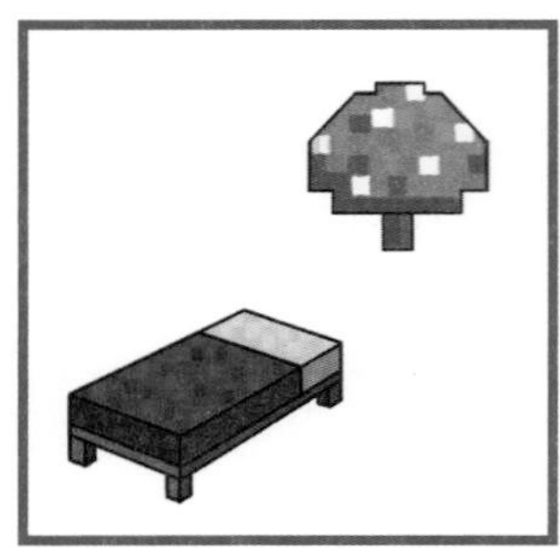
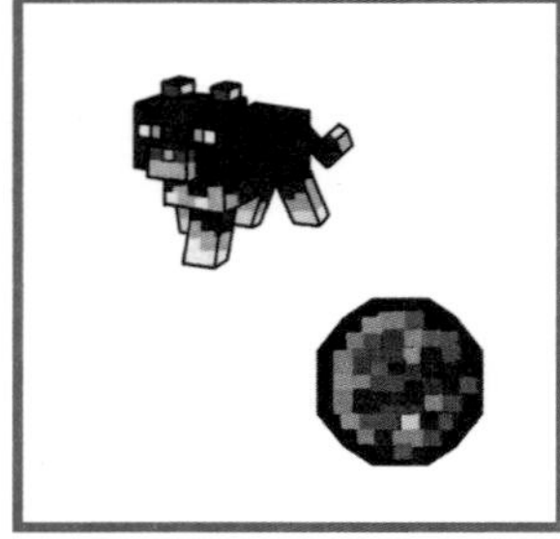

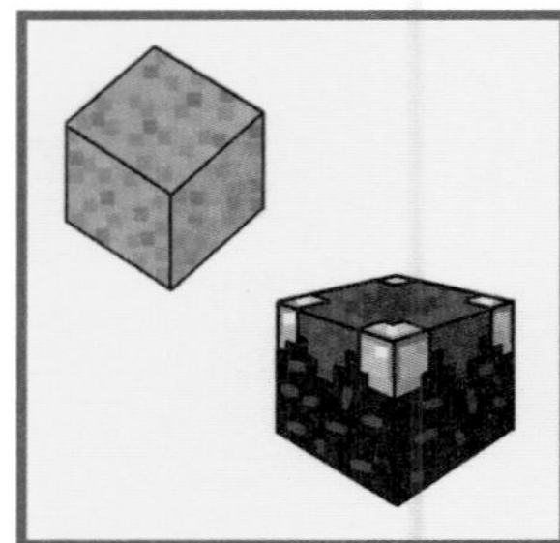

NAP TIME

Help the cat find the path to the warm furnace (where he will sit and nap until you feed him a fish).

Begin in one of the four boxes to the right of, or below, the cat (you'll have to guess which one), and follow the numbers and arrows. Each square tells you how many spaces to move and in what direction. Arrows leading off the grid are dead ends.

		3 ↓	5 ↓	3 ↓	1 ←	5 ↓	4 ←
		3 ↓	3 →	3 ←	3 ↓	1 ↑	3 ←
4 →	4 ↓	5 ↓	5 ↓	4 ↓	1 ↓	4 ←	1 ↑
7 →	1 ↓	1 →	2 ↑	3 ←	3 →	6 ←	3 ↑
1 ↑	5 →	2 ←	2 ↓	1 ←	2 ↑	2 ↑	2 ↓
4 →	2 ↓	5 →	2 →	4 ↓	4 ↑	5 ←	3 ↑
1 ↑	4 →	1 ↑	3 ←	2 ←	6 ↑		
6 →	2 →	2 ←	1 →	3 ↑	1 →		

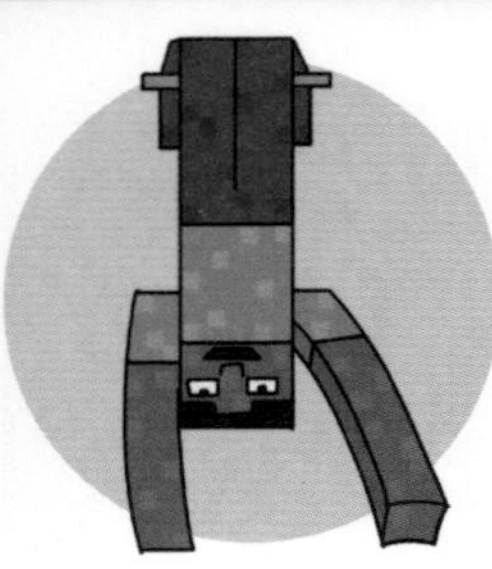

DIAMOND DASH

This room is full of creepers. Can you dash in, grab the diamonds, and get out without . . . you know . . . getting blown up?

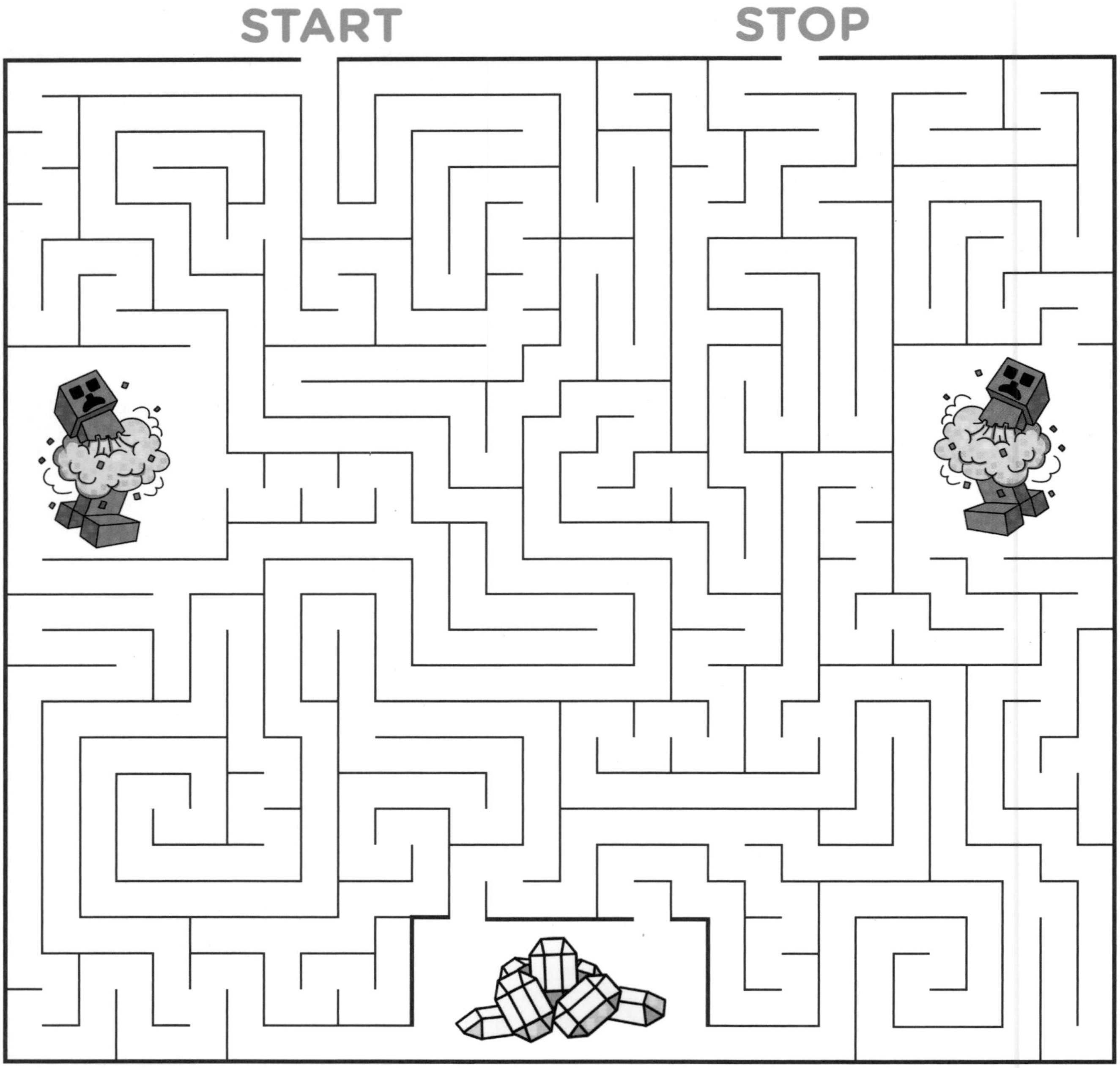

START

STOP

GOOD TRADES BAD TRADE

Five Minecraft players are trading with villagers. One is silly enough to try and trade with a nitwit.

Begin at the dot below each player's name and follow it downward. Every time you hit a horizontal line (one that goes across), you must take it. See where each player's path leads, and write each player's name below the correct trader on the line.

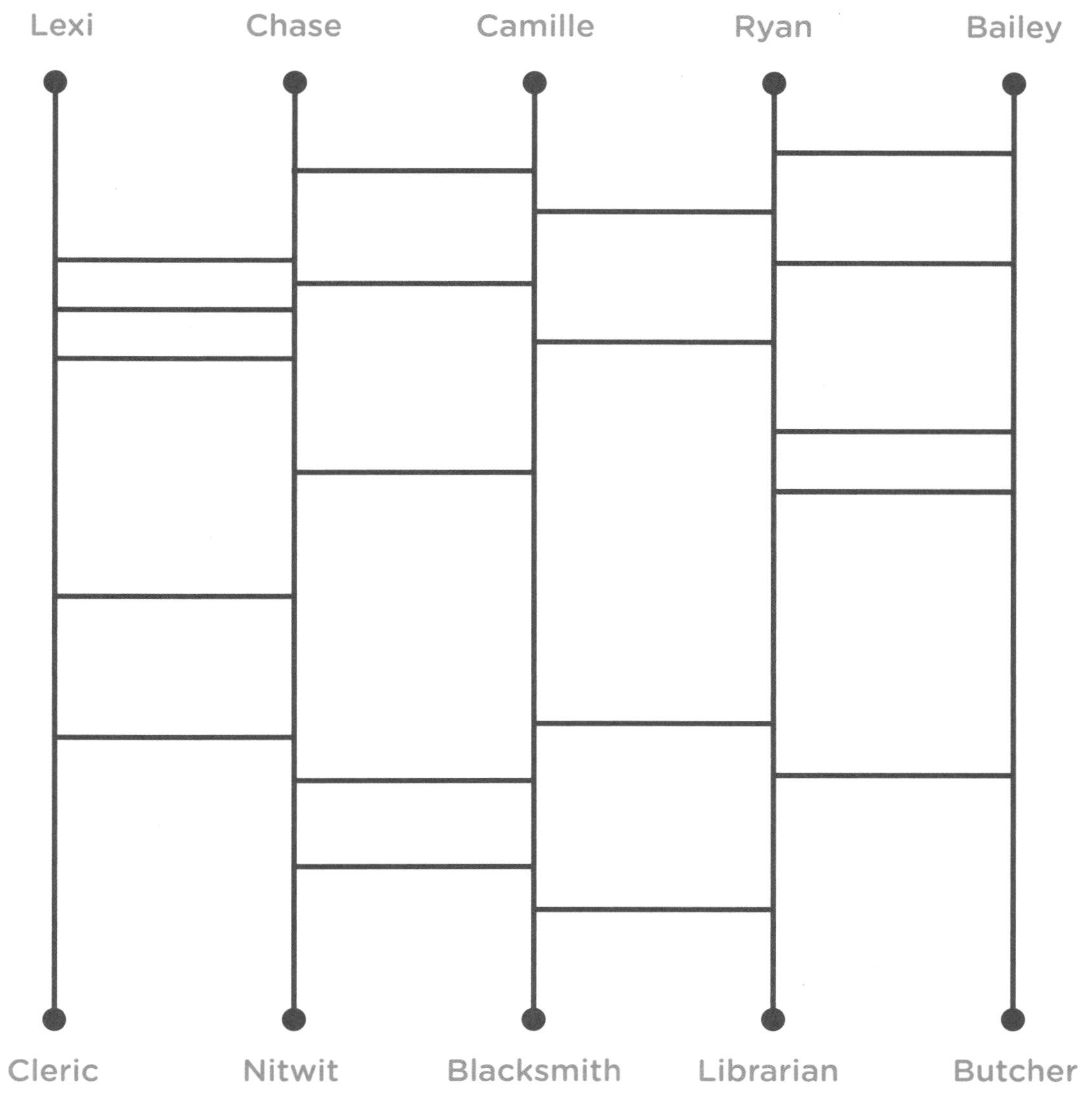

Lexi Chase Camille Ryan Bailey

Cleric Nitwit Blacksmith Librarian Butcher

__________ __________ __________ __________ __________

SMOOTHIES FOR SIX

You are making smoothies for six friends. For each smoothie, you need to add the following ingredients, in this order, to a blender:

Gather your ingredients below. You must pick up your first apple in the top row and your last watermelon slice in the bottom row.

Moving only up, down, left, and right, what path must you take to get all the ingredients for six smoothies?

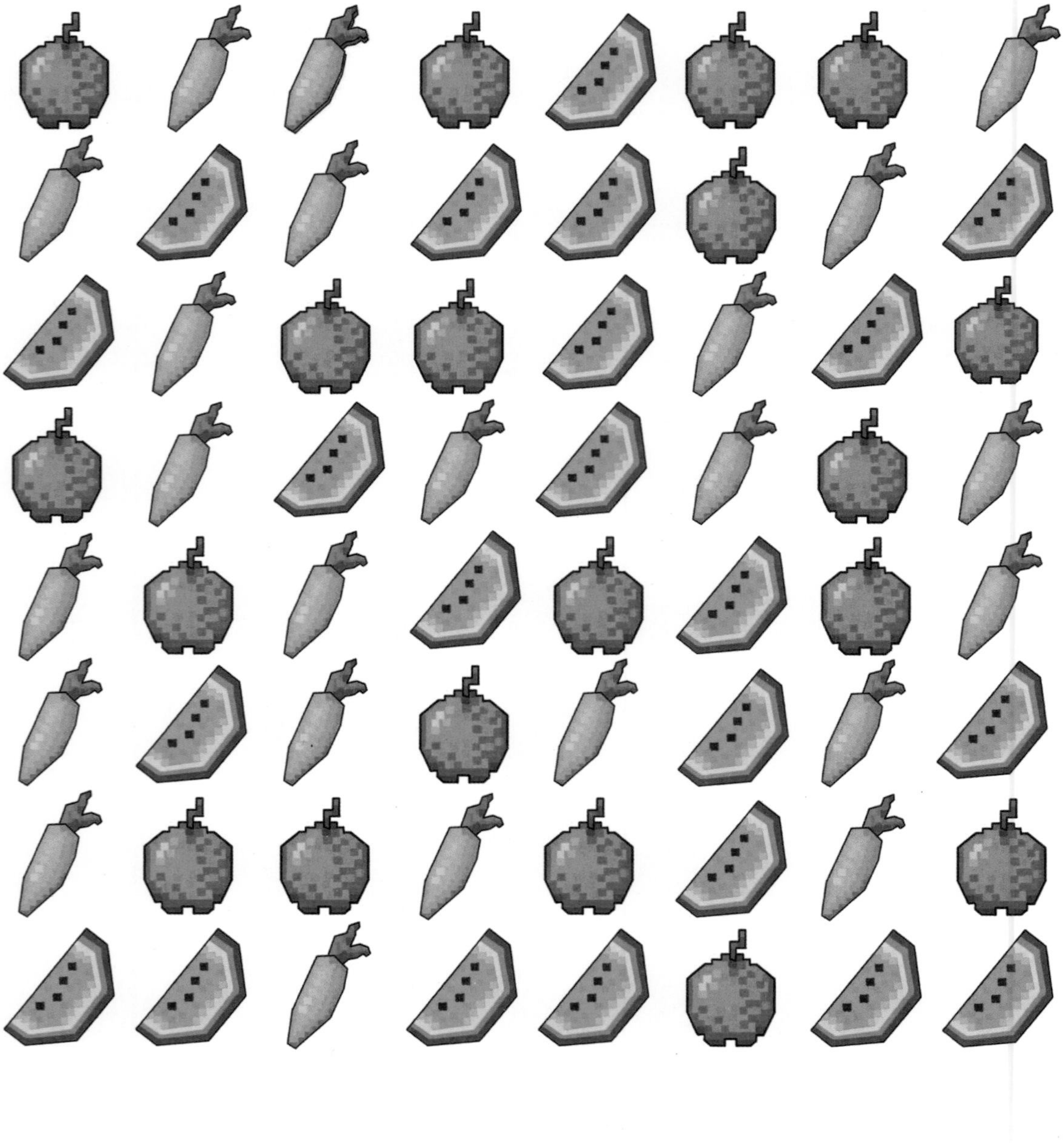

SPELLING BEE #3

Help the bee find its way through this maze to the flowers by spelling 4-letter words.

Make the words by adding NE after the given letters. Begin with the word MINE in the top row, and connect the real words until you reach the bottom row. (CRNE is not a real word!)

You can move up, down, left, right, or diagonally.

MINE	BU__	JE__	EA__	SC__	FI__	JE__	CR__
LA__	HE__	BR__	CR__	LO__	ST__	DO__	VI__
AT__	ZO__	MA__	DU__	IF__	UR__	SA__	FO__
GU__	CH__	MO__	GR__	OI__	FA__	TU__	OP__
OU__	HO__	NI__	QU__	MS__	BO__	RE__	LI__
DI__	KY__	EG__	EA__	CA__	PL__	AJ__	TO__
BL__	PI__	WU__	DR__	UR__	NO__	KR__	BR__
NE__	CO__	AU__	JU__	GO__	FE__	CL__	HU__

INTO BATTLE

Four Minecraft players are heading into battle with hostile mobs. Follow each player's path, under and over crossing paths, to discover who's fighting whom.

Ghast

Drowned

Scarrr	Clash
Jaction	Attax

Shulker

Evoker

CACTUS CROP COLLECTION

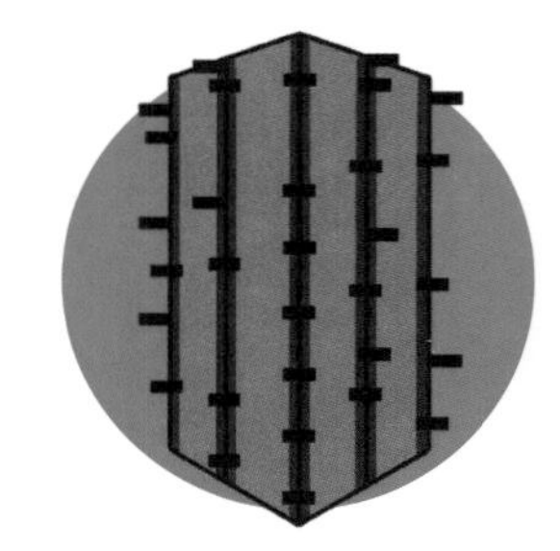

You've been growing cacti so you can build traps, and your cactus crop is ready to harvest.

To do this, draw a line from Start to Finish that passes through every cactus once. Your line can go up, down, left, or right, but not diagonally. Careful! Don't get stuck!

Finish **Start**

LAVA KNOWLEDGE

A little bit of lava knowledge will help you out here.

Find your way through this maze from START to FINISH. It will be easier if you correctly identify each statement as true or false.

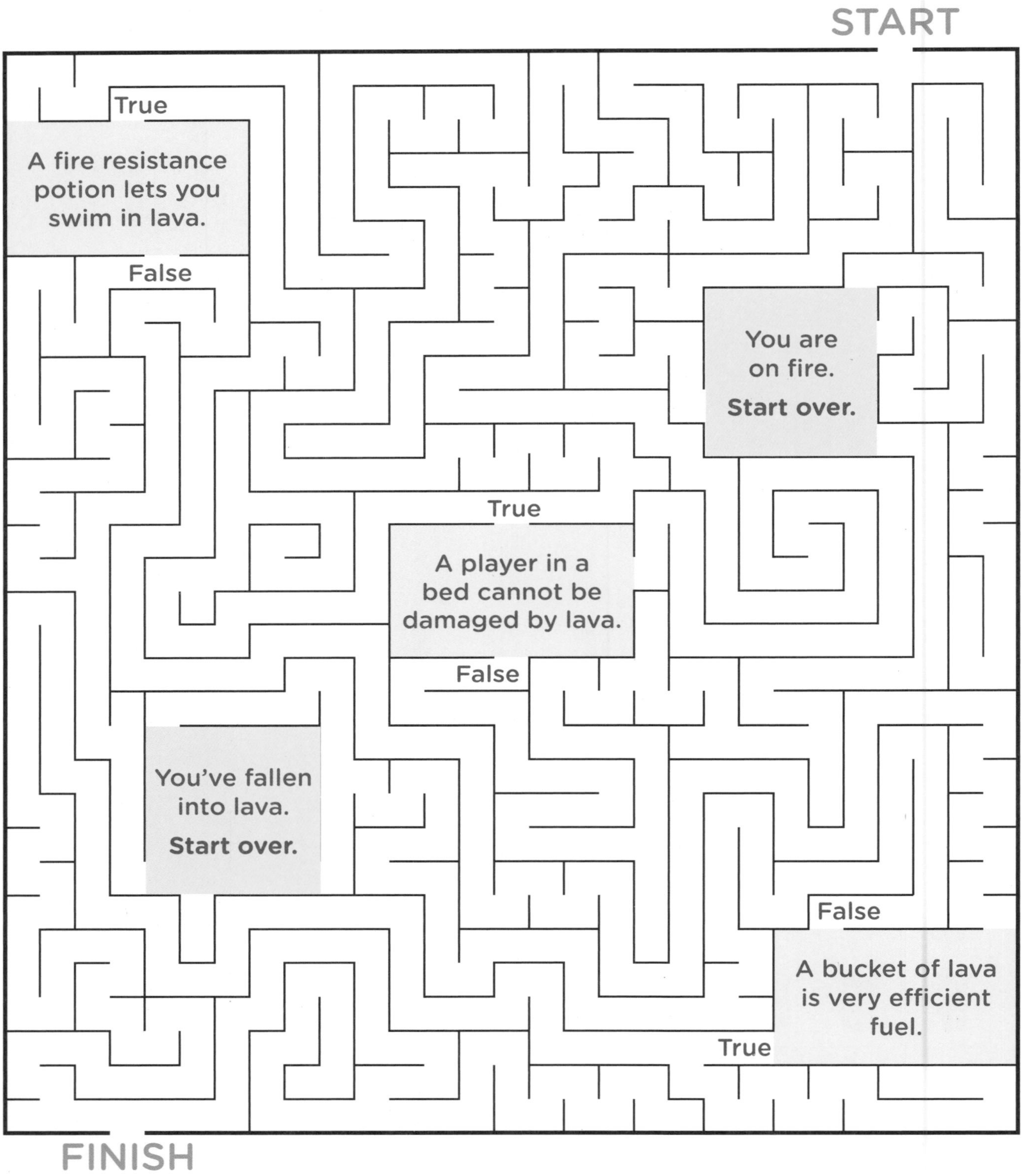

START

True

A fire resistance potion lets you swim in lava.

False

You are on fire.

Start over.

True

A player in a bed cannot be damaged by lava.

False

You've fallen into lava.

Start over.

False

A bucket of lava is very efficient fuel.

True

FINISH

HOP TO IT #4

Find your way from the top-left yellow box to the bottom-right yellow box by keeping one icon the same each time you hop boxes. There are two paths to take. See if you can find the right one!

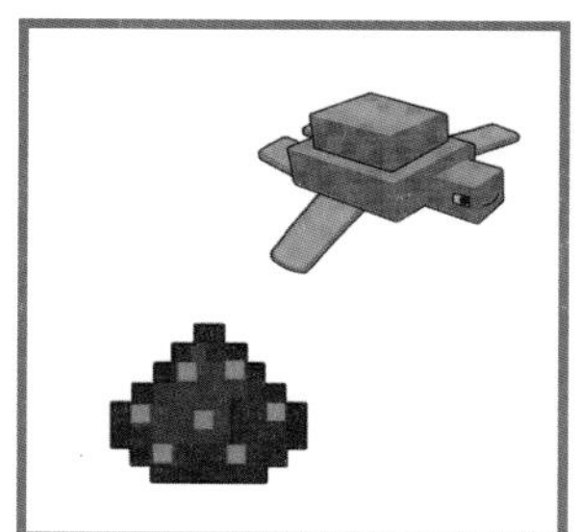

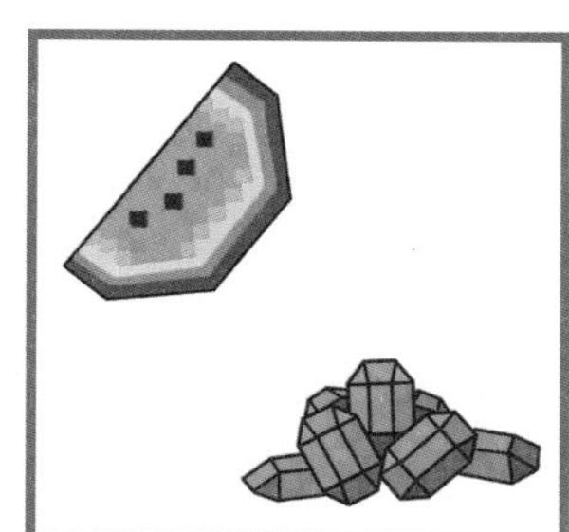

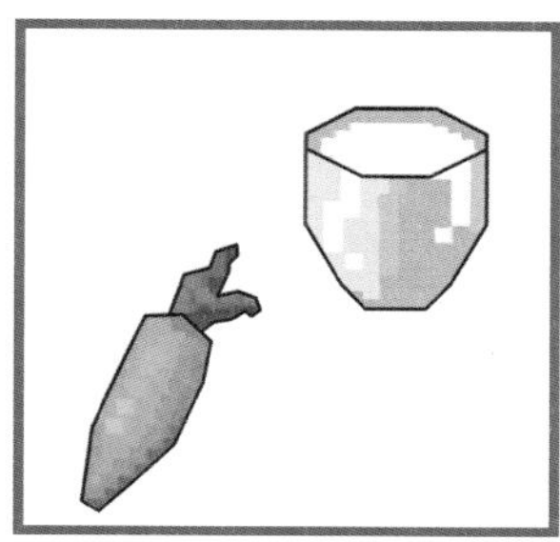
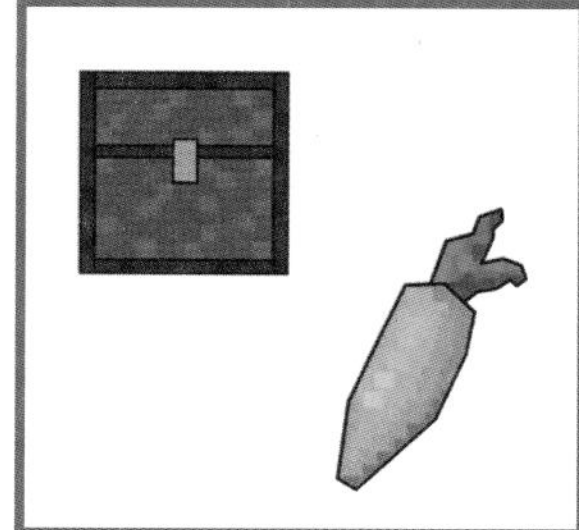
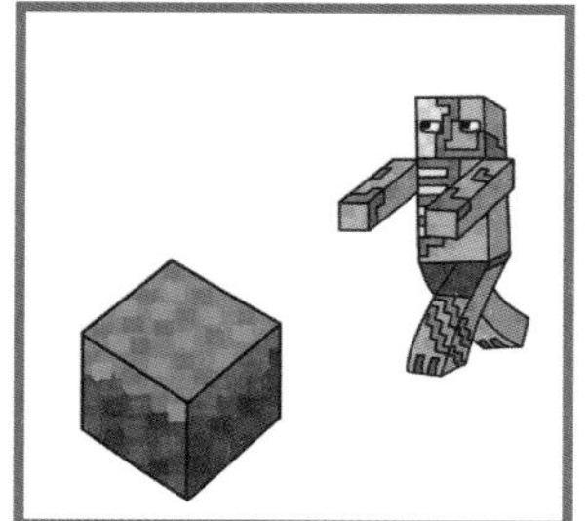
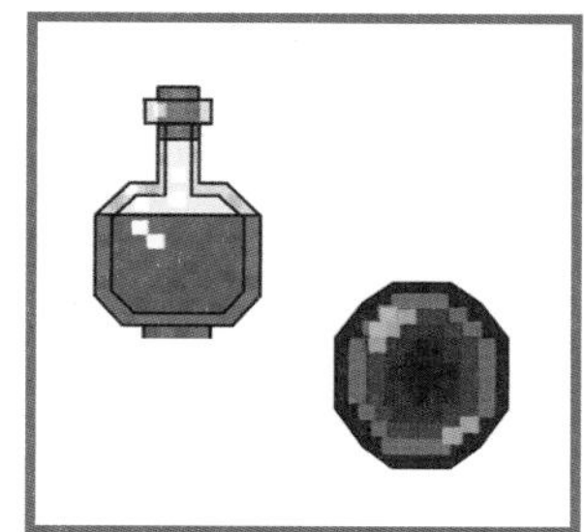

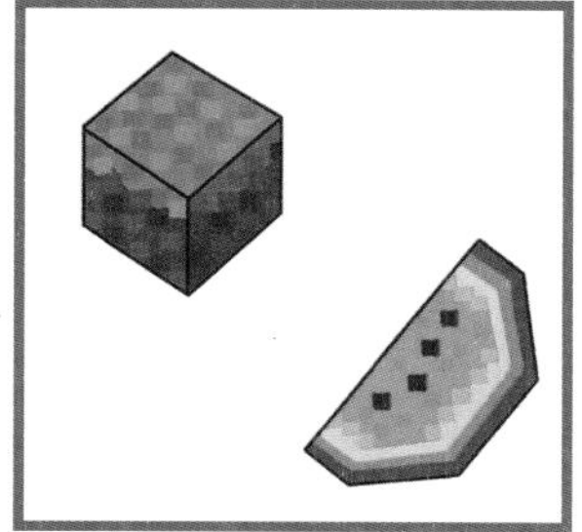
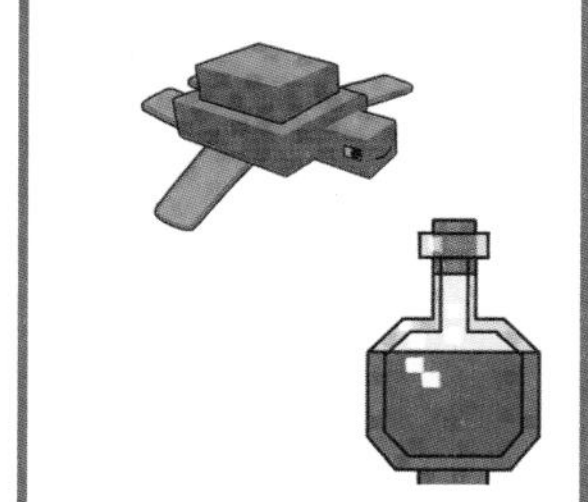

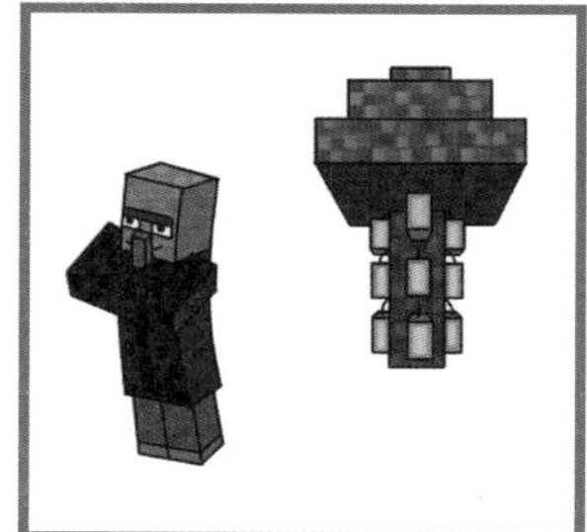

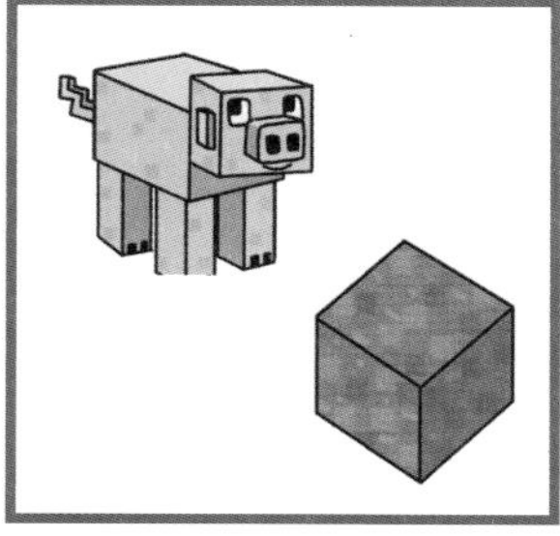

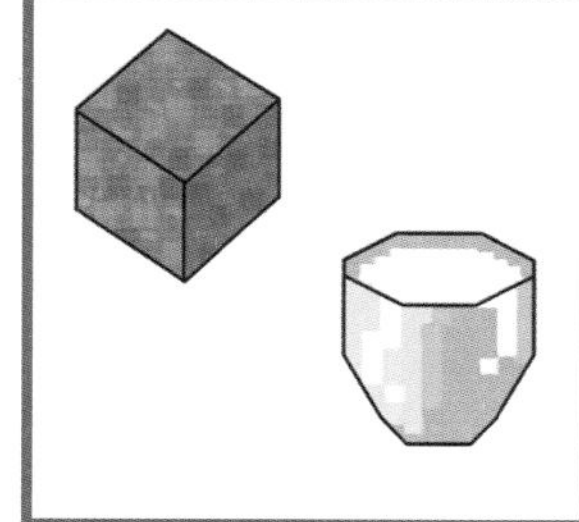
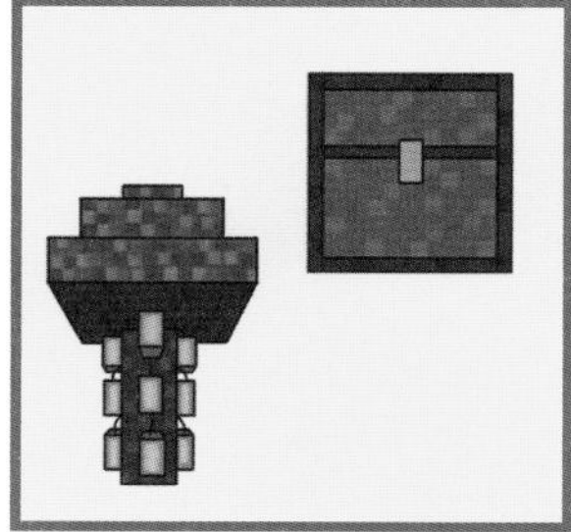

LOST BEACON

Steve needs to get to the beacon to gain power, but an unbreakable barrier stands between him and the beacon. He can only access it by following this tricky maze.

Begin in one of the four boxes above, below, or to the left of Steve (it's up to you to figure it out) and follow the numbers and arrows. Each square tells you how many spaces to move and in what direction. Arrows leading off the grid are dead ends.

Can you help Steve find the path to the beacon?

6→	7→	2↓	4←	3↓	2→	3↑	4↓
7→	3→	3↑	5→	1↓	1→	6↓	2↓
2↑	1←	4↓	4→	2↑	3↓	1←	4↓
2↑	1←	3↑			4↓	1←	2↓
2↓	4↓	2←			3↑	2←	2←
2↓	4↑	1←	3→	3→	5←	2↑	3←
5→	3↑	4→	1↓	3←	6↑	4↑	4←
7→	5↑	2↑	2←	1↑	1←	4←	6↑

AN ENCHANTED HOE

If you pick up the gold ingots and sticks before exiting this maze, you can craft a hoe that's enchanted with Unbreaking and Mending.

Can you collect all four items and find your way out of the maze?

START

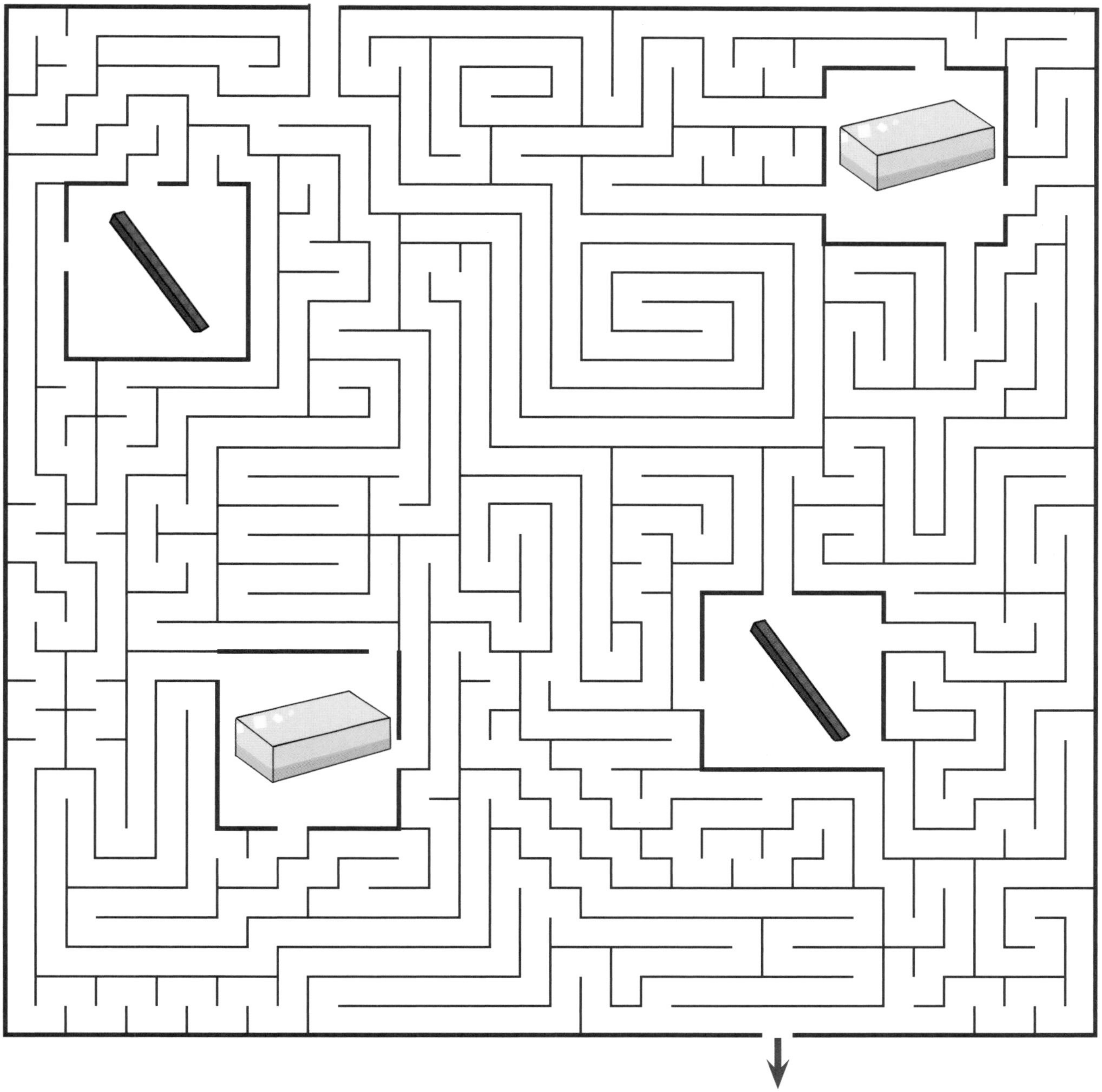

Did you collect all four items?

Yes → Congratulations! You've earned two enchantments for your new golden hoe.

No → Try again!

A VERY SMART PIG (AND A FUNNY GIRL)

Find your way through this maze to discover the answer to Steve's question below. Follow the lines to determine which letter goes on each numbered line.

Begin at the dot below each number and follow it downward. Every time you hit a horizontal line (one that goes across), you must take it. See what letter each number connects with.

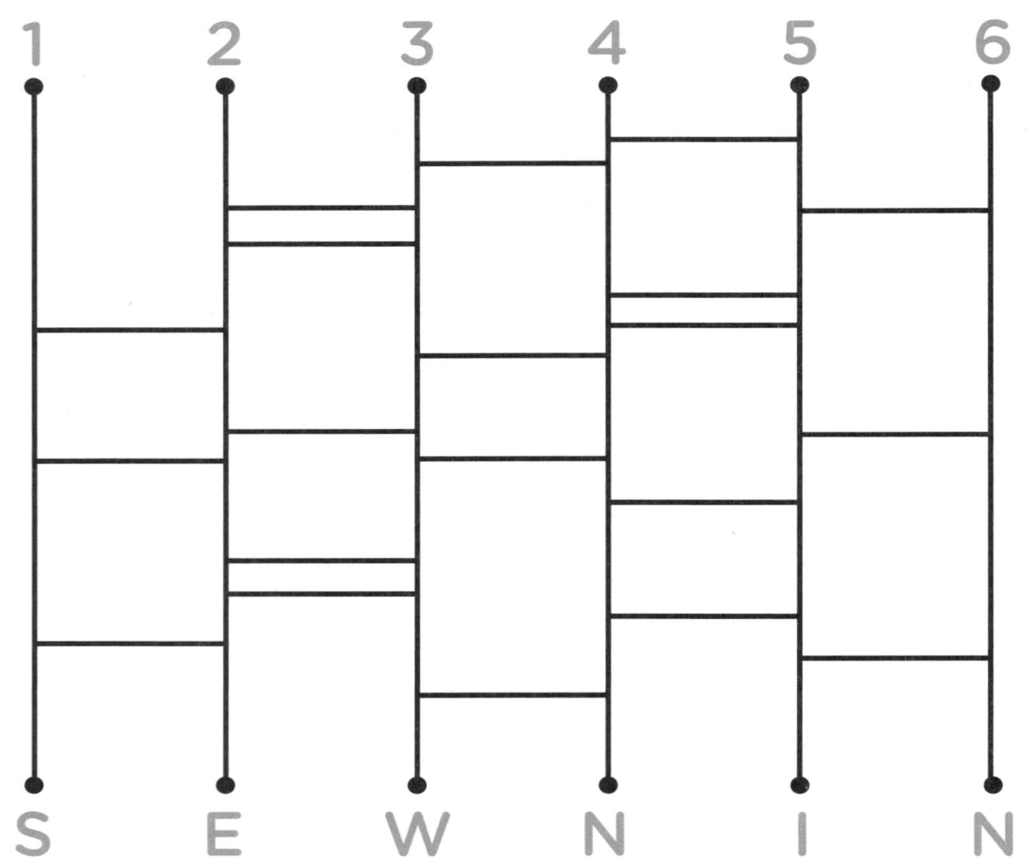

Alex: I have the smartest pig in Minecraft.

Steve: What's its name?

Alex: __ __ __ __ __ __ __ __

3 6 4 2 1 6 5 3

MAIN COURSE MIX-UP

You are collecting a week's worth of meat from the village butcher.

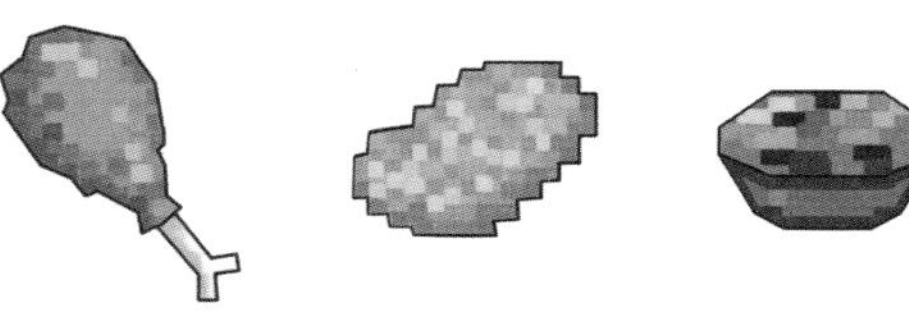

You must pick up your first chicken drumstick in the top row and your last rabbit stew in the bottom row.

Moving only up, down, left, and right, what path must you take?

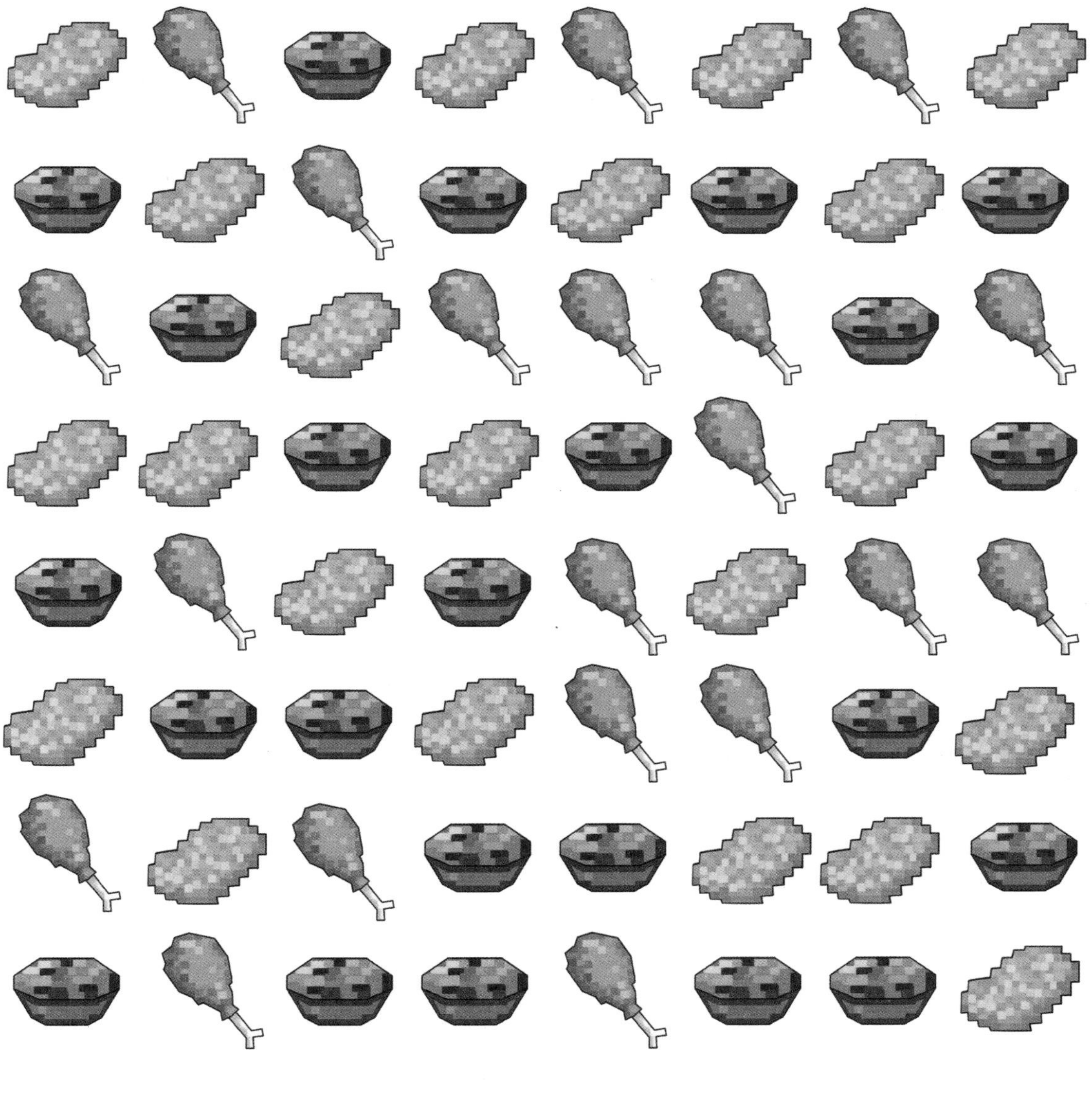

SPELLING BEE #4

Help the bee find its way through this maze to the flowers by spelling 4-letter words.
Make the words by adding IN between the given letters.
Begin with the word MINE in the top row, and connect the real words until you reach the bottom row. (HINR is not a real word!)
You can move up, down, left, right, or diagonally.

L__D	R__K	W__P	F__G	MINE	H__R	L__K	Z__G
G__D	L__T	N__D	W__G	K__T	N__E	B__T	S__Y
V__E	C__G	S__K	L__X	F__T	P__D	E__G	R__D
R__G	H__O	B__Y	J__T	L__P	T__Y	M__R	S__K
N__W	F__D	I__G	S__G	P__K	Z__T	B__D	G__G
W__K	H__L	P__E	A__W	D__F	T__C	P__T	T__T
F__E	Z__C	G__Z	F__Y	H__T	W__D	S__T	O__K
L__F	R__P	U__T	K__G	V__G	Y__U	M__B	K__Z

A SECRET MESSAGE

T	O	O	D	I	H	O	S
H	G	A	E	S	T	L	R
E	E	I	D	M	G	V	O
S	H	E	Z	A	N	I	F
E	T	G	T	I	O	N	S
A	T	E	C	U	R	T	S
R	E	Y	O	U	R	I	N

These are your instructions for solving this maze. Get the idea? Good!

P	L	E	H	N	A	L	U
Y	U	Z	B	D	C	F	F
O	P	Z	E	N	I	R	Y
U	E	L	I	F	M	A	A
S	V	E	N	O	E	M	L
O	L	S	G	I	N	A	P

_____ __ _ ________ _____ __ ____ ___

____ ___ ______ ________.

BEDS WANTED!

Four Minecraft players have not had their avatars go to bed for over six in-game days, and phantoms are prowling. They are all trying to get through this maze to a bed. Follow each player's path, under and over crossing paths, to discover which players, if any, find a bed. Who is finally getting some rest?

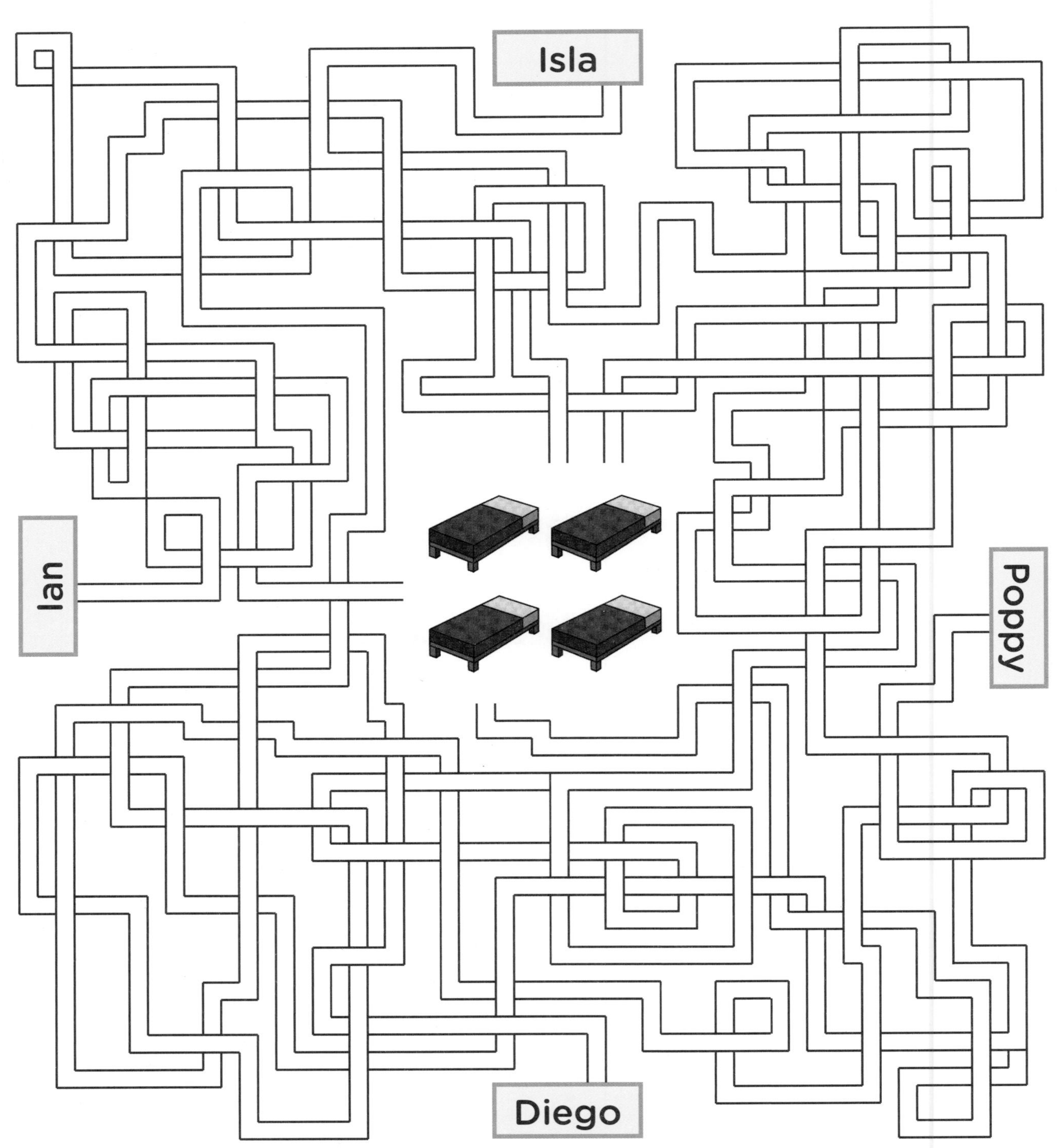

COBWEB DREAMS

A Minecrafter calling himself SpiderGuy dreams of building a mansion out of cobwebs. Help him collect all the cobwebs below.

To do this, draw a line from Start to Finish that includes each and every cobweb once. Your line can go up, down, left, or right, but not diagonally.

Start

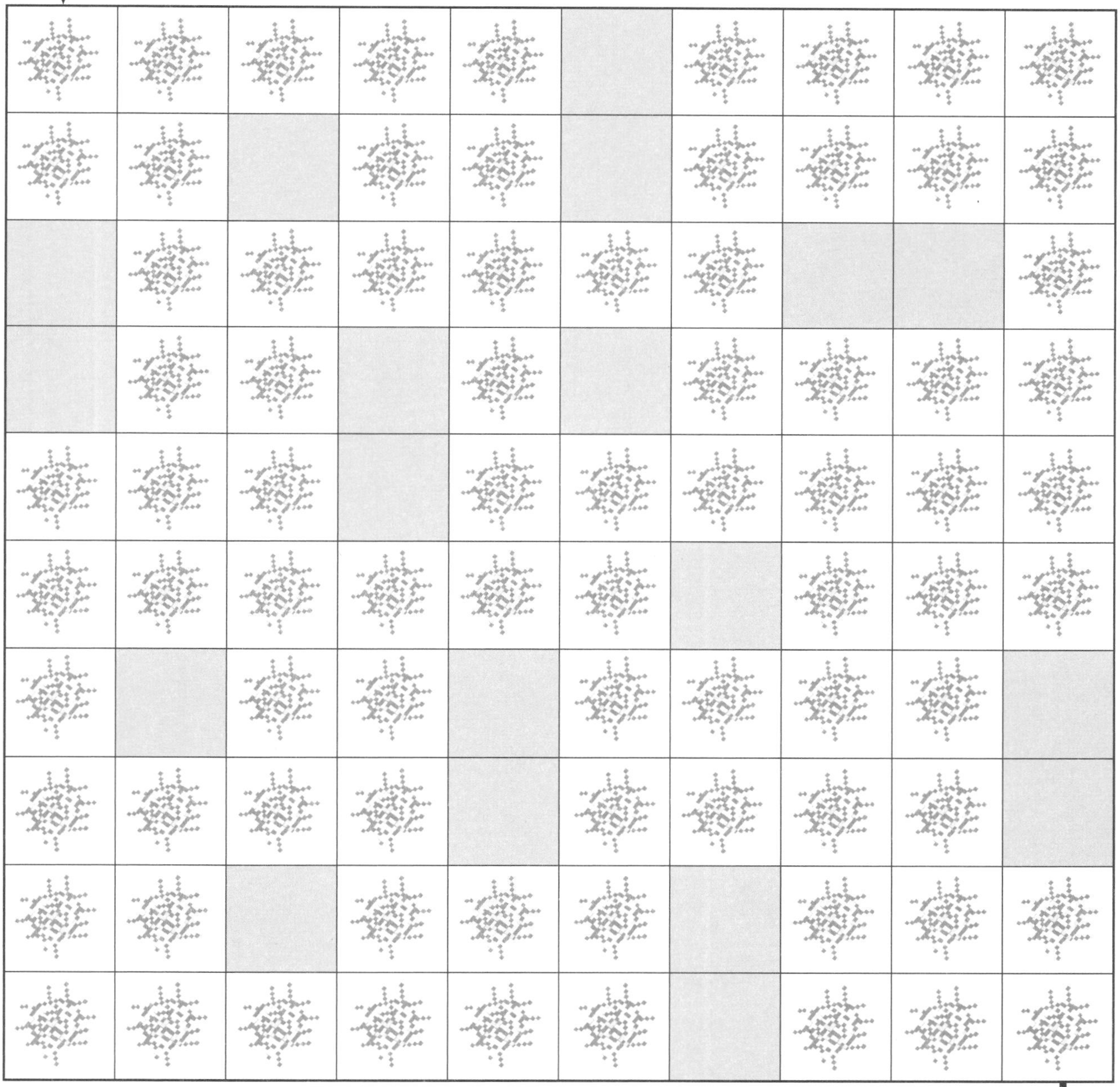

Finish

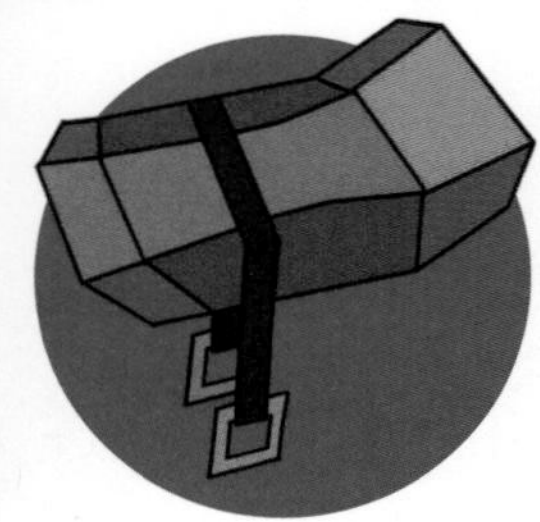

SADDLE UP!

Find your way through this maze from START to FINISH. It will be easier if you correctly identify each statement as true or false.

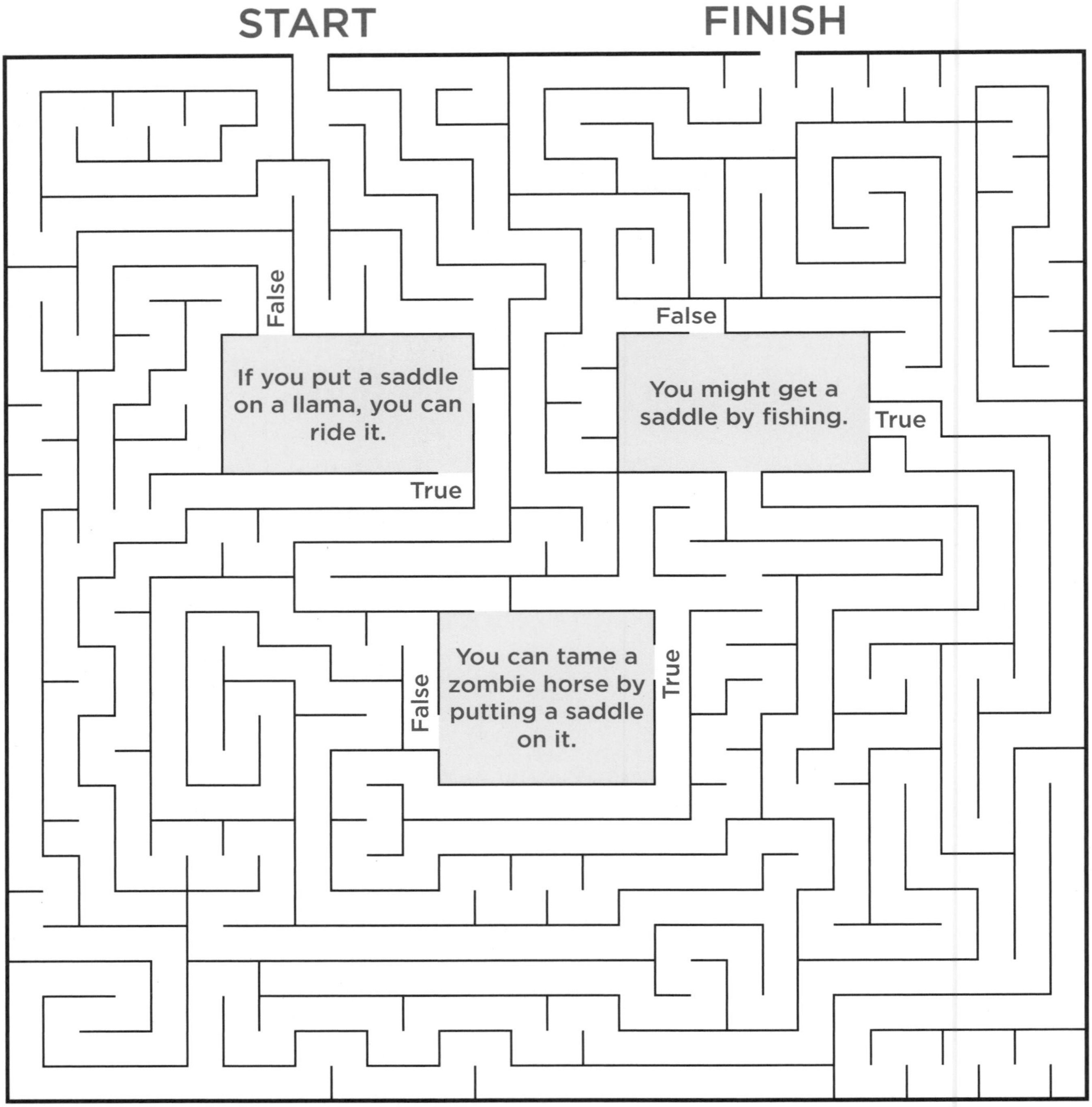

HOP TO IT #5

Find your way from the top-left yellow box to the bottom-right yellow box by keeping one icon the same each time you hop boxes. There are several paths to take. See if you can find the right one!

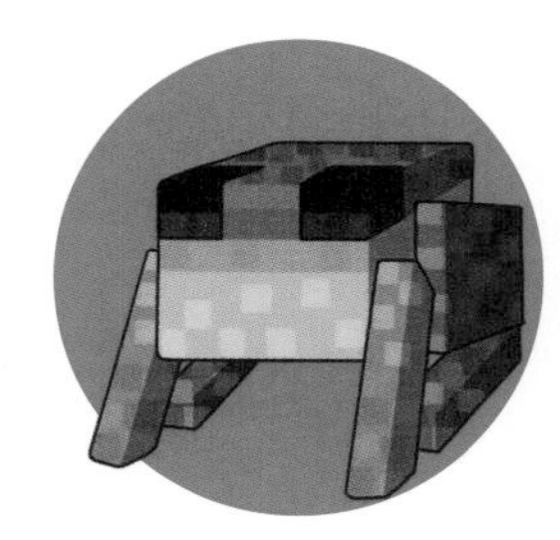

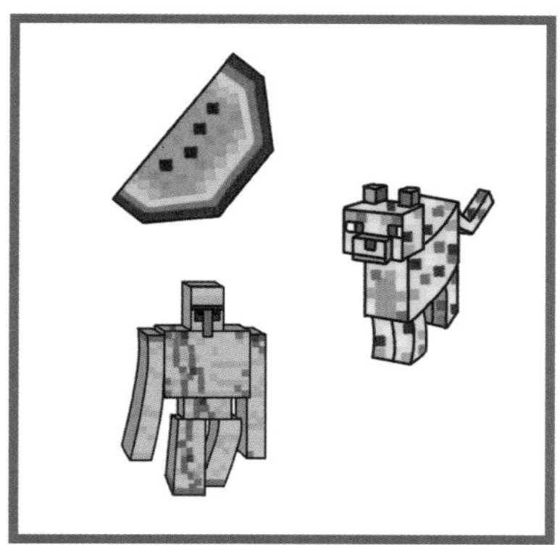

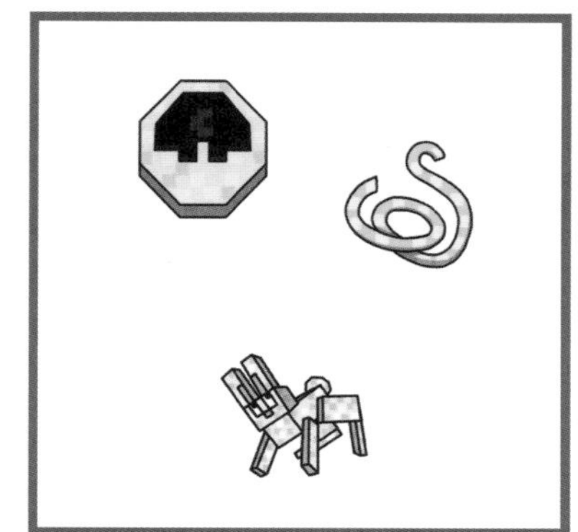

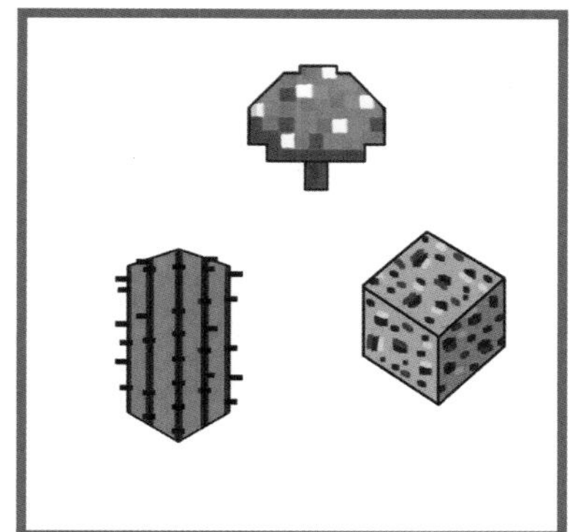

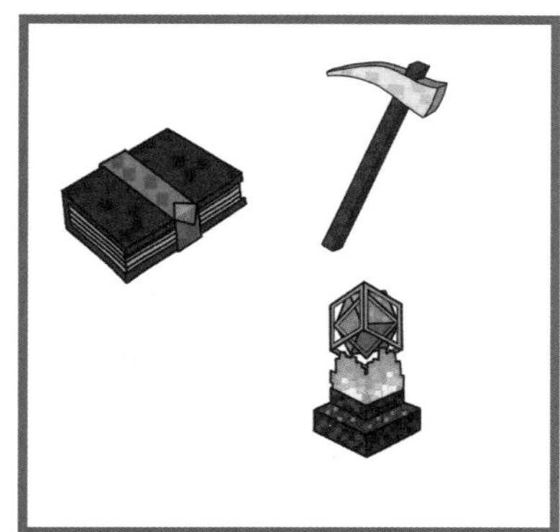

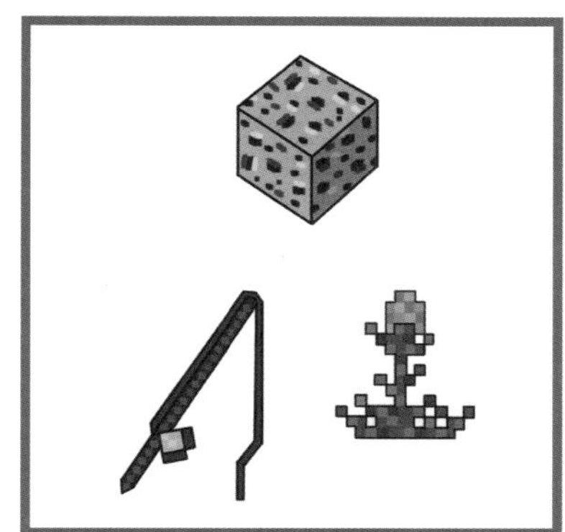

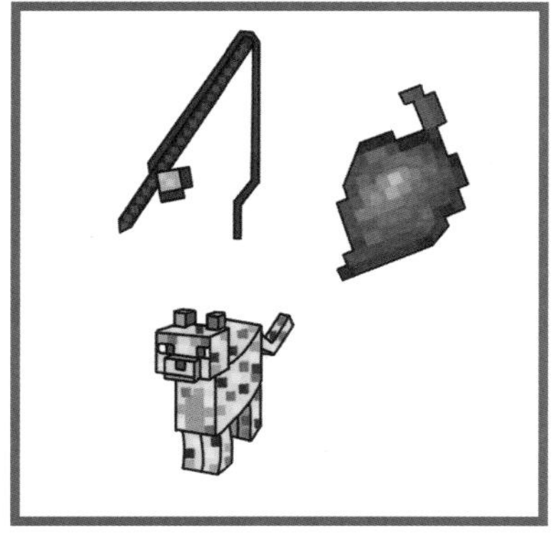

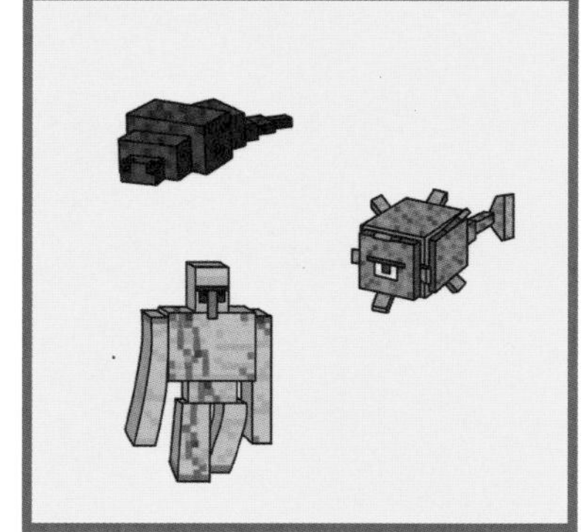

THE PEARLY PATH

Find the path to the Ender pearl and it is yours.

Begin in one of the four corner boxes (you'll have to guess which one), and follow the numbers and arrows. Each square tells you how many spaces to move and in what direction. Arrows leading off the grid are dead ends.

Can you find the path to the Ender pearl? Choose a corner and begin!

3 ↓	4 →	2 →	2 ↓	1 ←	4 ↓	3 ↓
3 ↓	5 →	2 →	5 ↓	1 ↓	5 ←	3 ←
6 →	3 ↓	3 ←	2 →	3 ←	2 →	2 ↓
2 →	3 ↑	3 ↓		3 ←	2 ↓	1 ←
1 →	4 ↑	3 ↑	1 ↑	1 ←	4 ←	4 ←
3 →	3 →	5 ↑	2 ↑	4 ←	3 ←	2 →
4 ↑	5 ↑	3 →	1 →	3 ↑	5 ↑	5 ←

MOB HOUSE

Try to make your way through this mob house without running into any mobs as you go.

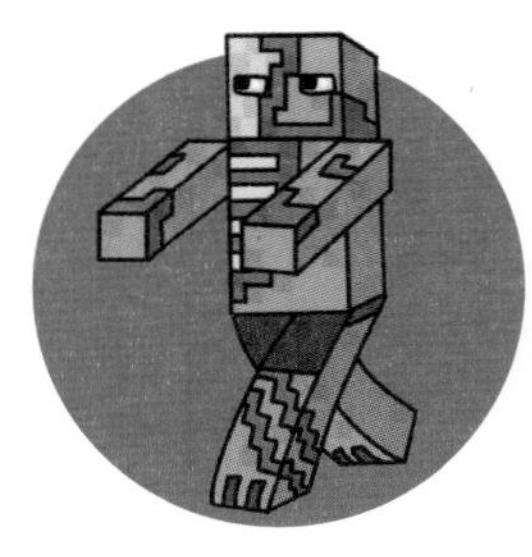

START

FINISH

SCAVENGER HUNT FINDS

Five Minecraft players have found between 1 and 5 objects for a scavenger hunt. How many has each player found?

To find out, begin at the dot below each player's name and follow it downward. Every time you hit a horizontal line (one that goes across), you must take it. See where each player's path leads, and write each name below the correct number. Who found the most?

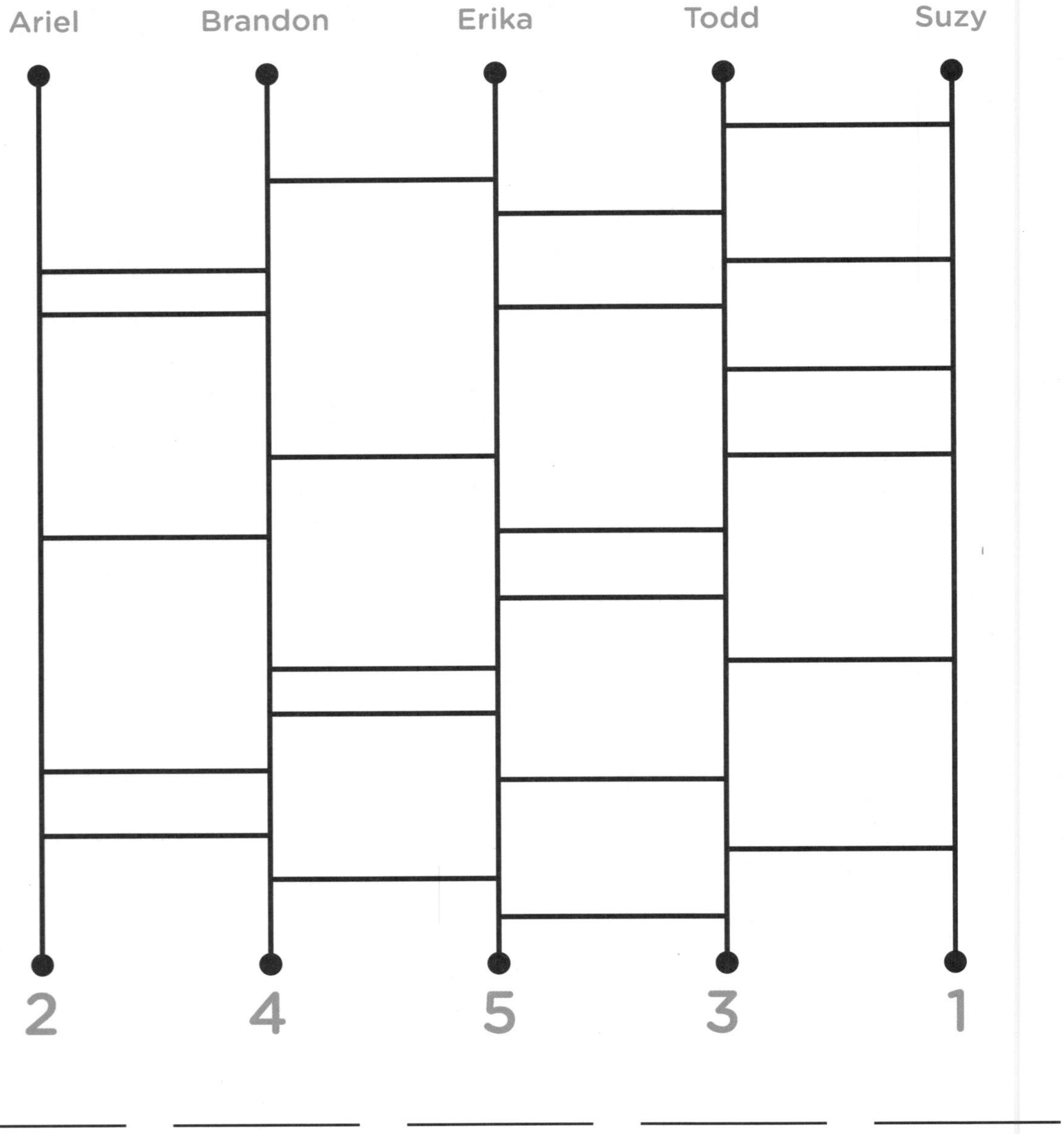

Ariel	Brandon	Erika	Todd	Suzy
2	4	5	3	1
________	________	________	________	________

MOOSHROOM SHEARING

It's time to shear the mooshrooms. You must pick up the first set of shears in the top row and wind up with your last cow on the bottom row. To get there, you must move from shears to mooshroom to cow, in that order, until you exit the herd at the bottom row.

Moving only up, down, left, and right, what path must you take?

SPELLING BEE #5

Help the bee find its way through this maze to the flowers by spelling 4-letter words.

Make the words by adding M before the given letters and E after the given letters. Begin with the word MINE in the top row, and connect the real words until you reach the bottom row. (MUDE is not a real word!)

You can move up, down, left, right, or diagonally.

MINE	_AL_	_UD_	_IK_	_AB_	_OC_	_IY_	_OZ_
_OR_	_OG_	_AF_	_AC_	_UH_	_IL_	_OI_	_EH
_IJ_	_IM_	_UK_	_AU_	_OV_	_UM_	_AD_	_YL_
_TL_	_SN_	_US_	_AK_	_OM_	_EO_	_IP_	_UT_
_AT_	_LL_	_UQ_	_EL_	_IS_	_OT_	_UU_	_IC_
_IV_	_IK_	_AN_	_OW_	_UL_	_OD_	_OP_	_AX_
_OZ_	_PR_	_UP_	_AR_	_AY_	_RT_	_IB_	_AI_
_UW_	_OL_	_CH_	_EV_	_AZ_	_AE_	_ID_	_OB_

WHERE AM I?

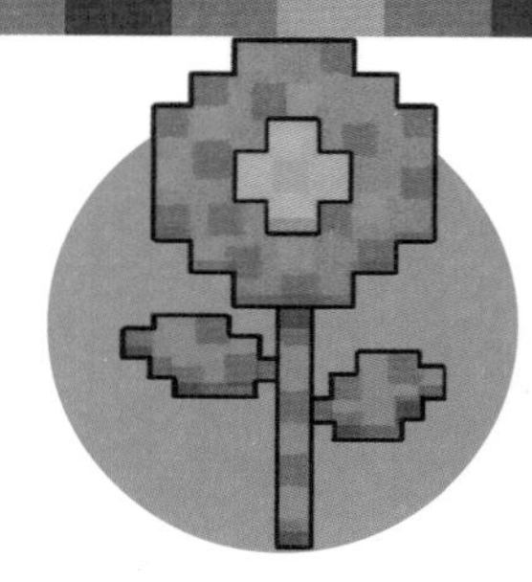

Four Minecraft players wandered into new biomes. Follow each player's path, under and over crossing paths, to discover where each is now.

Swamp

Deep Ocean

Ambler

Drifter

Gad2222

Journey-Man

Arctic

Jungle

'NOTHER NETHER STAR, PLEASE

Let's face it: Nether stars aren't easy to get in Minecraft. But you can collect a whole bunch here.

To do it, draw a line from Start to Finish that passes through every Nether star once. Your line can go up, down, left, or right, but not diagonally. On your mark, get set, collect!

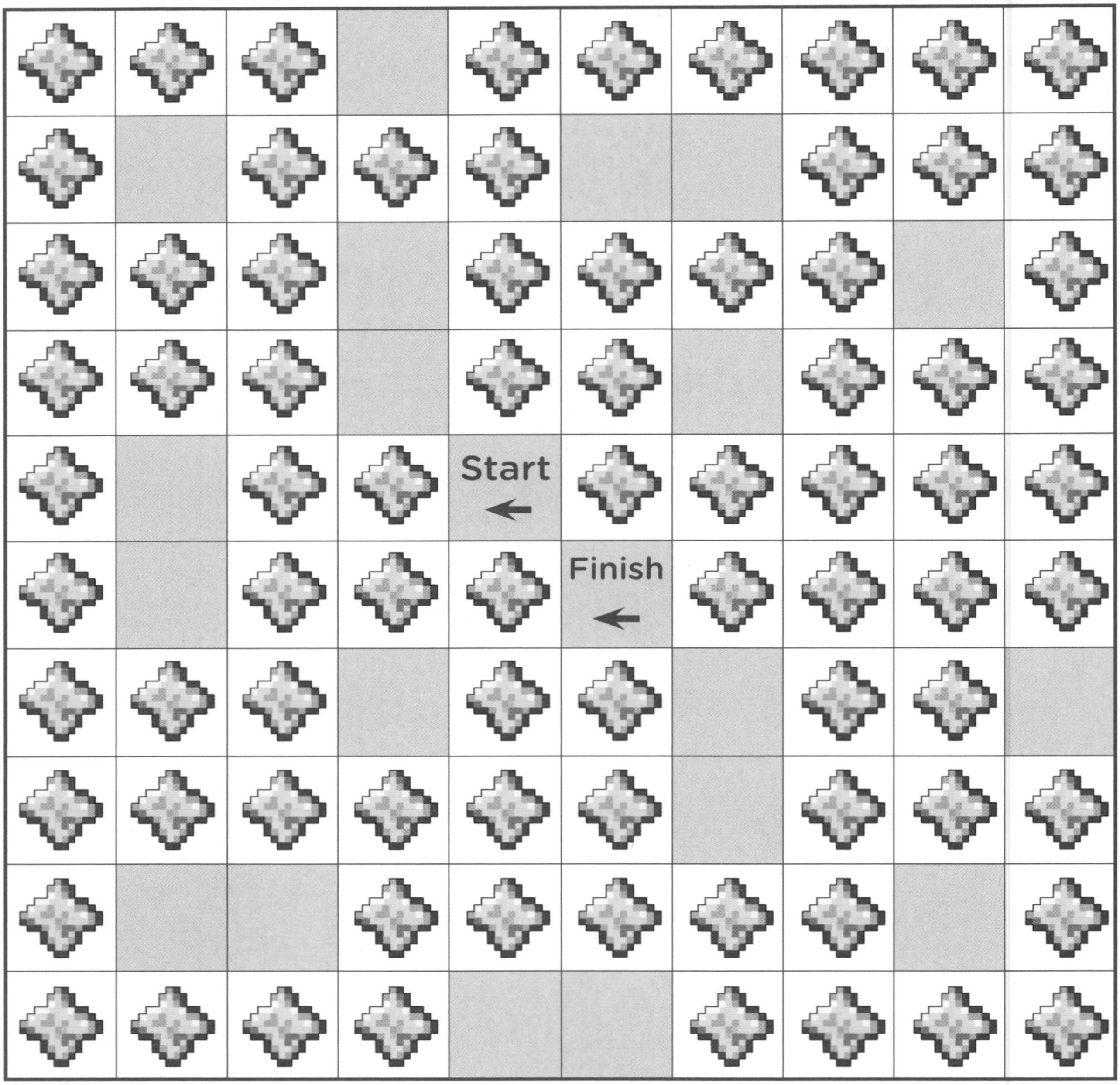

Start ←

Finish ←

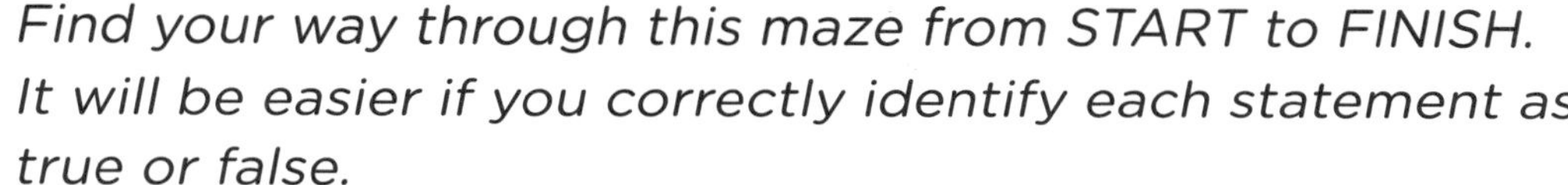

CHEST JESTS

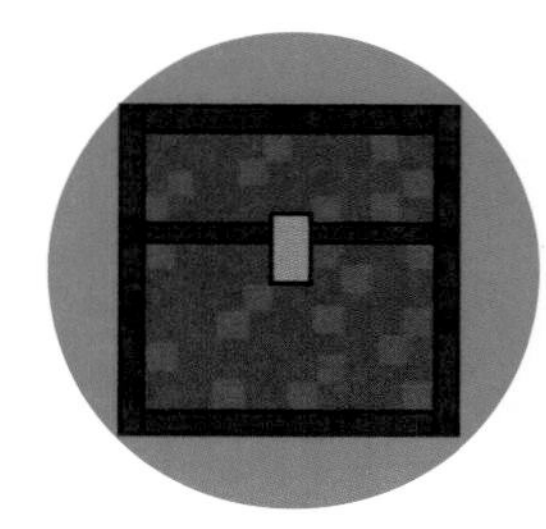

Chests can be funny things . . .

Find your way through this maze from START to FINISH. It will be easier if you correctly identify each statement as true or false.

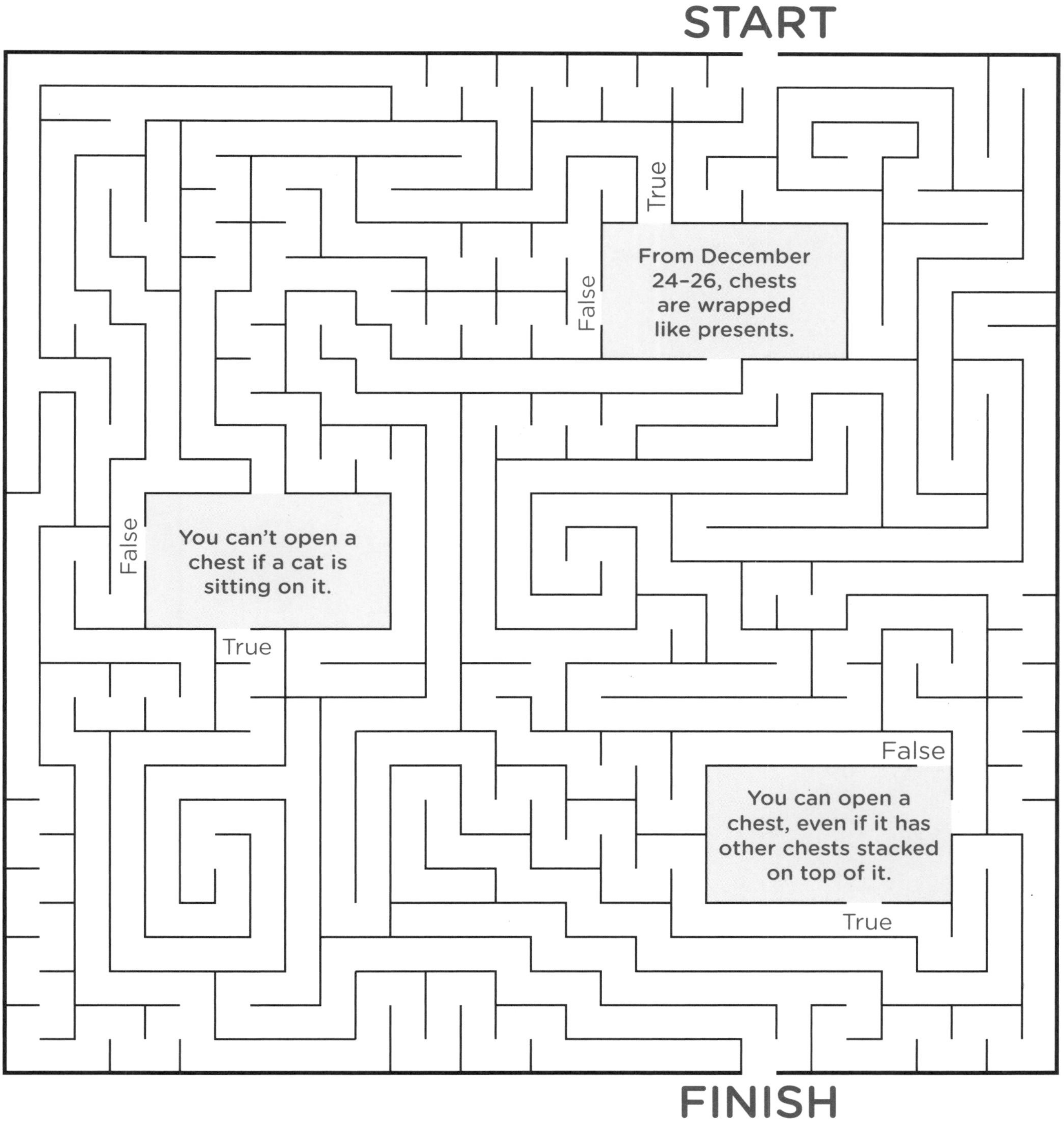

START

From December 24–26, chests are wrapped like presents.

True

False

You can't open a chest if a cat is sitting on it.

False

True

You can open a chest, even if it has other chests stacked on top of it.

False

True

FINISH

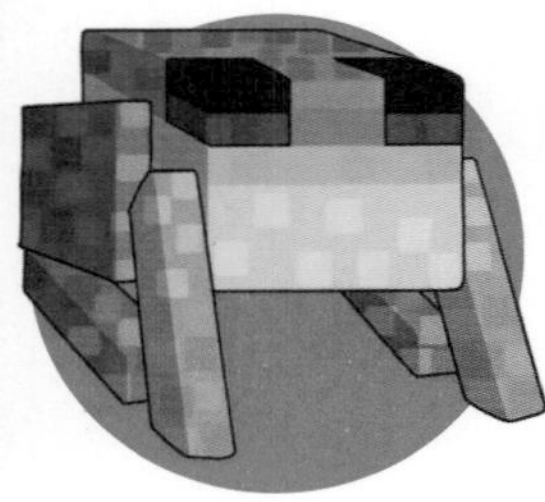

HOP TO IT #6

Find your way from the top-left yellow box to the bottom-right yellow box by keeping one icon the same each time you hop boxes. There are several paths to take. See if you can find the right one!

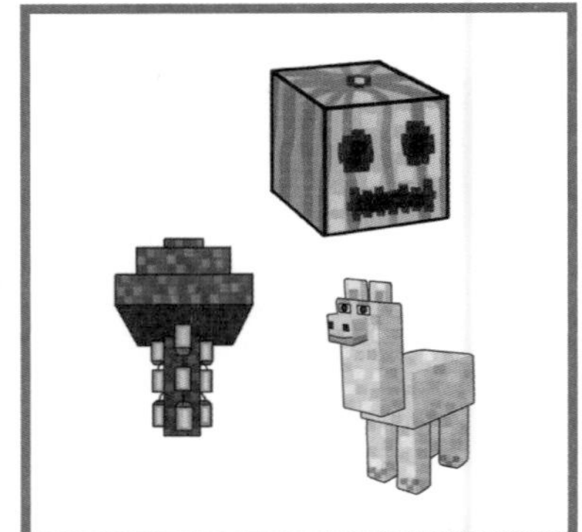

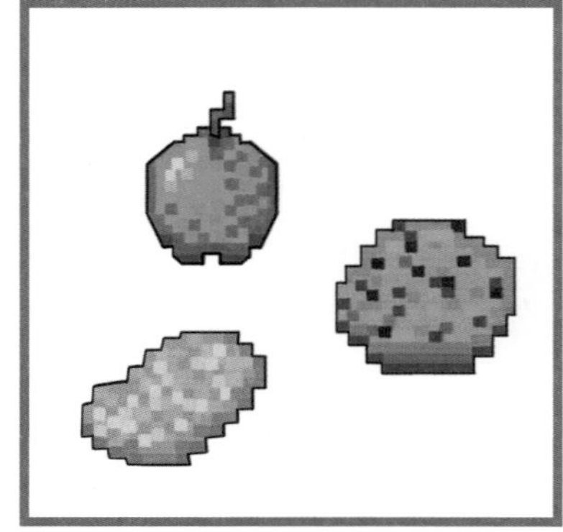
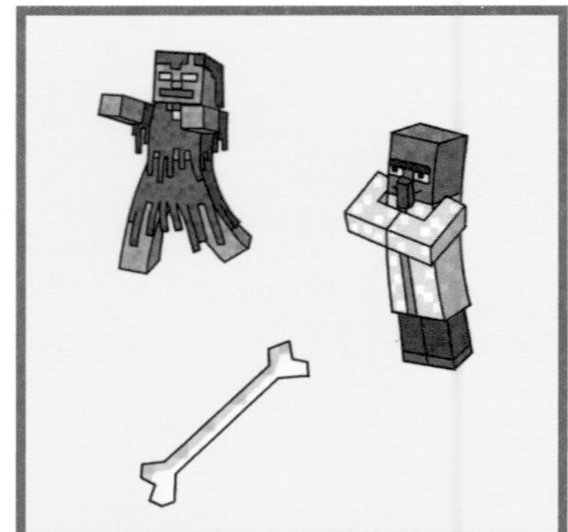

QUICK! YOU CAN SAVE US ALL!

Uh-oh. A TNT block will explode if you don't get to the center of this maze and flip the switch.

Begin in one of the four corner boxes (you'll have to guess which one), and follow the numbers and arrows. Each square tells you how many spaces to move and in what direction. Arrows leading off the grid are dead ends.

Can you find the path to the lever so you can flip it and prevent the TNT from exploding?

3 →	8 ↓	4 ↓	6 ↓	2 ↓	1 ←	8 ↓	2 ↑	5 ↓
7 →	3 ↓	2 ↓	2 ←	2 ↓	5 ←	6 ↓	2 ↓	6 ←
2 ↑	4 ↓	2 ←	1 →	3 →	4 ←	1 ↓	5 ↓	2 ←
1 ←	7 →	3 →	4 ↓	1 ↓	6 ←	3 ←	3 ↓	7 ←
4 →	1 ↑	2 ←	3 ←		4 ↑	2 ←	3 ←	3 ←
5 ↑	2 ↓	2 →	1 →	2 ↓	1 →	5 ↑	3 →	7 ←
2 →	4 →	1 ↑	5 →	2 ↑	4 ↑	4 ↓	2 ↓	4 ↑
1 ↑	4 →	5 ↑	1 ←	4 →	6 ↑	1 ↑	7 ←	6 ↑
5 →	2 ↑	8 ↑	7 ↑	4 ↑	3 ↑	3 ←	5 ←	4 ↑

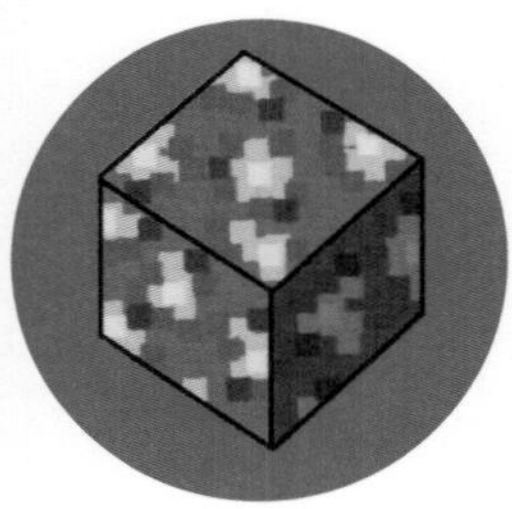

GO FOR GLOW

Can you find your way through this Nether maze to get to the glowstone? If you fall in the lava, go back to START and try again.

FINISH

START

LAUGH LINES

Follow the lines in the maze to determine which letter goes on each numbered line. If you follow the maze correctly, you'll find the answer to the joke.

Begin at the dot below each letter and follow it downward. Every time you hit a horizontal line (one that goes across), you must take it. See what number each letter connects with, and write that letter on the correct space.

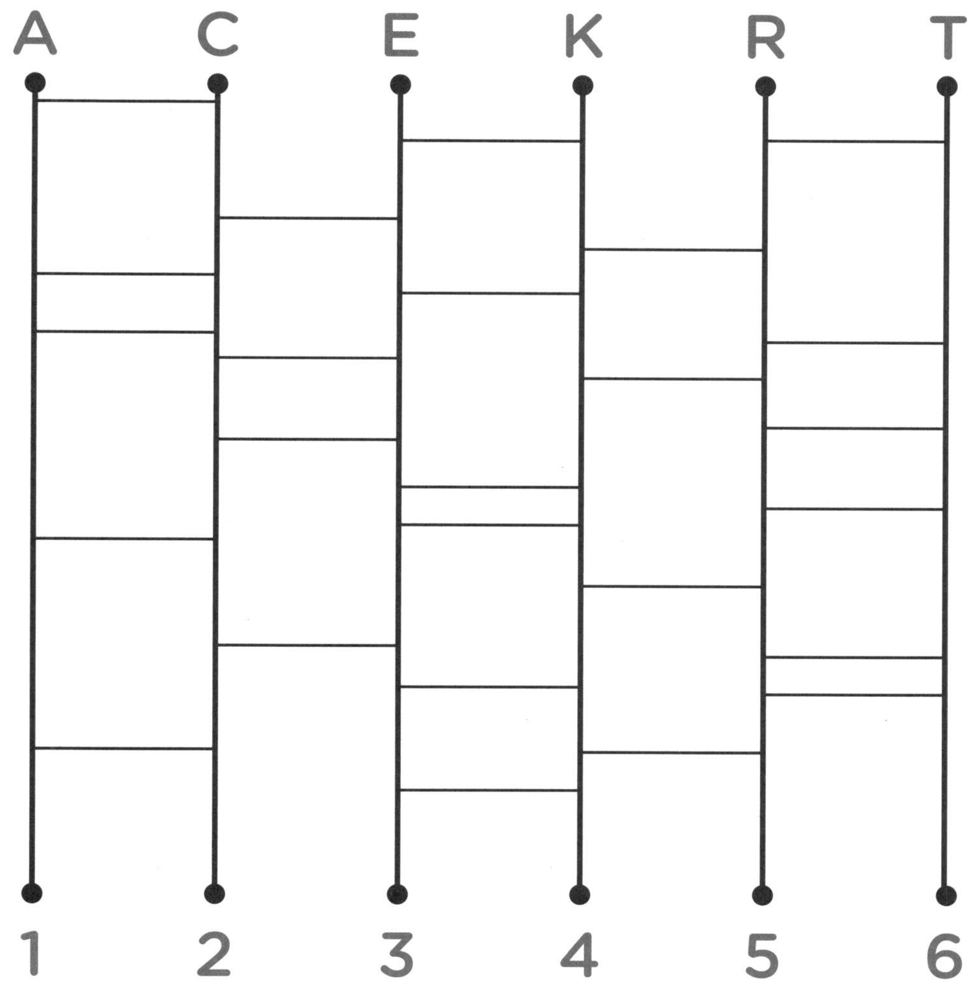

What's another name for a gold ingot?

__ __ __　___　__ __ __ __
2 4 3　1 4　5 4 2 6

MOB SCHOOL CARPOOL

It's your turn to drive the mobs to school. You must pick up all 16 mobs in a specific order or they will get mad and attack. You must pick up your first blaze in the top row and your last zombie pigman in the bottom row, and you must pick them up in this order:

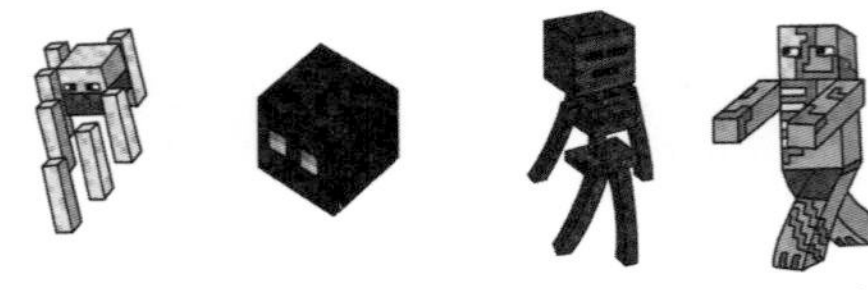

Moving only up, down, left, and right, what path must you take?

SPELLING BEE #6

Help the bee find its way through this maze to the flowers by spelling 4-letter words.

Make the words by adding I on the first space and E on the second space in each letter set. Begin with the word MINE in the top row, and connect the real words until you reach the bottom row. (ZIGE is not a real word!)

You can move up, down, left, right, or diagonally.

B_P_	S_B_	P_L_	R_P_	S_F_	F_D_	MINE	Z_G_
J_B_	P_M_	K_B_	C_C_	W_G_	L_M_	T_G_	F_N_
D_D_	H_R_	R_R_	Y_D_	P_P_	G_M_	S_Q_	K_L_
W_B_	H_V_	P_T_	Z_P_	W_S_	A_P_	T_D_	Q_T_
C_T_	O_N_	K_T_	F_B_	U_P_	F_V_	E_J_	H_K_
A_B_	C_M_	D_C_	W_R_	R_H_	Z_M_	Y_D_	N_C_
G_X_	T_M_	F_Y_	H_Q_	B_T_	G_V_	S_D_	J_M_
N_R_	W_G_	L_K_	S_C_	C_H_	T_F_	G_H_	C_E

CHICKEN HERDING

Uh-oh! The chickens have escaped from your farm, and now you must round them up. To do this, draw a line from Start to Finish that passes through every chicken once. Your line can go up, down, left, or right, but not diagonally. On your mark, get set . . . "Heeeeere, chicken-chicken-chicken!"

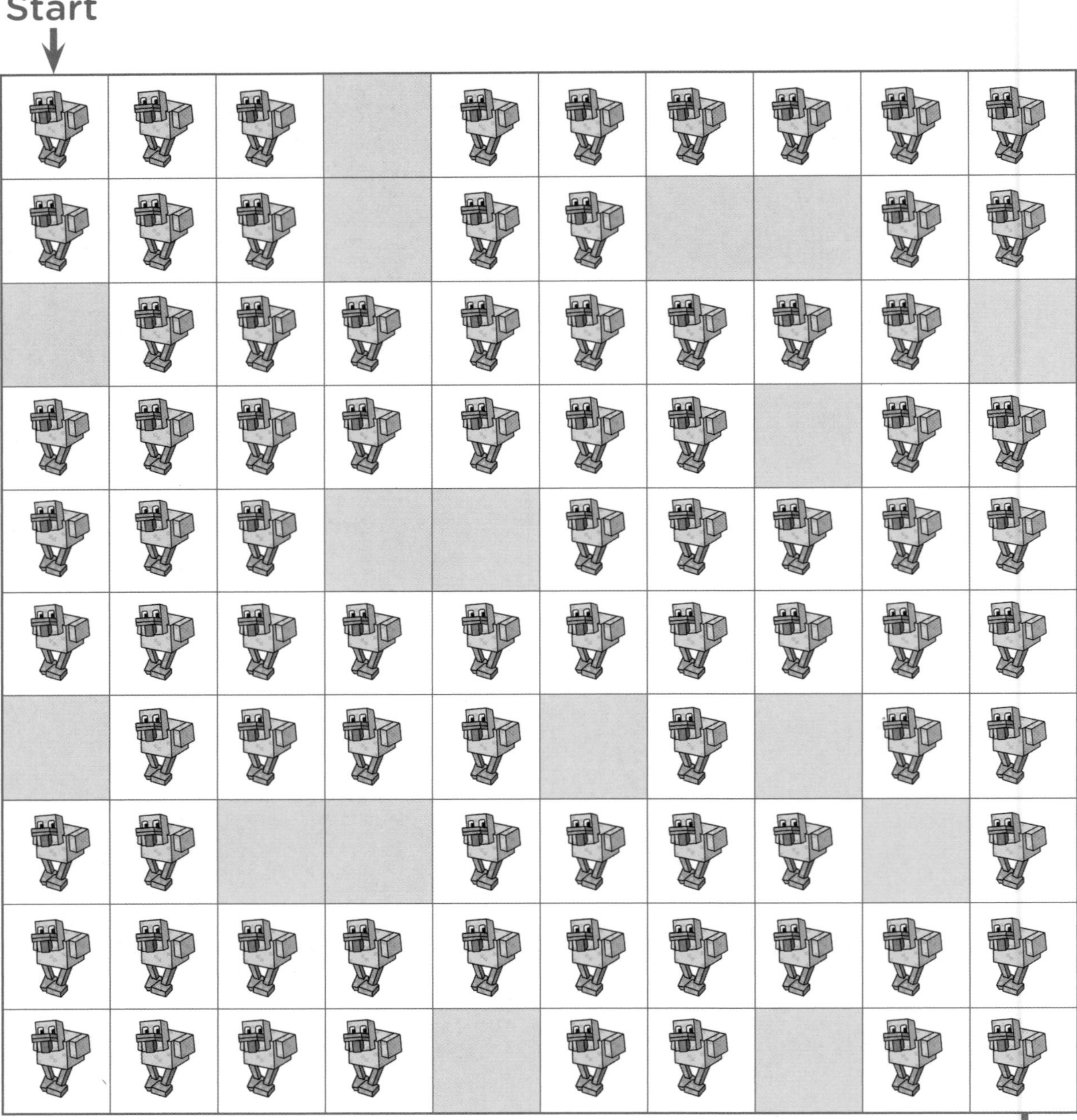

SHEDDING LIGHT ON REDSTONE TORCHES

Knowledge of redstone torches can illuminate the correct path here. Don't worry, though. If you're not up on redstone torches, you can feel your way.

Find your way through this maze from START to FINISH. It will be easier if you correctly identify each statement as true or false.

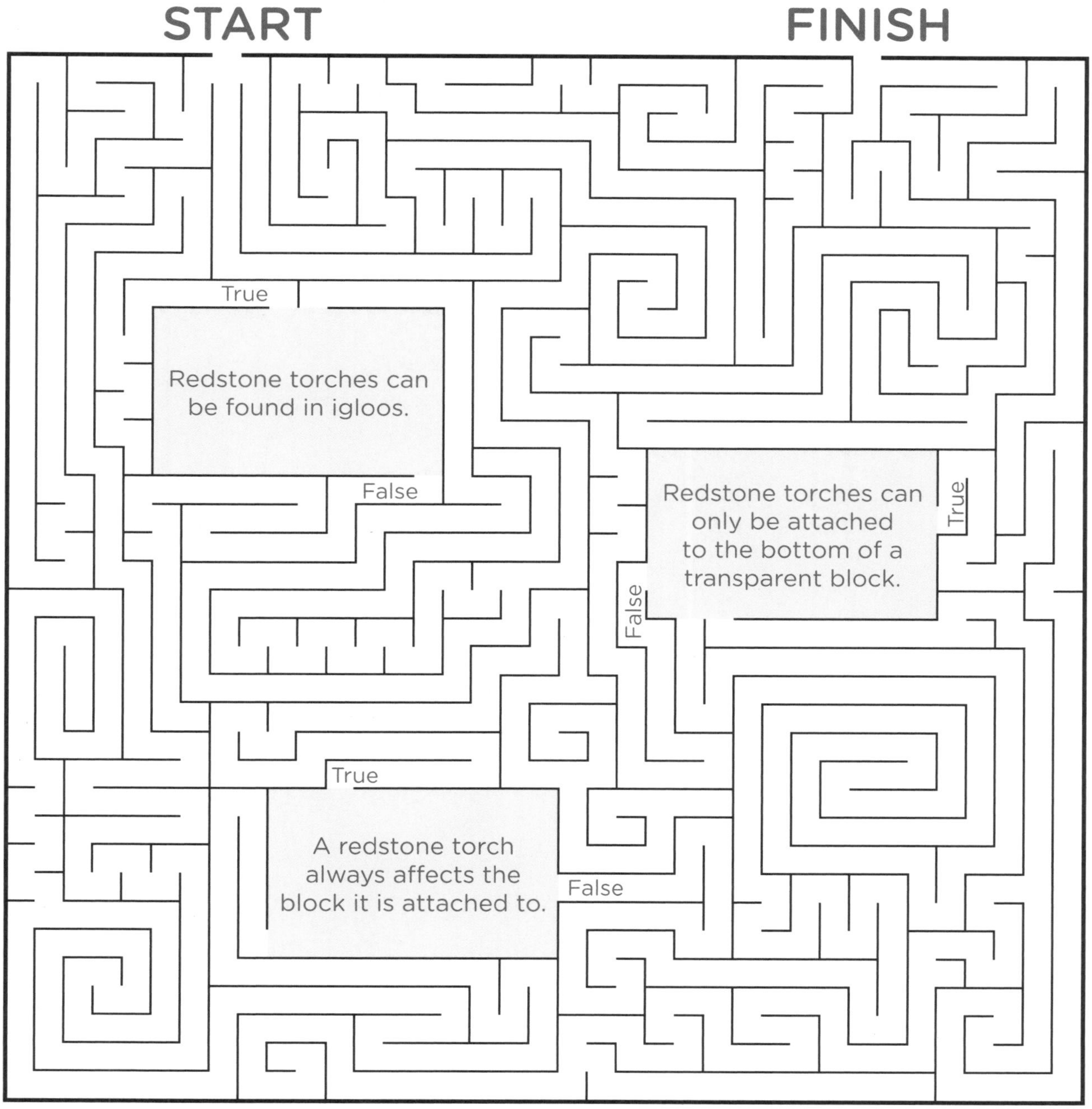

START

FINISH

True

Redstone torches can be found in igloos.

False

Redstone torches can only be attached to the bottom of a transparent block.

True

False

True

A redstone torch always affects the block it is attached to.

False

HOP TO IT #7

Find your way from the top-left yellow box to the lower-right yellow box by keeping one icon the same each time you hop boxes. There are several paths to take. See if you can find the right one!

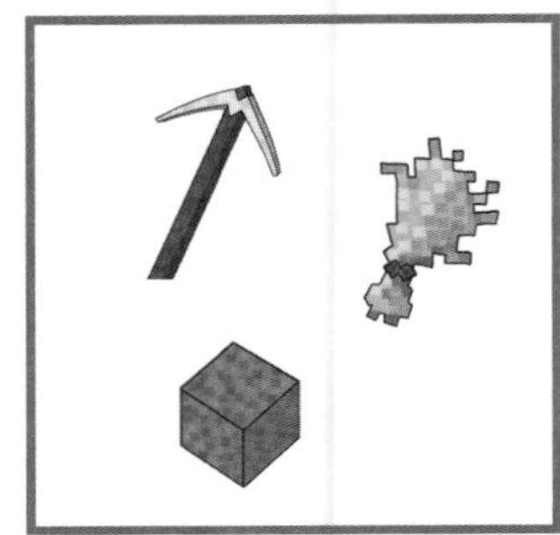
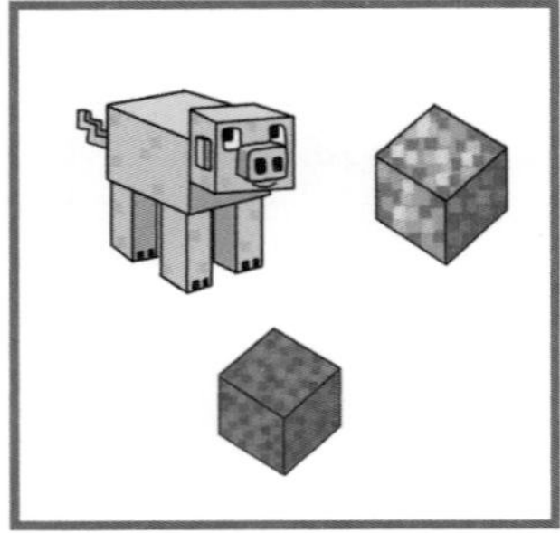
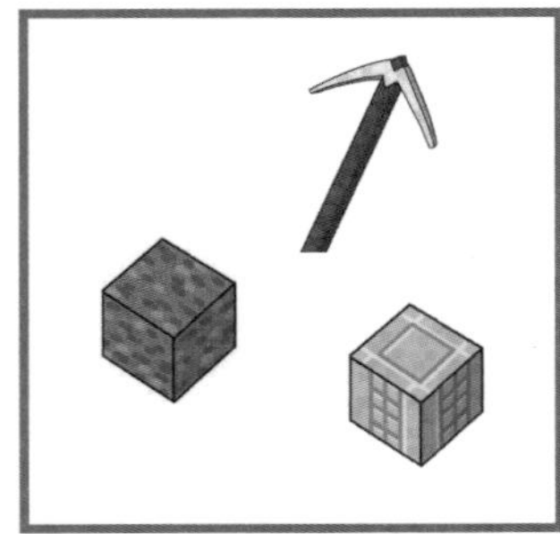
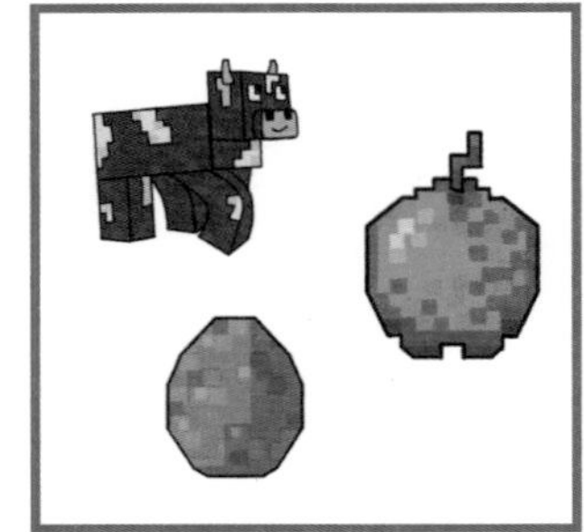

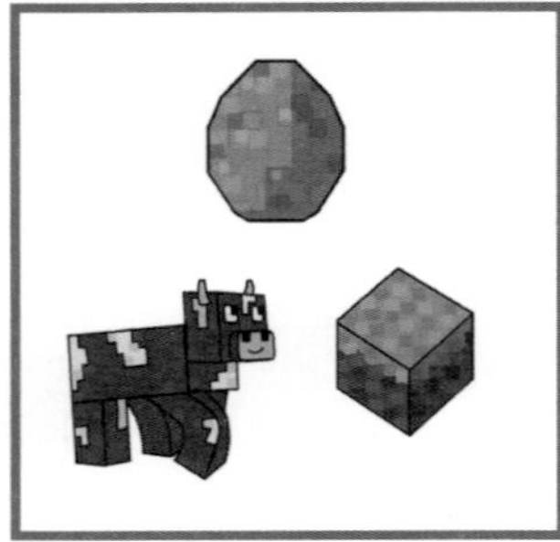

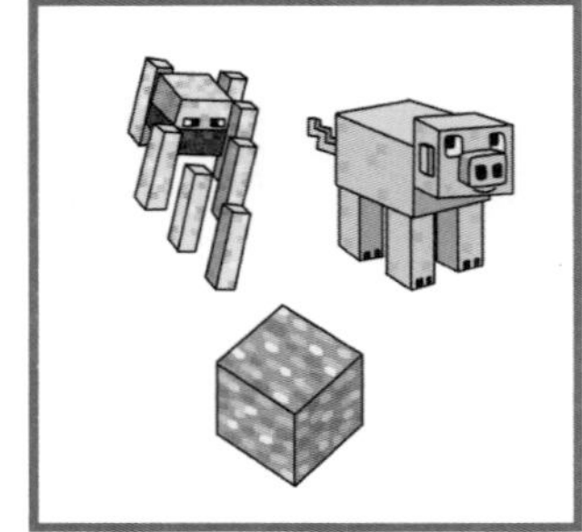

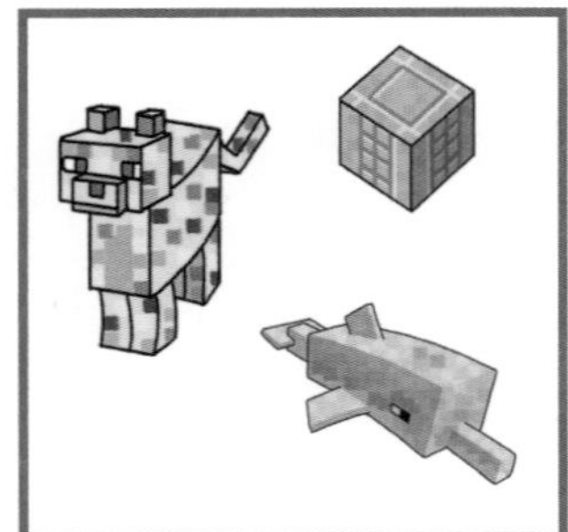
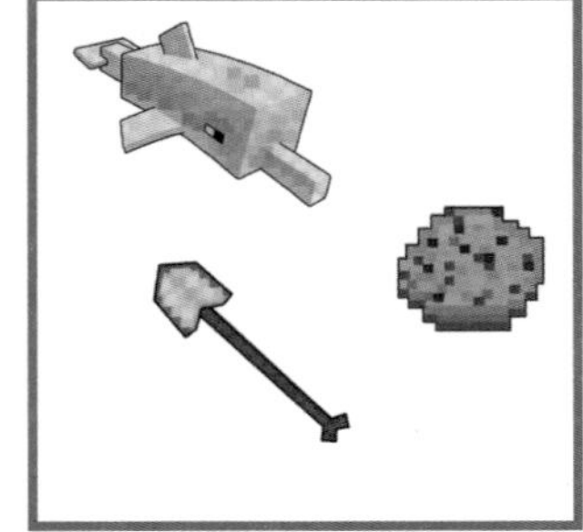
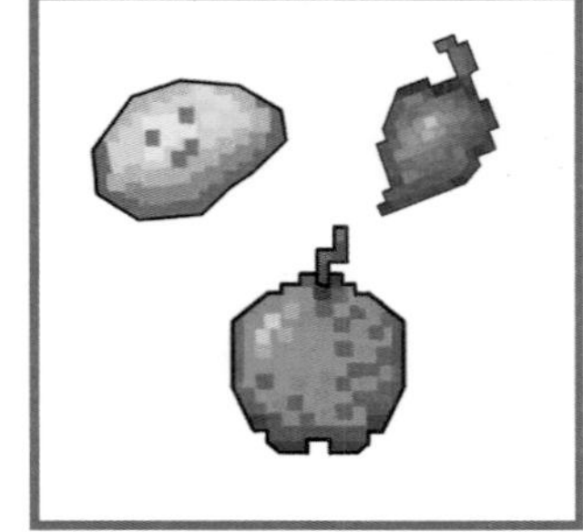

GO FOR THE GOLD

Make your way to the golden hoe so you can enchant it with Unbreaking.

Begin in one of the four corner boxes (you'll have to guess which one), and follow the numbers and arrows. Each square tells you how many spaces to move and in what direction. Arrows leading off the grid are dead ends.

Can you find the path to the hoe?

4 ↓	3 ↓	6 ↓	4 ←	3 ←	2 ←	5 ↓
5 →	1 ←	1 ↑	1 ↓	1 ←	4 ↓	4 ←
5 →	5 →	1 ↓	1 →	1 ↑	2 ↓	1 ↓
2 ↓	3 →	2 ←		2 ↑	3 ↑	1 ←
4 →	2 →	4 →	1 ↑	4 ↑	1 →	3 ↑
4 →	3 ↑	3 ↑	2 ←	1 ↓	3 ←	3 ←
4 ↑	5 ↑	1 →	2 ↑	1 →	5 ↑	5 ←

PURSUING PRISMARINE

Can you avoid the drowned and the guardian to reach the prismarine in the ocean monument? Give it a shot!

START

UNDEAD HUMOR

Uncover the answer to the joke by following the lines in the maze to determine which letter goes on each numbered line.

Begin at the dot below each letter and follow it downward.

Every time you hit a horizontal line (one that goes across), you must take it. See what number each letter connects with, then write that letter on the space with that number.

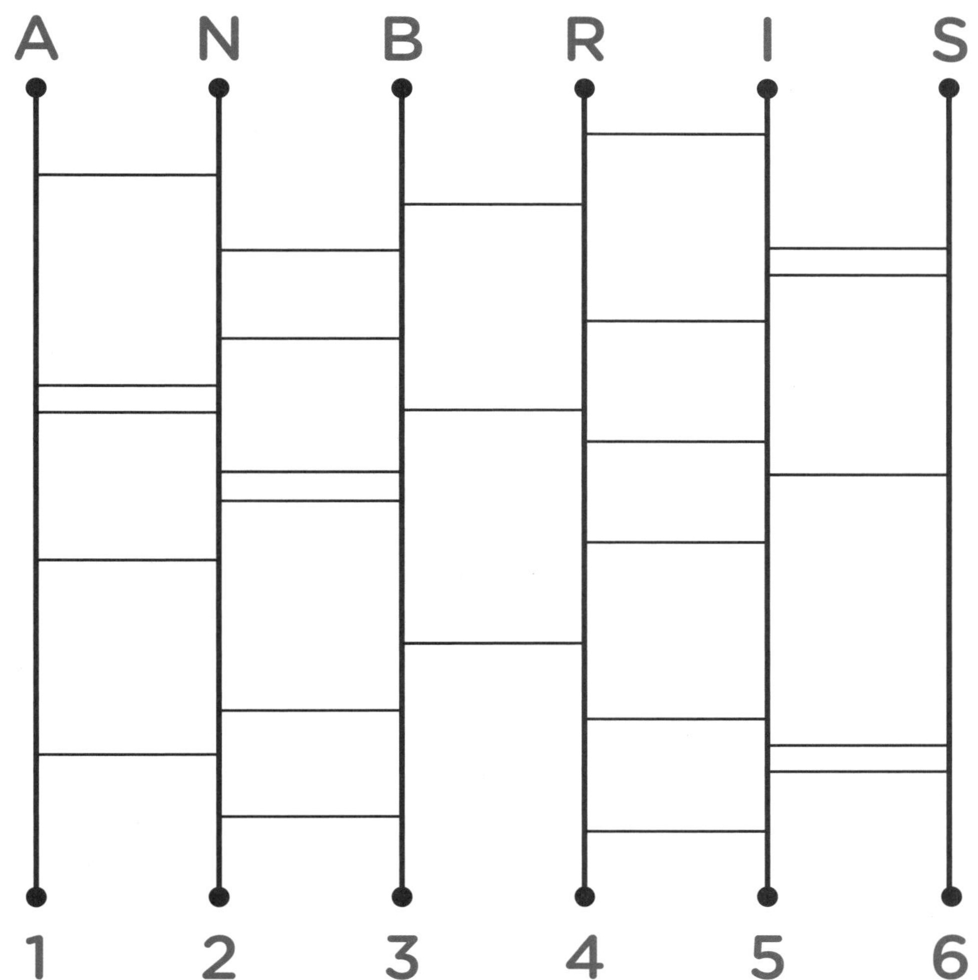

What did the zombie order for dinner?

__ __ __ __ __ __!

5 4 3 6 2 1

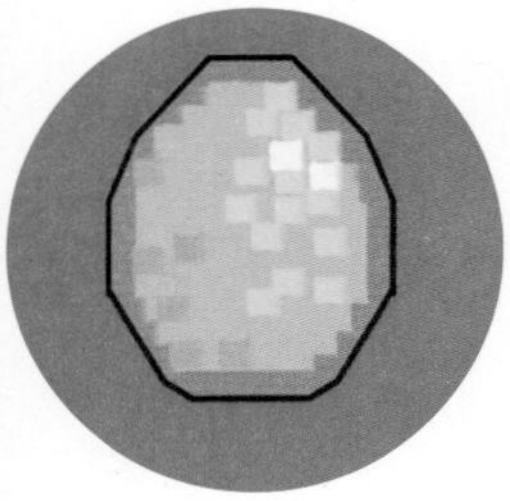

EGG HUNT

You are collecting two dozen spawn eggs. It's delicate work. If you don't do it correctly, the mobs will hatch and attack you!

You must pick up your first egg in the top row and your last egg in the bottom row, and you must pick them up in this order:

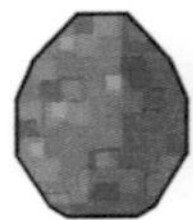  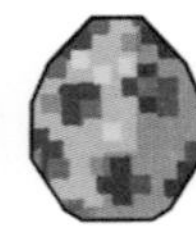 

Moving only up, down, left, and right, what path must you take?

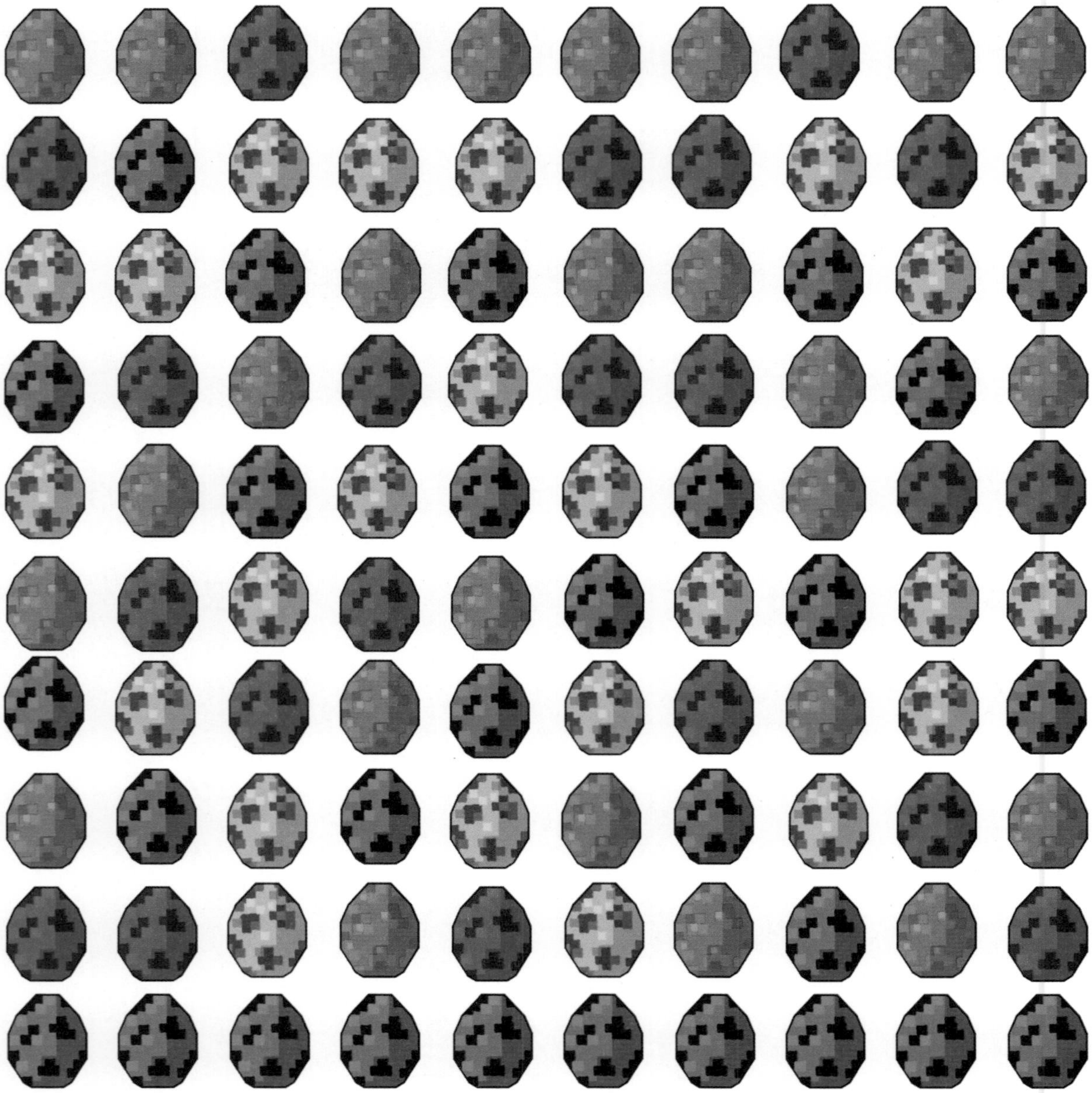

SPELLING BEE #7

Help the bee find its way through this maze to the flowers by spelling 5-letter words.

Make the words by adding CR before the given letters. Begin with the word CRAFT in the top row, and connect the real words until you reach the bottom row. (CRONG is not a real word!)

You can move up, down, left, right, or diagonally.

CRAFT	__OWD	__IDE	__UMP	__ESP	__YPT	__EPE	__ALK
__IMP	__ONG	__ASH	__OSH	__ESS	__USE	__EAT	__OON
__UDE	__ITE	__UMB	__ALM	__UGE	__ANE	__OLE	__AIL
__UEL	__OUG	__IFT	__EST	__EWL	__USH	__ISP	__EAN
__UST	__ACE	__IME	__ANG	__ODA	__ATE	__UBE	_ACK
__EEP	__PLE	__YNG	__AWL	__EAM	__ILF	__OPT	__EEK
__OLY	__EDO	__IFY	__OAP	__IGE	__IFE	__AVE	__ANK
__ELT	__UFF	__SPY	__ILL	__AZE	__OWN	__GST	__LPY

ANSWERS

CAVE EXPLORERS

Carlos, Cara, and Camilo find the cave. Cami does not.

REDSTONE ROUNDUP

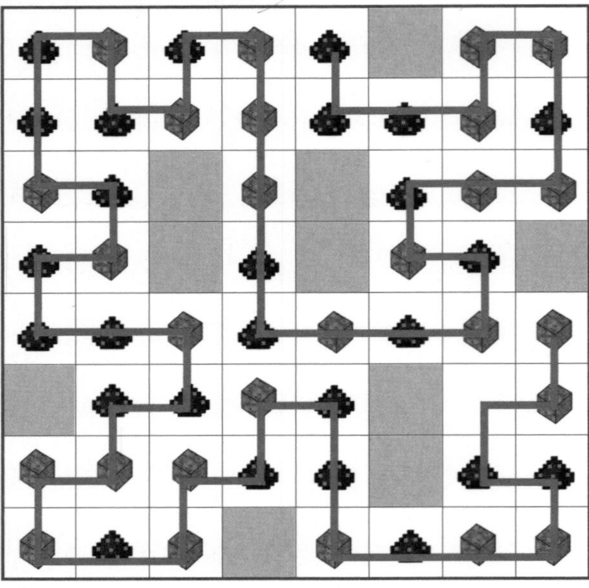

A DOG'S LIFE

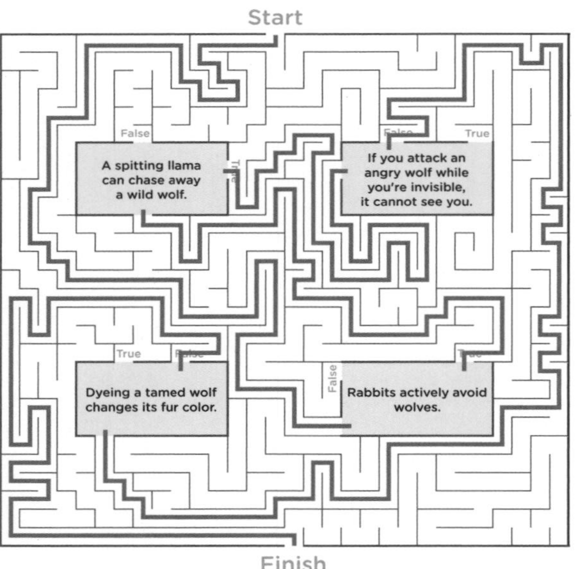

HOP TO IT #1

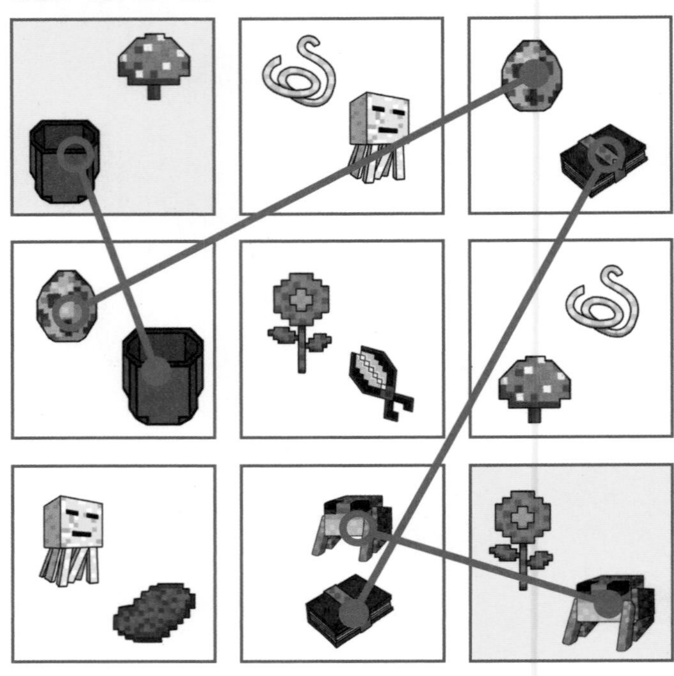

CAPTURE THE SWORD

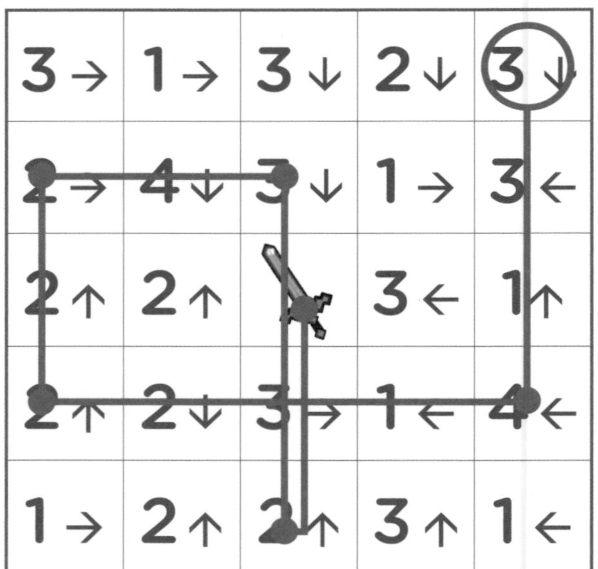

INTO THE FOREST

SPELLING BEE #1

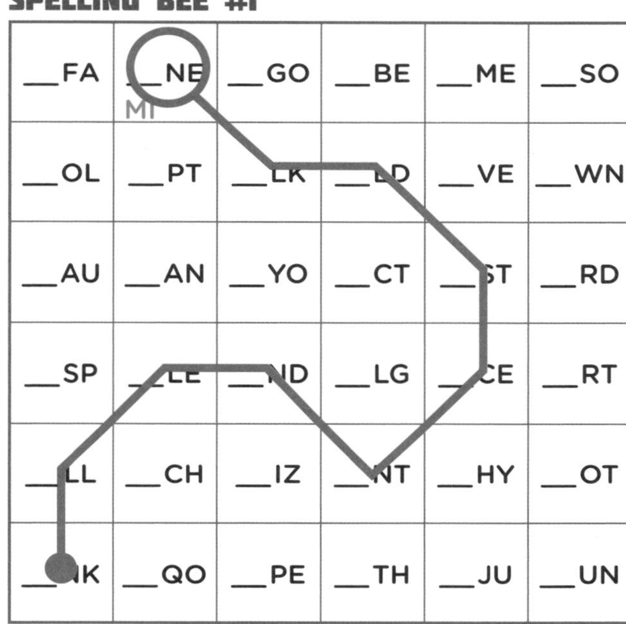

TOOLS FOR THE TAKING

Felicia - Diamond Shovel
Brett - Wooden Sword
Jenny - Iron Axe
Matao - Gold Pickaxe

FAVORITE THINGS

Garth Invader - Battle Mobs
MissyMosh - Build Redstone Devices
SharpShooedHer - Build Mazes
Speed Damon - Hunt for Treasure

SAFE SLIMES

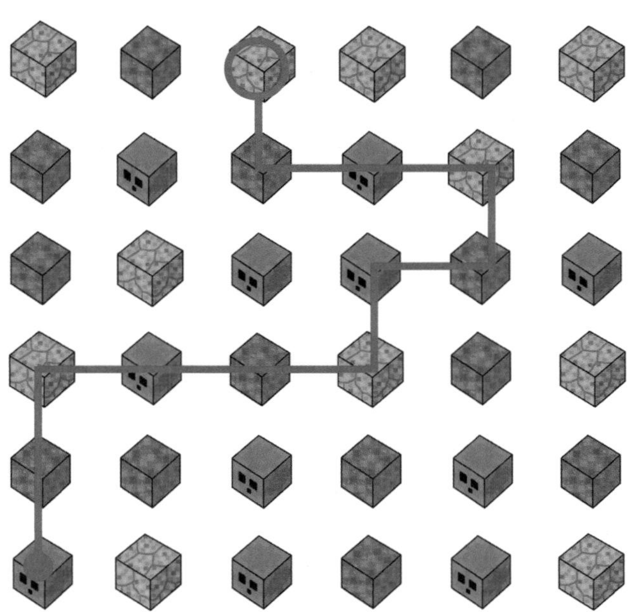

EGGCEPTIONAL SPAWNING

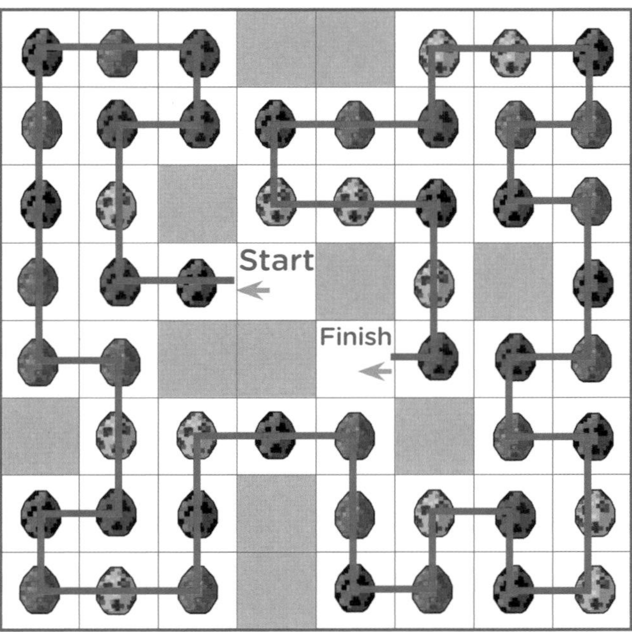

AROUND THE BLOCKS

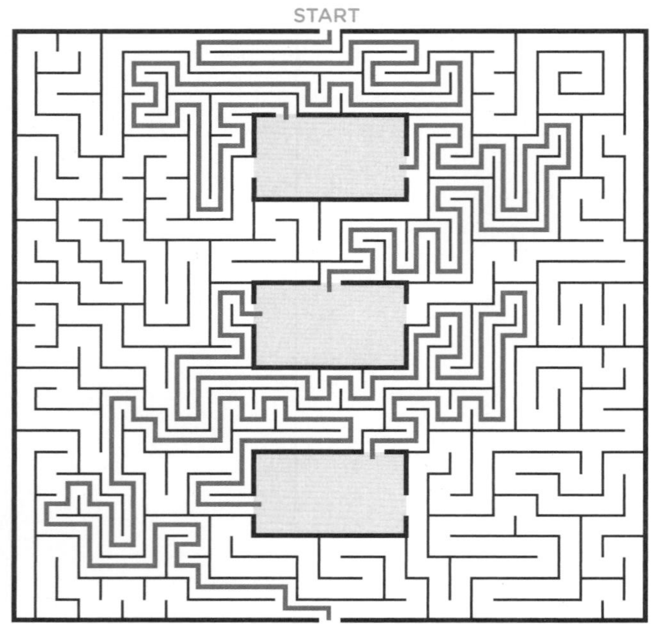

HOP TO IT #2

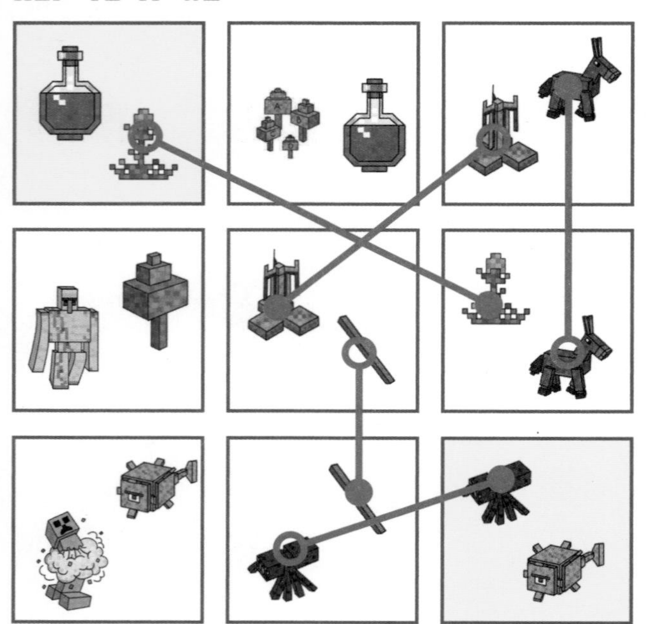

EMERALD FIND

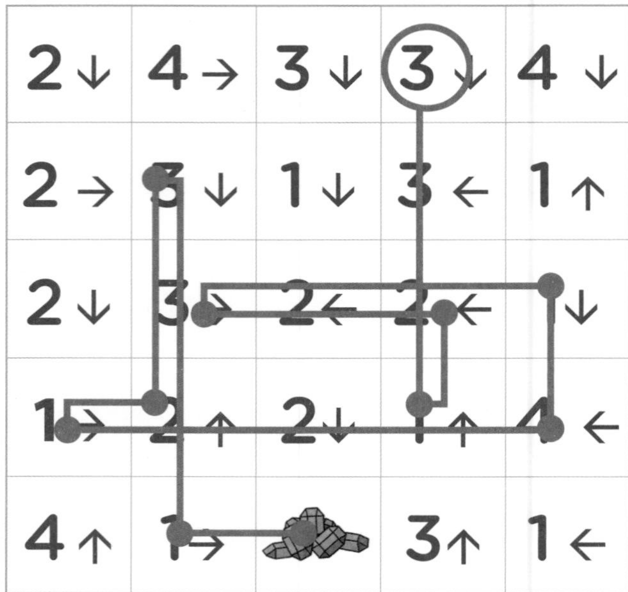

TEMPLE ESCAPE

RUN!

Tame wolf - Haki
Wither skeleton - Roberto
Zombie villagers - Bella
Stray - Mark

SPECIMEN COLLECTION

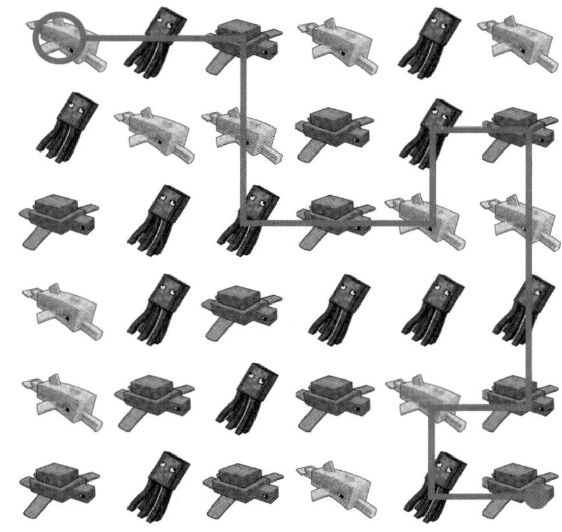

SPELLING BEE #2

_O_T	_E_G	_S_A	_I_Z	_I_E	_U_L
_I_O	_A_W	_Z_K	_E_D	M N _O_D	_A_F
_R_O	_Y_A	_U_R	_C_K	_I_H	_E_B
_I_X	_P_E	_A_Y	_J_I	_E_K	_O_O
_A_Q	_O_Z	_F_U	_Y_V	_U_N	_A_T
_U_F	_[illegible]_T	_W_O	_A_V	_E_K	_U_P

CHEST QUEST

Crazy Q is the only player to find the chest.

FROG FITNESS

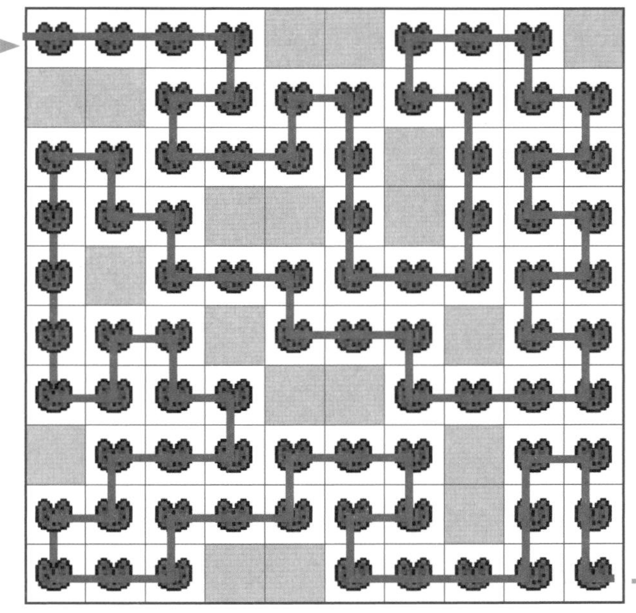

ENCHANTÉ

HOP TO IT #3

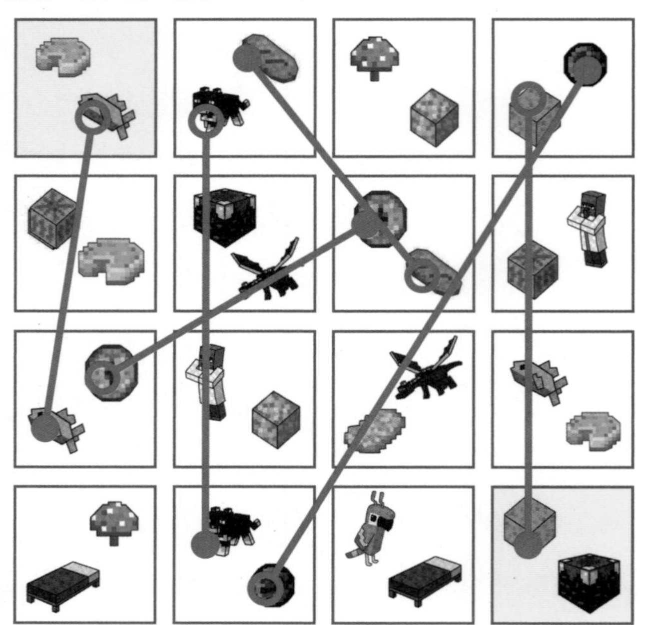

DIAMOND DASH

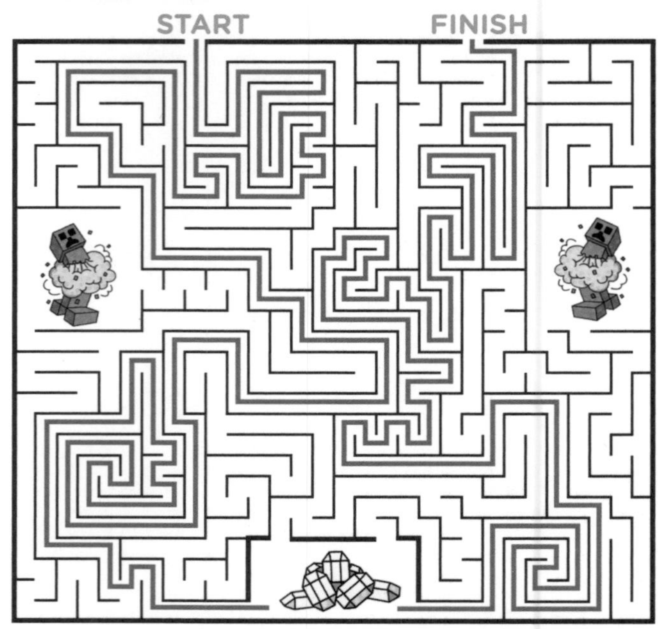

NAP TIME

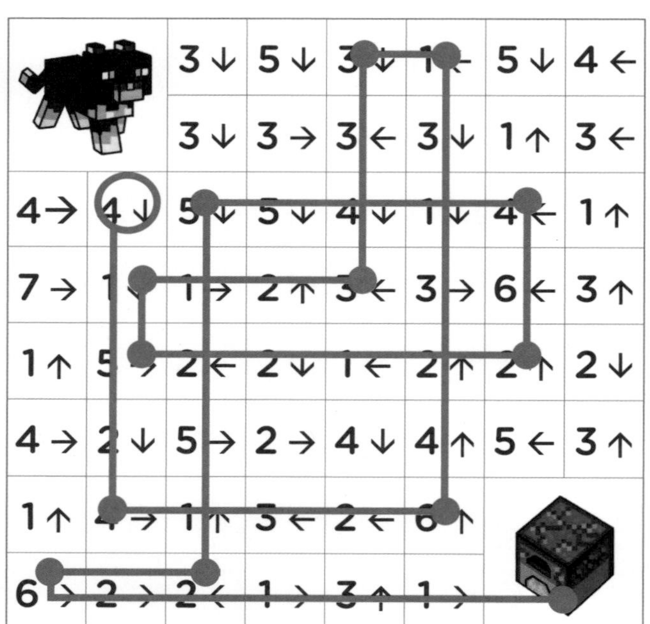

GOOD TRADES BAD TRADE

Lexi - Librarian
Chase - Blacksmith
Camille - Cleric
Ryan - Nitwit
Bailey - Butcher

SMOOTHIES FOR SIX

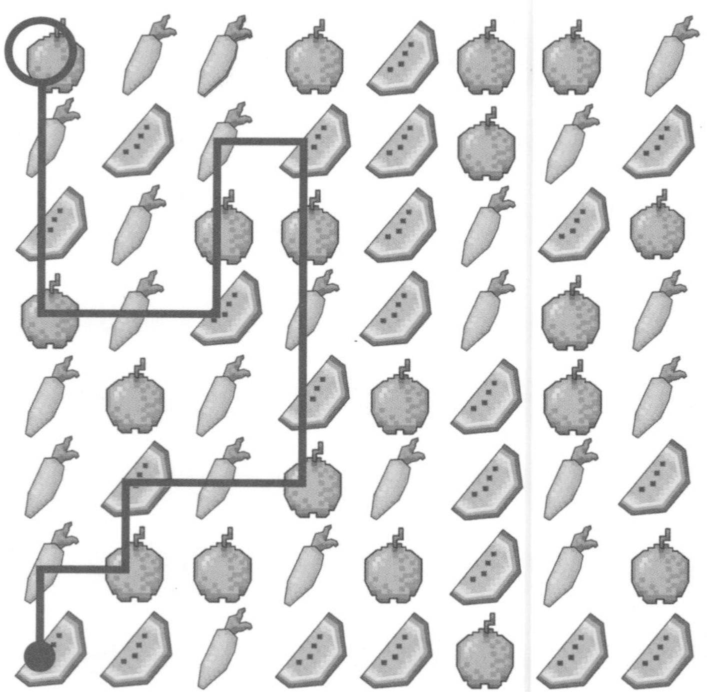

SPELLING BEE #2

MI__	BU__	JE__	EA__	SC__	FI__	JE__	CR__
LA__	HE__	BR__	CR__	LO__	ST__	DO__	VI__
AT__	ZO__	MA__	DU__	IF__	UR__	SA__	FO__
GU__	CH__	MO__	GR__	OI__	FA__	TU__	OP__
OU__	HO__	NI__	QU__	MS__	BO__	RE__	LI__
DI__	KY__	EG__	EA__	CA__	PL__	AJ__	TO__
BL__	PI__	WU__	DR__	UR__	NO__	KR__	BR__
NE__	CO__	AU__	JU__	GO__	FE__	CL__	HU__

NE

LAVA KNOWLEDGE

INTO BATTLE

Scarrr - Shulker
Clash - Evoker
Jaction - Ghast
Attax - Drowned

HOP TO IT #4

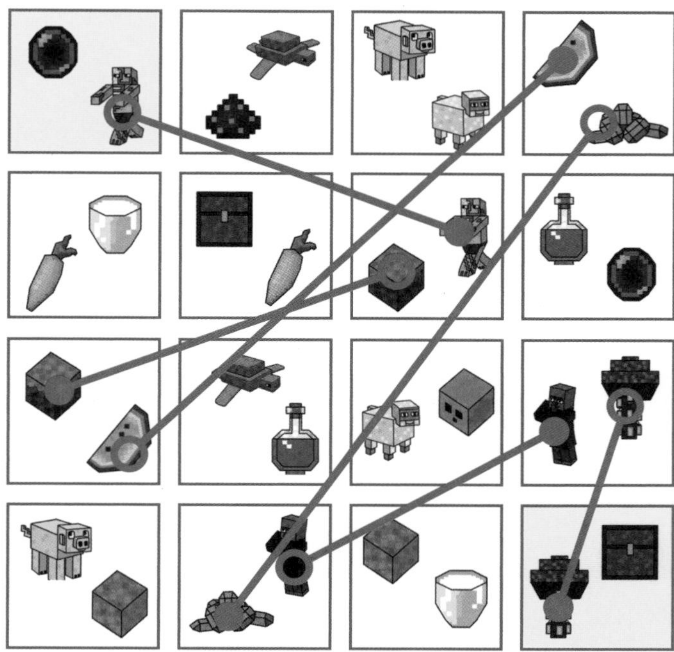

CACTUS CROP COLLECTION

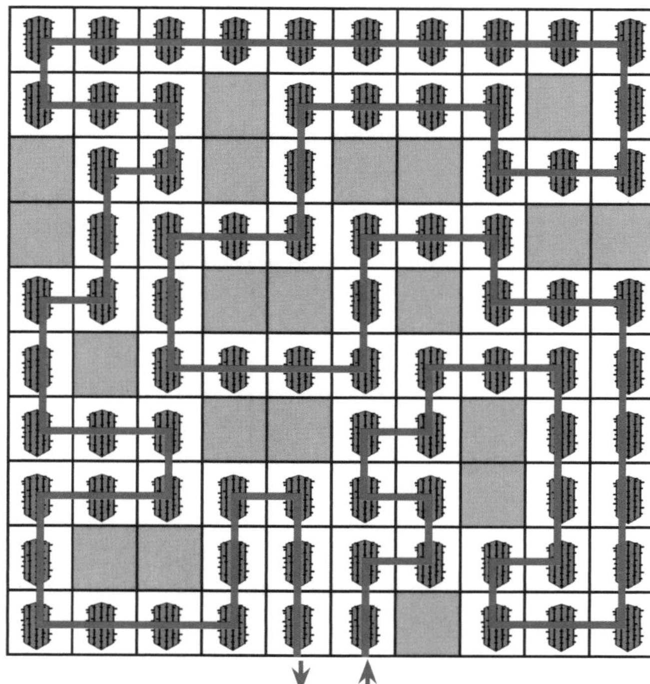

LOST BEACON

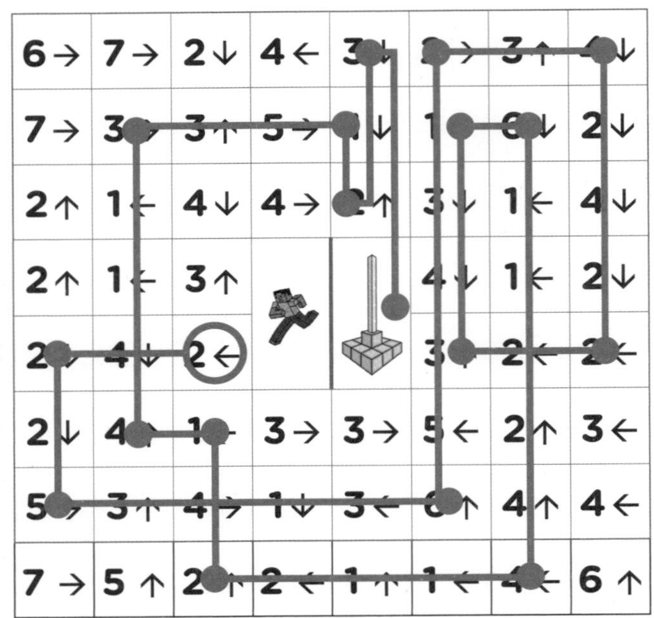

MAIN COURSE MIX-UP

AN ENCHANTED HOE

SPELLING BEE #4

L__D	R__K	W__P	F__G	M__E	H__R	L__K	Z__G
G__D	L__T	N__D	W__G	K__T (IN)	N__E	B__T	S__Y
V__E	C__G	S__K	L__X	F__T	P__D	E__G	R__D
R__G	H__O	B__Y	J__T	L__P	T__Y	M__R	S__K
N__W	F__D	I__G	S__C	P__K	Z__T	B__D	G__G
W__K	H__L	P__E	A__W	D__F	T__C	P__T	T__T
F__E	Z__C	G__Z	F__Y	H__T	W__D	S__T	O__K
L__F	R__P	U__T	K__G	V__G	Y__U	M__B	K__Z

A VERY SMART PIG (AND A FUNNY GIRL)

EINSWINE

A SECRET MESSAGE

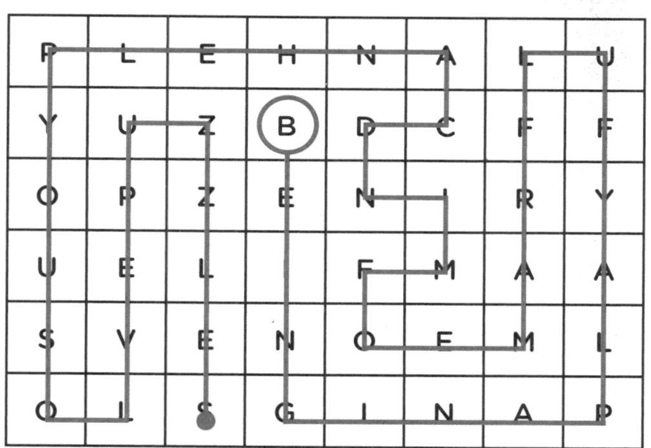

BEING IN A PLAYFUL FRAME OF MIND CAN HELP YOU SOLVE PUZZLES.

BEDS WANTED!

Poppy and Diego find beds.

COBWEB DREAMS

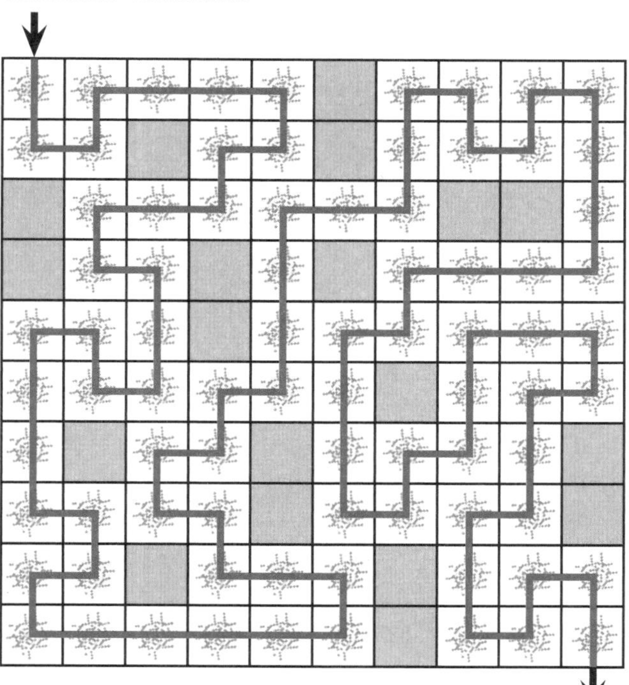

SADDLE UP!

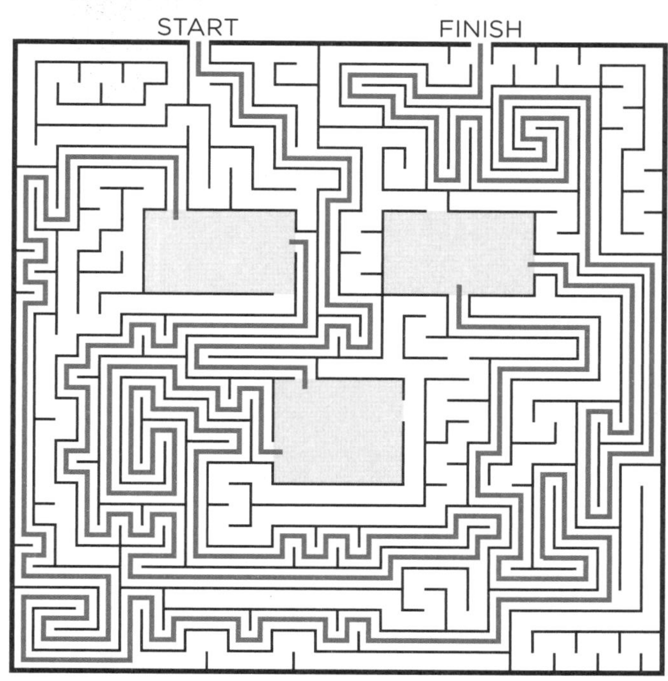

HOP TO IT #5

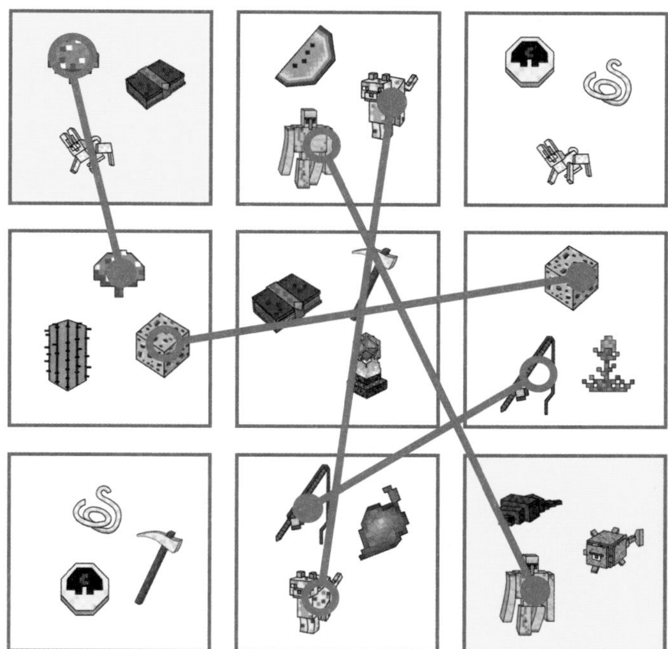

THE PEARLY PATH

3 ↓	4 →	2 →	2 ↓	1 ←	4 ↓	3 ↓
3 ↓	5 →	2 →	5 ↓	1 ↓	5 ←	3 ←
[illegible] →	3 ↓	3 ←	2 →	3 ←	2 →	2 ↓
2 →	3 ↑	3 ↓		3 ←	2 ↓	1 ←
1 →	4 ↑	3 ↑	1 ↑	1 ←	4 ←	4 ←
3 [illegible]	3 →	5 ↑	2 ↑	4 ←	3 ←	2 →
4 ↑	5 ↑	3 →	1 →	3 ↑	5 ↑	5 ←

MOOSHROOM SHEARING

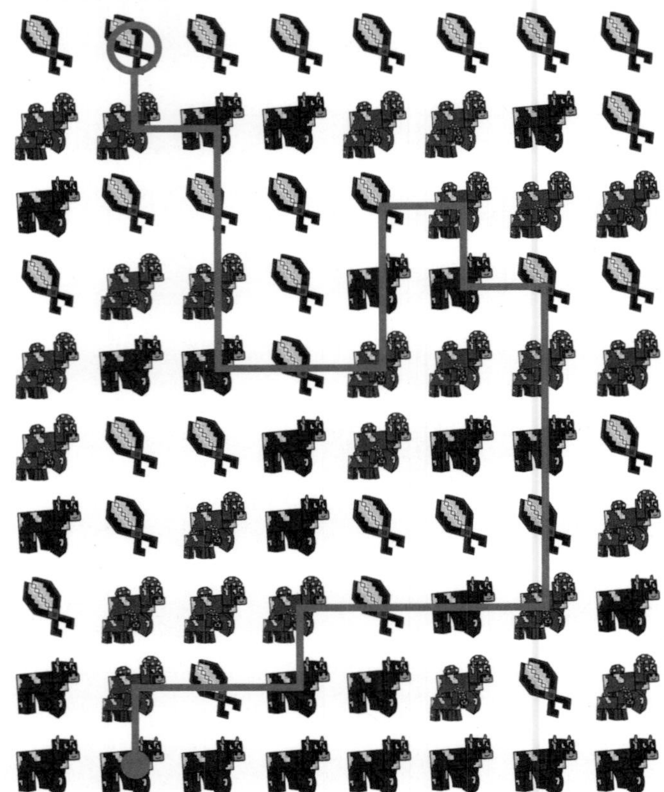

MOB HOUSE

SPELLING BEE #5

_IN_	_AL_	_UD_	_IK_	_AB_	_OC_	_IY_	_OZ_
_OR_	_OG_	_AF_	_AC_	_UH_	[illegible]	_OI_	_EH
_IJ_	_IM_	_UK_	_AU_	_OV_	_UM_	_AD_	_YL_
_TL_	_SN_	_US_	_AK_	_OM_	_EO_	_IP_	_UT_
_AT_	_LL_	_UQ_	_EL_	_IS_	_OT_	_UU_	_IC_
_IV_	_IK_	_AN_	_OW_	_UL_	_OD_	_OP_	_AX_
_OZ_	_PR_	_UP_	_AR_	_AY_	_RT_	_IB_	_AI_
_UW_	_OL_	_CH_	_EV_	[illegible]	_AE_	_ID_	_OB_

SCAVENGER HUNT FINDS

Ariel - 3

Brandon - 4

Erika - 1

Todd - 2

Suzy - 5

WHERE AM I?

Ambler and Drifter - Jungle

Gad2222 - Deep Ocean

Journey-Man - Arctic

'NOTHER NETHER STAR, PLEASE

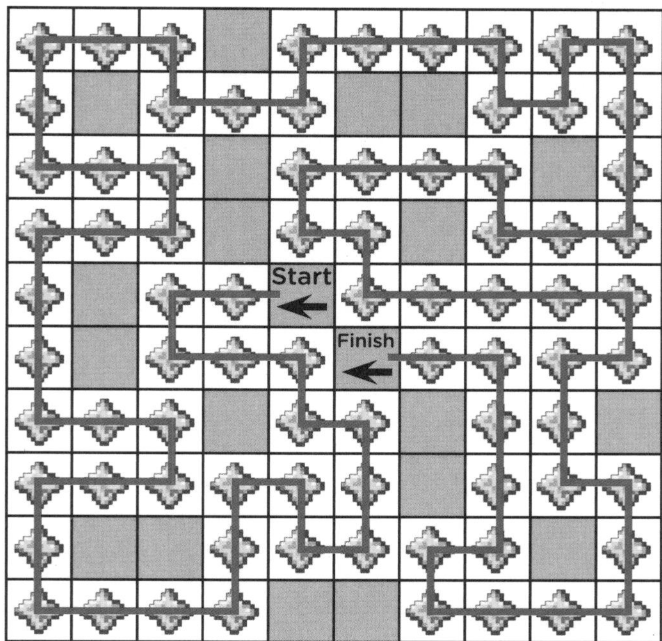

CHEST JESTS

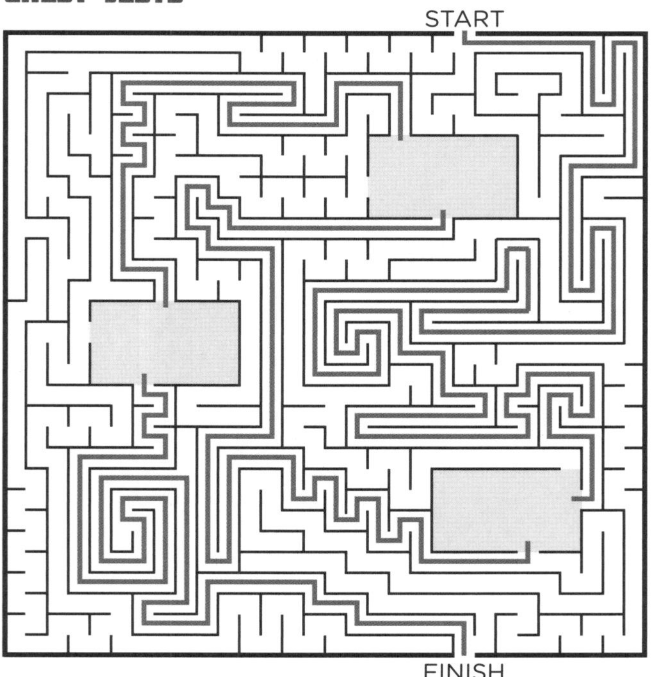

HOP TO IT #6

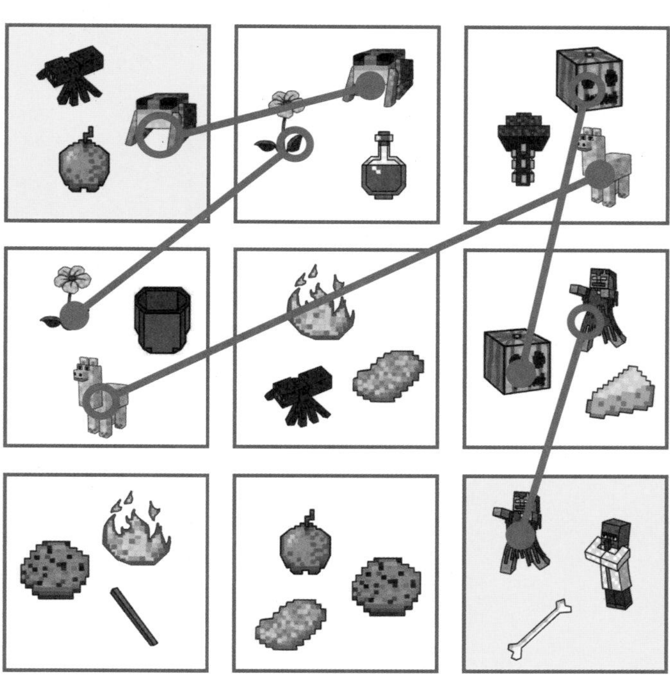

QUICK! YOU CAN SAVE US ALL!

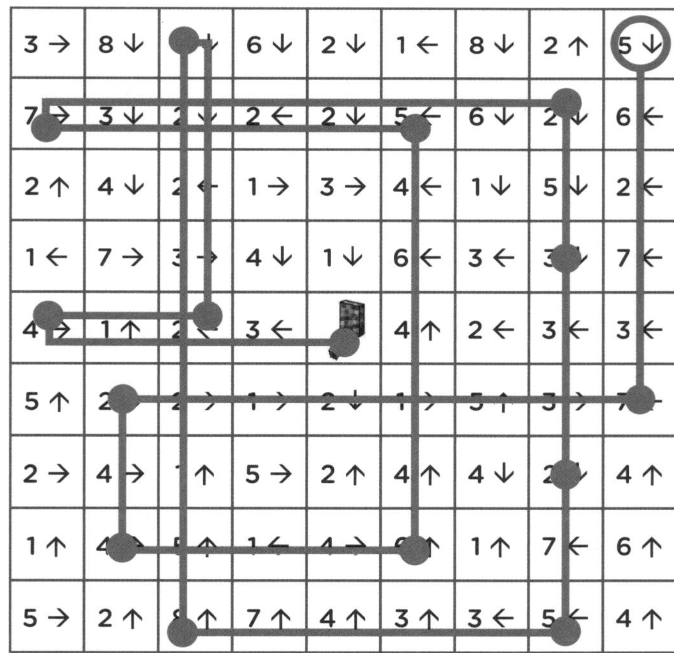

GO FOR GLOW

START

SPELLING BEE #6

B_P_	S_B_	P_L_	R_P_	S_F_	F_D_	M_N_	Z_G_
J_B_	P_M_	K_B_	C_C_	W_G_	L_M_	T_G_	F_N_
D_D_	H_R_	R_R_	Y_D_	P_P_	G_M_	S_Q_	K_L_
W_B_	H_V_	P_T_	Z_P_	W_S_	A_P_	T_D_	Q_T_
C_T_	O_N_	K_T_	F_B_	U_P_	F_V_	E_J_	H_K_
A_B_	C_M_	D_C_	W_R_	R_H_	Z_M_	Y_D_	N_C_
G_X_	T_M_	F_Y_	H_Q_	B_T_	C_V_	S_D_	J_M_
N_R_	W_G_	L_[illegible]_	S_C_	C_H_	T_F_	G_H_	C_E

I E

CHICKEN HERDING

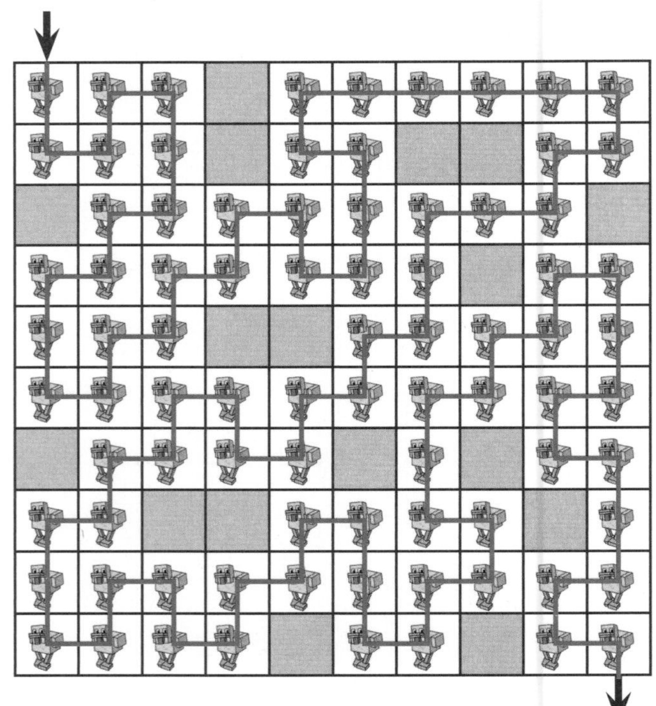

LAUGH LINES

KARAT CAKE

MOB SCHOOL CARPOOL

SHEDDING LIGHT ON REDSTONE TORCHES

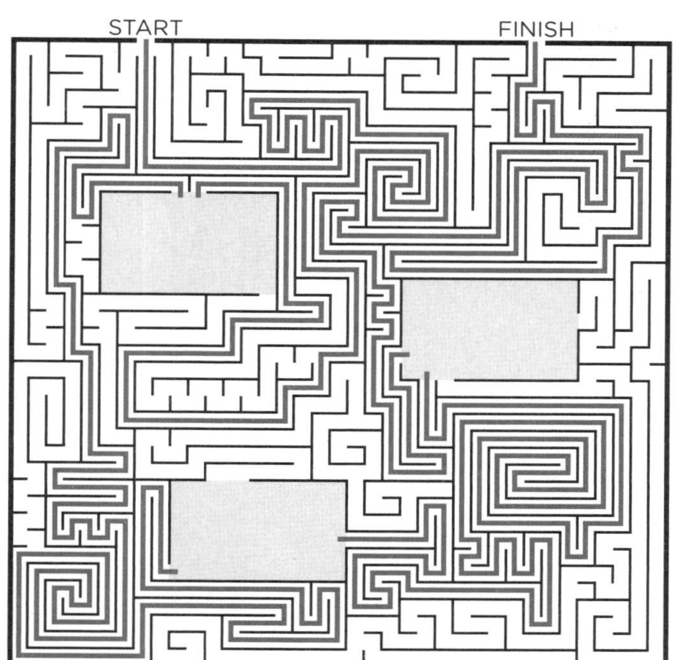

GO FOR THE GOLD

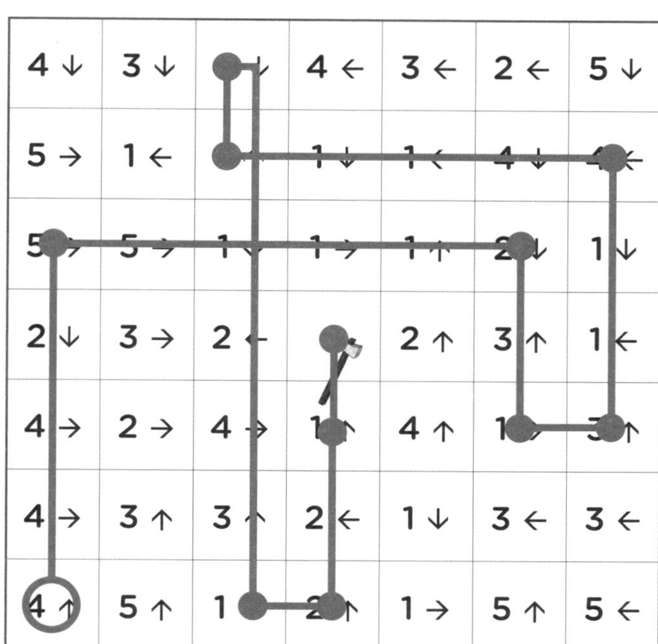

4 ↓	3 ↓	[illegible] ↓	4 ←	3 ←	2 ←	5 ↓
5 →	1 ←	[illegible]	1 ↓	1 ←	4 ↓	4 ←
5 →	5 →	1 ↓	1 →	1 ↑	2 ↓	1 ↓
2 ↓	3 →	2 ←	[illegible]	2 ↑	3 ↑	1 ←
4 →	2 →	4 →	1 ↑	4 ↑	1 [illegible]	3 ↑
4 →	3 ↑	3 ↑	2 ←	1 ↓	3 ←	3 ←
4 ↑	5 ↑	1 [illegible]	2 ↑	1 →	5 ↑	5 ←

HOP TO IT #7

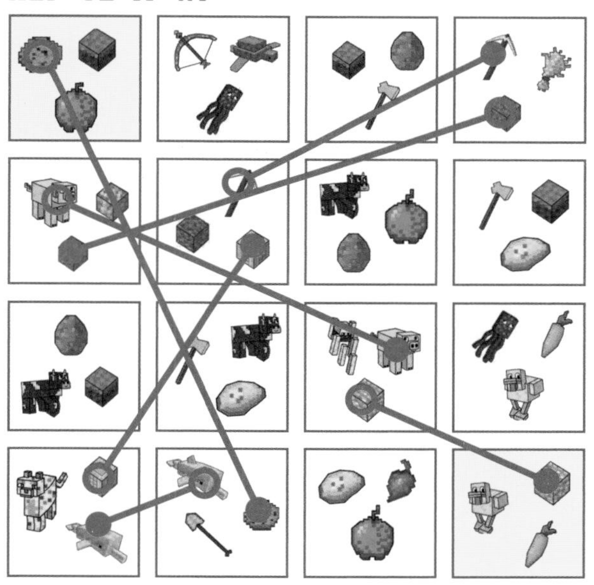

PURSUING PRISMARINE

UNDEAD HUMOR

BRAINS!

EGG HUNT

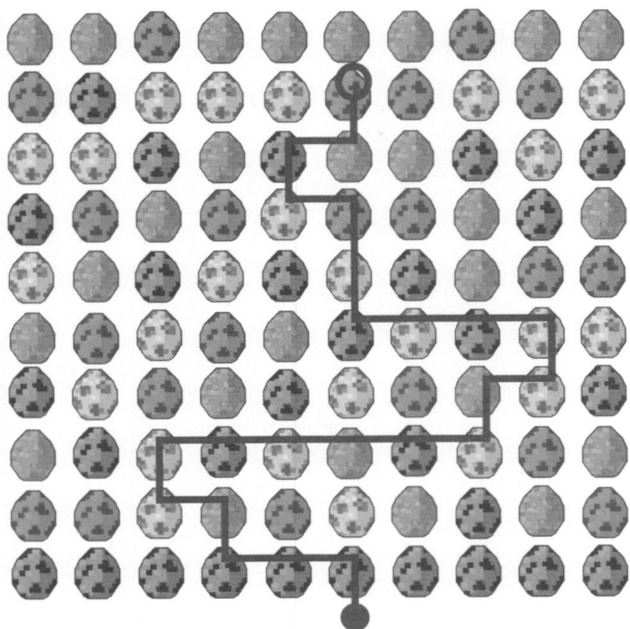

SPELLING BEE #7

CRAFT	__OWD	__IDE	__UMP	__ESP	__YPT	__EPE	__ALK
__IMP	__ONG	__ASH	__OSH	__ESS	__USE	__EAT	__OON
__UDE	__ITE	__UMB	__ALM	__UGE	__ANE	__OLE	__AIL
__UEL	__OUG	__IFT	__EST	__EWL	__USH	__ISP	__EAN
__UST	__ACE	__I[illegible]E	__ANG	__ODA	__[illegible]TE	__UBE	__ACK
__EEP	__PLE	__YNG	__AW[illegible]	__[illegible]AM	__ILF	__OPT	__EEK
__OLY	__EDO	__IFY	__OAP	__IGE	__IFE	__[illegible]VE	__ANK
__ELT	__UFF	__SPY	__ILL	__AZE	__[illegible]N	__GST	__LPY

ASTOUNDING ACTIVITIES FOR MINECRAFTERS

Puzzles and Games for Endless Fun!

Sky Pony Press
New York

TABLE OF CONTENTS

Wheel of Fortune #1
Alex Says: Tool Tip
The Mirror's Message
You Can Draw It: Wither
Shop Around the Block
Stay Away!
Enchanted Chest
Killer Joke
Gem Search
Buried Treasure
You Can Draw It: Ocelot
Favorite Thing to Do
Squared Up: Garden Plot
Homeward Bound
Life-Saving Steps
You Can Draw It: Llama
Fact of (Real) Life
Mystery Mob
Nether Finds
Who's Whose on the Farm?
Party Snack Pick-Up
Get Out!
You Can Draw It: Skeleton
Wishing You Good...
Rare Drop Scores
Lost Library
Uncommon Common Feature
Alex Says: Did You Know This about Zombies?
Wheel of Fortune #2
Saddle Search
Memo from Mirror
Squared Up: Let There Be Light
Cookie Feast
You Can Draw It: Witch
Enchanted Book
Long Laugh
Gettin' Crafty
True or False?
Go with the Flow Chart
Inside Info
Creeper Destroyers
Whoops!
What's for Dinner?
Score More Ore
Trading Jo(s)
The Locked Door
Zombie Friends
Alex Says: Own Your Mine Business
Wheel of Fortune #3
Hidden Armor
Reflections in the Water
Squared Up: Logical Loot
Flowers to Dye For
Ship Shape
Enchanted Trap Door
Tall Tale
Animals, Animals Everywhere
Letter Hunt
Math Mobs
So Much for Peaceful!
Baby's Favorite Toy
Hidden Hazard
Whose Biome is This?
Mob Drops
Surprise!
You Can Draw It: Creeper Family
What Zombies Want
Whodunnit?
Wheel of Fortune #4
Seed Finder
In the Beginning
You Can Draw It: Enderdragon
Bountiful Harvest
Name Shifting
Enchanted Bow and Arrow
Which Witch?
Pick a Potion
Text Strings
Additional Math Mobs
Flower Power
A Rare Find
Miner Humor
Drop Match
A Cold Reception
Answers

WHEEL OF FORTUNE #1

Start at the ▼.
Write every third letter on the spaces to reveal a fortune you want to claim.

F _ _ _ _ _ _ _ - _ _ _ _ _ _ _ _ _ _ _ _

_ _ _ _

ALEX SAYS: TOOL TIP

If you have ever played the game Simon Says, then you know how this game works: follow only the directions that begin with "Alex says" to reveal a helpful tool tip.

	1	2	3	4	5
A	IF	THE	DON'T	TO	YOU
B	WASTE	MINED	EMERALD	IRON	DIAMONDS
C	CAN'T	ON	GRIND	ISN'T	BE
D	A	KIND	REDSTONE	SHOVEL	BLIND

1. **Alex says**, "Cross off words with fewer than four letters in Row A and Column 5."
2. **Alex says**, "Cross off words that rhyme with *find*."
3. Cross off all Minecraft tools.
4. **Alex says**, "Cross off the ores in columns 3 and 4."
5. **Alex says**, "Cross off contractions in Row C."
6. **Alex says**, "Read the remaining words to reveal a tip from Alex."

Secret tip: ______________________________________

____

THE MIRROR'S MESSAGE

Circle letters on the top half of the grid that have correct mirror images on the bottom half. Write the circled letters in order on the spaces to uncover a ghastly detail you may not know.

T H U O W O R A K S P L E A M S H P O T

I O N S M U P S T H M I T T H I A E L O

W E B R H A L O C F O F A R G O H A S T

W E D ʁ H ∀ Γ Ø D Ⅎ O Ⅎ ∀ Ь ⅁ C H ∀ ƨ ⊥

I O И ƨ W ∩ ʁ ƨ ⊥ H Z I ⊥ ⊥ H Γ W E Γ O

⊥ K W O W O ʁ V K ƨ Ь Γ ƨ ∀ W ƨ H Ь O ⊥

__ __   __ __ __ __,   __ __ __ __ __ __ __

__ __ __ __ __ __ __ __   __ __ __ __ __   __ __ __   __ __ __

__ __ __ __ __ __   __ __ __ __ __   __ __   __   __ __ __ __ __ __

YOU CAN DRAW IT: WITHER

Use the grid to copy the picture. Examine each small square in the top grid, then transfer those lines to the corresponding square on the bottom grid.

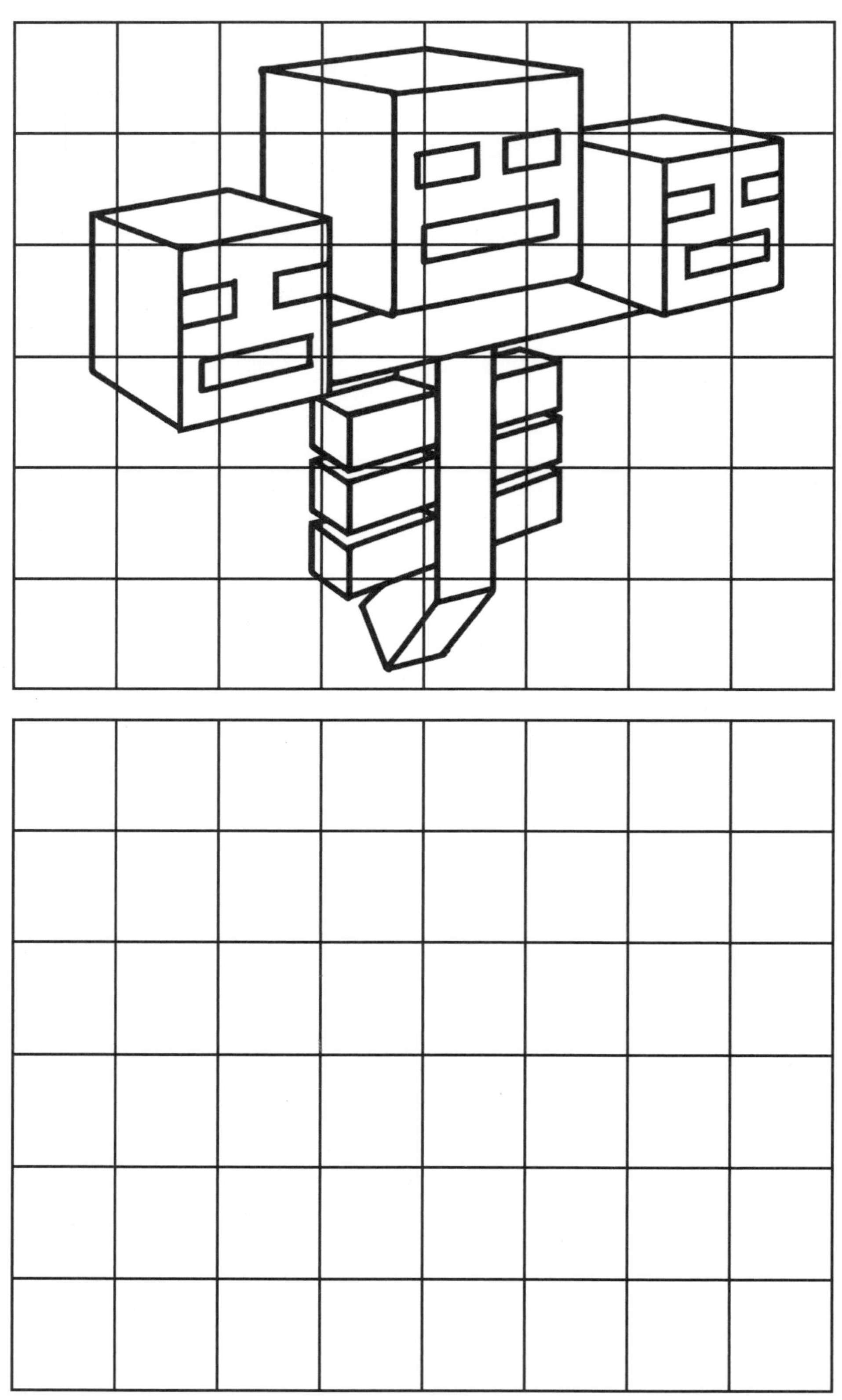

SHOP AROUND THE BLOCK

Minecraft player, Ew N. Ick, built a specialty shop that sells poisonous potato, rotten flesh, spider eye, and pufferfish. What is the name of this shop? Follow the directions in the flow chart to find out.

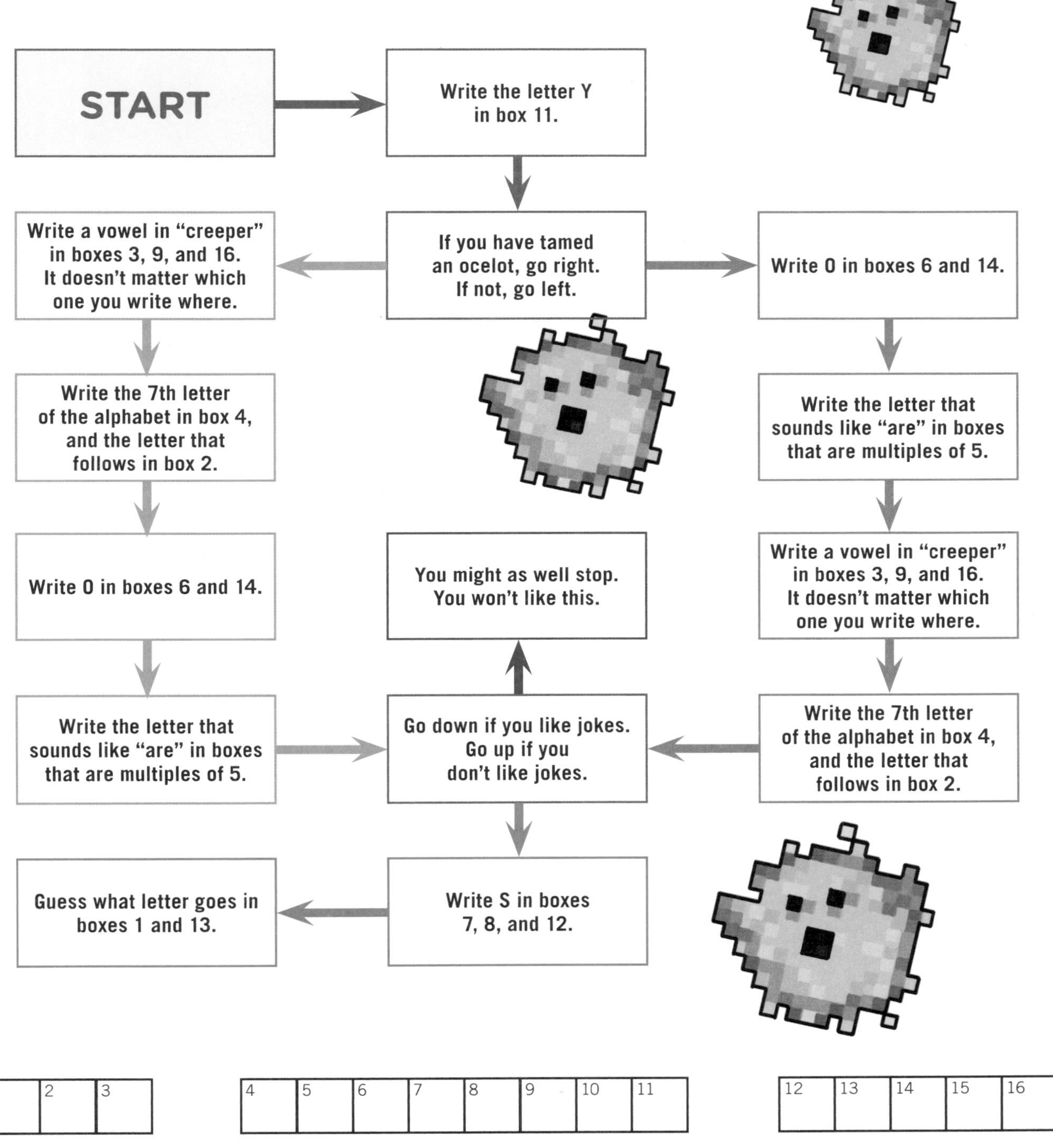

1	2	3

4	5	6	7	8	9	10	11

12	13	14	15	16

STAY AWAY!

The answers to the clues use each letter in the letter box. Write the answers to the clues on the numbered spaces, one letter on each blank. Then transfer the letters to the boxes with the same numbers. If you fill in the boxes correctly, you'll reveal something you should avoid if you're worried about zombie pigmen.

A E E H L N O P R R T T

Not now, but soon

___ ___ ___ ___ ___
1 2 3 4 5

Often a dog or cat, but sometimes a horse or snake

___ ___ ___
6 7 8

You can honk this on a car

___ ___ ___ ___
9 10 11 12

12	7	3	9	4	11

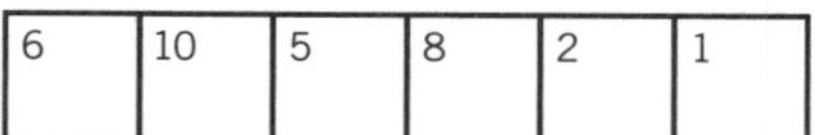

6	10	5	8	2	1

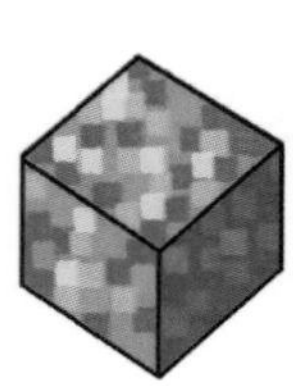
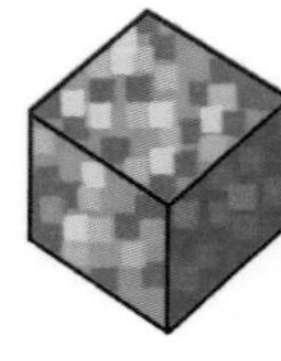
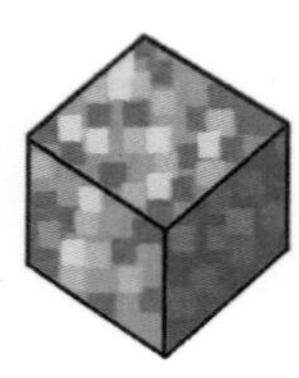

ENCHANTED CHEST

This End City chest is enchanted. To open it, you must press all nine buttons just once, in the correct order.

Follow the directions on the buttons. For instance, 2D means you must move your finger two buttons down. R=right, L=left, U=up. To open the chest, you must land on the F button last.

Which button do you have to press first to land on the F button last?

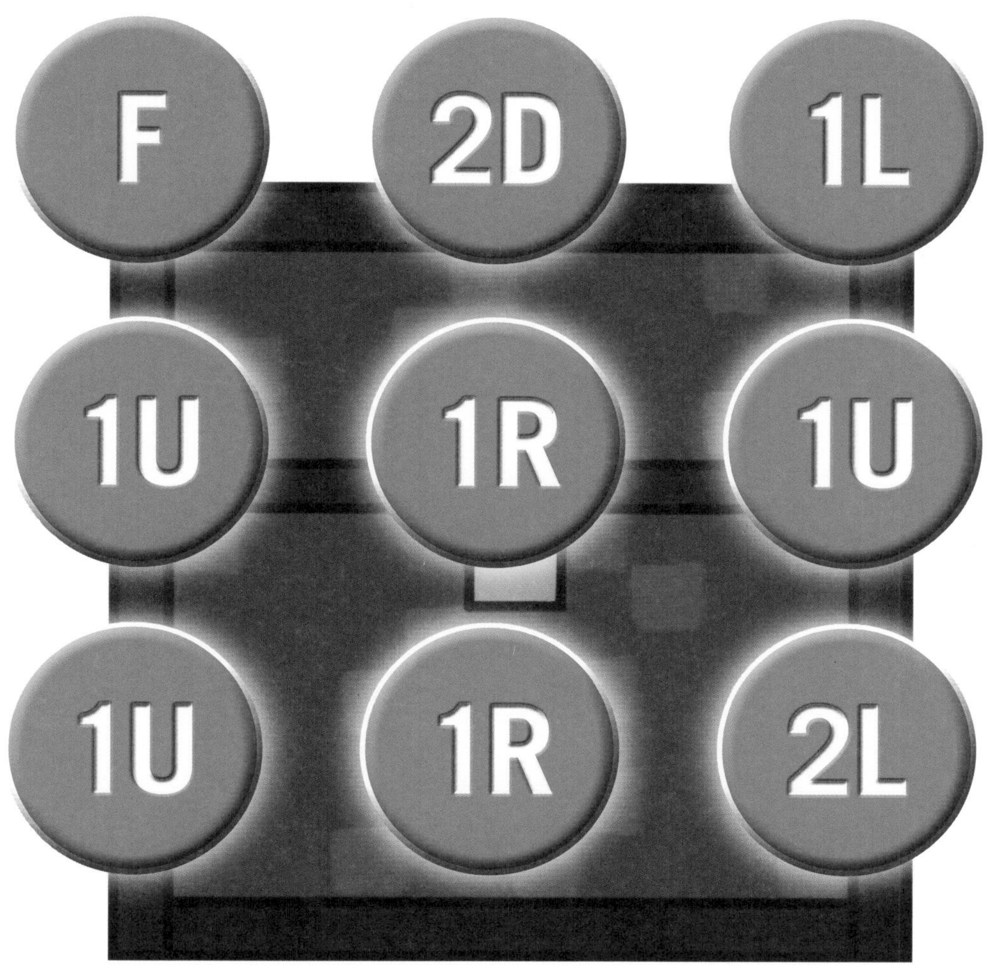

KILLER JOKE

In this crossword, you get to figure out where each word fits. Use the picture clues to guess the word answers, then see where each word fits best. If you fill in the puzzle correctly, you'll get a funny answer to the question below.

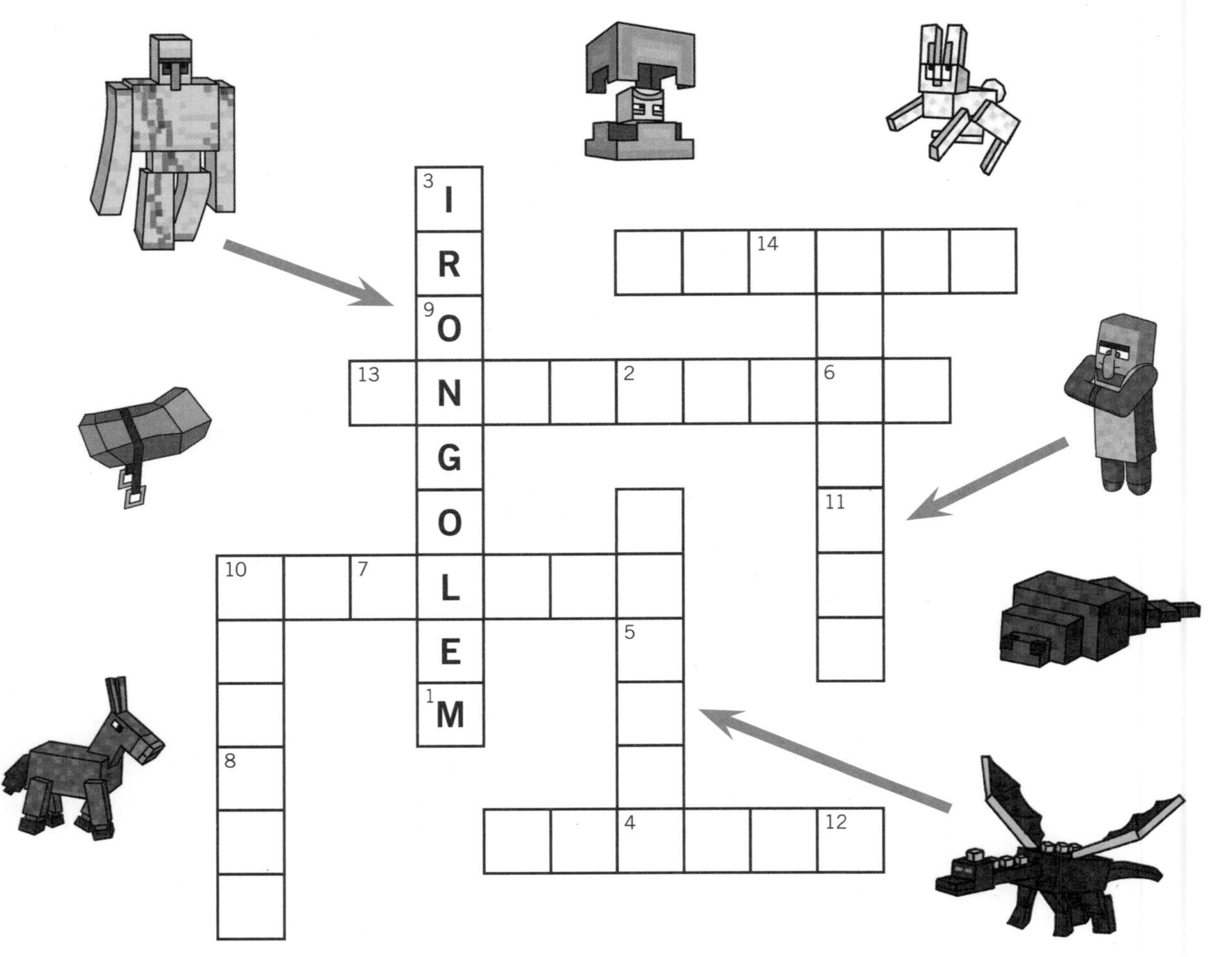

What's the difference between a killer rabbit and a counterfeit dollar bill?

__ __ __   __ __   __ __ __   __ __ __ __ __   __ __ __
9 4 13   3 10   14 5 8   1 9 4 13 12   5 4 8

__ __ __   __ __ __ __ __   __ __   __   __ __ __
6 11 13   9 6 11 13 2   3 10   5   1 5 8

__ __ __ __ __
14 7 4 4 12

GEM SEARCH

Can you find the emerald? It appears only once in a horizontal, vertical, or diagonal line.

L	A	E	D	L	E	R	E	M	E
E	R	A	M	E	M	A	M	D	R
D	M	L	D	E	E	E	L	E	A
A	L	E	D	L	R	A	D	M	D
E	L	A	R	E	M	E	E	L	D
M	A	D	R	A	A	D	A	E	L
E	L	R	D	M	L	R	E	D	A
R	M	D	A	R	E	L	A	L	R
A	E	A	L	M	A	E	D	E	E
D	E	M	E	R	E	D	L	A	M

BURIED TREASURE

Uncover the loot in the grid, and it is yours! Color every box that has an odd number to discover the name of the loot item.

13	27	9	78	77	4	92	29	50	55	3	61
44	35	10	70	83	1	18	15	16	28	97	14
26	41	62	56	21	66	49	7	38	60	19	32
12	19	8	74	5	30	2	63	54	32	43	6

YOU CAN DRAW IT: OCELOT

Use the grid to copy the picture. Examine each small square in the top grid, then transfer those lines to the corresponding square on the bottom grid.

FAVORITE THING TO DO

Follow each player's path, under and over crossing paths, to discover what each likes to do in Minecraft.

MOHIT JASMINE LU CLAIRE

BUILD SOLVE MAZES BATTLE MOBS BREW POTIONS

SQUARED UP: GARDEN PLOT

Each of the four vegetables in this puzzle can appear only once in each row, column, and the four inside boxes. Can you figure out how this garden plot is designed?

B = BEETROOT

C = CARROT

M = MELON

P = POTATO

			B
C	B		M
P		B	C
B			

HOMEWARD BOUND

Help the villager find his way back home.

START

STOP

LIFE-SAVING STEPS

Boxes connected by lines contain the same letter. Some letters are given; others have to be guessed. Fill in all the boxes to reveal the answer to this question:

What steps should you take if you meet a hostile mob while you are unarmed?

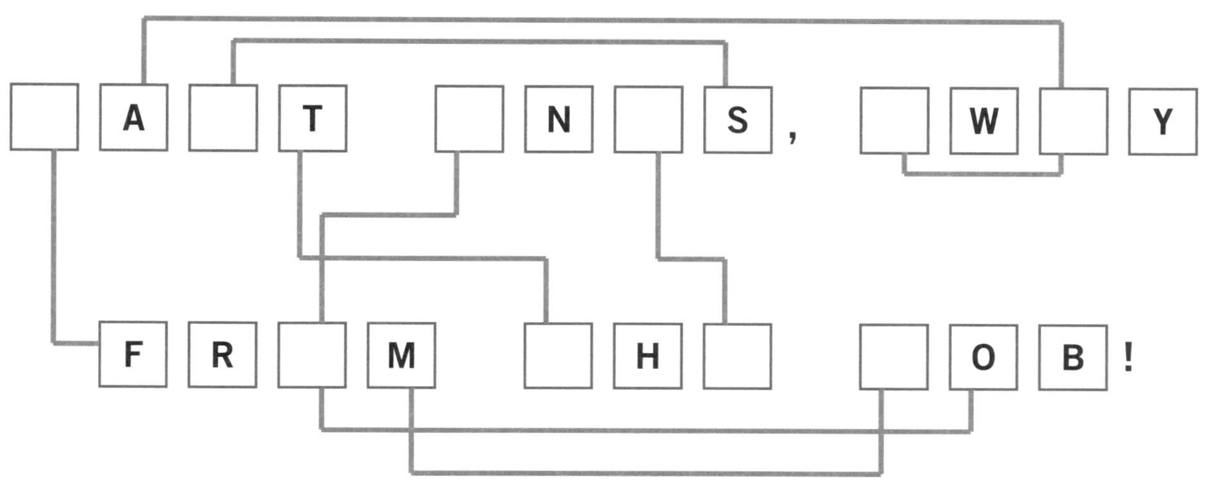

YOU CAN DRAW IT: LLAMA

Use the grid to copy the picture. Examine one small square in the top picture then transfer those lines to the corresponding square in the bottom grid.

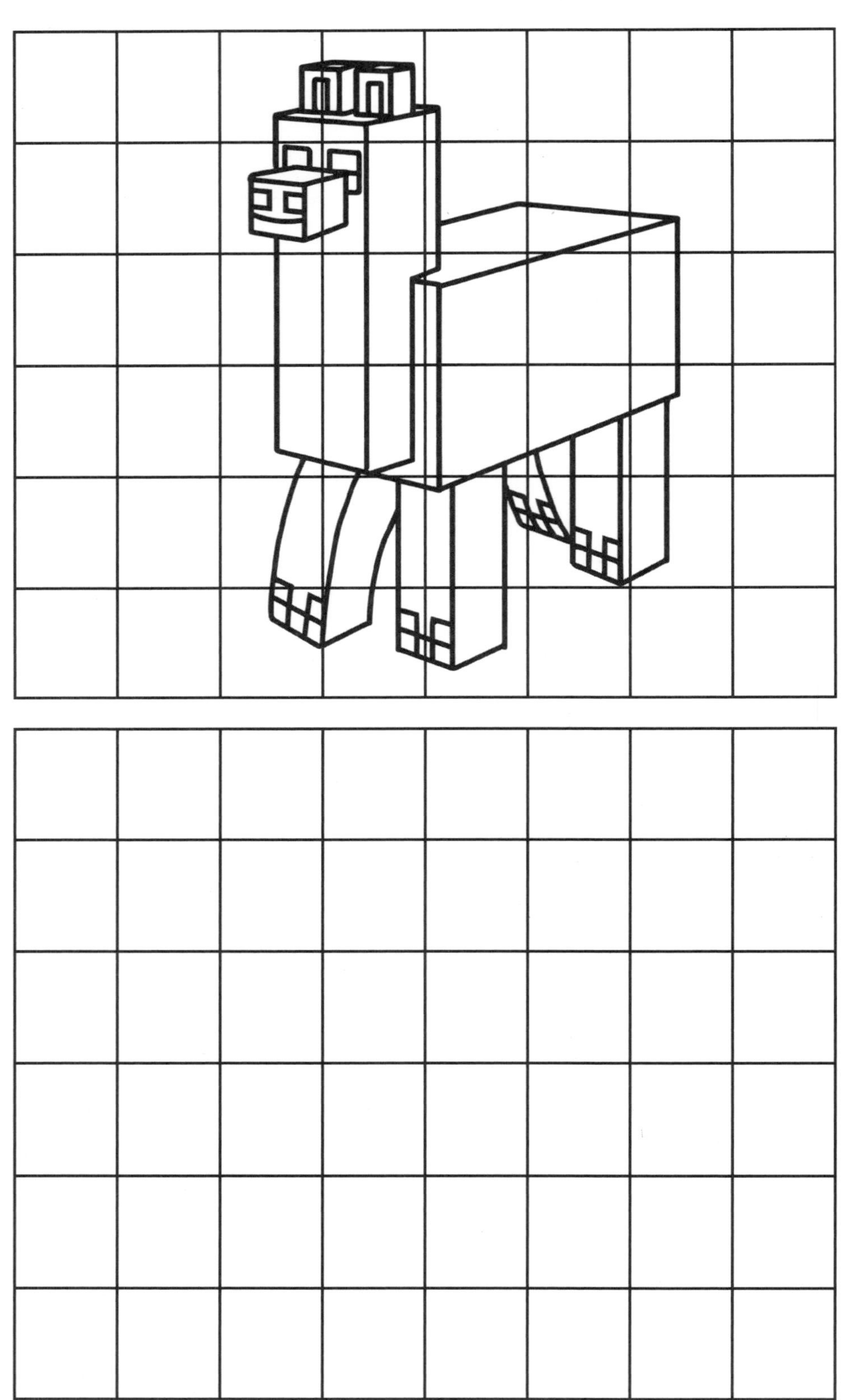

FACT OF (REAL) LIFE

The answer to the question will be revealed as you add letters to the empty boxes that come before, between, or after the given letters in the alphabet. If you get to Z, start all over again with A. The first letter has been written for you.

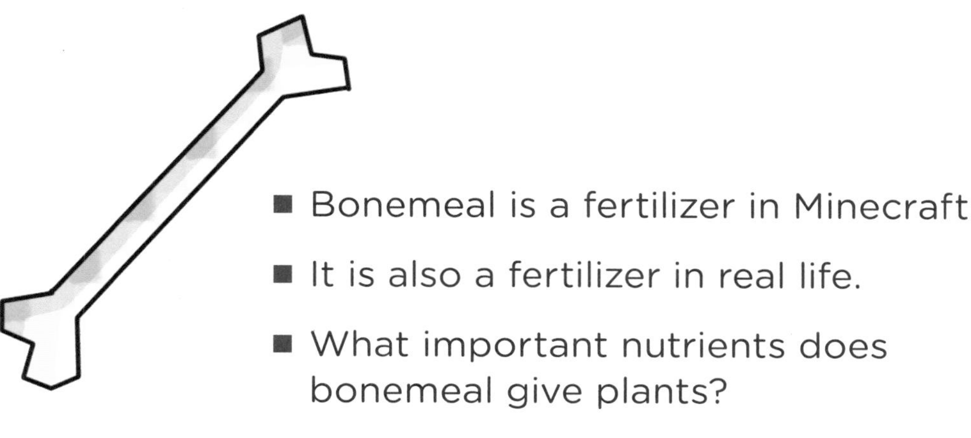

- Bonemeal is a fertilizer in Minecraft.
- It is also a fertilizer in real life.
- What important nutrients does bonemeal give plants?

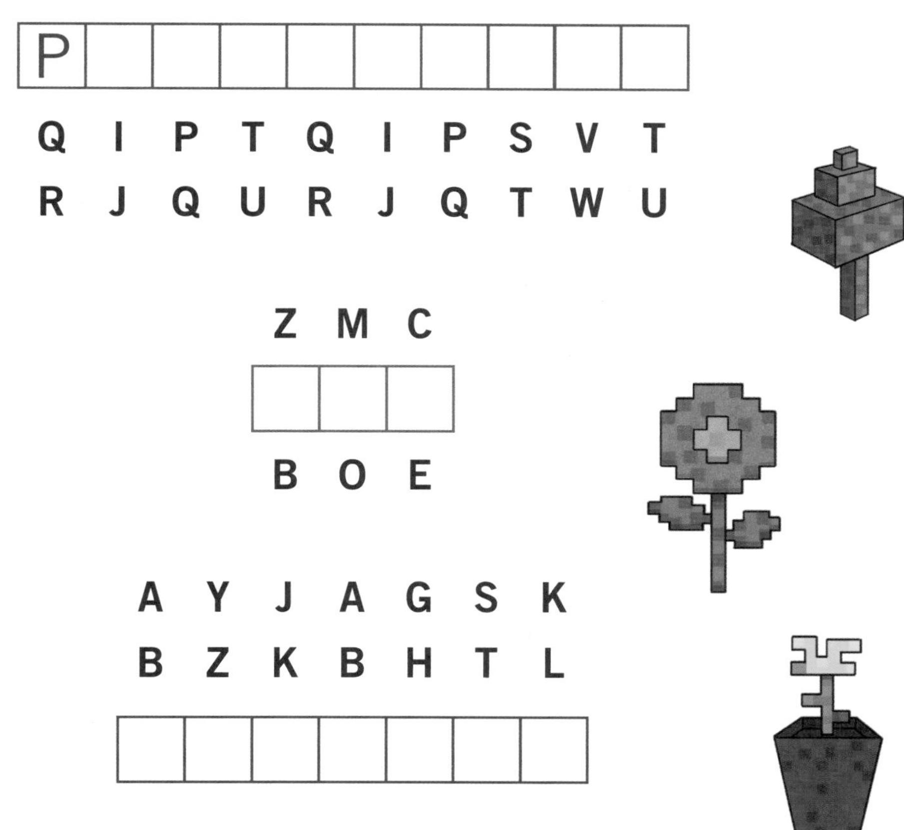

MYSTERY MOB

One mob on this page is real. The others are holograms. You must identify the one real mob from the clues below and circle it.

My first letter is in **PIGMAN**, but not in **ZOMBIE**

My second is in **FISH** and also in **WITHER**

My third is in **PARROT**, but not in **SPIDER**

My fourth is in **SHEEP**, but not **POLAR BEAR**

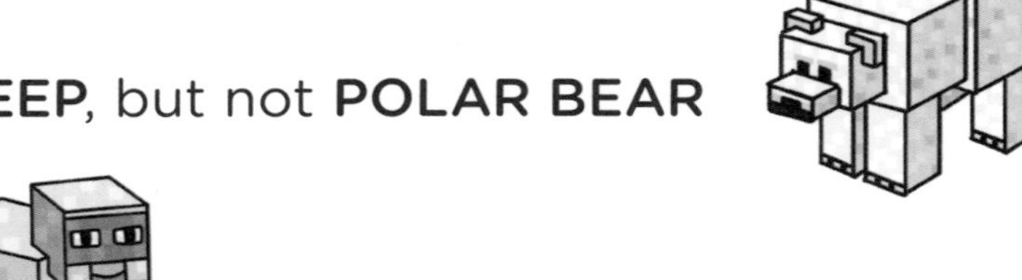

The fifth and fourth are next-door neighbors in the alphabet

NETHER FINDS

Find and circle names of ten things you can only collect or build if you visit The Nether. They might be forward, backward, up, down, or diagonal. Watch out! Every N has gone up in flames.

BLAZE ROD
GHAST TEARS
GLOWSTONE

MAGMA CREAM
NETHER BRICK

				🔥	B	L	A	Z	O	A	S				
				E	E	R	B	S	E	🔥	R				
				🔥	I	T	O	Z	G	E	A				
				O	C	U	H	L	F	T	E				
🔥	R	🔥	E	T	L	K	O	E	K	H	T	C	R	H	M
B	E	S	Z	S	A	🔥	T	C	R	E	T	A	E	A	K
T	L	T	A	W	G	E	B	E	M	R	S	R	G	S	C
G	F	🔥	H	O	H	T	L	B	S	B	A	M	T	O	I
H	D	E	S	L	A	C	A	S	R	R	H	C	O	U	R
A	A	Z	E	G	W	R	Z	W	T	I	G	🔥	K	L	B
🔥	🔥	C	E	E	M	E	E	T	S	C	E	🔥	W	S	R
🔥	E	T	H	E	R	B	R	I	C	K	F	E	🔥	C	E
R	W	T	A	R	L	A	O	O	U	S	A	T	W	O	H
O	E	W	H	U	T	M	D	W	E	T	I	H	R	S	T
🔥	L	O	O	E	M	A	E	R	C	A	M	G	A	M	E
D	G	S	S	S	R	T	O	T	🔥	I	S	A	🔥	D	🔥
				T	T	W	S	A	B	R	I				
				A	H	M	A	G	A	S	M				
				R	E	A	D	R	W	A	S				
				E	🔥	C	E	A	T	E	🔥				

NETHER BRICK FENCE
NETHER BRICK STAIRS

NETHER RACK
NETHER WART
SOUL SAND

WHO'S WHOSE ON THE FARM?

Use the clues to figure out which animal belongs to which player.

- BlockBuster's animal is facing left.
- Creeper Hunter's animal is dyed.
- iBuild's animal is not pink.
- Masterminer's animal carries a chest.

	CHICKEN	DONKEY	SHEEP	PIG
BlockBuster				
iBuild				
Creeper Hunter				
Masterminer				

PARTY SNACK PICK-UP

You are picking up snacks for a party. You need to collect four pumpkin pies, four cookies, and four melon slices.

You must pick up your first snack in the top row and your last snack in the bottom row, and you must pick them up in this order:

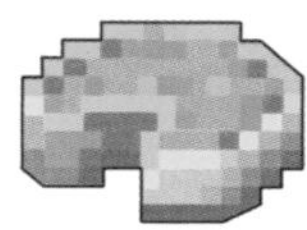 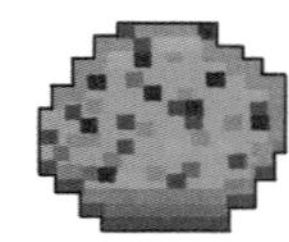 

Moving only up, down, left, and right, what path must you take?

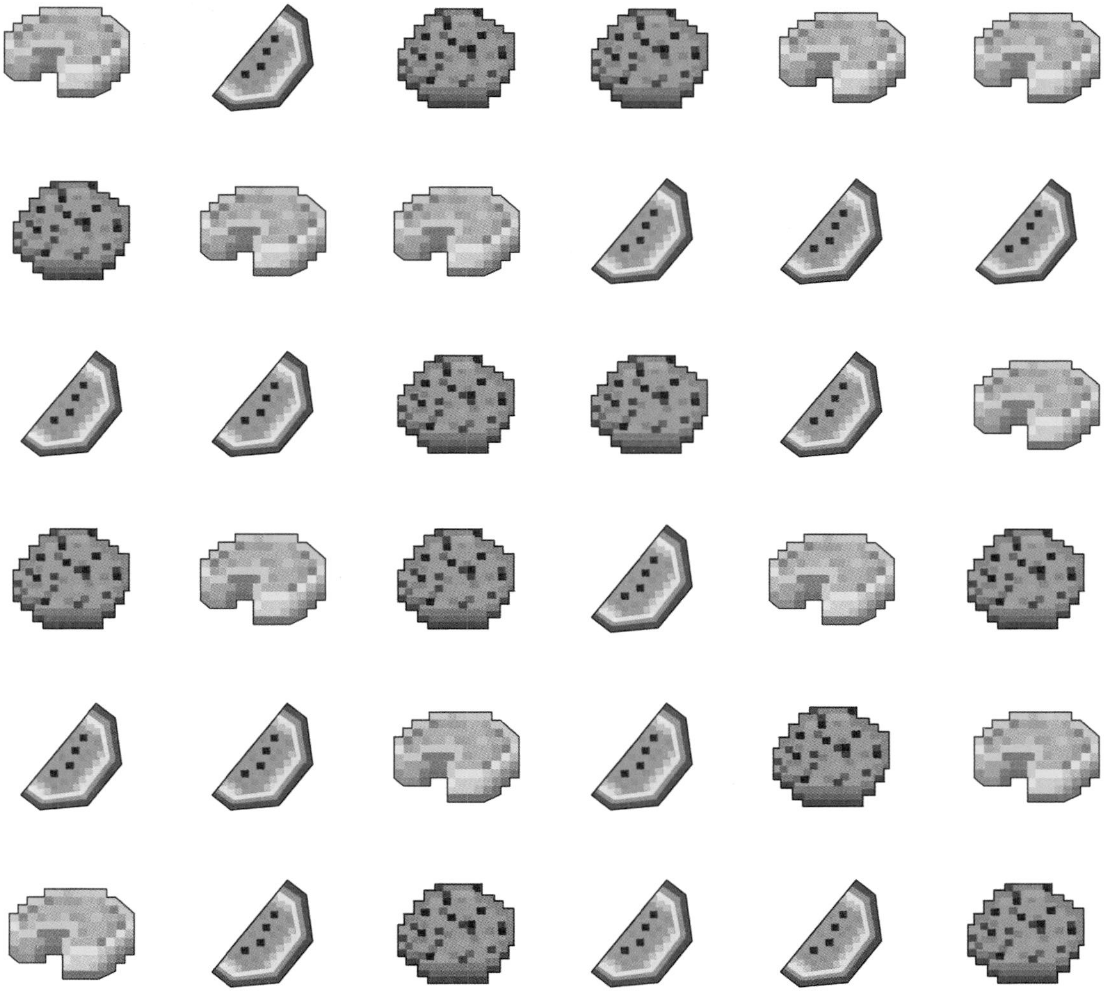

GET OUT!

Can you find your way out of this maze alive?

YOU CAN DRAW IT: SKELETON

Use the grid to copy the picture. Examine each small square in the top grid, then transfer those lines to the corresponding square on the bottom grid.

WISHING YOU GOOD . . .

Every word in Column B contains the same letters as a word in Column A, plus one letter. Draw a line between word "matches," then write the extra letter on the space provided. Unscramble the column of letters to reveal our wish for your Minecraft avatar—and for you, too. And your family. And friends. And pets. Well, you get the idea.

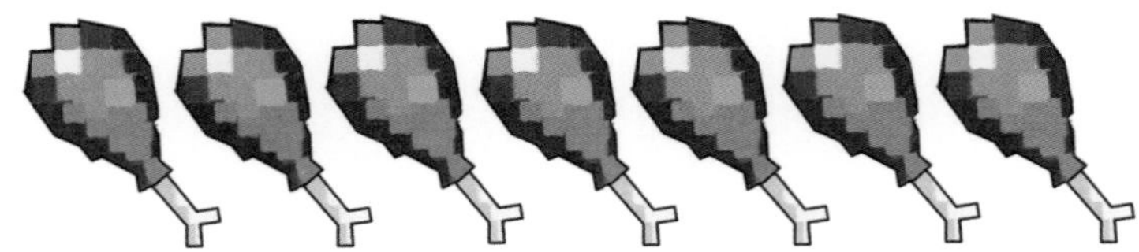

COLUMN A	COLUMN B	EXTRA LETTER
Term	**Ocean**	__
Dared	**Heart**	__
Rate	**Crash**	__
Once	**Death**	__
Scar	**Meter**	__
Head	**Ladder**	__

__ __ __ __ __ __

RARE DROP SCORES

Four Minecraft players scored rare drops today. Who collected what?

To find out, begin at the dot below each player's name and follow it downward. Every time you hit a horizontal line (one that goes across), you must take it. See where each player's path leads.

KIM MALIK TALIA CAMERON

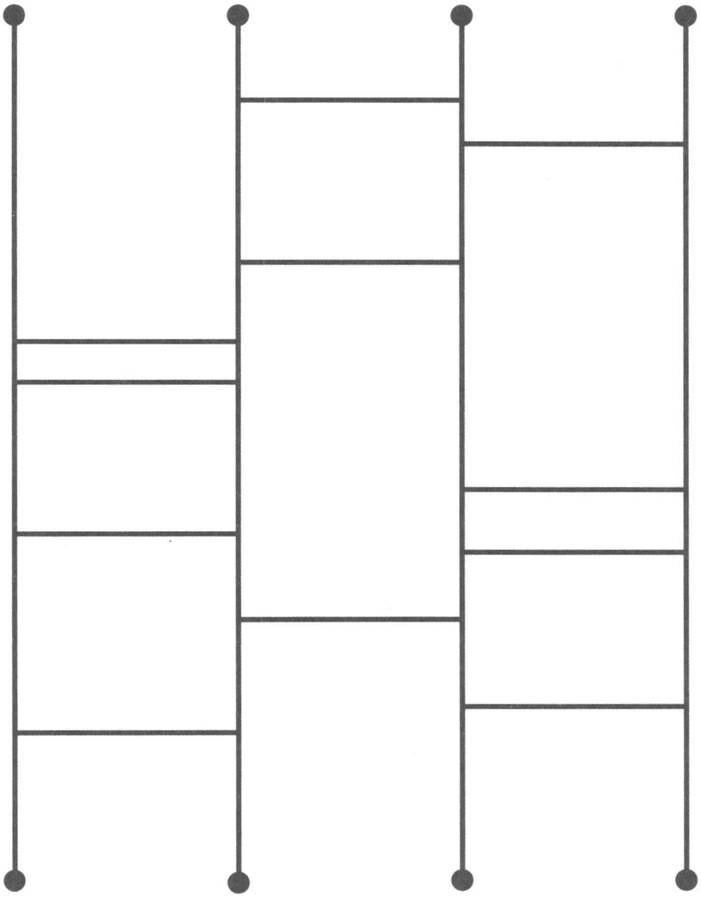

NETHER STAR ENDER PEARLS BLAZE ROD GHAST TEAR

LOST LIBRARY

Four players are racing to find a book of maps in the library in a woodland mansion. Follow each player's path, under and over crossing paths, to discover who finds the book that will save them all.

UNCOMMON COMMON FEATURE

In this crossword, you get to figure out where each word fits! Use the picture clues to guess the word answers, then see where each word fits best. If you fill in the puzzle correctly, you'll discover something uncommon that a few villagers have in common. Got that?

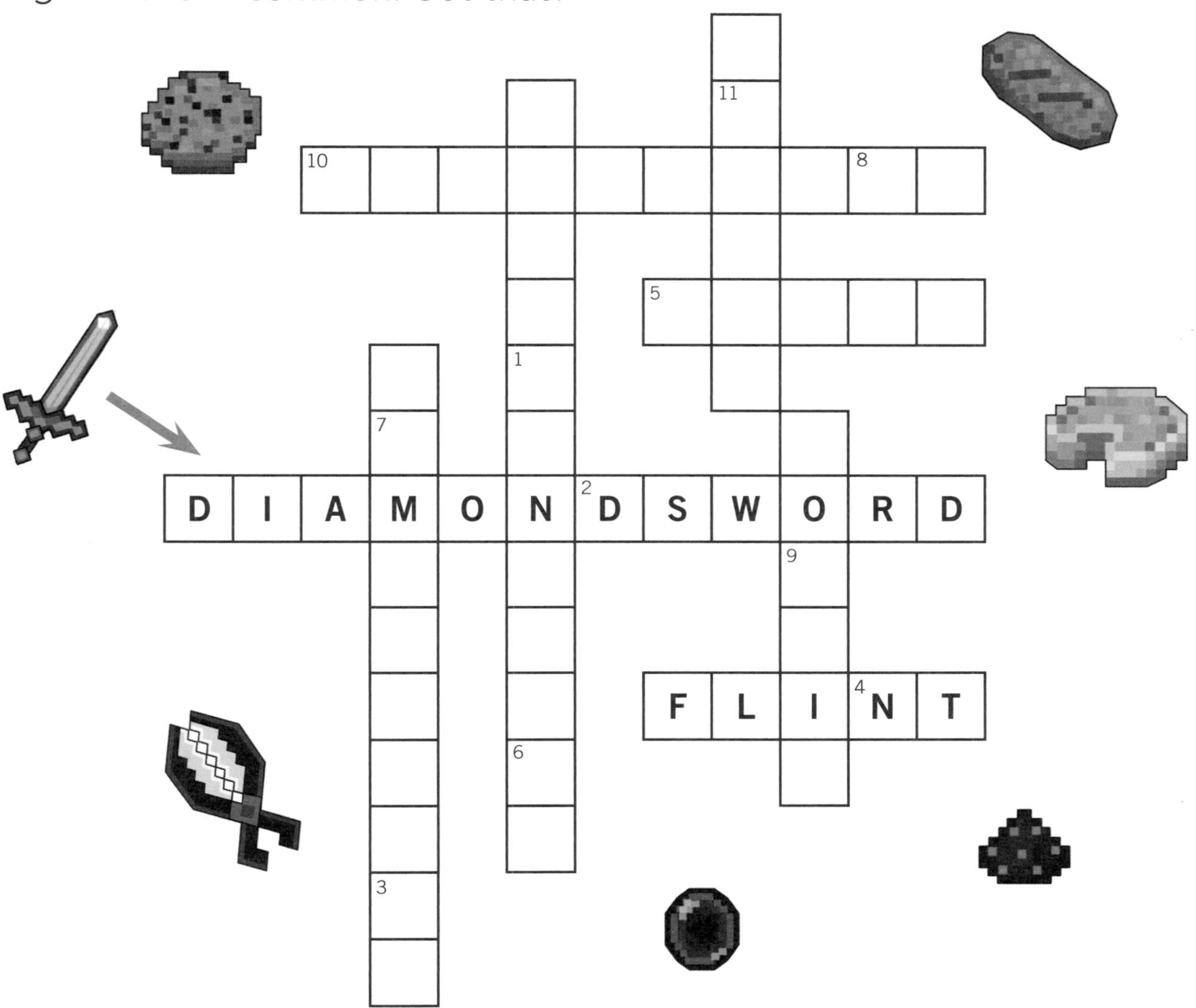

What do a librarian, priest, and nitwit have in common?

__ __ __ __ __ __   __ __ __ __ __   __ __
7 4 7 6 10 2   11 9 9 2 6   9 4

__ __ __ __ __   __ __ __ __ __
1 11 10 3 8   8 9 5 10 6

ALEX SAYS: DID YOU KNOW THIS ABOUT ZOMBIES?

If you have ever played the game Simon Says, then you know how this game works: follow only the directions that begin with "Alex says" to reveal a tip about zombies.

	1	2	3	4	5
A	WHO	IF	HOW	ZOMBIES	THROW
B	FIND	ARMOR	SWORDS	FOUR	THEY
C	ALLOW	THIRTY-ONE	FIVE	CAN	WEAR
D	TRIDENT	IT	BOWS	RUN	NOW

1. **Alex says**, "Cross off words that are numbers."
2. **Alex says**, "Cross off words that rhyme with *cow* or *moo*."
3. Cross off all nouns (people, places, things).
4. **Alex says**, "Cross off verbs (action words) in rows A and D."
5. **Alex says**, "Cross off Minecraft weapons in columns 1 and 3."
6. **Alex says**, "Read the remaining words to reveal something you should know about zombies."

Secret tip: ____

____

WHEEL OF FORTUNE #2

Start at the ▼. Write every third letter on the spaces to reveal a fortune you want to claim.

_ _ _ _ _ _ _   _ _   _ _ _ _ _ _

_ _ _ _ _ _ _ _ _

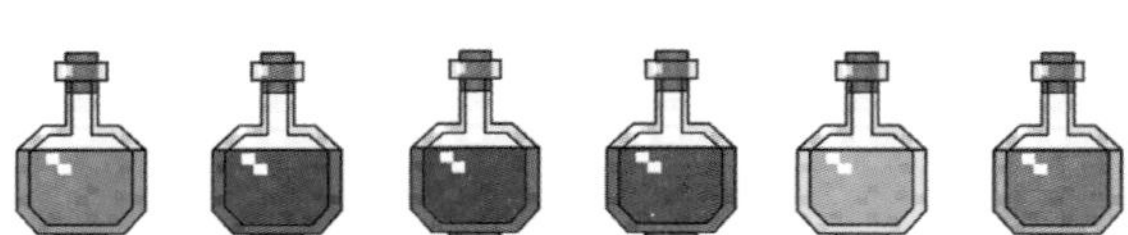

SADDLE SEARCH

Can you find the saddle? It appears spelled correctly only once in a horizontal, vertical, or diagonal line.

E S A D D E L A E S

L D L S A S E D L A

D S E A E S D A D D

D A L D D A L E D E

S L D S S E L S D L

A A D L D D A D A S

S L A D A S L D S D

D S S S D A D S L A

E L D A S L S D A S

E D D A E S A D D L

MEMO FROM MIRROR

Circle letters on the top half of the grid that have correct mirror images on the bottom half. Write the circled letters in order on the spaces to reveal a helpful tip.

W H E D O N O R U T S L V E B C E P O N

A B E O J D I N M T S Z H E N L A E T H

E R I K T W I L E L E X K P L Y O D E G

E ꓤ I ⅄ ⊥ W I Γ Ⅎ Γ E X X Ь Γ ⊥ O D E D

∀ B E Ǿ Ь D I И W ⊥ Z И H E И I Λ E ⊥ H

M ∀ ⊥ D O И O Ь И ⊥ ƨ Γ ∀ E Ь D E Ь O И

_ _   _ _ _   _ _ _ _ _ _   _ _   _   _ _ _

_ _   _ _ _   _ _ _ _ _ _.

_ _   _ _ _ _   _ _ _ _ _ _ _.

SQUARED UP: LET THERE BE LIGHT

Each of the four light sources in this puzzle can appear only once in each row, column, and the four inside boxes. Can you fill each empty box below with the correct letter?

B = BEACON

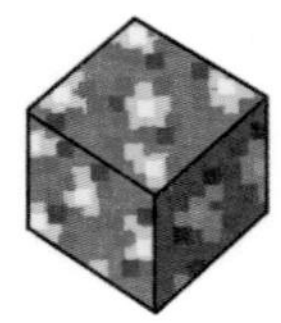

G = GLOWSTONE

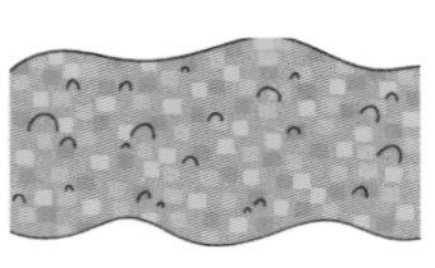

L = LAVA

T = TORCH

B			L
	T	G	
	L	B	
T			G

COOKIE FEAST

It's an all-you-can-eat cookie maze! Your job is to eat every single cookie. To do this, draw a line from Start to Stop that passes through every cookie once. Your line can go up, down, left, or right but not diagonally. On your mark, get set, munch!

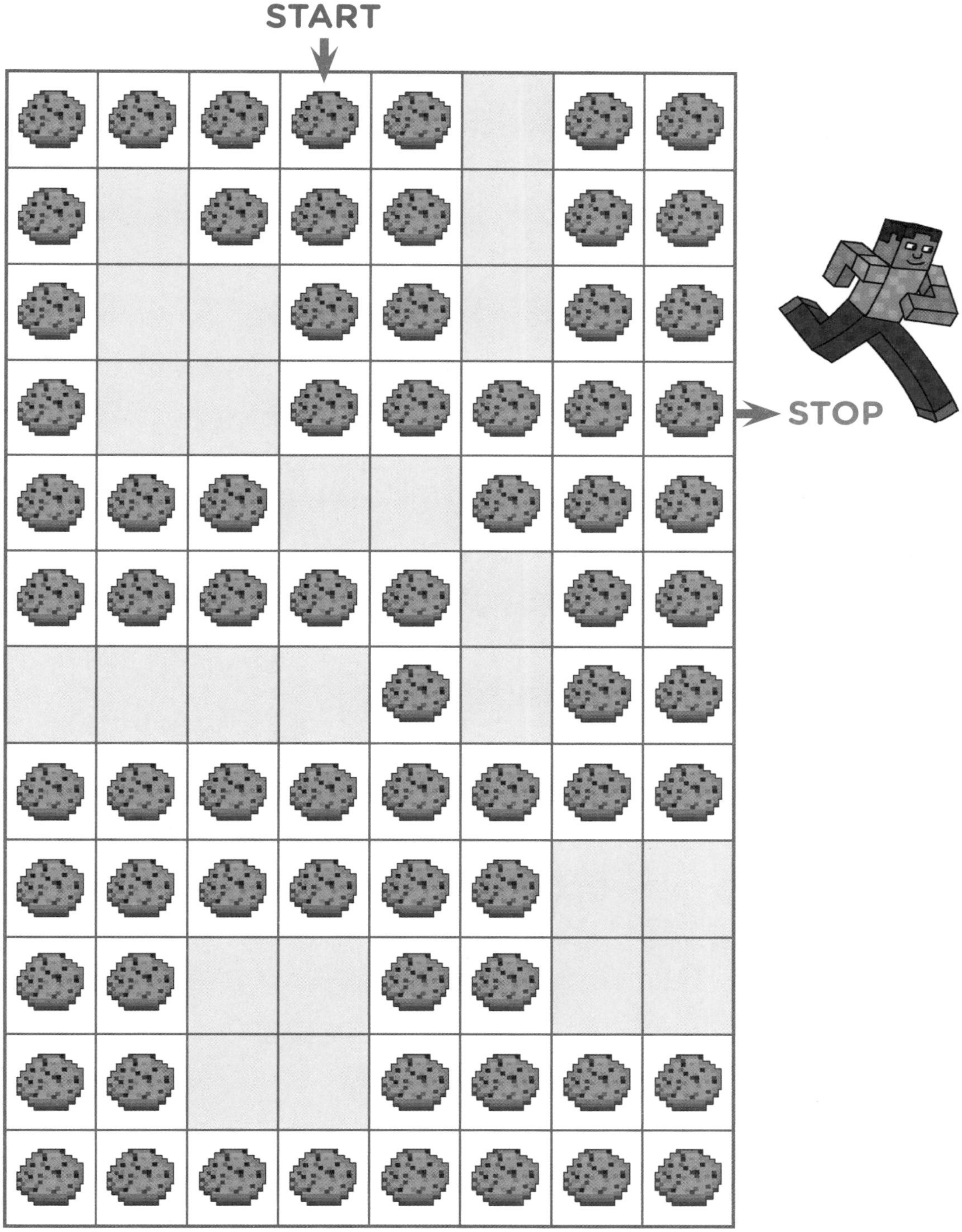

START

STOP

YOU CAN DRAW IT: WITCH

Use the grid to copy the picture. Examine each small square in the top grid, then transfer those lines to the corresponding square on the bottom grid.

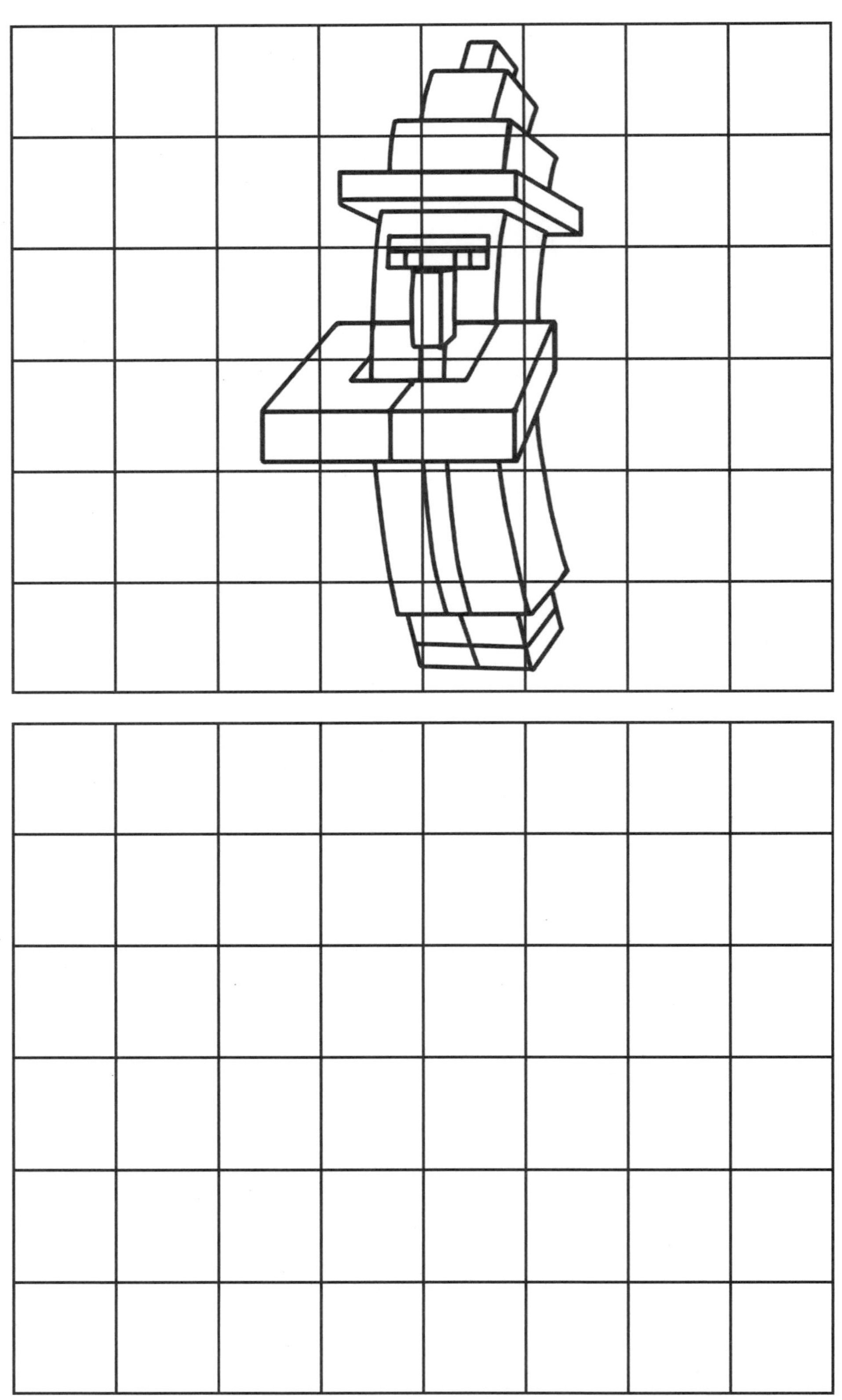

ENCHANTED BOOK

This book is enchanted. To open it and use it, you must press all nine buttons just once, in the correct order.

Follow the directions on the buttons. For instance, 2D means you must move your finger two buttons down. R=right, L=left, U=up. To open the book, you must land on the F button last.

Which button do you have to press first to land on the F button last?

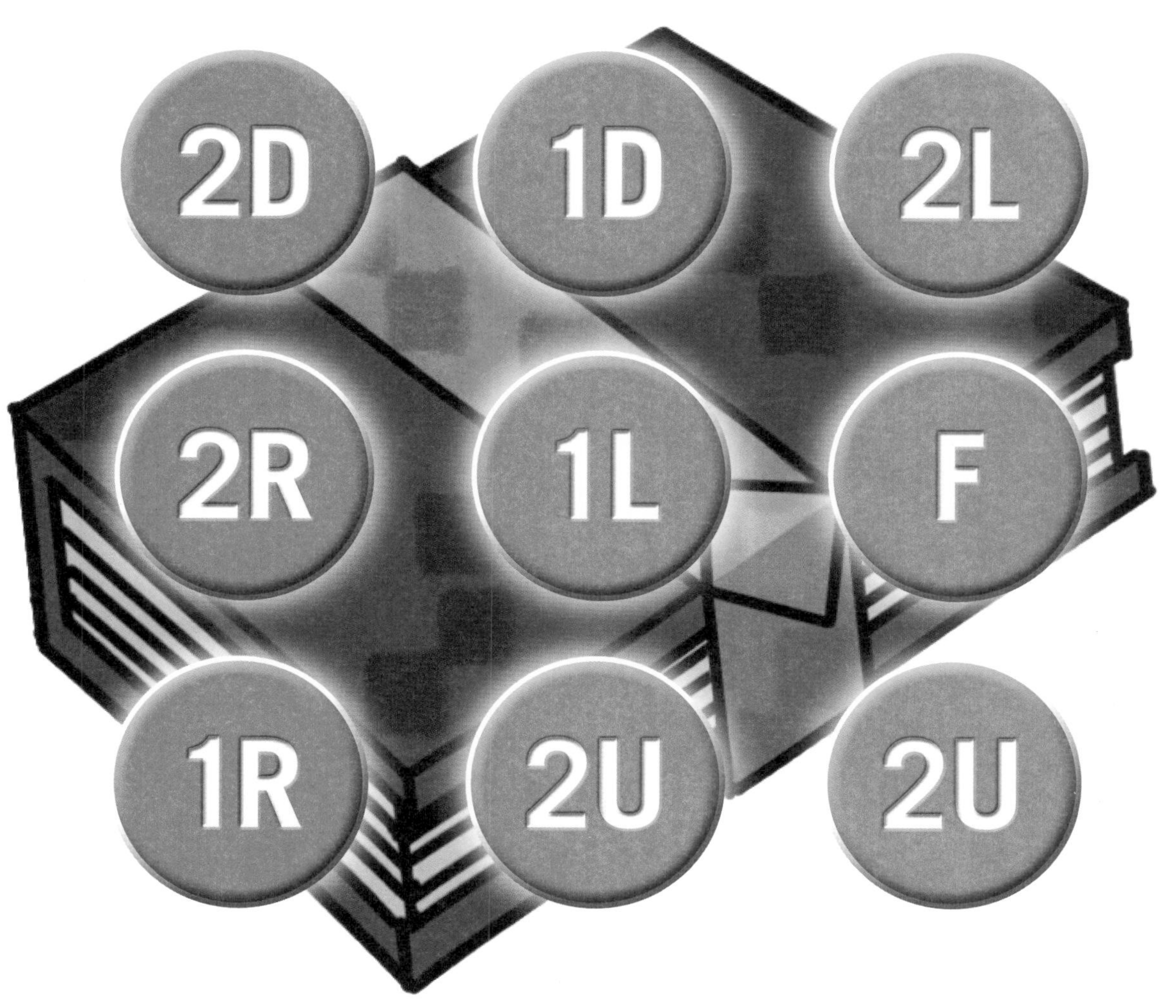

LONG LAUGH

The answer is written below. Read it.

Hint: *It helps to hold the page at eye level and shut one eye.*

What did the skeleton bring to the mob potluck picnic?

GETTIN' CRAFTY

Find and circle the names of nine things you craft in Minecraft. They might be forward, backward, up, down, or diagonal. Write unused letters on the spaces, in order from top to bottom and left to right, to reveal a tenth thing you can craft.

Hint: *Circle individual letters instead of the whole word at once. The first one has been done for you.*

BANNER	COOKIE	SHIELD
BEACON	HELMET	~~SHOVEL~~
BUCKET	LADDER	STRING

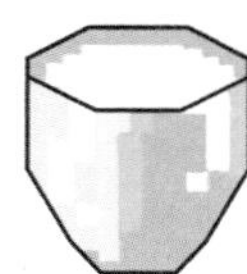

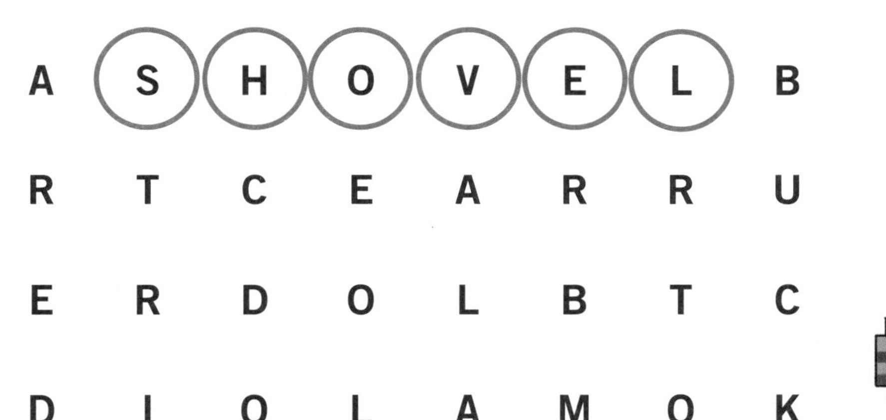

A	S	H	O	V	E	L	B
R	T	C	E	A	R	R	U
E	R	D	O	L	B	T	C
D	I	O	L	A	M	O	K
D	N	N	N	E	O	E	E
A	G	N	A	K	I	S	T
L	E	T	I	I	C	H	K
R	B	E	A	C	O	N	S

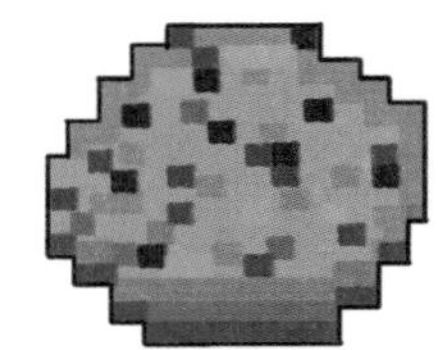

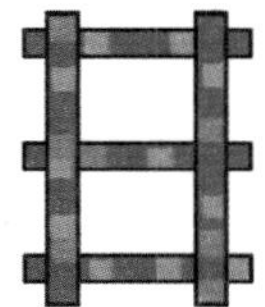

_ _ _ _ _ _ _ _ _ _ _ _ _ _ _ _

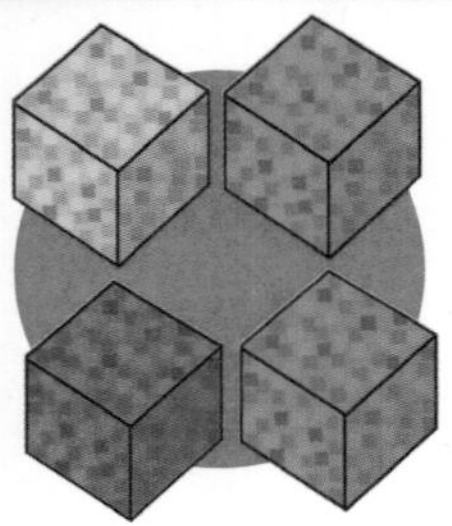

TRUE OR FALSE?

Find your way through this maze from Start to Finish. It will be easier if you answer the questions correctly.

START

True

A parrot will die if you feed it a cookie.

False

True

False

You cannot open a chest with an anvil on it.

True

False

Villagers can see invisible players.

True

Endermen can drop whole melons instead of slices.

False

STOP

GO WITH THE FLOW CHART

Follow the instructions in the flow chart to reveal one of the most exciting things you can build in Minecraft. Do you know how to build this?

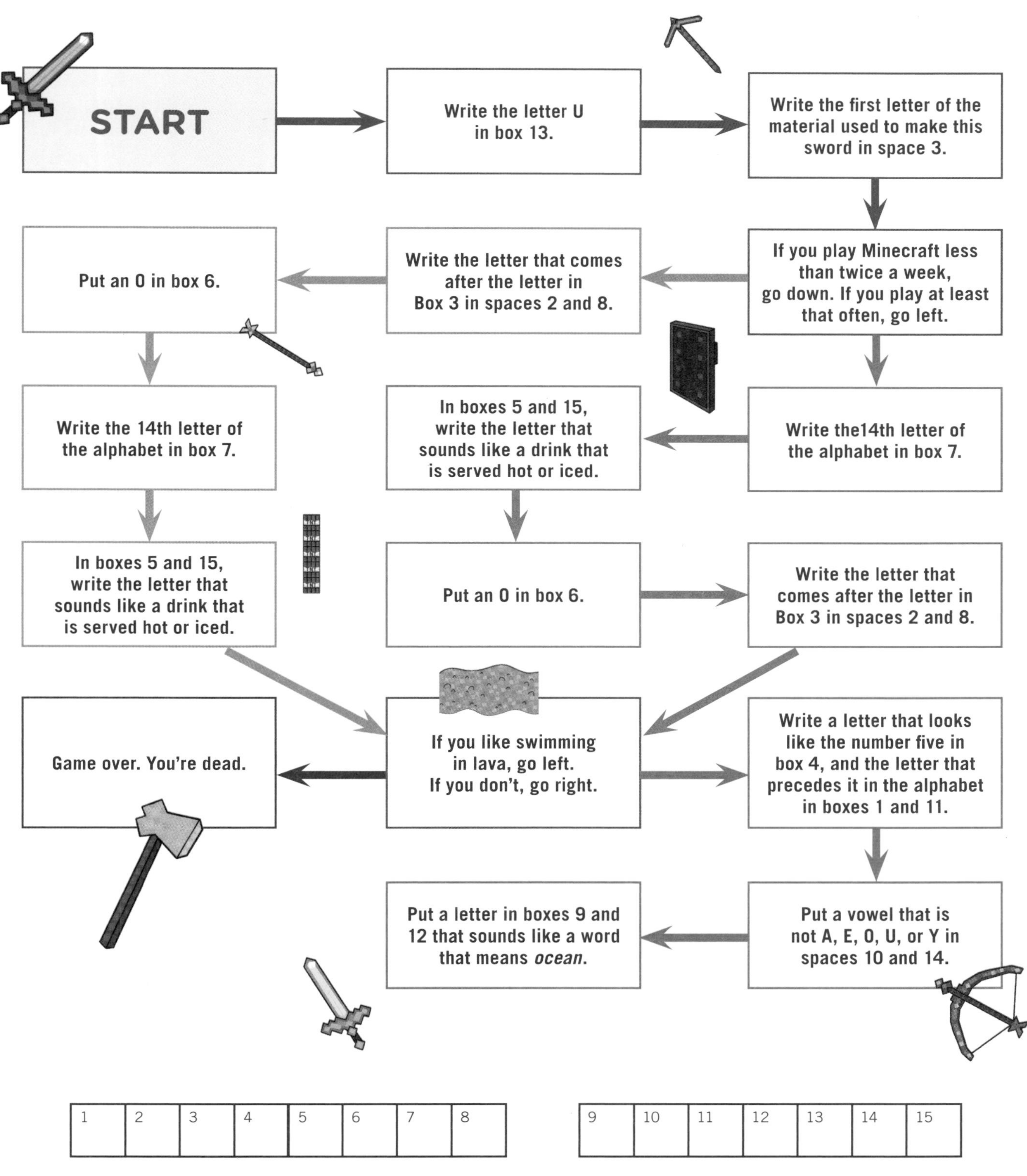

INSIDE INFO

Use the key to reveal a fun feature in Minecraft. Then use the key to decipher what you might call this feature.

A	B	C	D	E	G	H	I	K	L	M	N	O	P	R	S	T	W

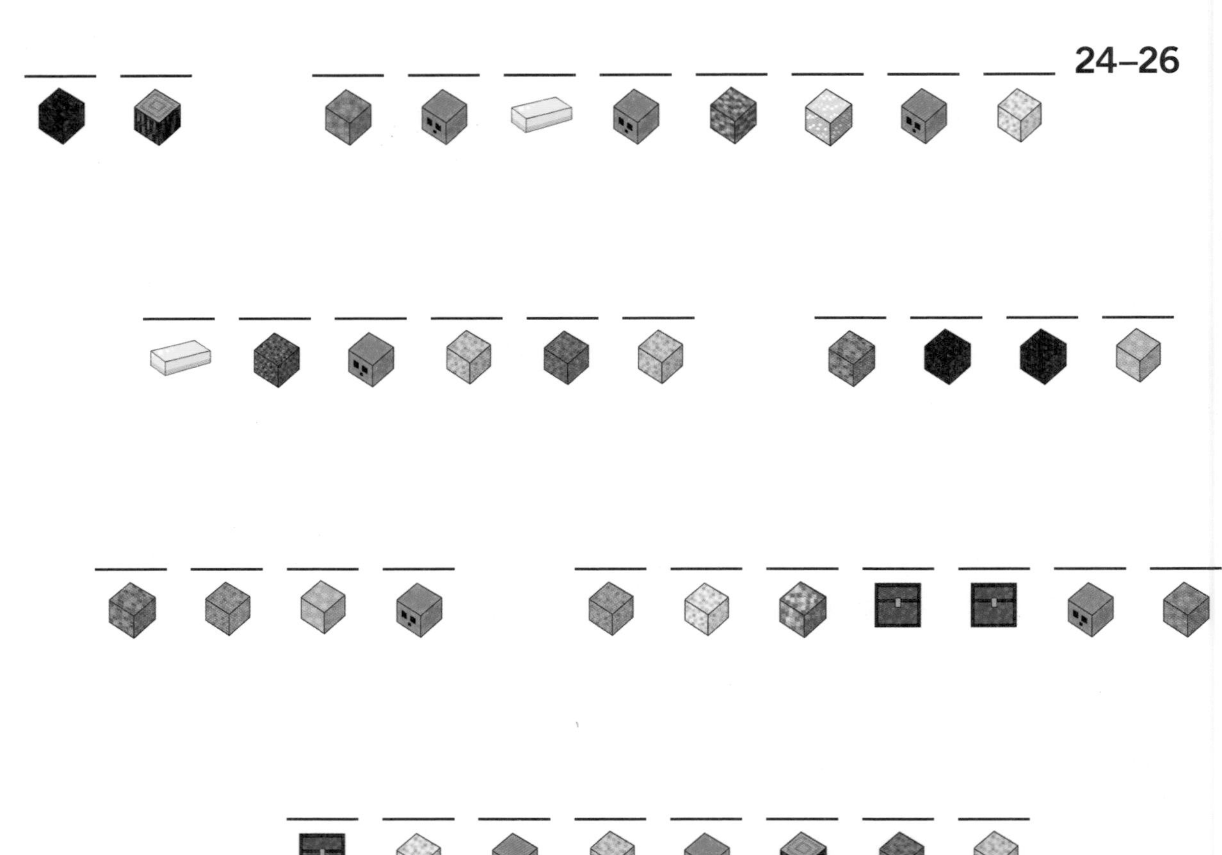

CREEPER DESTROYERS

Each of the five players below destroyed a different number of creepers (with five being the maximum). The numbers in the circles give you a hint. They show how many creepers were killed by both players whose squares touch the number. Use your addition facts to figure out how many creepers each player destroyed.

Hint: *Do Xavier last!*

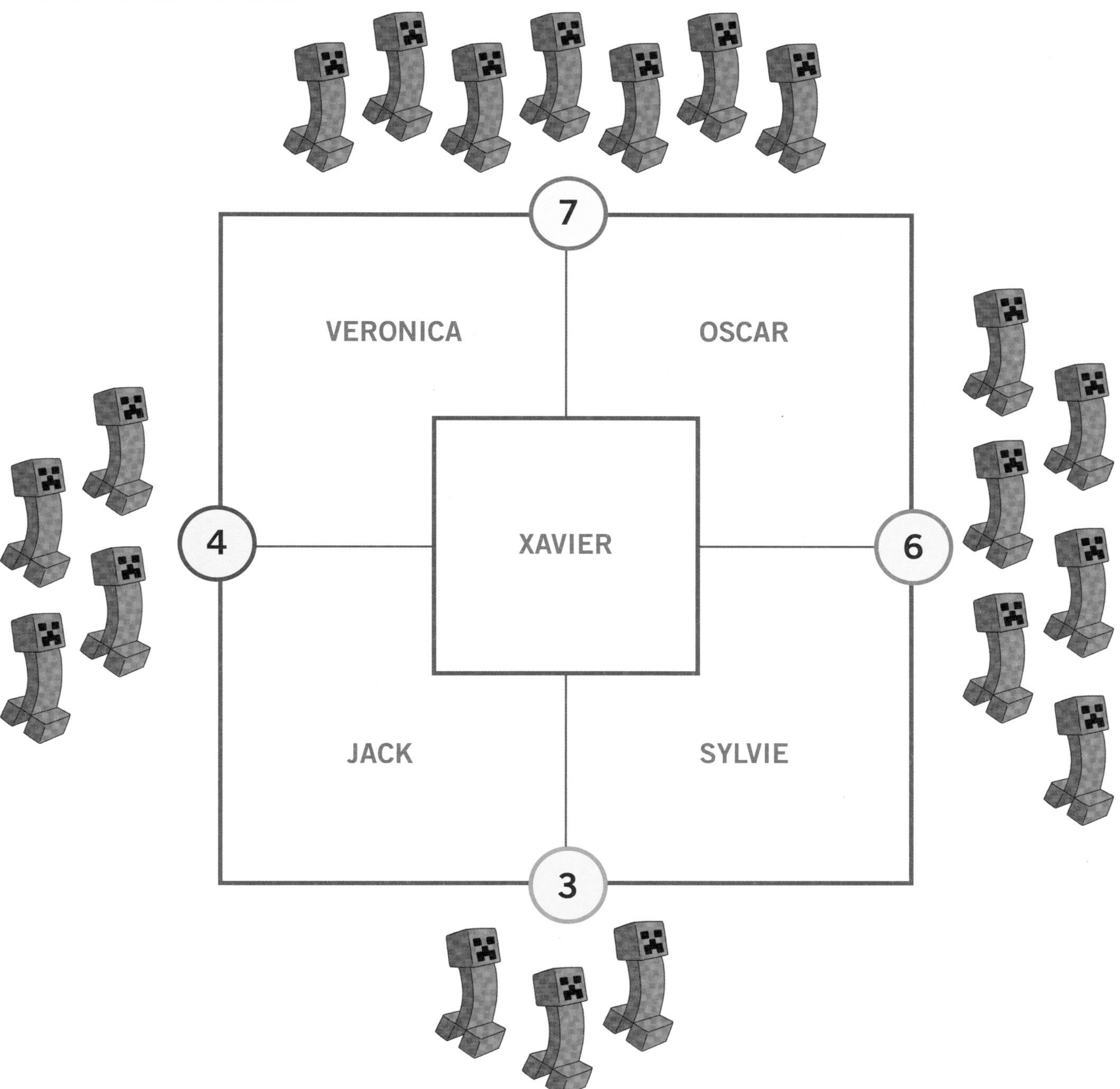

WHOOPS!

The answers to the clues use each letter in the letter box. Write the answers to the clues on the numbered spaces Then transfer the letters to the boxes with the same numbers. If you fill in the boxes correctly, you'll reveal the answer to the joke.

A A E N N P R S S T T

Clue	Spaces
Material that hangs below a basketball hoop	_ _ _ (3 2 4)
Resting sessions for babies	_ _ _ _ (5 6 7 8)
A glowing ball of gas visible in the sky at night	_ _ _ _ (9 10 11 12)

What did Alex get when she accidentally splashed her mom and dad with a Potion of Invisibility?

10	12	6	5	8	7	11	12	2	3	4	9

WHAT'S FOR DINNER?

Use the clues to figure out what each player eats to restore saturation and hunger levels.

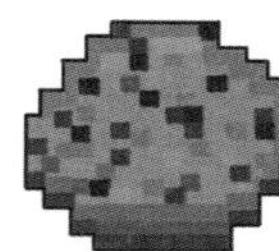

YUM!

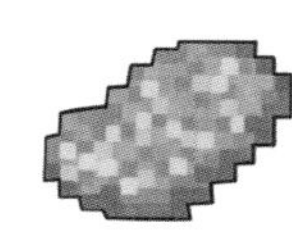

- A zombie dropped Enderslayer's dinner.
- Of these four players, 4321Blastoff gets the most hunger points from her meal.
- Neither Emperor Nethero nor 4321Blastoff ate something yellow; either Enderslayer or Call me Fishmale ate something orange.

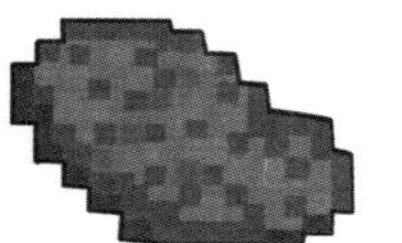

- Call me Fishmale's dinner is not grown as a crop, but Enderslayer's is.
- Either Emperor Nethero or Call me Fishmale caught his dinner while fishing.

YUM!

	ROTTEN FLESH	PUFFERFISH	POTATO	CARROT
Emperor Nethero				
Call me Fishmale				
Enderslayer				
4321Blastoff				

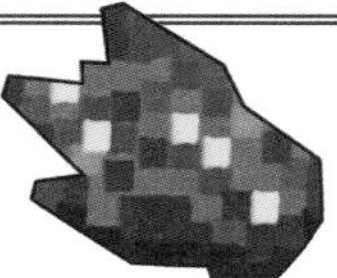

SCORE MORE ORE

It's a mining bonanza! To find your way through this maze, pick up six blocks each of iron ore, lapis lazuli, and redstone.

You must pick up your first block in the top row and your last block in the bottom row, and you must pick them up in this order:

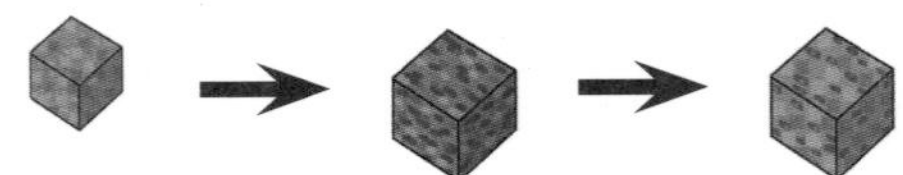

Moving only up, down, left, and right, what path must you take?

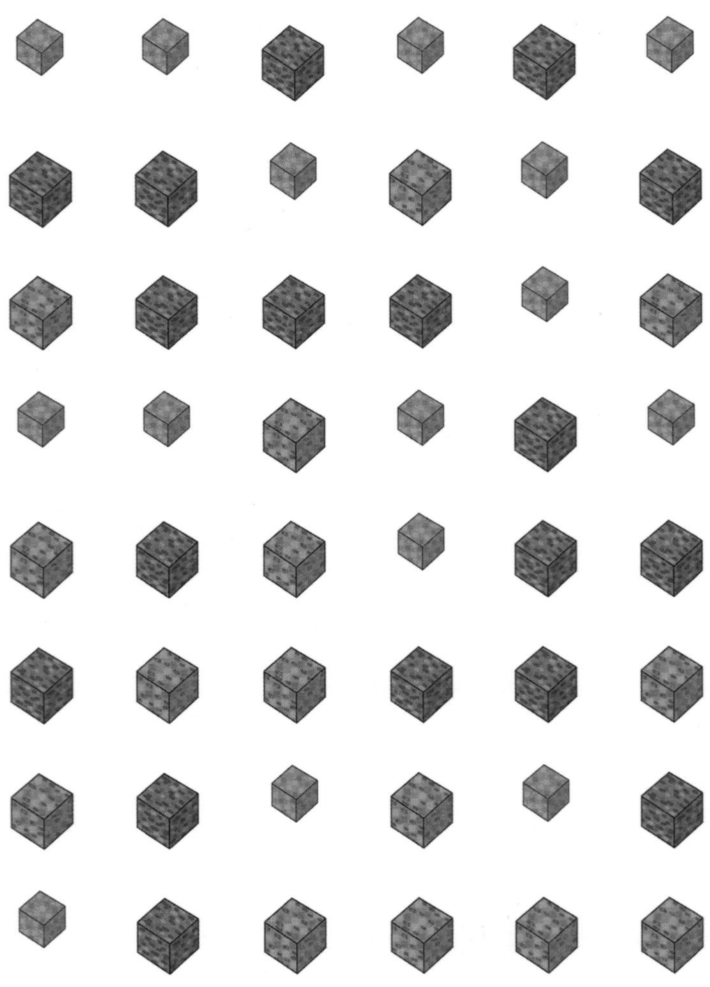

TRADING JO[S]

Four Minecraft players, who all go by "Jo," are trading with villagers. Who is trading with whom?

To find out, begin at the dot below each player's name and follow it downward. Every time you hit a horizontal line (one that goes across), you must take it. See where each player's path leads.

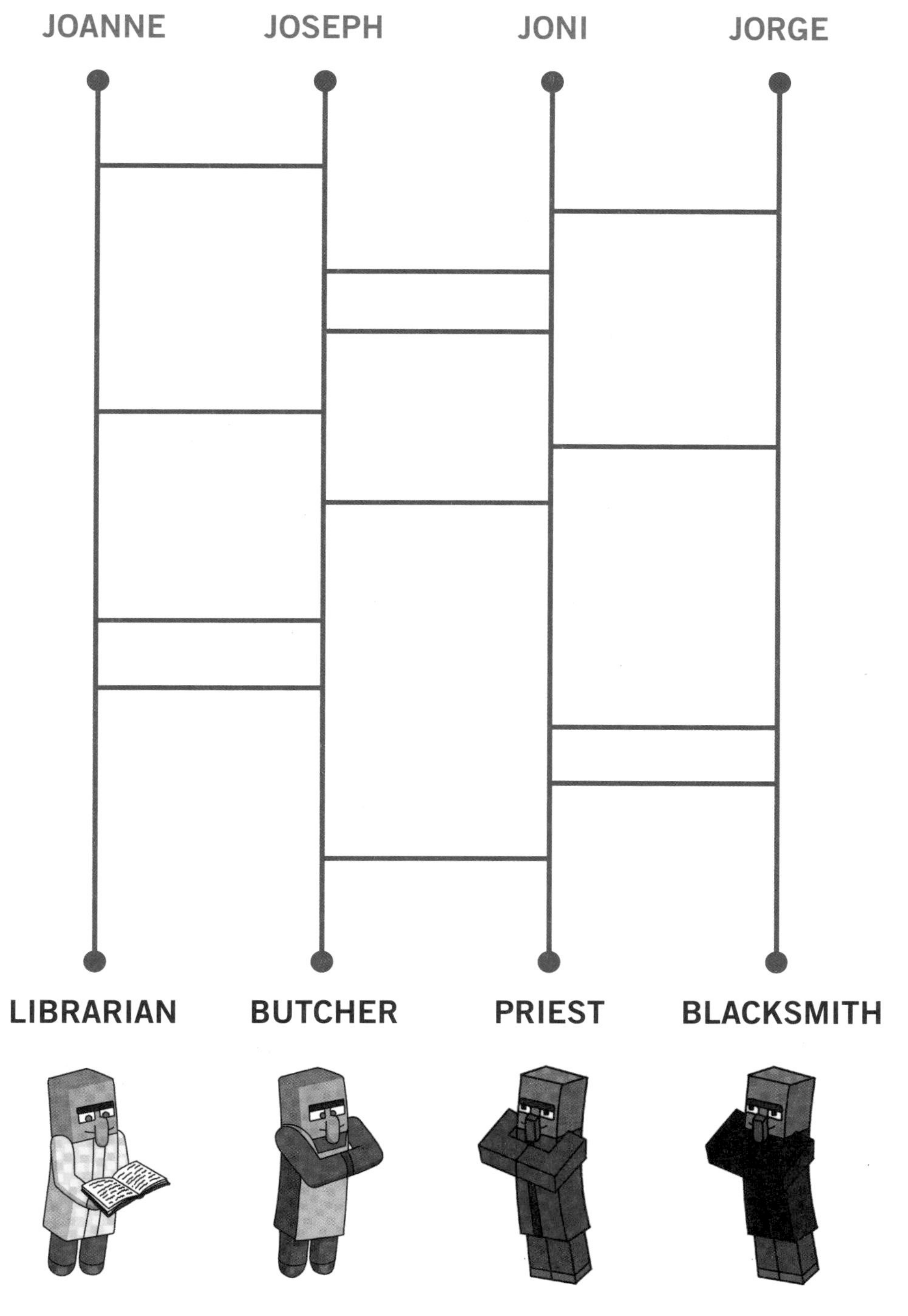

THE LOCKED DOOR

Four players are racing to find the end portal that works. Follow each player's path, under and over crossing paths, to the portal they encounter, then follow the path from there to see whose portal leads to the Ender dragon.

ZOMBIE FRIENDS

In this crossword, you get to figure out where each word fits! Use the picture clues to guess the word answers, then see where each word fits best. If you fill in the puzzle correctly, you'll discover the answer to the joke.

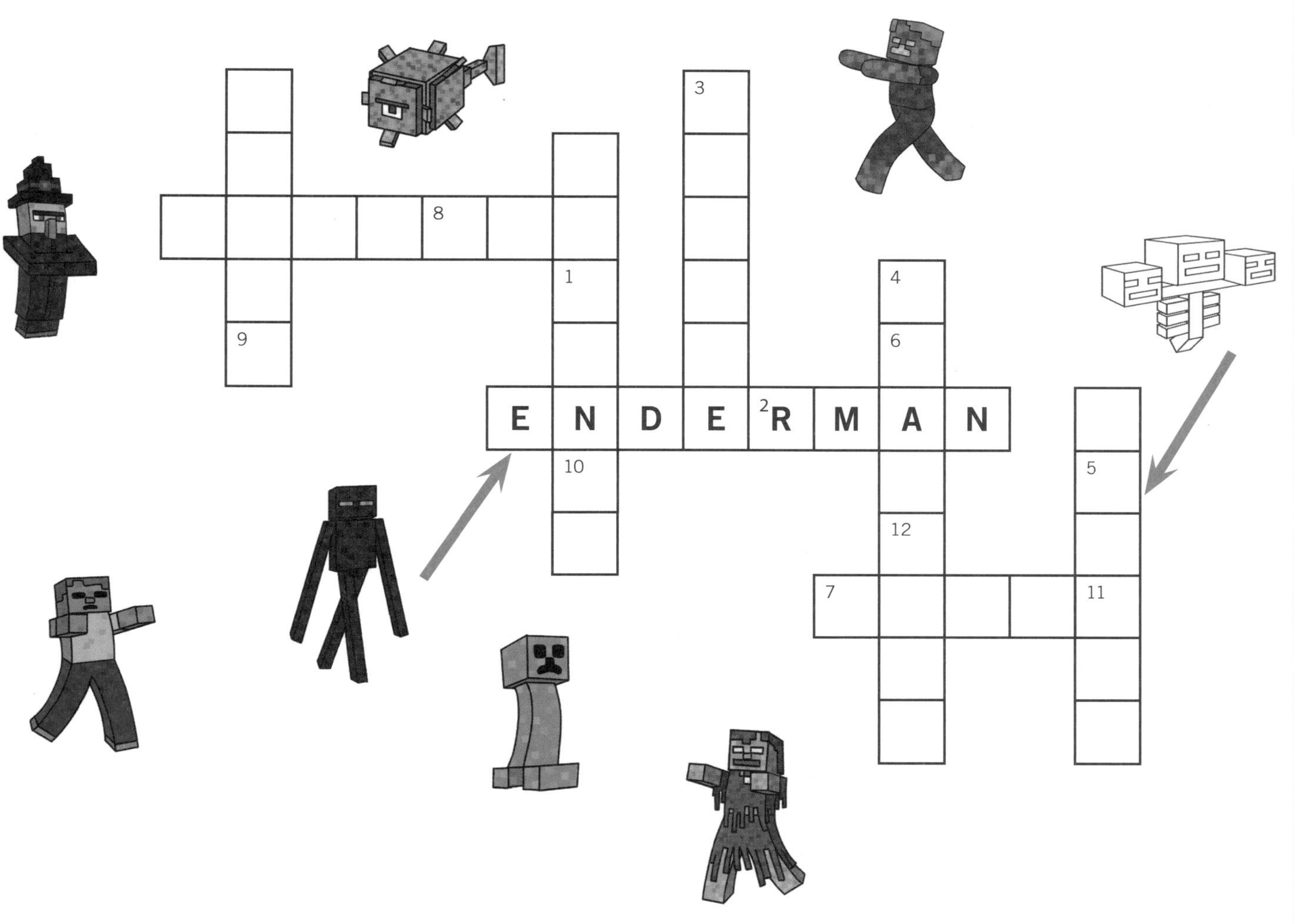

What did the zombie's friends say when he introduced his girlfriend?

___ ___ ___ ___ , ___ ___ ___ ___ ___ ___ ___ ___ ___ ___ ___
4 10 10 3 , 7 11 10 2 10 12 5 12 9 1 6

___ ___ ___ ___ ___ ___ ___ ___ ?
12 5 4 11 10 2 6 8 ?

ALEX SAYS: OWN YOUR MINE BUSINESS

If you have ever played the game Simon Says, then you know how this game works: follow only the directions that begin with "Alex says" to reveal a mining tip.

	1	2	3	4	5
A	A	SPIDER EYE	CAKE	SPOT	LOCATE
B	UNDER	FIND	GLASS BOTTLE	DISCOVER	DIAMONDS
C	DEEP	ACHE	IN	LAYER	STEAK
D	AND	TWELVE	OF	REDSTONE DUST	AGAIN

1. **Alex says**, "Cross off words that begin with vowels in column 1 and row D."
2. Cross off words that have two of the same letter.
3. **Alex says**, "Cross off items that are commonly dropped by witches."
4. **Alex says**, "Cross off words that mean *find* in columns four and five."
5. **Alex says**, "Cross off words that rhyme with *break*."
6. **Alex says**, "Read the remaining words to reveal a mining tip."

Mining tip: ___________________________________

____

WHEEL OF FORTUNE #3

Start at the ▼.
Write every third letter on the spaces to reveal a treasure you want to claim.

HIDDEN ARMOR

Can you find the phrase "horse armor"? It appears spelled correctly only once in a horizontal, vertical, or diagonal line.

M	R	H	O	R	S	E	A	R	M	O	H
A	O	O	R	M	R	A	S	R	O	H	S
H	O	R	S	E	A	R	M	R	O	A	E
O	E	S	S	R	O	M	S	R	O	H	O
R	H	E	A	E	R	E	S	A	S	M	M
S	R	O	M	R	A	E	S	R	O	H	R
E	S	A	O	H	A	R	M	A	O	O	A
A	E	R	E	R	O	M	E	R	S	M	E
R	O	M	M	H	S	S	S	M	A	E	S
R	H	O	A	E	R	E	S	R	O	H	R
O	O	R	R	O	M	R	A	E	S	R	O
R	A	M	H	R	A	E	S	R	O	H	H

REFLECTIONS IN THE WATER

Circle letters on the bottom half of the grid that have correct mirror images in the top half. Write the circled letters in order on the spaces to reveal a weapon tip.

R O W P N T R I I D E N C T B A K C K L E S

M E N T B C K R I N G S S S Y O U E A R T H

S A H I L O P Y A L T W R Y E N C H E A N T

Z A V T L O R Y A L T M K Y E N C H B A N T

M E N T B G X R I N G S N N Y O U D B R T H

R O W L N T R I J D E N O T B A X C K I B Z

_ _______ _____________

______ ____

______ _______ ____

SQUARED UP: LOGICAL LOOT

Each loot item below is found just once in each column, each row, and each of the four inner boxes. B represents bone, R represents rotten flesh, and so on. Can you fill every empty square with the right letter?

B = BONE

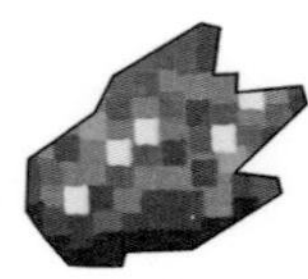

R = ROTTEN FLESH

S = STICK

W = WATER BOTTLE

	B		W
R			
			S
W		B	

FLOWERS TO DYE FOR

Your job is to make the most dye possible. That means collecting every flower in this maze. To do this, draw a line from Start to Stop that passes through every flower once. Your line can go up, down, left, or right but not diagonally. On your mark, get set, gather!

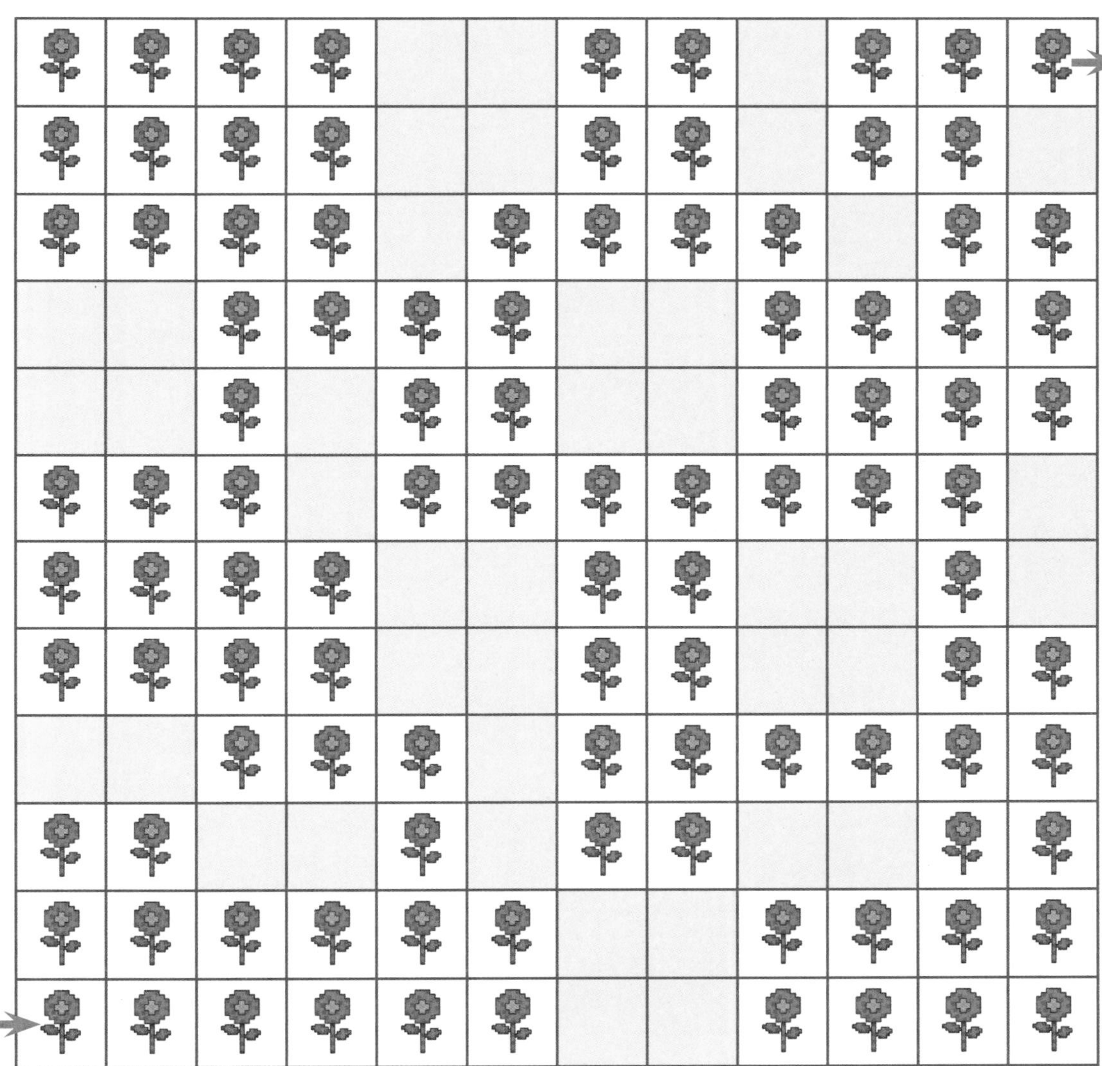

SHIP SHAPE

Boxes connected by lines contain the same letter. Some letters are given; others have to be guessed. Fill in all the boxes to reveal some of the cool things about the Update Aquatic. Then transfer the letters in the numbered boxes to the spaces with the same numbers to reveal the answer to the joke.

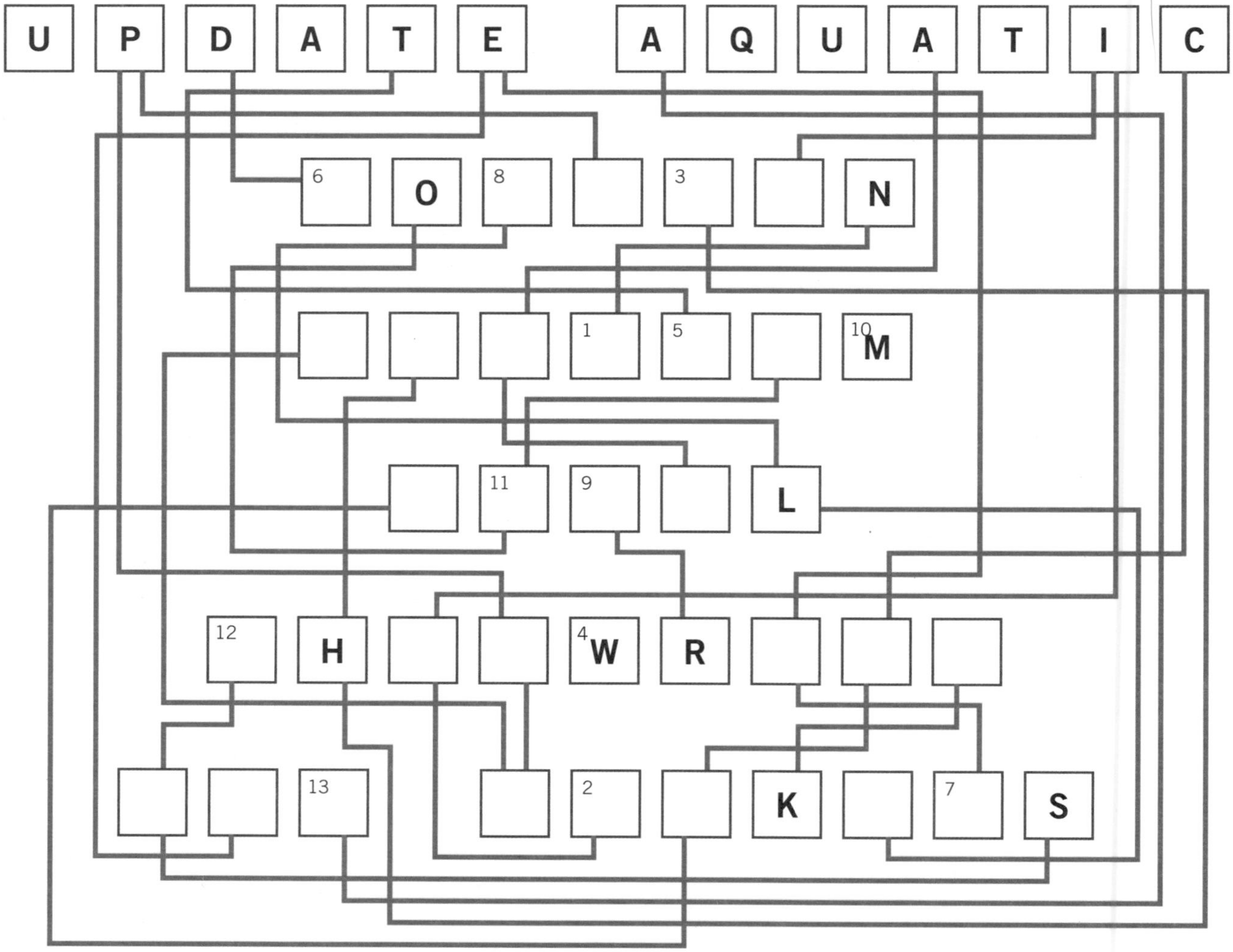

U P D A T E A Q U A T I C

6 | O | 8 | | 3 | | N

| | | 1 | 5 | | 10 M

| 11 | 9 | | L

12 | H | | | 4 W | R | | |

| | 13 | | 2 | | K | | 7 | S

What happened in the wreck between the red ship and the blue ship?

__ __ __   __ __ __ __ __ __ __
5 3 7   12 13 2 8 11 9 12

__ __ __ __   __ __ __ __ __ __ __ __
4 7 9 7   10 13 9 11 11 1 7 6

ENCHANTED TRAP DOOR

This trap door is enchanted. To open it, you must press all twelve buttons just once, in the correct order.

Follow the directions on the buttons. For instance, 2D means you must move your finger two buttons down. R=right, L=left, U=up. To open the trap door, you must land on the F button last.

Which button do you have to press first to land on the F button last?

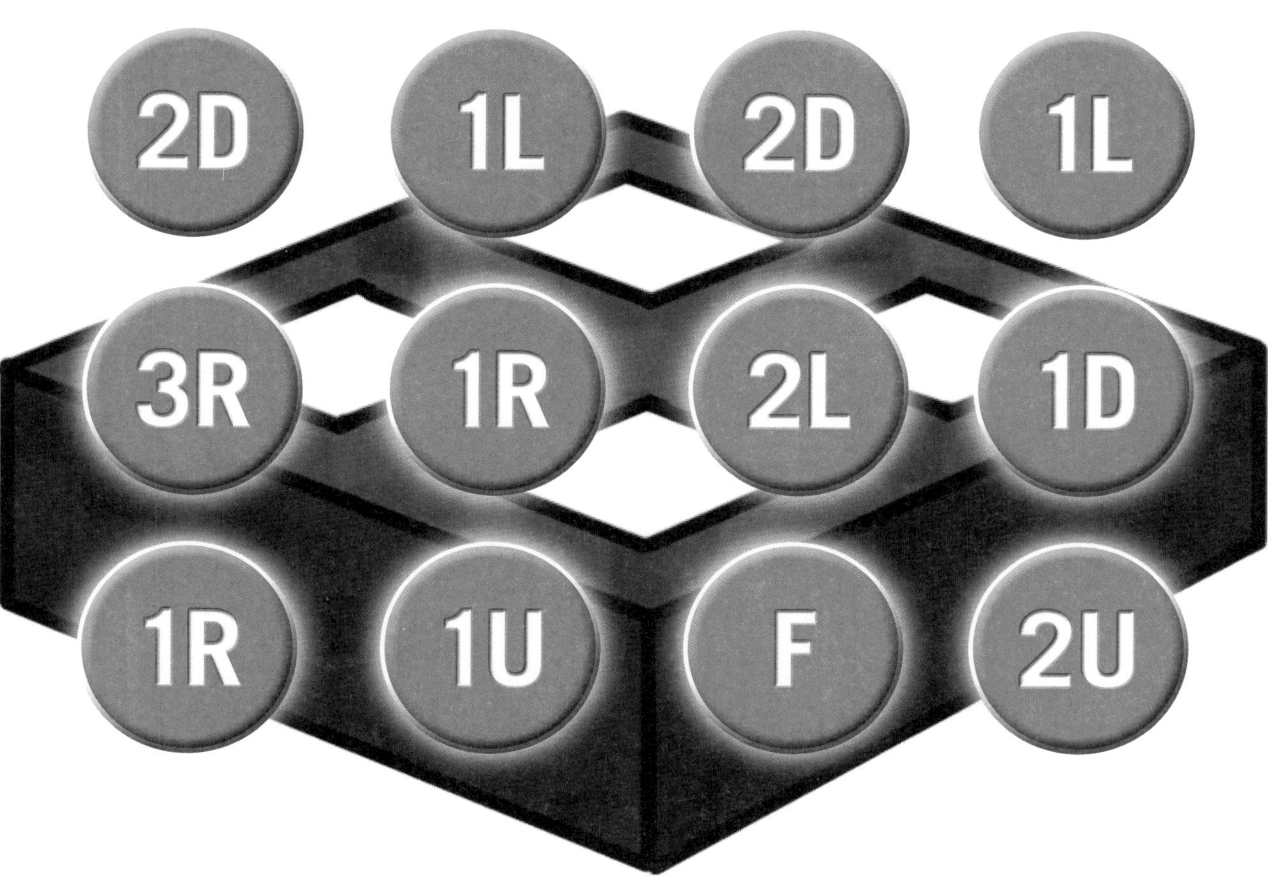

TALL TALE

Did you hear about the famous skeleton artist?

There's a funny answer to this question, and it's hidden in the lines below. See if you can read it.

Hint: *It helps to hold the page at eye level and shut one eye.*

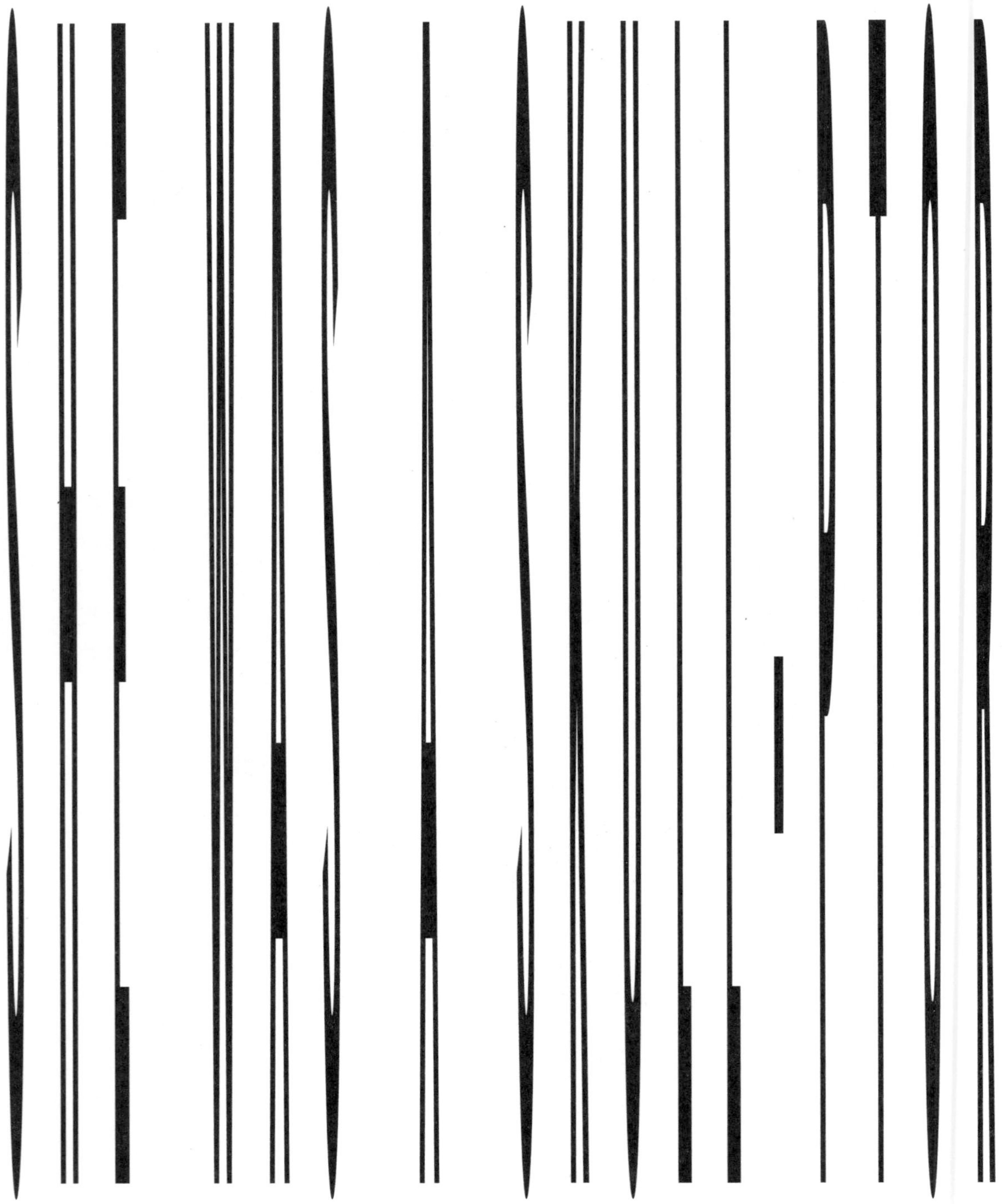

ANIMALS, ANIMALS EVERYWHERE

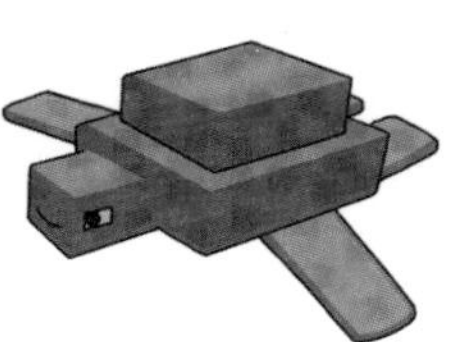

Find and circle the names of 17 animals in the wordfind. They might be forward, backward, up, down, or diagonal. Write unused letters on the blank spaces, in order from top to bottom and left to right, to discover a tip for protecting crops from animals.

Hint: *Circle individual letters instead of whole words. We've found one to get you started.*

S	B	H	U	Y	E	K	N	O	D	E	I
A	P	L	O	D	A	L	D	I	L	R	S
L	T	U	I	R	T	S	L	U	L	P	D
M	A	N	F	O	S	D	M	A	I	I	O
O	W	O	L	F	N	E	A	D	M	L	L
N	A	E	T	K	E	E	E	T	O	A	P
G	C	P	O	L	A	R	B	E	A	R	H
O	R	O	R	W	A	S	F	T	E	P	I
A	T	U	R	T	L	E	D	I	Y	E	N
S	U	P	A	D	I	U	Q	S	S	E	P
L	Y	O	P	F	N	E	K	C	I	H	C
W	H	(R)	(A)	(B)	(B)	(I)	(T)	E	A	S	T

CHICKEN
DOLPHIN
DONKEY
HORSE
LLAMA
MULE
OCELOT
PARROT
POLAR BEAR
PUFFERFISH
~~RABBIT~~
SALMON
SHEEP
SPIDER
SQUID
TURTLE
WOLF

LETTER HUNT

Identify the shared letter in each group of four words. Only one letter is in all four words. Write that shared letter on the space provided, then transfer the letters from the spaces to the boxes with the same numbers. If you fill in the boxes correctly, you'll earn a rare reward.

1. ____	TROPICAL, BEHAVIOR, MINECART, GHAST
2. ____	PUFFERFISH, HOSTILE, PHANTOM, ACHIEVEMENT
3. ____	PLAYERS, REDSTONE, TRANSPARENT, ANIMALS
4. ____	PASSIVE, TAMEABLE, MECHANISM, SILVERFISH
5. ____	ENDERMITE, UTILITY, MOUNTAIN, COBBLESTONE
6. ____	INVENTORY, FLOWER, CREATIVE, DRAGON
7. ____	PRISMARINE, DISPENSER, GUARDIAN, SPAWN

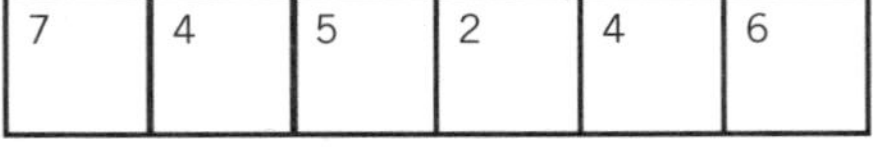

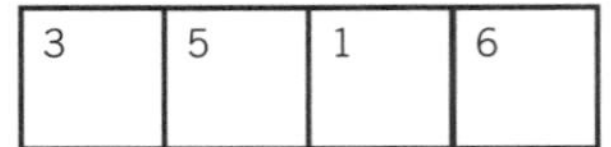

MATH MOBS

The numbers at the end of the rows are linked to the images in the grid.

What number goes in the circle?

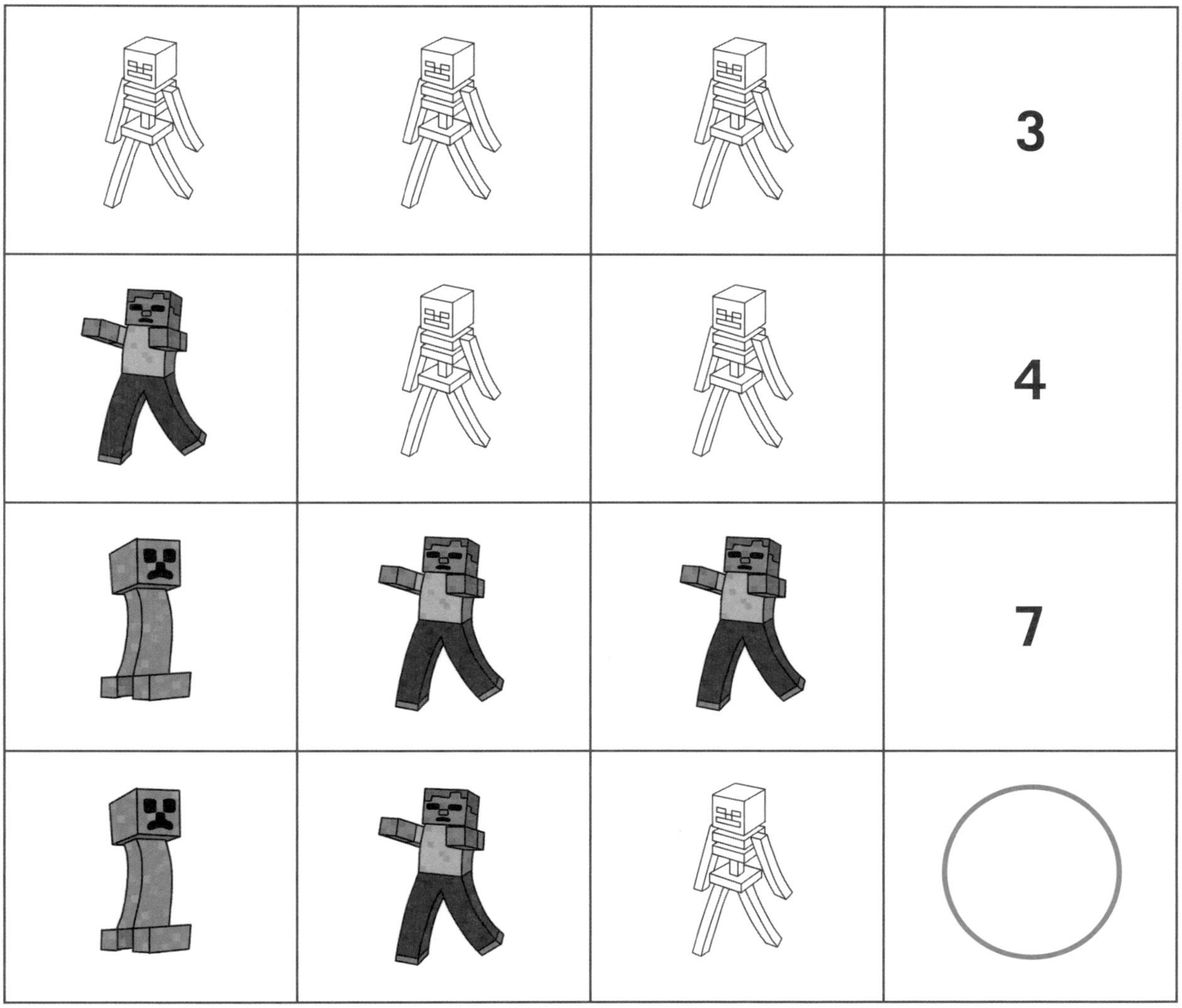

			3
			4
			7
			◯

SO MUCH FOR PEACEFUL!

Use the key to reveal something you'll want to watch out for even when playing in peaceful mode.

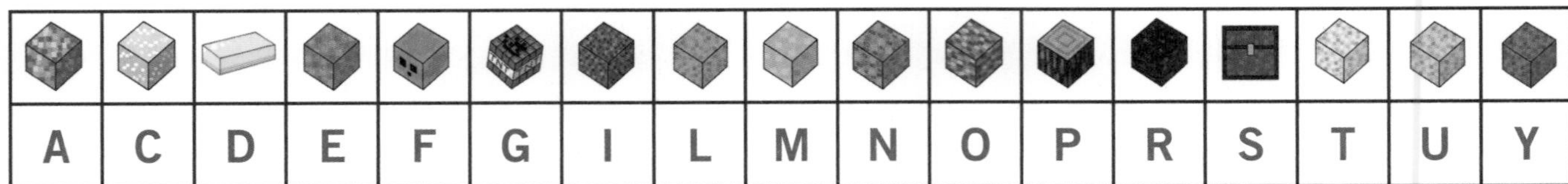

A	C	D	E	F	G	I	L	M	N	O	P	R	S	T	U	Y

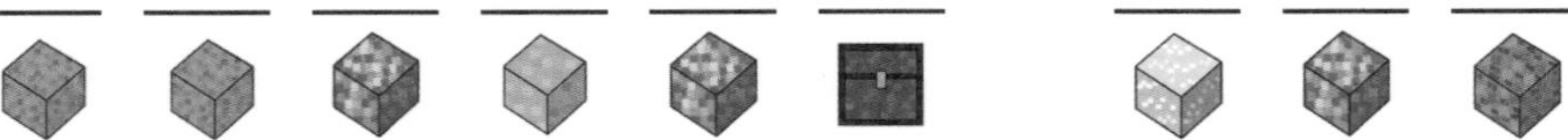

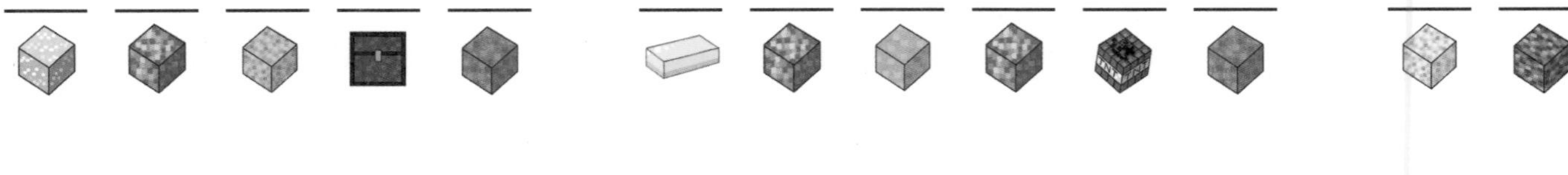

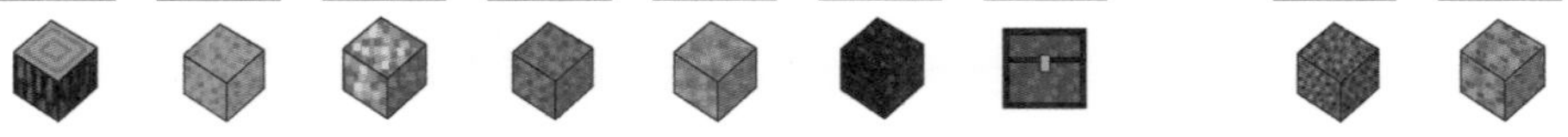

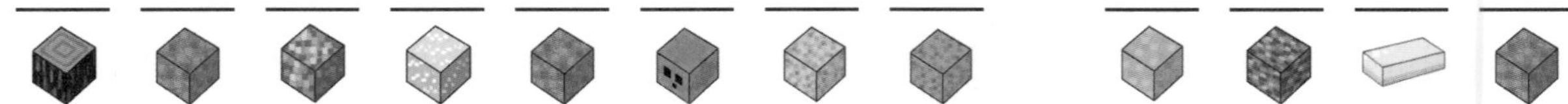

BABY'S FAVORITE TOY

Every word in Column B contains the same letters as a word in Column A, plus one letter. Draw a line between word "matches," then write the extra letter on the space provided. Transfer the numbered letters from the column to the spaces at the bottom to discover the answer to the joke.

COLUMN A	COLUMN B	
Stored	**Redstone**	___ 1
Groan	**Wither**	___ 2
Canoe	**Layer**	___ 3
White	**Dragon**	___ 4
Snorted	**Destroy**	___ 5
Rely	**Beacon**	___ 6

What is a baby zombie's favorite toy?

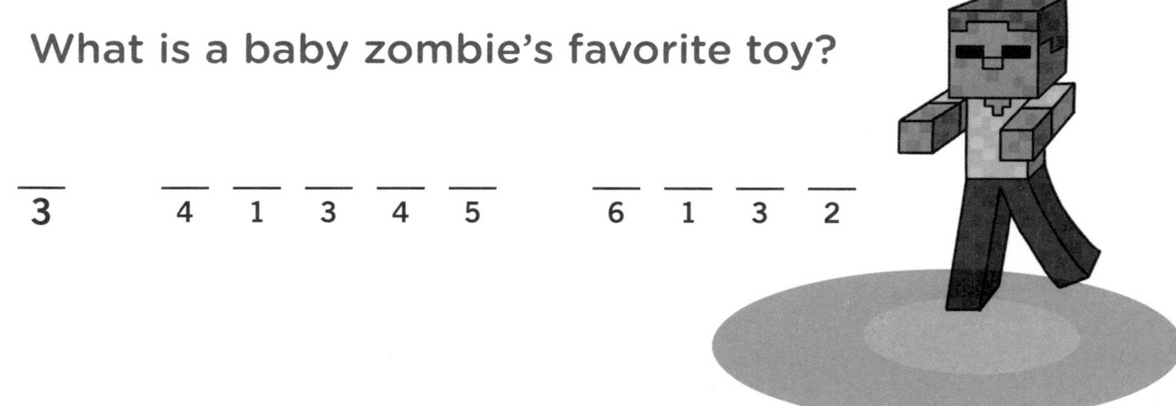

___   ___ ___ ___ ___ ___   ___ ___ ___ ___

3   4 1 3 4 5   6 1 3 2

HIDDEN HAZARD

Uncover the danger in the grid, if you dare. Color every box that has an even number, and be prepared to protect yourself.

Can't see the danger? Try turning the page on its side and holding it in front of a mirror.

72	46	20	16	4	32	64	88
29	98	54	23	21	11	83	23
41	63	67	30	2	65	13	49
35	7	93	47	61	68	18	27
50	78	26	90	74	10	82	6
25	97	59	31	47	5	15	61
53	12	70	82	22	46	38	3
34	89	71	19	79	95	53	18
56	75	39	1	29	71	95	66
5	66	72	38	16	8	44	23
17	45	67	85	35	47	59	35
55	36	16	94	3	20	52	57
80	13	27	14	25	65	83	34
48	11	15	91	51	37	51	98
33	64	58	20	6	78	82	81
21	71	85	5	45	93	57	43
52	68	18	90	13	43	1	63
69	9	97	42	76	82	34	77
1	33	31	98	7	49	29	50
73	27	15	16	90	66	32	85
8	84	56	62	55	45	9	21
17	61	91	87	73	37	11	69
44	6	79	37	74	26	8	41
81	55	30	14	51	77	99	22
89	57	65	98	41	15	63	78
96	18	76	28	50	32	96	46
33	7	39	53	17	99	3	31
43	20	56	2	48	22	70	87
4	25	67	59	67	19	9	62
16	49	39	3	19	75	19	88
38	42	66	18	30	24	96	72

WHOSE BIOME IS THIS?

Use the clues to figure out where each player is exploring.

- Either MineQueen or ZipDooDa should watch out for guardians.
- Knowitall says, "Llamas and emerald ore occur naturally here."
- Squ88mish is looking at a blue terracotta block inside a sandstone structure or a squid.
- MineQueen is not in a place to harvest cocoa pods, and neither is Knowitall.
- ZipDooDa sees a parrot or a fossil.

	MOUNTAINS	DESERT	DEEP OCEAN	JUNGLE
Squ88mish				
MineQueen				
ZipDooDa				
Knowitall				

MOB DROPS

Draw a line between the mob and the item it drops when destroyed. No diagonal lines allowed. No two lines will cross or share a square. If you do it correctly, no two lines will cross or share a square.

Example:

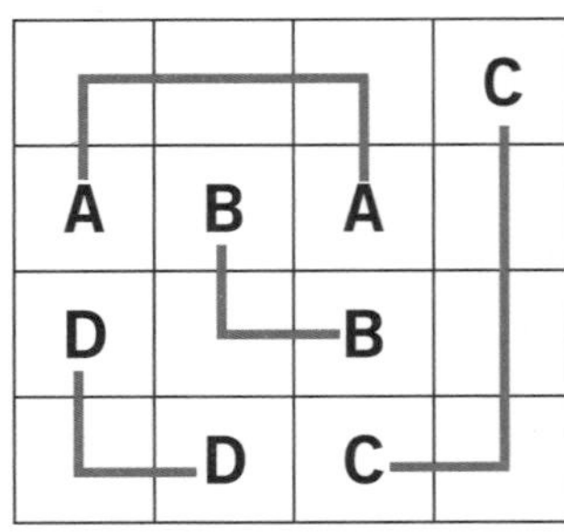

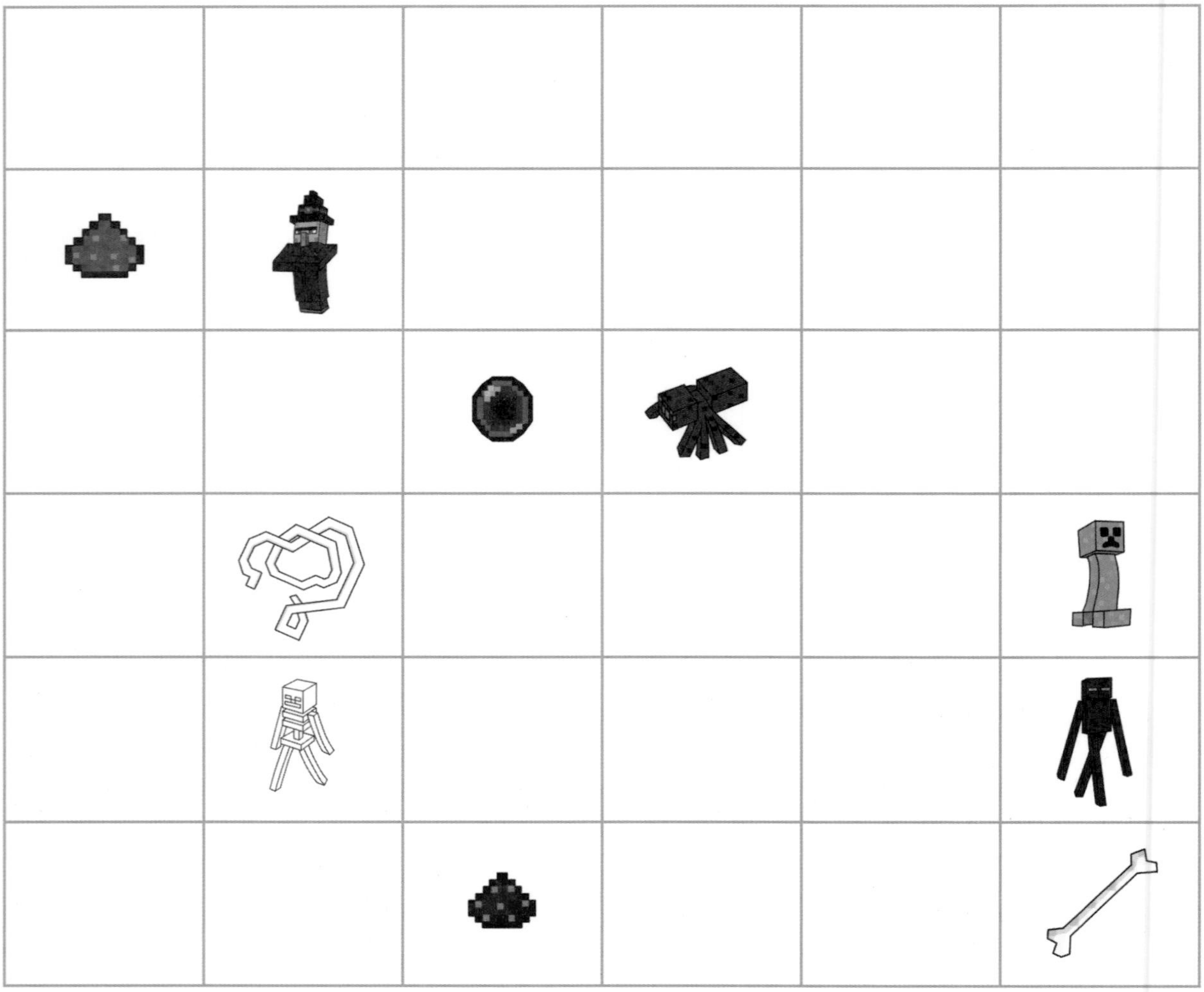

SURPRISE!

Four Minecraft players accidentally trip a wire that opens a door and reveals a surprise. Three players get harmless surprises, but one gets a dangerous surprise. Which player gets which surprise?

To find out, begin at the dot below each player's name and follow it downward. Every time you hit a horizontal line (one that goes across), you must take it. See where each player's path leads.

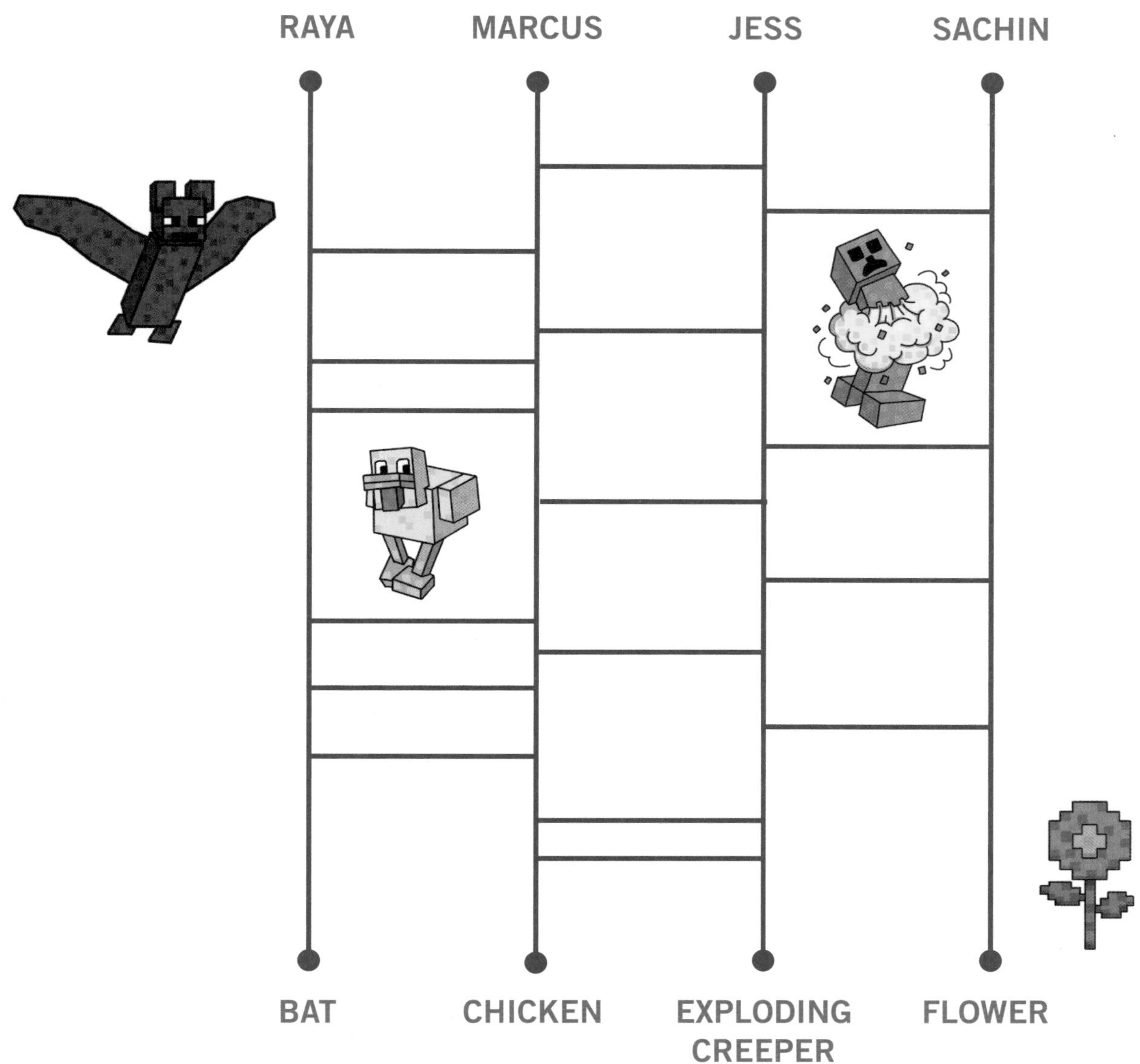

YOU CAN DRAW IT: CREEPER FAMILY

Use the grid to copy the picture. Examine each small square in the top grid, then transfer those lines to the corresponding square on the bottom grid.

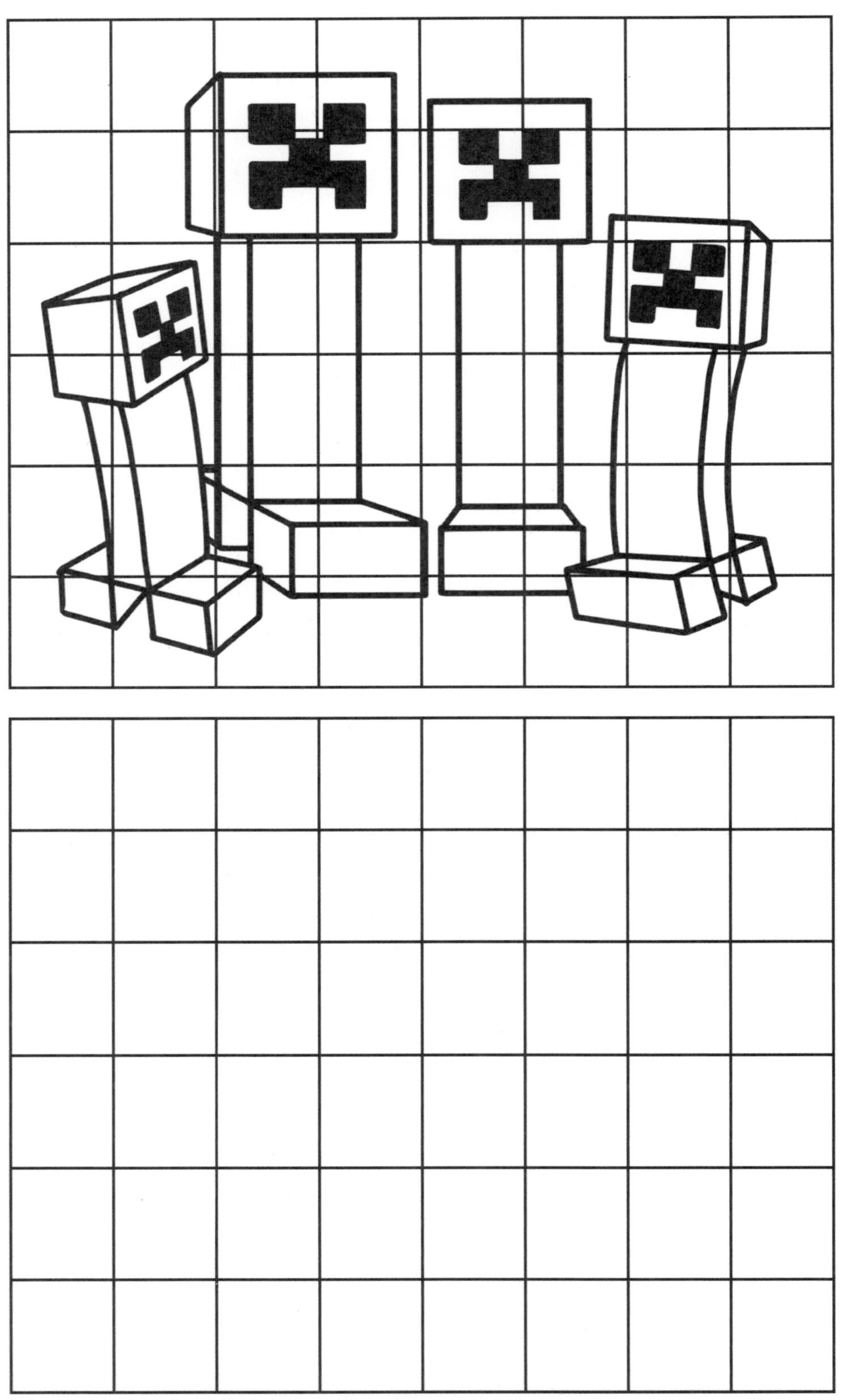

WHAT ZOMBIES WANT

In this crossword, you get to figure out where each word fits! Use the picture clues to guess the word answers, then see where each word fits best. If you fill in the puzzle correctly, you'll discover the answer to the joke.

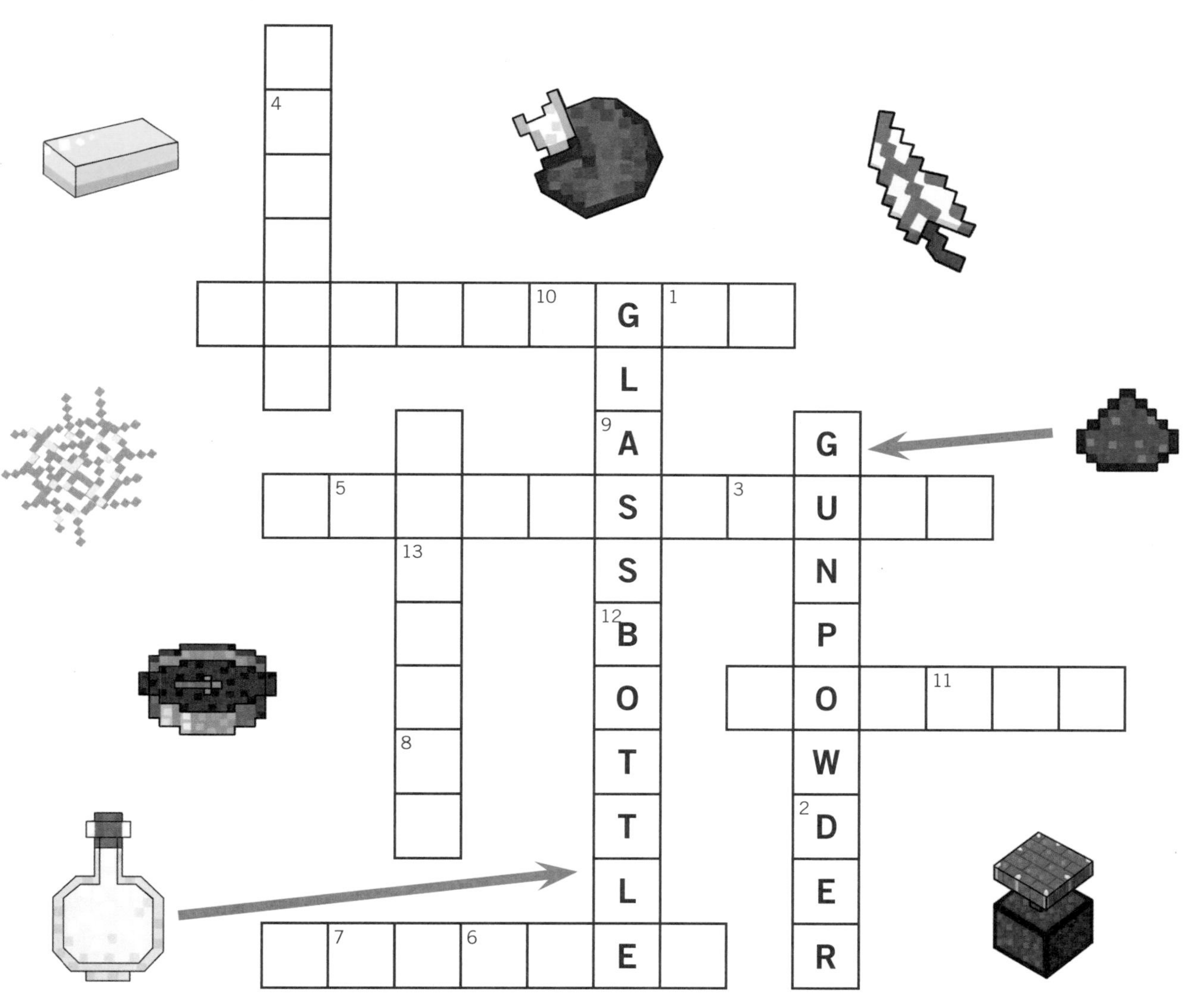

Why did the zombie attack the skeleton?

__ __   __ __ __ __ __ __   __ __ __
4 6   11 9 10 6 7 2   5 4 8

__ __ __ __   __ __ __   __ __ __ __ __ __
12 1 10 7   9 10 2   13 9 3 3 1 11

WHODUNNIT?

Two mobs have done you serious damage. Recover full health by figuring out whodunnit.

Write the name of the pictured mob on the spaces. Use the fractions to circle one or more of the letters in the name. Transfer the circled letters to the boxes to reveal whodunnit. We've done the first one for you.

LAST 1/5 OF		1. P U F F E R F I (S H)
MIDDLE ½ OF		2. ___ ___ ___ ___
LAST ½ OF		3. ___ ___ ___ ___ ___ ___
FIRST 1/5 OF		4. ___ ___ ___ ___ ___
FIRST 2/3 OF		5. ___ ___ ___
SECOND ¼ OF		6. ___ ___ ___ ___ ___ ___ ___ ___
MIDDLE 1/5 OF		7. ___ ___ ___ ___ ___

1 S	H	2		3		

4	5		6		7

WHEEL OF FORTUNE #4

Start at the ▼.
Write every third letter on the spaces to reveal something simple with a super-impressive name.

___ ____ __________

__________ _______

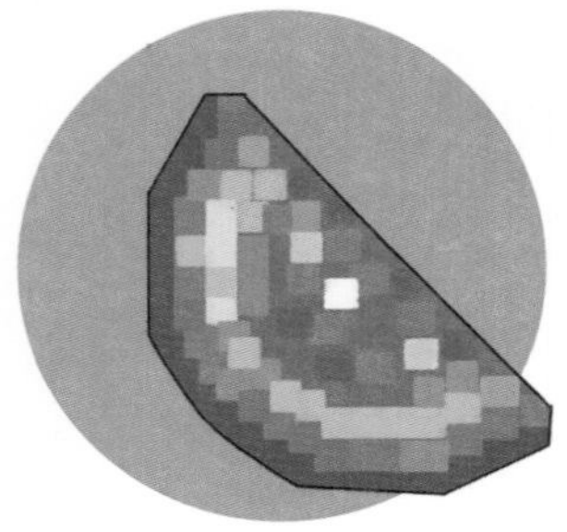

SEED FINDER

Can you find the melon seeds? They appear only once in a horizontal, vertical, or diagonal line.

M	O	S	E	E	S	N	O	L	E	M	S
E	E	D	M	E	L	O	N	S	E	D	N
L	M	E	O	M	S	L	E	L	E	M	O
O	M	E	L	E	E	N	O	E	S	L	L
N	E	N	L	E	D	N	M	S	D	E	E
S	L	O	S	O	S	E	E	E	O	M	N
E	O	L	O	E	N	O	E	N	L	O	O
E	N	E	E	E	L	S	E	M	E	N	L
S	E	M	O	N	O	L	E	E	M	S	E
L	S	S	D	E	E	S	N	E	L	E	M
O	N	M	E	L	O	N	S	E	D	D	O
N	D	S	S	E	N	O	L	E	M	S	L

IN THE BEGINNING . . .

Circle letters on the bottom half of the grid that have correct mirror images in the top half. Write the circled letters in order on the spaces to reveal a behind-the-scenes fact about Minecraft.

E ∩ N ⊥ O B ʎ E O B ь C I ⅁ Λ D M C E И

Γ ⅁ ь Γ ∀ ⅁ Z H E M O ⊥ B ⊥ ƨ W E D ᴚ ᴚ

O M ᴚ I ⅁ Λ K I N ∀ Γ B Z W Γ ʎ Ø N Λ I

O W R I G A R I N A L E S N L Y O U V I

L C J L A G S M E M O L B I S W E B P R

E A L T O B X E G F P D I G A C M O E N

_ _ _ _ _ _ _ _ _ _, _ _ _ _ _ _ _

_ _ _ _ _ _ _ _

_ _ _ _ _ _ _ _ _ _ _

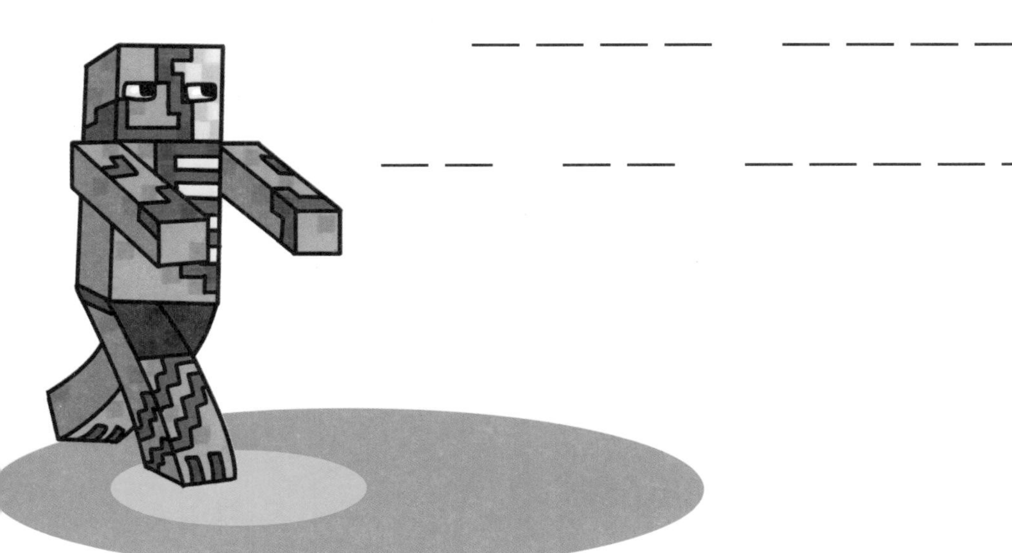

YOU CAN DRAW IT: ENDERDRAGON

Use the grid to copy the picture. Examine each small square in the top grid, then transfer those lines to the corresponding square on the bottom grid.

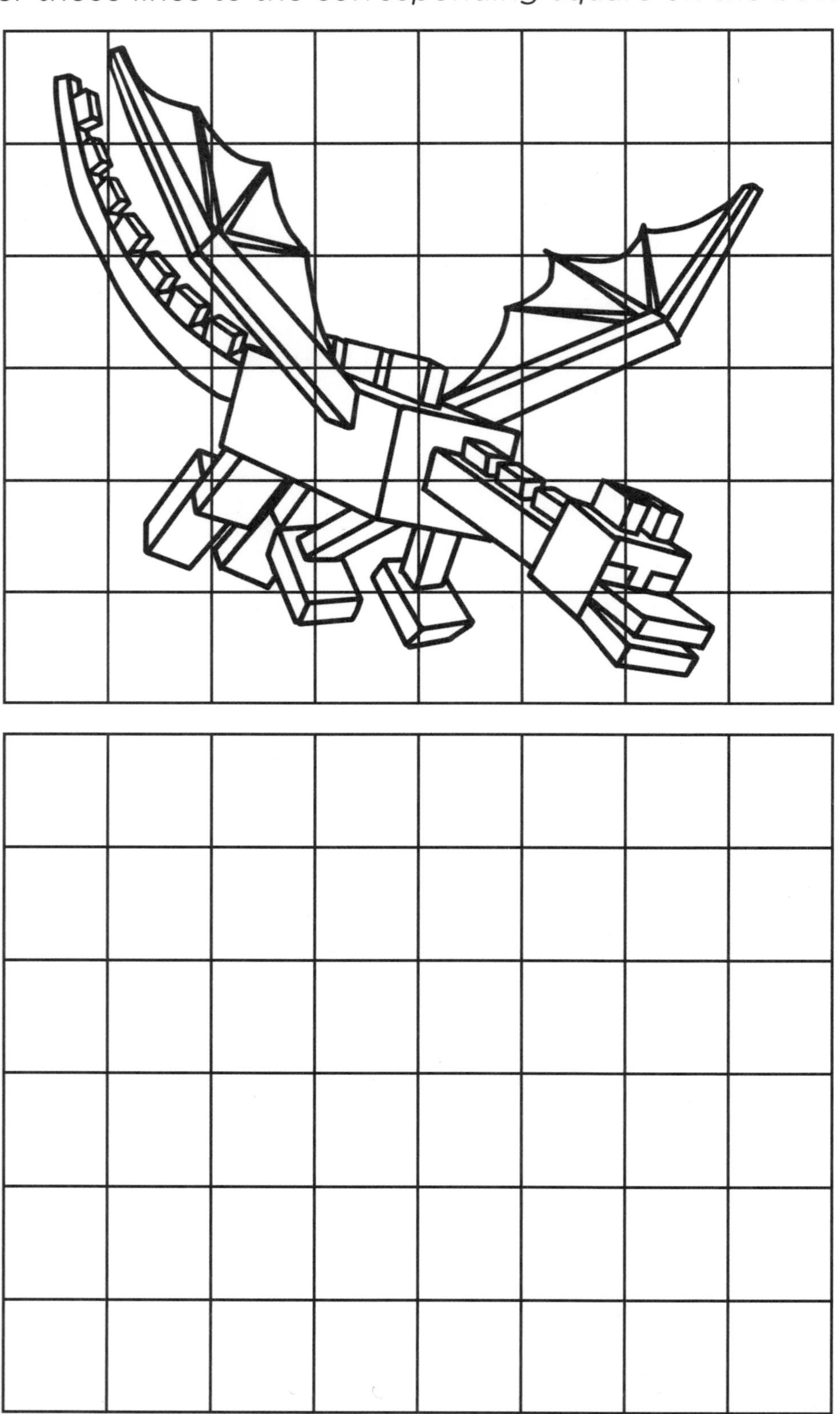

BOUNTIFUL HARVEST

You will soon head out on an adventure. You need all the food in your inventory that you can collect. That means picking up every edible item in this maze. To do this, draw a line from Start to Stop that passes through every piece of food once. Your line can go up, down, left, or right but not diagonally. On your mark, get set, stock up!

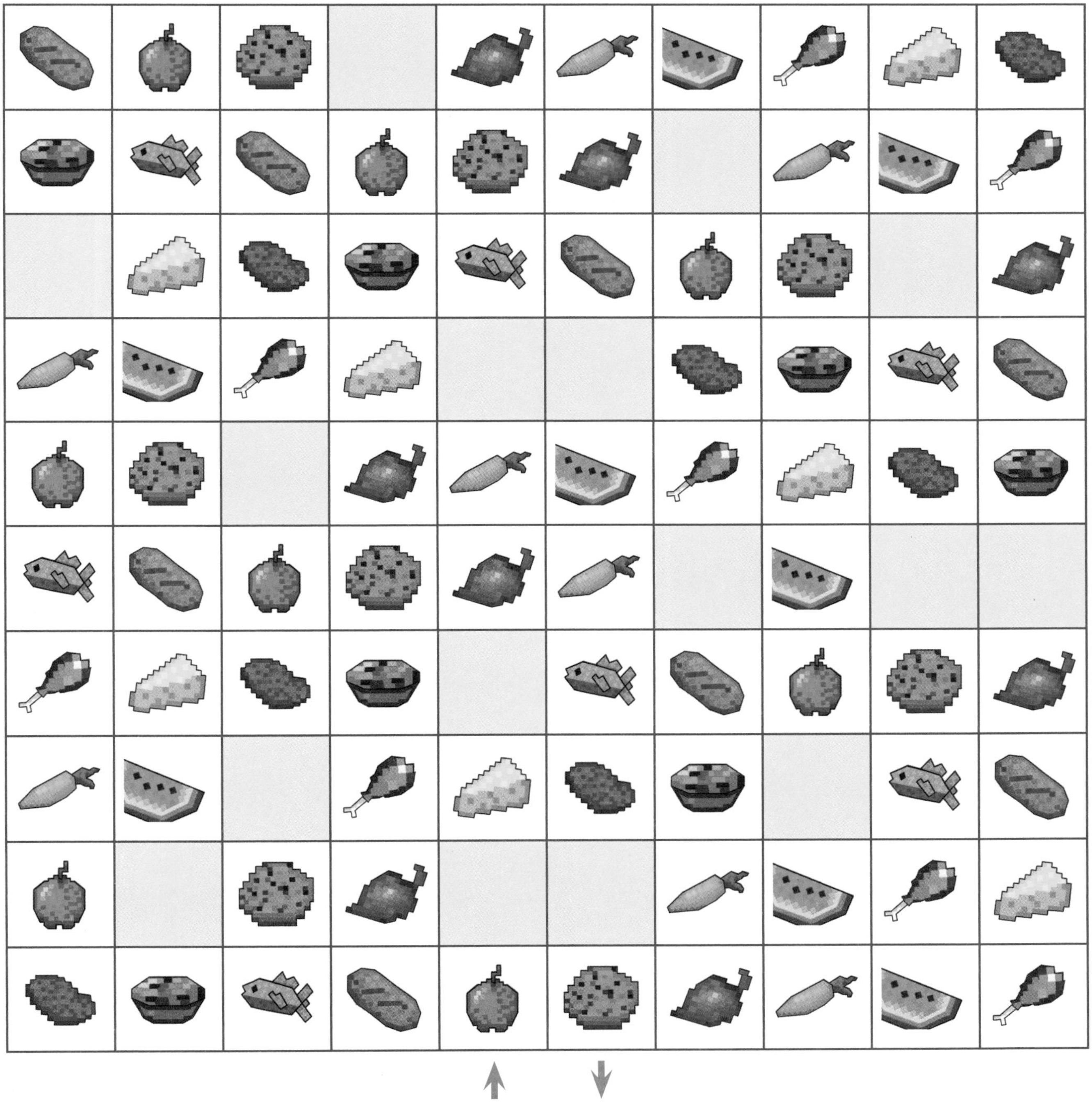

START STOP

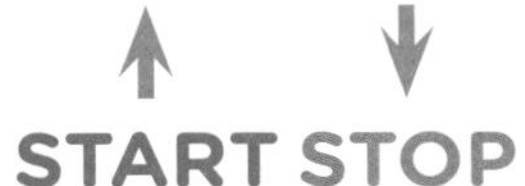

NAME SHIFTING

Follow the instructions to transform this mob's name to its nickname.

1. Write the **name of this mob** on the space to the right.	
2. Move **the second vowel** to the end of the name.	
3. Change the **middle two letters** of the name to the first two letters of the alphabet.	
4. Change the **second letter** of the name to something that when combined with the first letter, it makes a sound that means "be quiet."	
5. Make the **first letter** the fourth letter in the name, and change it to the fourth letter of the alphabet.	
6. Make the **first half** of the name swap positions with the second half of the name.	

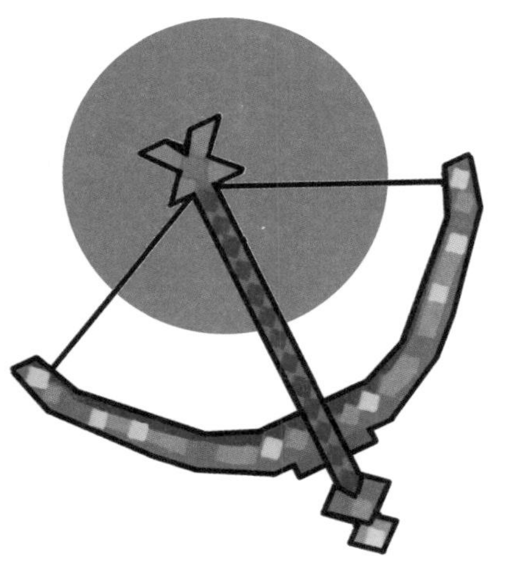

ENCHANTED BOW AND ARROW

The bow and arrow are enchanted. To use them, you must press all sixteen buttons just once, in the correct order.

Follow the directions on the buttons. For instance, 2D means you must move your finger two buttons down. R = right, L = left, U = up. To use the bow and arrow, you must land on the F button last.

Which button do you have to press first to land on the F button last?

3D	2D	1L	2D
1R	2R	1R	2D
2U	1R	1D	3L
2U	F	2U	3U

WHICH WITCH?

What do you call a witch that spawns in the desert?

The answer is written below. Read it.

Hint: *It helps to hold the page at eye level and shut one eye.*

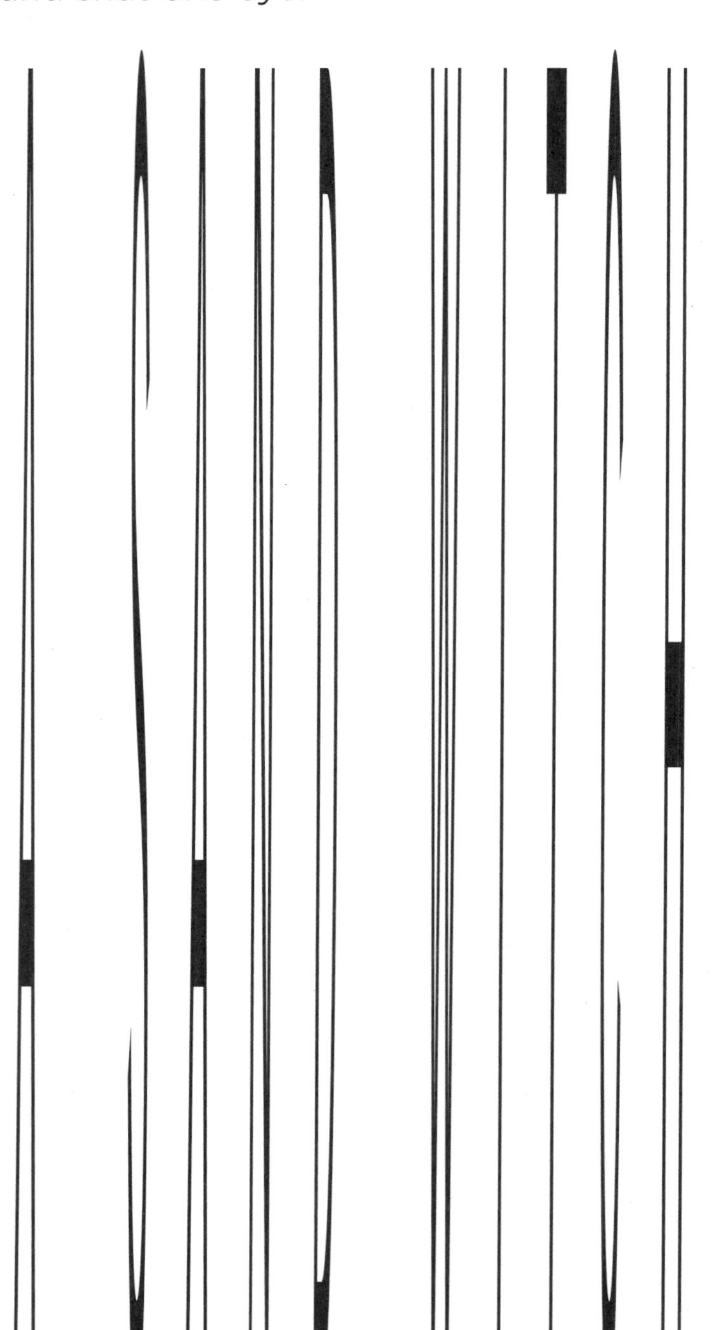

PICK A POTION

Find and circle the names of 14 potions in the wordfind. They might be forward, backward, up, down, or diagonal. Write unused letters on the blank spaces, in order from top to bottom and left to right, to discover something useful to know.

Hint: *Circle individual letters instead of whole words. We've found one to get you started.*

ANTIDOTE
DECAY
ELIXIR
EYEDROPS
HEALING
INVISIBILITY
NIGHT VISION
POISON
REGENERATION
~~SLOWNESS~~
STRENGTH
SWIFTNESS
TONIC
TURTLE MASTER

A N I S H E A L I N G R
I N N S T T Y A C E D E
A N V T D R A M A T G T
S W I F T N E S S O E S
I V S C P L O N T D I A
N O I S I V T H G I N M
O N B X C N A N K T I E
L L I A O P O L A N H L
Y R L S E R A T T A O T
N O I T A R E N E G E R
N O T S L O W N E S S U
P E Y E D R O P S C E T

TEXT STRINGS

Identify the shared letter in each group of four words. Only one letter is in all four words. Write that shared letter on the space provided, then transfer the letters from the spaces to the boxes with the same numbers. If you fill in the boxes correctly, you'll reveal an advanced feature of Minecraft. Do you know how to use this feature?

3. ____	DIAMOND, SLIMEBALL, MULTIPLAYER, EXTREME
2. ____	BEETROOT, EXPLORER, PORKCHOP, PISTON
4. ____	ENVIRONMENT, FERMENTED, LUMINANCE, COMPARATOR
8. ____	COORDINATES, NAUTILUS, SLOWNESS, SHIPWRECK
7. ____	GUARDIAN, CAULDRON, WOODLAND, DESERT
5. ____	VINDICATOR, FURNACE, QUARTZ, MINESHAFT
6. ____	SKELETON, SWIFTNESS, INGREDIENT, OBSIDIAN
1. ____	RESISTANCE, MYCELIUM, TORCH, RECIPE

1	2	3	4	5	6	7	8

ADDITIONAL MATH MOBS

The numbers at the end of the rows and columns are linked to the images in the grid. What number goes in the circle?

Hint: *Start with the column of pigs.*

			11
			10
			12
			9
8	18		

FLOWER POWER

Use the picture-number combination under each space to find the correct letter on the grid. The correct letter is the one where the picture and number intersect. If you fill in the spaces correctly, you'll discover a Minecrafting secret.

1	L	H	W	U	R
2	V	T	M	G	D
3	E	J	A	I	F
4	S	O	C	B	N

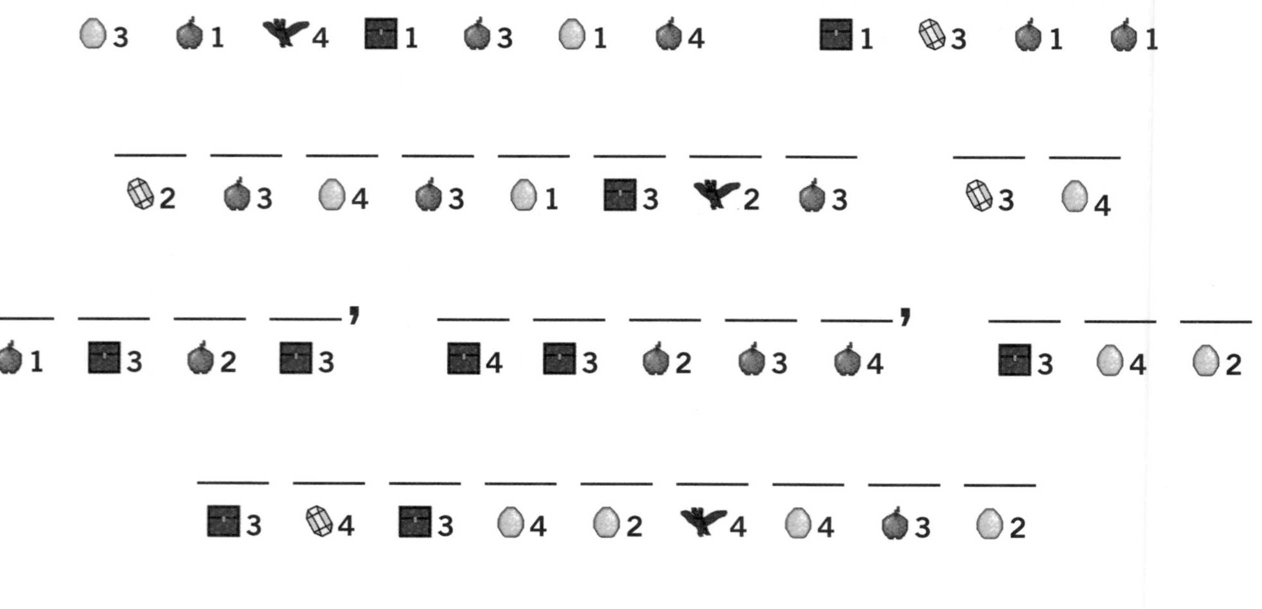

A RARE FIND

Every word in Column B contains the same letters as a word in Column A, plus one letter. Draw a line between word "matches," then write the extra letter on the space provided.

Unscramble the column of letters to reveal a rare find.

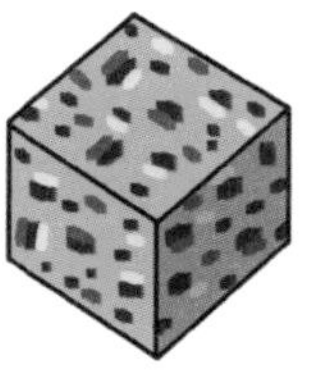

COLUMN A	COLUMN B	
Dasher	**Hardcore**	___
Yoked	**Player**	___
Early	**Golem**	___
Charred	**Spider**	___
Pride	**Sheared**	___
Mole	**Donkey**	___

What rare find did you just reveal?

__ __ __ __ __ __

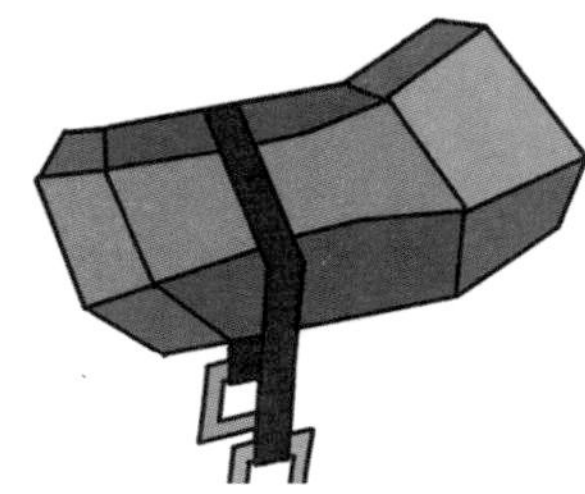

MINER HUMOR

What do you get when you throw a piano down a mineshaft?

To find out, color every box that contains a multiple of five.

77	9	63	41	51	82	10	1	68	79	70	92	38	12	23	29	73	2	14	29
70	25	5	20	95	50	6	52	33	27	17	50	90	58	41	97	11	63	47	36
91	52	8	69	48	89	30	9	73	11	44	18	42	15	10	65	85	40	12	54
97	35	80	55	60	40	98	93	2	16	87	91	92	64	55	84	22	76	5	67
76	86	17	3	78	81	15	72	47	67	51	78	4	26	80	7	13	23	52	25
7	90	65	75	45	30	49	96	24	82	1	10	75	60	45	30	20	90	35	39
85	4	56	41	61	74	38	23	37	96	25	31	83	72	95	38	81	47	11	31
54	68	79	98	26	16	6	69	73	57	64	8	14	66	21	52	59	19	33	89
36	40	85	60	5	35	50	14	95	53	8	79	53	39	24	3	73	1	21	9
20	86	23	11	59	21	9	49	42	26	2	26	66	62	88	47	27	94	62	38
46	17	94	62	7	49	84	18	94	48	15	67	17	34	5	93	42	13	96	13
60	70	15	20	85	90	5	31	4	81	37	85	25	80	40	30	55	70	56	51
46	69	36	78	2	60	31	86	99	57	24	77	61	18	65	41	68	3	95	59
28	4	92	14	42	78	55	39	92	22	12	6	13	34	83	28	32	16	88	5
71	30	80	75	25	30	46	51	73	53	87	43	32	27	87	48	61	10	30	81
10	58	36	22	61	4	32	12	2	18	53	56	29	8	44	71	22	91	19	32
64	82	83	34	62	83	54	88	58	13	40	95	20	70	90	65	15	5	30	15
74	75	90	85	20	10	72	43	62	5	69	27	44	87	14	19	79	74	7	48
15	44	55	66	49	39	55	81	59	19	97	63	48	1	74	37	57	12	24	18
90	52	98	80	76	99	40	88	53	28	34	30	90	27	41	35	26	64	29	96
33	20	89	21	60	25	59	66	16	77	65	79	3	55	82	6	20	68	86	57
57	43	7	21	33	89	28	39	54	73	50	93	76	63	25	54	90	71	37	46
91	66	32	71	3	15	63	67	84	97	1	10	45	5	60	85	17	46	86	31
85	45	30	60	75	33	77	6	43	58	75	82	36	84	24	44	58	69	8	92
99	62	88	90	5	67	43	91	89	94	56	9	77	19	5	71	29	76	47	98
74	14	57	42	83	10	23	34	61	84	80	60	25	15	70	10	5	35	20	65
51	93	22	42	95	68	49	16	78	95	68	38	87	11	50	56	73	28	94	33

Can't read it? Try turning the page on its side.

DROP MATCH

Draw a line between the object and the item it drops when mined. No diagonal lines allowed. No two lines will cross or share a square.

Example:

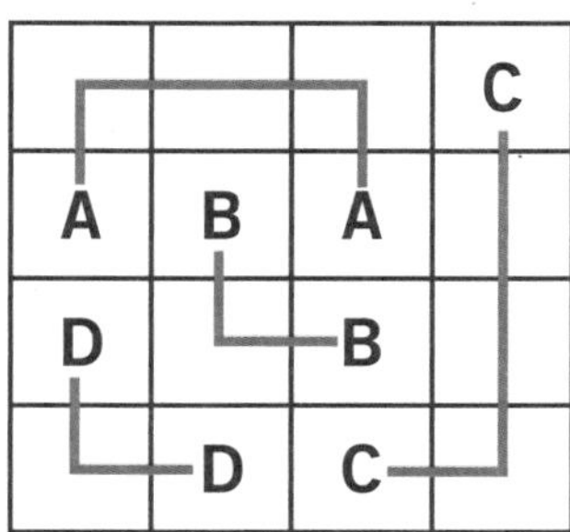

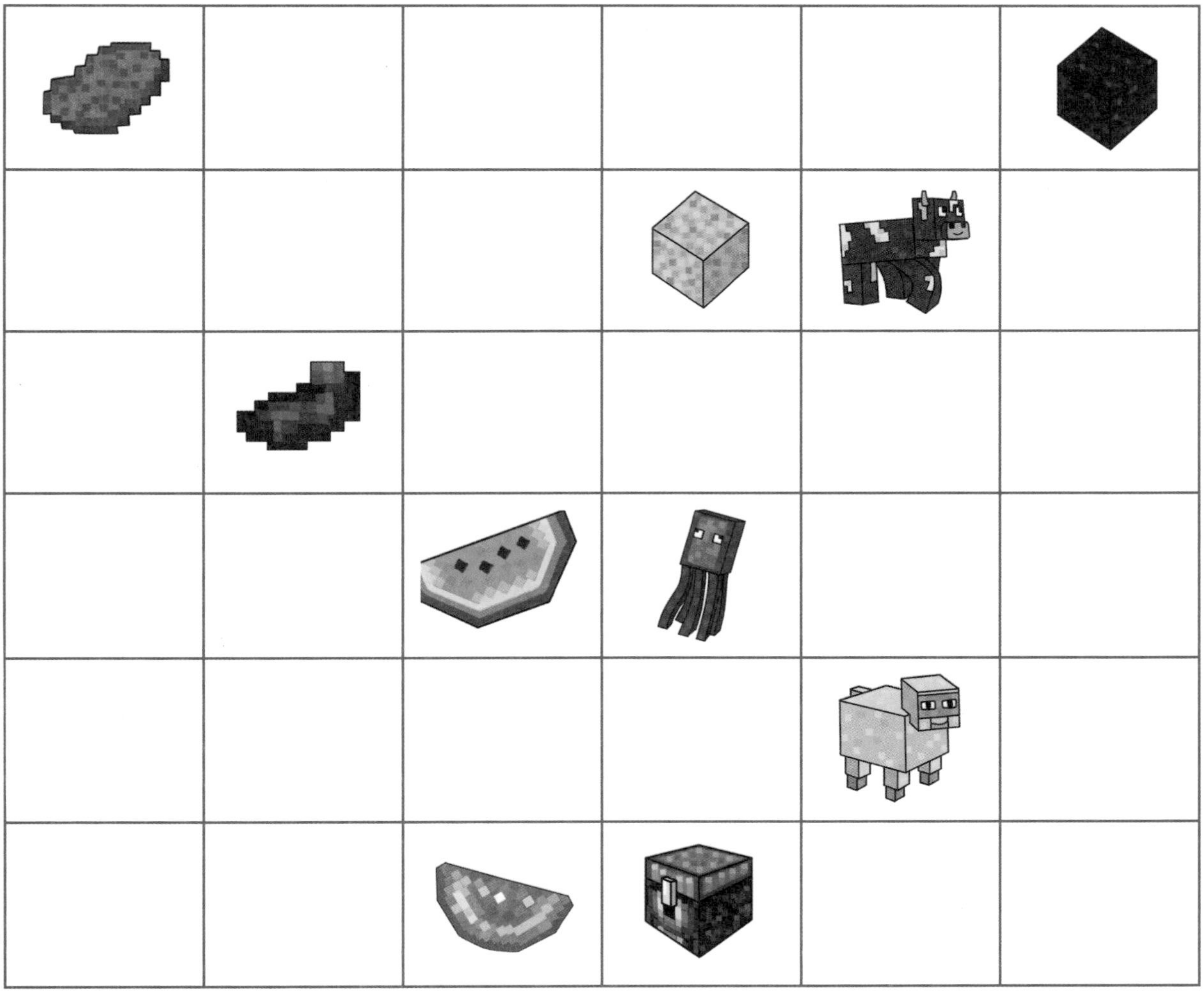

A COLD RECEPTION

The answers to the clues use each of the letters in the letter box. Write the answers to the clues on the numbered spaces Then transfer the letters to the boxes with the same numbers. If you fill in the boxes correctly, you'll reveal the answer to the joke.

B E F I O R S T T

A group of things that go together, sometimes called a "matched ___"   ___ ___ ___ (1 2 3)

Lie   ___ ___ ___ (4 5 6)

Go bad, spoil   ___ ___ ___ (7 8 9)

What do you get from a hostile wolf in the Snowy Taiga?

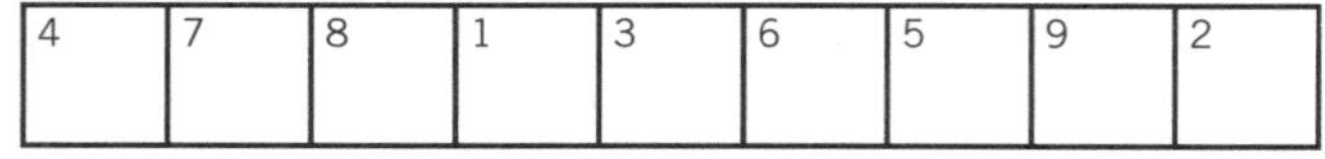

4	7	8	1	3	6	5	9	2

ANSWERS

WHEEL OF FORTUNE #1

FORTUNE-ENCHANTED PICK

ALEX SAYS: TOOL TIP

DON'T WASTE DIAMONDS ON A SHOVEL.

It may last longer, but there are better uses for diamonds.

THE MIRROR'S MESSAGE

TO WORK, SPLASH POTIONS MUST HIT THE LOWER HALF OF A GHAST.

SHOP AROUND THE BLOCK

THE GROSSERY STORE

STAY AWAY!

LATER, PET, HORN

NETHER PORTAL

ENCHANTED CHEST

F	2D	1L
1U	1R	1U
1U	1R	2L

The red button is the first one pressed.

KILLER JOKE

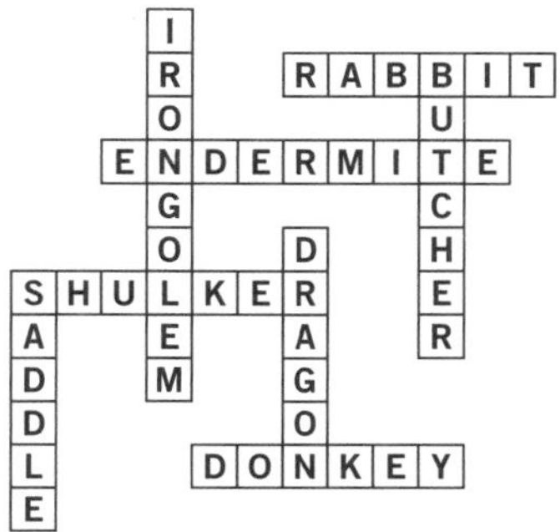

What's the difference between a killer rabbit and a counterfeit dollar bill?

ONE IS BAD MONEY AND THE OTHER IS A MAD BUNNY!

GEM SEARCH

L	A	E	D	L	E	R	E	M	E
E	R	A	M	E	M	A	M	D	R
D	M	L	D	E	E	E	L	E	A
A	L	E	D	L	R	A	D	M	D
E	L	A	R	E	M	E	E	L	D
M	A	D	R	A	A	D	A	E	L
E	L	R	D	M	L	R	E	D	A
R	M	D	A	R	E	L	A	L	R
A	E	A	L	M	A	E	D	E	E
D	E	M	E	R	E	D	L	A	M

BURIED TREASURE

			78		4	92		50			
44		10	70			18		16	28		14
26		62	56		66			38	60		32
12		8	74		30	2		54	32		6

FAVORITE THING TO DO

Mohit - Battle mobs

Jasmine - Build

Lu - Solve mazes

Claire - Brew potions

SQUARED UP: GARDEN PLOT

M	P	C	B
C	B	P	M
P	M	B	C
B	C	M	P

HOMEWARD BOUND

LIFE-SAVING STEPS

FAST ONES, AWAY FROM THE MOB!

FACT OF (REAL) LIFE

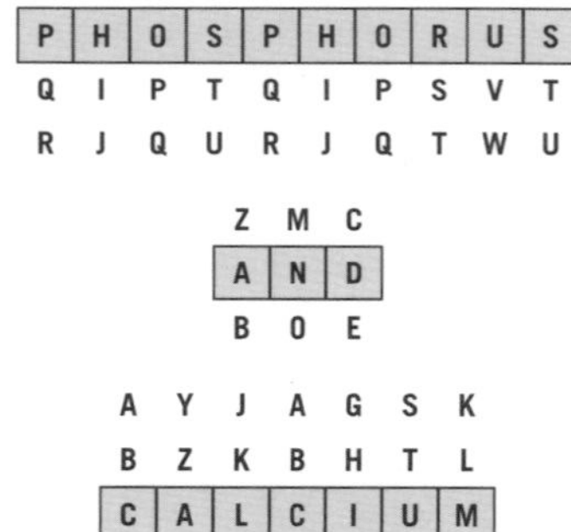

MYSTERY MOB

GHAST

The ghast is real. Watch out for fireballs!

NETHER FINDS

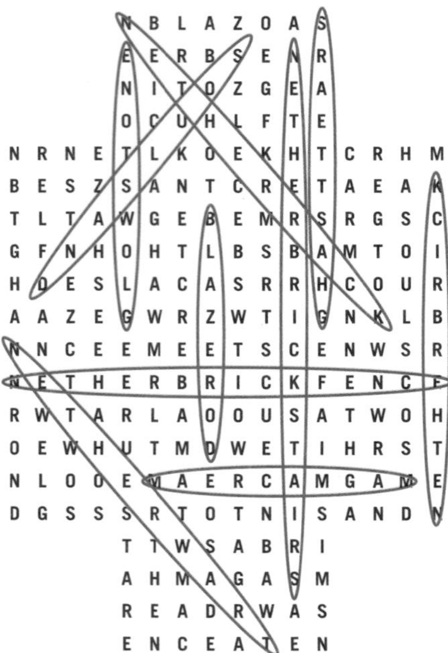

WHO'S WHOSE ON THE FARM

BlockBuster - Pig

iBuild - Chicken

Creeper Hunter - Sheep

Masterminer - Donkey

PARTY SNACK PICK-UP

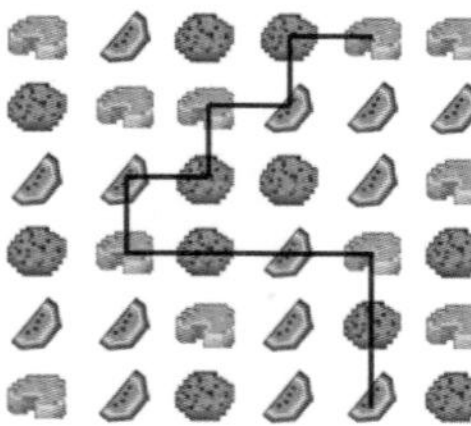

GET OUT!

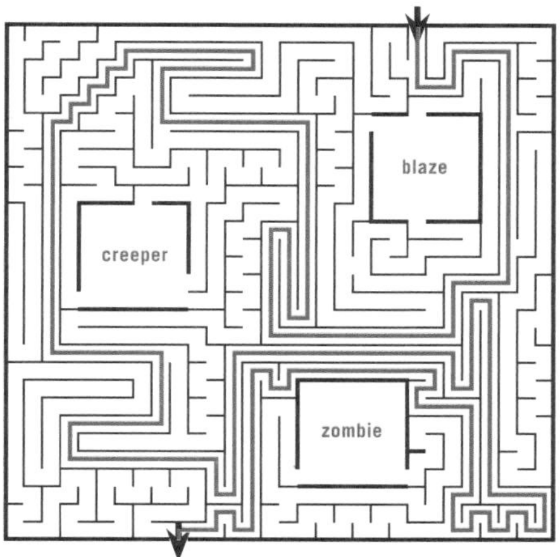

WISHING YOU GOOD . . .

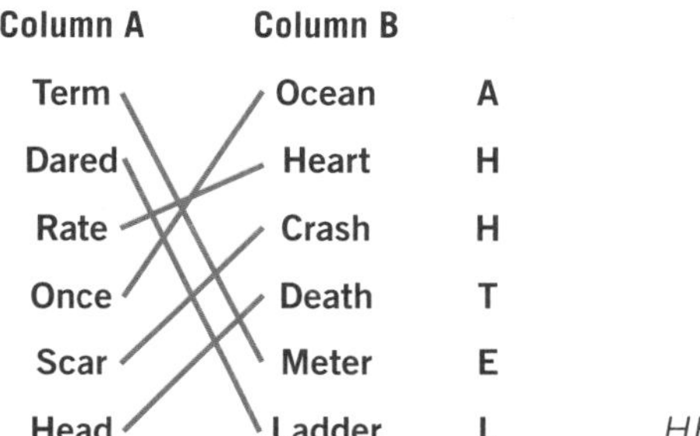

HEALTH

RARE DROP SCORES

Kim - Ghast Tear

Malik - Blaze Rod

Talia - Nether Star

Cameron - Ender Pearls

LOST LIBRARY

MASH finds the library.

UNCOMMON COMMON FEATURE

What do a librarian, priest, and nitwit have in common?

UNUSED HOODS ON THEIR ROBES.

It's true. You'll find hoods in their textures, but they aren't used.

ALEX SAYS: DID YOU KNOW THIS ABOUT ZOMBIES?

IF ZOMBIES FIND ARMOR, THEY CAN WEAR IT.

So don't leave it lying around, okay?

WHEEL OF FORTUNE #2

POTION OF WATER BREATHING

SADDLE SEARCH

E	S	A	D	D	E	L	A	E	S
L	D	L	S	A	S	E	D	L	A
D	S	E	A	E	S	D	A	D	D
D	A	L	D	D	A	L	E	D	E
S	L	D	S	S	E	L	S	D	L
A	A	D	L	D	D	A	D	A	S
S	L	A	D	A	S	L	D	S	D
D	S	S	S	D	A	D	S	L	A
E	L	D	A	S	L	S	D	A	S
E	D	D	A	E	S	A	D	D	L

MEMO FROM MIRROR

DO NOT SLEEP ON A BED IN THE NETHER.
IT WILL EXPLODE.

SQUARED UP: LET THERE BE LIGHT

B	G	T	L
L	T	G	B
G	L	B	T
T	B	L	G

COOKIE FEAST

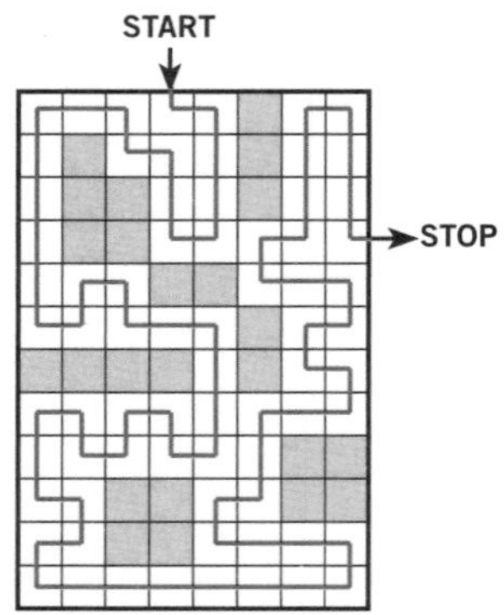

ENCHANTED BOOK

The red button is the first one pressed.

LONG LAUGH

What did the skeleton take to the mob potluck?

SPARE RIBS

GETTIN' CRAFTY

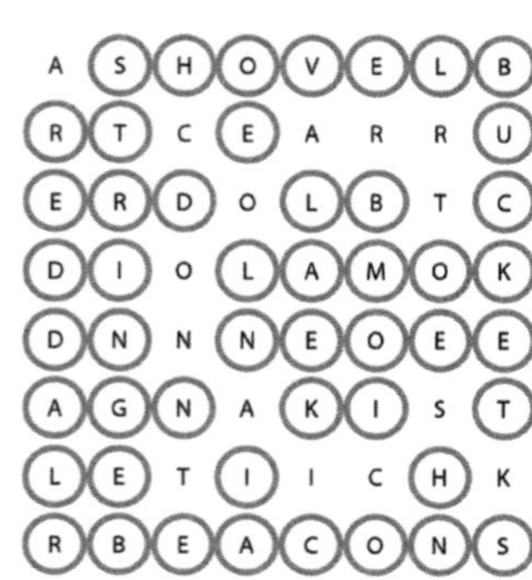

A CARROT ON A STICK

TRUE OR FALSE?

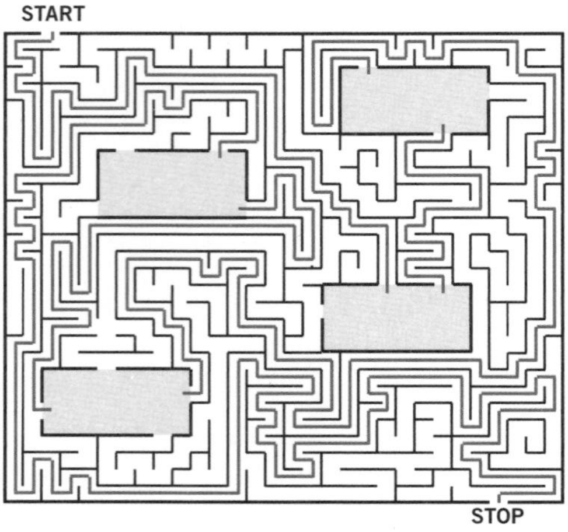

GO WITH THE FLOW CHART

REDSTONE CIRCUIT

INSIDE INFO

ON DECEMBER 24-26, CHESTS LOOK LIKE WRAPPED PRESENTS

CREEPER DESTROYERS

Jack - 1; Sylvie - 2; Veronica - 3; Oscar - 4; Xavier - 5

WHOOPS!

NET, NAPS, STAR

What did Alex get when she accidentally splashed her mom and dad with a Potion of Invisibility?

TRANSPARENTS

WHAT'S FOR DINNER?

Emperor Nethero - Potato

Call me Fishmale - Pufferfish

Enderslayer - Carrot

4321Blastoff - Rotten flesh

SCORE MORE ORE

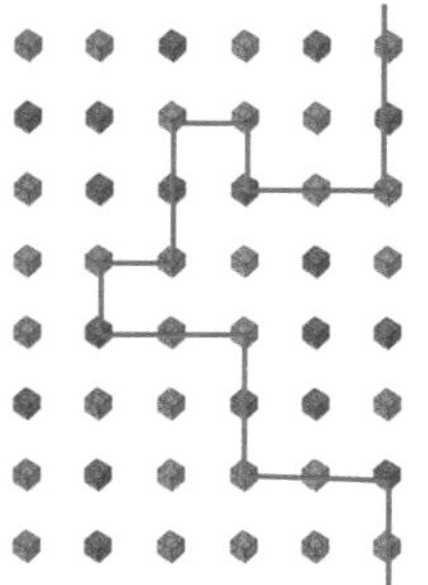

TRADING JO(S)

Joanne - Librarian

Joseph - Butcher

Joni - Priest

Jorge - Blacksmith

THE LOCKED DOOR

Liam - red, Ami - green, Lain - yellow, Ali - blue

Lain's yellow wool "key" unlocks the door.

ZOMBIE FRIENDS

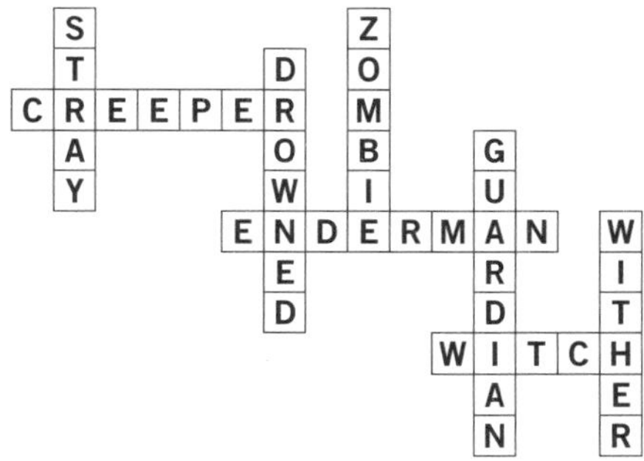

What did the zombie's friends say when he introduced his girlfriend?

GEEZ, WHERE DID YOU DIG HER UP?

ALEX SAYS: OWN YOUR MINE BUSINESS

FIND DIAMONDS DEEP IN LEVEL TWELVE.

It's the best place to mine for diamonds.

WHEEL OF FORTUNE #3

ENCHANTED DIAMOND CHESTPLATE

HIDDEN ARMOR

M	R	H	O	R	S	E	A	R	M	O	H
A	O	O	R	M	R	A	S	R	O	H	S
H	O	R	S	E	A	R	M	R	O	A	E
O	E	S	S	R	O	M	S	R	O	H	O
R	H	E	A	E	R	E	S	A	S	M	M
S	R	O	M	R	A	E	S	R	O	H	R
E	S	A	O	H	A	R	M	A	O	O	A
A	E	R	E	R	O	M	E	R	S	M	E
R	O	M	M	H	S	S	S	M	A	E	S
R	H	O	A	E	R	E	S	R	O	H	R
O	O	R	R	O	M	R	A	E	S	R	O
R	A	M	H	R	A	E	S	R	O	H	H

REFLECTIONS IN THE WATER

A LOYALTY ENCHANTMENT BRINGS YOUR THROWN TRIDENT BACK

SQUARED UP: LOGICAL LOOT

S	B	R	W
R	W	S	B
B	R	W	S
W	S	B	R

FLOWERS TO DYE FOR

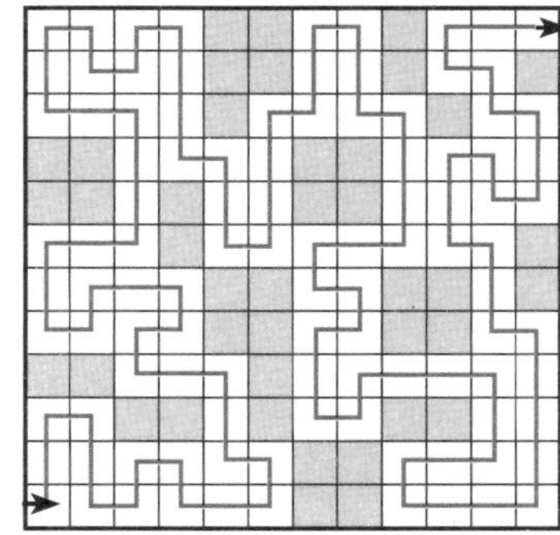

SHIP SHAPE

UPDATE AQUATIC

DOLPHIN

PHANTOM

CORAL

SHIPWRECK

SEA PICKLES

What happened in the wreck between the red ship and the blue ship?

THE SAILORS WERE MAROONED

ENCHANTED TRAP DOOR

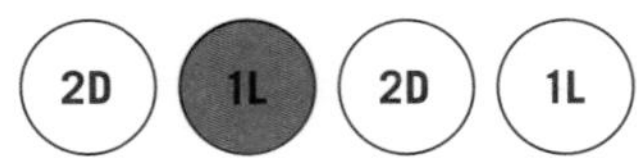

The red button is the first one pressed.

TALL TALE

Did you hear about the famous skeleton artist?

SHE WAS A SKULL-PTOR

ANIMALS, ANIMALS EVERY-WHERE

S B H U Y E K N O D E I
A P L O D A L D I L R S
L T U I R T S L U L P D
M A N F O S D M A I I O
O W O L F N E A D M L L
N A E T K E E E T O A P
G C P O L A R B E A R H
O R O R W A S F T E P I
A T U R T L E D I Y E N
S U P A D I U Q S S E P
L Y O P F N E K C I H C
W H R A B B I T E A S T

BUILD A DIRT ISLAND IN A LAKE TO GROW A STEADY SUPPLY OF WHEAT

LETTER HUNT

NETHER STAR

MATH MOBS

6

SO MUCH FOR PEACEFUL!

LLAMAS CAN CAUSE DAMAGE TO PLAYERS IN PEACEFUL MODE

BABY'S FAVORITE TOY

What is a baby zombie's favorite toy?

A DEADY BEAR

HIDDEN HAZARD

29			23	21	11	83	23
41	63	67			65	13	49
35	7	93	47	61			27
25	97	59	31	47	5	15	61
53							3
	89	71	19	79	95	53	
	75	39	1	29	71	95	
5							23
17	45	67	85	35	47	59	35
55				3			57
	13	27		25	65	83	
	11	15	91	51	37	51	
33							81
21	71	85	5	45	93	57	43
				13	43	1	63
69	9	97					77
1	33	31		7	49	29	
73	27	15					85
				55	45	9	21
17	61	91	87	73	37	11	69
		79	37				41
81	55			51	77	99	
89	57	65		41	15	63	
33	7	39	53	17	99	3	31
43							87
	25	67	59	67	19	9	
	49	39	3	19	75	19	

WHOSE BIOME IS THIS?

Squ88mish - Desert

MineQueen - Deep ocean

ZipDooDa - Jungle

Knowitall - Mountains

MOB DROPS

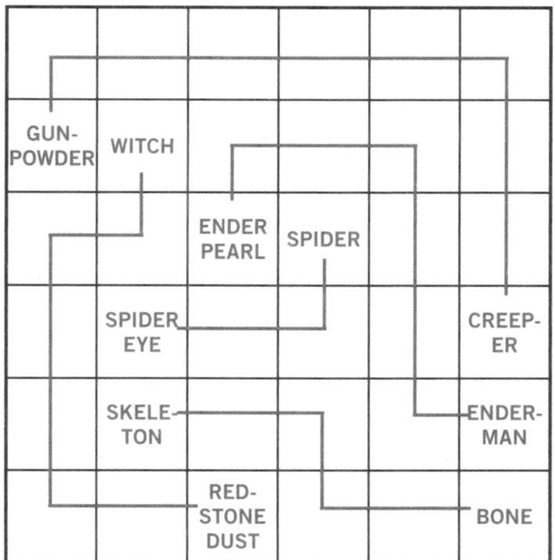

SURPRISE!

Raya - Chicken

Marcus - Bat

Jess - Flower

Sachin - Creeper

WHAT ZOMBIES WANT

Why did the zombie attack the skeleton?

IT WANTED HIS BONE AND MARROW

WHODUNNIT?

PUFFERFISH, MULE, EVOKER

SQUID, PIG, ENDERMAN, HORSE

SHULKER

SPIDER

WHEEL OF FORTUNE #4

PER BEND SINISTER INVERTED BANNER

Do you know what this banner looks like?

SEED FINDER

M O S E E S N O L E M S
E E D M E L O N S E D N
L M E O M S L E L E M O
O M E L E E N O E S L L
N E N L E D N M S D E E
S L O S O S E E E O M N
E O L O E N O E N L O O
E N E E E L S E M E N L
S E M O N O L E E M S E
L S S D E E S N E L E M
O N M E L O N S E D D O
N D S S E N O L E M S L

IN THE BEGINNING . . .

ORIGINALLY, VILLAGE MOBS WERE TO BE PIGMEN

BOUNTIFUL HARVEST

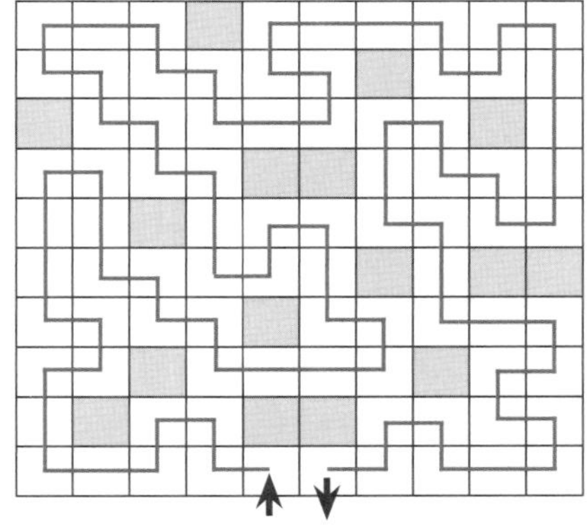

NAME SHIFTING

SKELETON

SKELTONE

SKEABONE

SHEABONE

HEADBONE

BONEHEAD

ENCHANTED BOW AND ARROW

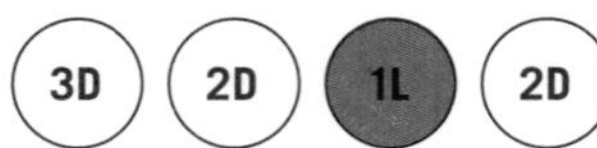

3D	2D	1L	2D
1R	2D	1R	2D
2U	1R	1D	3L
2U	F	2U	3U

The red button is the first one pressed.

WHICH WITCH?

What do you call a witch that spawns in the desert?

A SAND WITCH

PICK A POTION

A	N	I	S	H	E	A	L	I	N	G	R
I	N	N	S	T	T	Y	A	C	E	D	E
A	N	V	T	D	R	A	M	A	T	G	T
S	W	I	F	T	N	E	S	S	O	E	S
I	V	S	C	P	L	O	N	T	D	I	A
N	O	I	S	I	V	T	H	G	I	N	M
O	N	B	X	C	N	A	N	K	T	I	E
L	L	I	A	O	P	O	L	A	N	H	L
Y	R	L	S	E	R	A	T	T	A	O	T
N	O	I	T	A	R	E	N	E	G	E	R
N	O	T	S	L	O	W	N	E	S	S	U
P	E	Y	E	D	R	O	P	S	C	E	T

AN INSTANT DAMAGE IV POTION CAN KILL A PLAYER AT ONCE

TEXT STRINGS

COMMANDS

ADDITIONAL MATH MOBS

16

FLOWER POWER

FLOWERS WILL GENERATE IN LAVA, CAVES, AND ABANDONED MINESHAFTS

A RARE FIND

SPONGE

MINER HUMOR

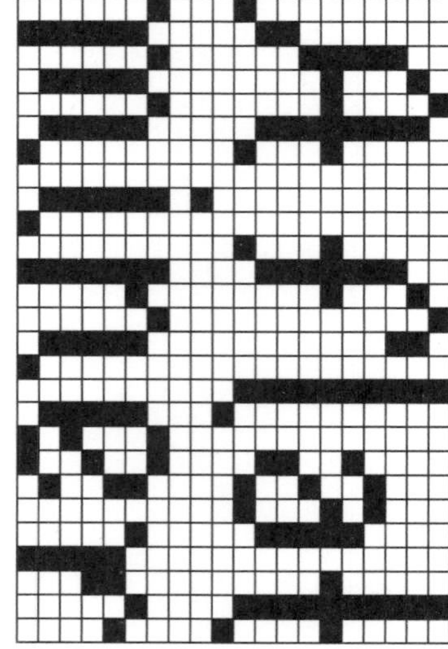

DROP MATCH

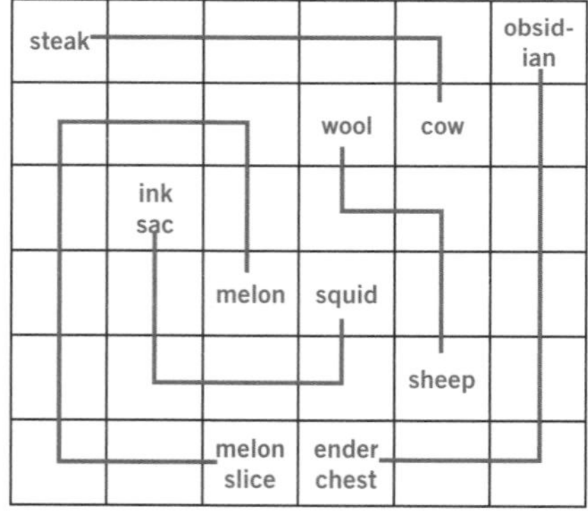

A COLD RECEPTION

SET, FIB, ROT

What do you get from a hostile wolf in the snowy taiga?

FROSTBITE

CERTIFICATE OF ACHIEVEMENT

CONGRATULATIONS

This certifies that

____

became a

MINECRAFT PUZZLE BOSS

on ____________.
Date

____

Signature

ALSO AVAILABLE